A Treatise On
Domestic Economy

A Treatise On Domestic Economy

Catherine Beecher

Introduction by Kathryn Kish Sklar

SCHOCKEN BOOKS • NEW YORK

First published by SCHOCKEN BOOKS 1977

Introduction copyright © 1977 by Schocken Books Inc.

Library of Congress Cataloging in Publication Data

Beecher, Catharine Esther, 1800-1878.
  A treatise on domestic economy.

  (Studies in the life of women)
  Reprint of the 1970 ed. published by Source
Book Press, New York, which was a reprint of the
1841 ed. published by Marsh, Capen, Lyon, and Webb,
New York.
  1. Home economics. I. Title.

TX445.B46 1976   640   76-9145

Manufactured in the United States of America

INTRODUCTION TO THE PAPERBACK EDITION

CATHARINE BEECHER's 1841 *Treatise on Domestic Economy for the Use of Young Ladies at Home and at School* was part of a burgeoning genre of self-help and self-improvement literature written in the spirit of democratic individualism during the ante-bellum period. Between 1840 and 1860 manual mania touched almost every aspect of American life and was especially vigorous in the domestic arena. Guides to courtship behavior, child rearing, character building, health maintenance, and marital felicity were produced and consumed in great abundance by Americans who believed that traditional knowledge of such topics no longer passed intact from parents to children or that traditional wisdom no longer met the needs of the rising generation.[1] Technological and marketing changes in book production and distribution spurred the increase in manuals by making relatively cheap editions available by 1840 on a national scale. Catharine Beecher was one of several prominent authors who supported herself by the sale of her printed advice.[2]

As one of the most eminent of such self-appointed counselors, Beecher produced eleven such manuals, several of which were either companion pieces to her *Treatise* or rewritings of it between 1838 and 1873. Supplementing certain aspects of the *Treatise* were her *Letters to Persons Who Are Engaged in Domestic Service* (1842), *Miss Beecher's Domestic Receipt Book* (originally published in 1846 and reprinted fourteen times before 1873), *Letters to the People on Health and Happiness* (1855), and *Physiology and Calisthenics for Schools and Families* (1856). Most of the *Treatise* was included verbatim in her later publications: *The American Woman's Home, or Principles of Domestic Science* (1869, co-authored with Beecher's younger sister, Harriet Beecher Stowe), *Principles of Domestic Science* (1870), *The New Housekeeper's Manual* (1873), and *Miss Beecher's Housekeeper and Healthkeeper* (1873). On child-rearing and character-building she produced *The Moral Instructor for Schools and Families* (1838) and *The Religious Training of Children in the School, the Family, and the Church* (1864).

From Boston to Burlington, Iowa, where she was hailed upon her arrival in the city as a "household divinity," Beecher's name was synonymous with the new values and behavior reshaping American domestic life in the nineteenth century. Although the *Treatise* was first published in 1841 by a small Boston firm that sold most of its stock over its own counter or relied on traveling book agents, in 1842 the book was reprinted and distributed by the more modern methods adopted by Harper & Brothers who specialized in supplying a network of retail bookstores with volumes on consignment.[3] Reprinted annually from 1842 to 1857, the *Treatise* enjoyed its hegemony in American domestic affairs during the same years that book marketing became more responsive to popular demand and feminism flowered into a political movement.

Beecher's manual was the first to depict the full behavioral details and to present the full ideological argument for the spiritualized, specialized, and politicized view of motherhood that we associate with the Victorian era and have come to call "the feminine mystique" in our own time. As such it stood in sharp contrast with its nearest competitor, Lydia Maria Child's *The American Frugal Housewife*, first published in 1830 and reprinted through 1850. Child's manual resembled traditionally straightforward household guides that had since the eighteenth century provided recipes and directions for rural family life. Many early nineteenth-century survivors in this genre were addressed to both men and women and assumed that they worked together within the household. Such was the case with H. I. Harwell's *The Domestic Manual: Or Family Directory, Containing Receipts in Arts, Trades, and Domestic Economy*, published in New London, Connecticut, in 1816, and Thomas Green Fassenden's *The Husbandman and Housewife: A Collection of Valuable Receipts and Directions Relating to Agriculture and Domestic Economy*, published in Bellows Falls, Vermont, in 1820. John Aikin's *The Arts of Life:* 1. Of *Providing Food,* 2. Of *Providing Clothing,* 3. Of *Providing Shelter . . . for the Instruction of Young Persons*, published in Boston in 1803 was written as letters addressed to "My Dear Boy." Like Fassenden's manual that discussed heartburn next to horseshoes, Child's *Frugal Housewife* presented an unvarnished listing of traditional directives and did not address a self-consciously female constituency. *A Treatise on Domestic Economy* cost twice as much as Child's manual, but for fifty cents instead of twenty-five cents the purchaser obtained a guide to domestic politics as well as advice on domestic economy.

By the time Beecher wrote the *Treatise* she was an expert at orchestrating the collective consciousness of contemporary mothers and daughters. Born in 1800 and narrowly escaping marriage by the death of her fiancé in a shipwreck, Beecher devoted the years between 1823 and 1841 to the advancement of female education. As the founder of Hartford Female Seminary in the 1820s and as a publicist for the need to employ and train women as teachers in the West in the 1830s, she had already met with considerable success in appealing to a self-consciously female constituency. Her *Treatise* was the chief means by which she continued to link this constituency to her own career advancement. Based on its popularity and sales, her career reached new heights in the 1840s and 1850s, providing her with financial independence that freed her both from her father's support and from the drudgery of keeping school.

Beecher gathered data for the *Treatise* during her widespread travels in the North and West in the 1830s. Her sharp eye for domestic detail was recorded by Edward King after Beecher visited his family in Chillicothe, Ohio, in 1835. "She asked more questions than one could answer in a day," King wrote his daughter,

> Why the fields were so square! Why there were not better houses! Why the current ran where it did! Whose property was this and that! She asked innumerable questions about the house, how long it had been built, why the walls were so thick, when everybody slept, why Lizzy slept in that room, whether mother managed her farm, whether she gave orders to the men, whether labor was difficult to procure, what was the price of help, why this fence was built and that.[4]

While her travels gave her knowledge of a wide variety of domestic economies, Beecher's married siblings provided her with more intimate information about American family life. Two years before she wrote *A Treatise* Beecher lived in her father's house not far from the marital home of her younger sister, Harriet. Harriet had married Calvin Stowe in 1836 at the age of twenty-six. Nine months after the wedding she gave birth to twin girls and was pregnant again a few months thereafter. After visiting Harriet about this time Catharine described her plight in a letter to another married sister:

> Harriet has one baby put out for the winter, the other at home, and
> number three will be here the middle of January. Poor thing, she bears up
> wonderfully well, and I hope will live through this first tug of matrimonial
> warfare, and then she says she shall not have any more *children, she knows
> for certain* for one while. Though how she found this out I cannot say, but
> she seems quite confident about it.[5]

Although a spinster herself, Catharine Beecher was fully aware of the
profound changes in economic production and human reproduction that
were reshaping the contours of American domestic life in the middle of
the nineteenth century. The importance of her *Treatise* as an historical
document lies in her effort to interpret these changes in ways that
promoted female interests.

Qualitative motherhood was the basic means the *Treatise* used to turn
social change to female advantage. Democratic individualism mandated a
new view of motherhood, the *Treatise* suggested, in which the *kind* of
children a family raised mattered more than the number. The book's first
chapter was a paean to the potential of American democracy accompanied
by a warning that only women could make it work:

> The success of democratic institutions, as is conceded by all, depends upon
> the intellectual and moral character of the mass of the people. If they are
> intelligent and virtuous, democracy is a blessing; but if they are ignorant
> and wicked, it is only a curse. . . . It is equally conceded, that the formation
> of the moral and intellectual character of the young is committed mainly to
> the female hand.[6]

Beecher's view of the relationship between childhood and society was an
essentially modern one. Rather than viewing society as a traditional set of
established controls and early childhood as a time when the will must be
broken to conform to those controls, she saw society as having an
uncontrolled growth, except as it was regulated by values internalized
and developed during early childhood.

Seeing it possible to exert in early childhood an influence of lifelong
personal and social significance, the *Treatise* extolled the importance of
the right kind of mothering and urged women to make the most of their
maternal influence. Such influence could provide leverage for other
female advances, particularly in the field of education. The *Treatise* urged
training for domestic responsibilities commensurate with that obtained by
men for their duties in the public arena:

Are not the most responsible of all duties committed to the care of woman? Is it not her profession to take care of mind, body, and soul? And that, too, at the most critical of all periods of existence? And is it not as much a matter of public concern that she should be qualified for her duties as that ministers, lawyers, and physicians should be prepared for theirs? And is it not as important to endow institutions that shall make a superior education accessible to all classes, for females, as much as for the other sex? [7]

Viewing the domestic sphere as a specialized segment of modern society with a complex social task to perform, the *Treatise* rejected the notion that women were naturally equipped to succeed in their socially mandated work. It urged readers to approach the female life cycle as a work cycle and prepare for it as a man would prepare for a vocation. Not passive submission to their biological identity, or the invalidism that frequently accompanied it, nor fetching dependency on their husbands, but active control of their immediate life circumstances was the model the *Treatise* held out to its readers.

Treatise readers were primarily middle-class women with property-owning fathers and husbands. The lives of such women differed considerably from those their grandmothers had known around 1800. Three basic changes had taken place in the space of as many generations. The profundity of these economic, demographic, and social changes can be measured by the fact that they produced fundamental alterations in an arena of human experience historically immune to change—the family.

Early outcroppings of the changes in marketing and technology that we call the "industrial revolution" were visible by 1800, but these were initially compatible with traditional patterns of family life. Although, for example, between 1790 and 1810 factories with spinning jennys produced yarn more cheaply and in greater volume than ever before—thus rendering home spinning relatively obsolete—finished cloth was, until the introduction of the power loom at Waltham in 1815, woven on home looms rather than in factories.[8] The grandmothers of *Treatise* readers could, therefore, as married women engage in income-producing work at home and meet their child-care responsibilities at the same time. Whereas the relationship between home and factory in 1800 had been one between primary and auxiliary producer, by 1840 that relationship had become one between consumer and producer. The inability of home looms to compete with factory looms can be seen in the precipitous fall in the price of a yard of plain shirting from forty-two cents in 1815 to thirteen cents in 1820 to seven-and-a-half cents in 1830.[9] Although the *Treatise* provided directions for the gardening and poultry work traditionally done by women and described how to make candles, soap, lye, and starch, the book assumed that "domestic economy" consisted primarily in the judicious household expenditure of money earned outside the home, rather than the organization of economic production within the home.

Mid-nineteenth-century work options within the home were more limited than they had been, but some new ones did emerge to replace the old. Taking in boarders was one of these. The *Treatise* seems to have provided for this option in its cottage designed "for persons of moderate circumstances, especially for young housekeepers, who are making their first essays in domestic affairs," since this cottage was described as accommodating "six grown persons," provided the parents and their "one or two children" sleep in the parlor.[10] In freeing the main bedroom of the house through this cramped parlor arrangement, Beecher's *Treatise* could conceivably have intended to make room for extended kin or apprentices—two categories of people traditionally appended to the nuclear household. The bedroom behind the kitchen was probably designed for a servant or servants. The word "adults" leaves in doubt the identity of the six persons not included in the nuclear family, but the presence of these non-family members was clearly worth the elaborate design as well as the inconvenience of the family bedroom in the parlor.

The *Treatise* argued that young women were less well trained for domestic duties than they had been, and there is evidence to suggest that this generation was more strongly oriented toward work outside the household during the years immediately preceding marriage than women had been in the past. Although the grandmothers of *Treatise* readers had been able to teach in the sex-segregated "women's schools" that became widespread in New England and elsewhere between 1780 and 1820, for example, the generation that matured between 1840 and 1860 enjoyed vastly increased teaching opportunities, since women were by that time replacing men as the teachers of coeducational primary schools. By 1850, approximately one out of five native-born Massachusetts women taught school, the vast majority doing so between the ages of seventeen and twenty-five, most of them without further education than that available to them in their own towns.[11] With an average age at marriage of about twenty-three, and with only 10 percent remaining unmarried, this generation may have been destined for lives as wives and mothers, but as young women their options were not limited to those of the domestic arena. The attractions of a stint of work outside the home before marriage were summarized in an 1855 letter written by one young teacher to another:

> I regard it as a great misfortune for a young lady never to go away from home. It gives her an opportunity to learn the different ways of people, and to study the most important of all studies—human nature. I would not exchange the knowledge I have acquired by living in different communities for all I could learn in two years at school. It seems to me that those persons who teach very near home lose half the advantages of the teacher's situation.[12]

The *Treatise* was adopted for use in the public schools of Massachusetts in 1842, and was probably read by young women who attended public high schools built after a state statute provided for such schools in 1824.[13] These schools would have contained a high percentage of young women who subsequently taught in primary schools and spent the years preceding marriage away from home. Perhaps with this reading constituency in mind, the *Treatise* focused on the gap that developed between female experience before marriage and the conditions women encounted in marital life.

For 90 percent of mid-nineteenth century married women, wifehood was accompanied by motherhood, and motherhood, for women of all classes brought with it a very real struggle against infant mortality. Mid-nineteenth-century child-care responsibilities included life and death dimensions that are absent from our post-penicillin and post-antibiotic lives. One of the basic assumptions of the *Treatise* was that child-care at this "critical period of existence" was a female responsibility. This responsibility may, more than any other, have prompted the purchase of manuals like the *Treatise*. Many women may have felt as Elizabeth Cady Stanton did after the birth of her first child in 1842: "Having gone through the ordeal of bearing a child, I was determined if possible to keep him, so I read everything I could find on the subject." [14] Stanton's attitude toward infant mortality was that it could be prevented, and such was the *Treatise*'s view as well. Citing statistics from J. B. Comb's writings on English infant mortality, the manual warned against the use of pacifying opiates, such as "Godfrey's Cordial," and provided an up-to-date summary of current medical opinion on infant care.

Infant mortality rates declined slowly throughout the nineteenth century, but the rate at which children were born fell even more rapidly. Demographic historians see the century as a time of "demographic transition" from the high death rates and high birth rates characteristic of traditional populations to the low death and low birth rates characteristic of our own twentieth-century population. This transition took place in England and western Europe as well as the United States. More people lived longer, so the population as a whole increased rapidly, but fewer babies were born to individual women.[15]

The *Treatise's* emphasis on qualitative motherhood reflected demographic fact as well as political and educational theory. From 1830 to 1880 the number of white children under five years of age per one thousand women of child-bearing age declined by a third. Between 1800 and 1930 the number of young children per one thousand mature women declined by two-thirds. This dramatic reduction in the number of children women bore began before significant industrialization or urbanization had taken place, and the decade of the most rapid decline was between 1840 and 1850 when rural birth rates declined more rapidly than urban rates.[16] Although the causes of the demographic transition still elude complete historical explanation, its effect on the female life cycle was to introduce longer intervals between births, some of quite prolonged duration. In an age before artificial contraceptive techniques, such intervals must have been maintained largely through sexual abstinence.

Historians have noted that Victorian sexual ideology facilitated family limitation. Although the control of sexual expression was not unique to the Victorian period, the controls that era imposed on marital sexuality were new and did coincide with the early stage of birth-rate decline that preceded artificial contraceptive techniques. Only a few Victorians advocated the deliberate control of births within marriage, but many adhered to the new beliefs that married women experienced no sexual passion akin to their husbands' and that sexual "expenditures" were debilitating for both sexes. The *Treatise* certainly viewed sexual arousal as a life-threatening activity when it advised mothers that "children may inflict evils on themselves, which not unfrequently terminate in disease, delirium, and death." [17] It was in this context of Victorian sexuality that the manual's discussion of childbirth and invalidism took place.

In its emphasis on female debility the manual gave weight to the view that American women were no longer willing to bear children as frequently as they had in the past. Childbirth, the most "natural" of female responsibilities, was viewed as highly problematic:

> It would seem as if the primeval curse, that has written the doom of pain and sorrow on one period of a young mother's life, in this Country had been extended over all; so that the hour never arrives, when "she forgetteth her sorrow for joy that a man is born into the world."

Female despair over the burdens of child-bearing were dramatically presented through vivid personal testimony:

> The Writer has repeatedly heard mothers say, that they had wept tears of bitterness over their infant daughters, at the thought of the sufferings which they were destined to undergo; while they cherished the decided wish that these daughters should never marry. At the same time, many a reflecting young woman is looking to her further prospects, with very different feelings and hopes from those which Providence designed.[18]

The personal histories of many nineteenth-century women suggest that invalidism was a contraceptive strategy. After Harriet Beecher Stowe bore her fifth child in seven years of marriage in 1843, her "matriomonial warfare"—announced five years earlier—began in earnest. That birth brought with it a prolonged illness, the effects of which lingered for years. She did not give birth to her next child until 1849, thus omitting between 1843 and 1849 two children whose births were prevented by some kind of direct intervention. Perhaps the topic of sexual abstinence had been broached between Harriet and her husband after her illness of 1843, for in the following summer Calvin Stowe wrote his wife:

> With you, every desire I have, mental and physical, is completely satisfied and filled up, and leaves me nothing more to ask for. My enjoyment with you is not weakened by time nor blunted by age, and every reunion after separation is just as much of a honey-moon as was the first month after the wedding. Is not your own experience and observation a proof of what I say?[19]

"I love you as I now love God and I can conceive of no higher love," Harriet replied, adding that her love contained "no passion" of the senses, and that she "never knew yet or felt the pulsation" of such passion.[20] A year later Harriet described herself to Calvin as an invalid whose physical activities were sharply curtailed:

> I feel no life, no energy, no appetite, or rather a growing distaste for food; in fact I am becoming quite etheral . . . I suffer from sensible distress in the brain, as I have done more or less since my sickness last winter, a distress which some days takes from me all power of planning or executing anything.[21]

Concerned with the ill-effects of repeated child-bearing on their health, but married to men with traditional views of the appropriateness of sexual passion in marriage, many other Victorian women besides Harriet Beecher Stowe found invalidism the most effective contraceptive strategy available to them

While acknowledging invalidism as a fact of life among middle-class women, *A Treatise* nevertheless viewed such disability as a self-defeating life strategy. The problems associated with the female life cycle and the female constitution could be avoided, the manual insisted, if women prepared for their life work as men prepared for their vocations, and if they introduced in the home the same rational procedures that characterized the marketplace. The critical fact in a woman's life was not whether she was pious, but whether she controlled her life circumstances or they controlled her. Urging readers to "systematize" as much of domestic life as possible, the *Treatise* suggested that they compose a list of all their "religious intellectual, social, and domestic" duties, and use time as the standard by which they measured their priorities:

> Let a calculation be made, whether there be time enough, in the day or week, for all these duties. If there be not, let the least important be stricken from the list, as not being duties, and which must be omitted.

The critical importance of such a system was emphasized:

> Without attempting any such systematic employment of time, and carrying it out, so far as they can control circumstances, most women are rather driven along, by the daily occurrences of life, so that, instead of being the intelligent regulators of their own time, they are the mere sport of circumstances. There is nothing, which so distinctly marks the difference between weak and strong minds, as the fact, whether they control circumstances, or circumstances control them.[22]

The imposition of system and the assertion of female control frequently went hand in hand in the *Treatise*. Personal anecdotes dramatized strategies that extended and consolidated female decision-making in the domestic arena, as in the case of the woman who

> kept an account of all her disbursements, for one year. This she submitted to her husband and obtained his consent, that the same sum should be under her control, the coming year, for similar purposes, with the understanding, that she might modify future apportionments, in any way her judgement and conscience might approve.[23]

Yet in spite of these economic and demographic changes between 1800 and 1840, and the behavioral changes they created in women's lives, the legal status of women in 1840 was largely unchanged from what it had been in 1740. Then, as in the mid-nineteenth century, single women enjoyed rights that married women lacked, including the right to own property or retain their own wages. In keeping with theories of democratic individualism, the *Treatise* emphasized the voluntary nature of this surrender of rights upon marriage:

> No woman is forced to obey any husband but the one she chooses for herself; nor is she obliged to take a husband, if she prefers to remain single.[24]

The manual explained that "opinion" and "practice" had established

> that women have an equal interest in all social and civil concerns; and that no domestic, civil, or political, institution is right that sacrifices her interest to promote that of the other sex.

But, the *Treatise* continued,

> In order to secure her the more firmly in all these privileges, it is decided, that, in the domestic relation, she take a subordinate station, and that, in civil and political concerns, her interests be intrusted to the other sex. . . .[25]

While this view reflected the current legal status of women, it differed in one basic essential from the spirit of that status, for it saw women as a group with interests unique to their sex, different from those of men, and therefore "intrusted to" rather than subsumed within those "of the opposite sex." Although married women did not have a legal identity separate from that of their husbands', by 1840 many women married to property-owning husbands had experienced an autonomous social identity as members of such female associations as The American Female Moral Reform Society. (At its founding in 1839 this organization linked more than four hundred ongoing local chapters.[26]) Therefore while most local, state, and national governments did not recognize married women as having a social, economic, or political identity separate from their husbands, many, if not most middle-class married women were members of socially, economically, and politically autonomous female associations— particularly the charitable and educational associations to which the *Treatise* indirectly referred.

The *Treatise*'s contribution to women in these contradictory circumstances was to endorse the "equal interest" that "opinion" and "practice" gave to women "in all social and civil concerns," and to explain the continued "subordinate station" of married women as the result of society's need for "superior and subordinate relations" in order to "go forward harmoniously." Thus the book extended the boundaries of autonomous female activity without challenging the social and economic hierarchies that moderated the "irresistible" progress of "democratic equality." The book contains a variety of subthemes linking the advancement of female interests with those of middle-class and Evangelical interests.

A Treatise on Domestic Economy is a patchwork of old and new, combining, for example, original and effective designs for labor-saving devices with an assumption that every household would prefer to employ servants if it could find native-born women willing to perform such work. Yet in its cross currents of continuity and change the modern reader receives a vivid depiction of the everyday reality inhabited by mid-nineteenth-century women in property-owning families.

KATHRYN KISH SKLAR

New Haven, Connecticut
July, 1976

NOTES

1. For a methodological discussion of the historical use of manuals, see Jay Mechling, "Advice to Historians on Advice to Mothers," *Journal of Social History*, Vol. 9, no. 1 (Fall 1975), pp. 44–63.

2. For biographical information on Beecher, see Kathryn Kish Sklar, *Catharine Beecher: A Study in American Domesticity* (New York: Norton, 1976). See also: Kathryn Kish Sklar, "Catharine Beecher's *A Treatise on Domestic Economy:* A Document in Domestic Feminism," in Earl A. French and Diana Royce, eds., *Portraits of a Nineteenth Century Family: A Symposium on the Beecher Family* (Hartford, Conn.: The Stowe-Day Foundation, 1976).

3. W. S. Tryon, "Book Distribution in Mid-Nineteenth Century America," *Papers of the Bibliographic Society of America*, Vol. 41 (3rd Quarter, 1947), pp. 210–30.

4. Edward King to Sarah King, December 24, 1834, King Family Papers, Cincinnati Historical Society, Cincinnati, Ohio.

5 Catharine Beecher to Mary Beecher Perkins, undated (1838), Beecher-Stowe Collection, Folder 17, Schlesinger Library, Cambridge, Mass.

6. *A Treatise,* p. 13.

7. Ibid., p. 30.

8. Rolla M. Tryon, *Household Manufactures in the United States, 1640–1860: A Study in Industrial History* (Chicago: University of Chicago Press, 1917), pp. 302–3.

9. Ibid., p. 272.

10. *A Treatise,* p. 275.

11. Maris Vinovskis, *Women in Education in Ante-Bellum America,* Center for Demography and Ecology, The University of Wisconsin, Madison, Working Paper 73-7, Table no. A6.

12. L. D. Gleason to My Dear Jenny, Leicester Academy, March 8, 1855, Leicester Academy Papers, American Antiquarian Society, Worcester, Mass.

13. George Emerson, *Education in Massachusetts: Early Legislation and History* (Boston: Wilson & Son, 1869), p. 25.

14. Elizabeth Cady Stanton, *Eighty Years and More: Reminiscences, 1815–1897* (New York: Schocken, 1971, reprint of 1898 original), p. 114.

15. For a discussion of the demographic transition, see Ansley J. Coale, "The History of the Human Population," *The Human Population* (New York: Scientific American, 1973).

16. Wilson H. Grabill, Clyde V. Kiser, and Pascal K. Whelpton, "A Long View," in Michael Gordon, ed., *The American Family in Social-Historical Perspective* (New York: St. Martin's, 1973), pp. 374–97, esp. 388.

17. *A Treatise,* p. 233.

18. Ibid., pp. 19–20.

19. Calvin Stowe to Harriet Beecher Stowe, June 30, 1844, Beecher-Stowe Collection, Folder 61.

20. Harriet Beecher Stowe to Calvin Stowe, July 19, 1844, Beecher-Stowe Collection, Folder 69.

21. Harriet Beecher Stowe to Calvin Stowe, June 16, 1845, in Annie Fields, *Life and Letters of Harriet Beecher Stowe* (Cambridge: Riverside Press, 1897), pp. 110–11.

22. *A Treatise,* p. 148.

23. Ibid., p. 178.

24. Ibid., p. 3.

25. Ibid., p. 4.

26. Carroll Smith Rosenberg, "Beauty, the Beast and the Militant Woman: A Case Study in Sex Roles and Social Stress in Jacksonian America," *American Quarterly,* Vol. 23 (1971), pp. 562–84.

TO

AMERICAN MOTHERS,

WHOSE

INTELLIGENCE AND VIRTUES HAVE INSPIRED ADMIRATION AND RESPECT,

WHOSE

EXPERIENCE HAS FURNISHED MANY VALUABLE SUGGESTIONS, IN THIS WORK,

WHOSE

APPROBATION WILL BE HIGHLY VALUED,

AND WHOSE

INFLUENCE, IN PROMOTING THE OBJECT AIMED AT,

IS RESPECTFULLY SOLICITED,

THIS WORK IS DEDICATED,

BY

THEIR FRIEND AND COUNTRYWOMAN,

THE AUTHOR.

PREFACE.

THERE are two questions, which the Writer wishes to answer, in the Preface, as the most proper place, though it is feared that many of those, who will be disposed to ask them, may be among those who " never read a preface."

The first, is, How came the Author to write such a book ? She answers, Because she has herself suffered from the want of such knowledge, in early life ; because others, under her care, have suffered from her ignorance ; and because many mothers and teachers, especially in reference to matters pertaining to health, have so much occasion to sympathize in the regret with which this acknowledgement is made.

The care of a female seminary, for some twelve years, and subsequent extensive travels, have given such a view of female health, in this Nation, and of the causes which tend to weaken and destroy the constitution of young women, together with the sufferings consequent on a want of early domestic knowledge and habits, that, though others may be better qualified to attempt some efficient remedy, the

Writer has been led to contribute, at least what was in her power, for this end.

For more than ten years, she has vainly striven to induce various medical gentlemen, among her personal friends, to prepare a short and popular work on Physiology and Hygiene, for the use of female schools; but, failing in the effort, much of what could have been better presented by a medical writer, is inwoven in this volume, as a substitute for what it is hoped may yet be furnished by some abler hand.

The second question, is, What qualifications has the Writer, which entitle her to be received as authority on the various topics embraced in this Work?

In reply to this, she would say, that, being the eldest of a large family, she has, from early life, been accustomed to the care of children, and to the performance of most domestic duties. It has also been her good fortune to reside, most of her life, in the families of exemplary and accomplished house-keepers, and under the supervision of such friends, most of the domestic operations, detailed in this Work, have been performed by the Writer.

But much in these pages is offered, not as the results of her own experience, but rather as glean-ings from the experience of those more competent to instruct in such matters; and in gaining them, the Writer has often had to learn her own deficien-cies, by the light of superior excellence in others. Nothing is here presented, which has not received the sanction of some of the most judicious and experienced mothers and housekeepers in this Nation.

The articles on business not ordinarily performed by females, are sanctioned by those who are considered the highest authorities on the respective subjects, as are all the topics pertaining to Physiology and Hygiene.

There is one suggestion, which may be offered, to mothers and teachers who have to look back on past measures and labors, and their present results. It is painful, after years of toil and anxiety, to discover, that, in some important respects, mistakes have been made, which have entailed suffering and sorrow on ourselves, and on the objects of our care. This often tends to prevent a sensitive and conscientious mind from fairly judging of views, which, if true, will implicate the wisdom of past measures.

But there is one consideration, which may rectify this sinister tendency ; and that is, that we are never to blame ourselves for not acting according to knowledge and evidence not within our reach. In regard to the subject of health, especially, mothers and teachers have never had the facilities afforded for gaining the knowledge which they have needed, and their consequent mistakes should be regarded by themselves and by others, as misfortunes demanding sympathy, rather than as just occasions for reproach. The resemblance of this Work, in one portion, to Miss Leslie's House-Book, makes it proper to state, that this was planned in all its minutiæ, and partly completed, before that was seen, or any thing known about it, except the name.

NOTE.

On page 38, a mistake occurs, which the Writer is particularly anxious to have corrected. The last paragraph but one should read thus :

In the early years of female life, reading, writing, needle-work, drawing, and music, should alternate with domestic pursuits ; and one hour a day devoted to some study, in addition to the above employments, would be all that would be needful to prepare for a thorough education, after growth is attained and the constitution established.

The system of Calisthenics, referred to on page 34, is one devised by the Writer, and which has been adopted in several female seminaries. It has proved much more useful and interesting than previous methods; and the Author is now preparing a volume for the press, in which this system will be fully exhibited, with many recent improvements.

On p. 32, line 7, *for* eighty, *read* ninety.
   "   "   " 27, *read* neatly painted tubs.
   "   "   note, *read* Benjamin Godfrey, Esq.
   "   35, line 26, *for* Chalmers, *read* Chambers.

CONTENTS.

CHAPTER I.

PECULIAR RESPONSIBILITIES OF AMERICAN WOMEN.

CHAPTER II.

DIFFICULTIES PECULIAR TO AMERICAN WOMEN.

CHAPTER III.

REMEDIES FOR THESE DIFFICULTIES.

CHAPTER IV.

ON DOMESTIC ECONOMY AS A BRANCH OF STUDY.

CHAPTER V.

ON THE CARE OF HEALTH.

CHAPTER VI.

ON THE PREPARATION OF HEALTHFUL FOOD.

CHAPTER VII.

ON HEALTHFUL DRINKS.

CHAPTER VIII.

ON CLOTHING.

CHAPTER IX.

ON CLEANLINESS.

CHAPTER X.

ON EARLY RISING.

CHAPTER XI.

ON DOMESTIC EXERCISE.

CHAPTER XII.

ON DOMESTIC MANNERS.

CHAPTER XIII.

ON THE PRESERVATION OF A GOOD TEMPER IN A HOUSEKEEPER.

CHAPTER XIV.

ON HABITS OF SYSTEM AND ORDER.

CHAPTER XV.

ON GIVING IN CHARITY.

CHAPTER XVI.

ON ECONOMY OF TIME AND EXPENSES.

CHAPTER XVII.

ON HEALTH OF MIND.

CHAPTER XVIII.

ON THE CARE OF DOMESTICS.

CHAPTER XIX.

ON THE CARE OF INFANTS.

CHAPTER XX.

ON THE MANAGEMENT OF YOUNG CHILDREN.

CHAPTER XXI.

ON THE CARE OF THE SICK.

CHAPTER XXII.

ON ACCIDENTS AND ANTIDOTES.

CHAPTER XXIII.

ON DOMESTIC AMUSEMENTS.

CHAPTER XXIV.

ON SOCIAL DUTIES.

CHAPTER XXV.

ON THE CONSTRUCTION OF HOUSES.

CHAPTER XXVI.

ON FIRES AND LIGHTS.

CHAPTER XXVII.

ON WASHING.

CHAPTER XXVIII.

ON STARCHING, IRONING, AND CLEANSING.

CHAPTER XXIX.

ON WHITENING, CLEANSING, AND DYEING.

CHAPTER XXX.

ON THE CARE OF PARLORS.

CHAPTER XXXI.

ON THE CARE OF BREAKFAST AND DINING-ROOMS.

CHAPTER XXXII.

ON THE CARE OF CHAMBERS AND BEDROOMS.

CHAPTER XXXIII.

ON THE CARE OF THE KITCHEN, CELLAR, AND STOREROOM.

CHAPTER XXXIV.

ON SEWING, CUTTING, AND MENDING.

CHAPTER XXXV.

ON THE CARE OF YARDS AND GARDENS.

DOMESTIC ECONOMY.

CHAPTER I.

THE PECULIAR RESPONSIBILITIES OF AMERICAN WOMEN.

American Women should feel a peculiar interest in Democratic Institutions. The maxim of our Civil Institutions. Its identity with
the main principle of Christianity. Relations involving subordination; why they are neecful. Examples. How these relations are
decided in a Democracy. What decides the Equity of any Law or
Institution. The principle of Aristocracy. The tendency of Democracy in respect to the interests of Women. Illustrated in the
United States. Testimony of De Tocqueville. In what respects
are Women subordinate? and why? Wherein are they equal or
superior in influence? and how are they placed by courtesy? How
can American Women rectify any real disadvantages involved in
our Civil Institutions? Opinion of De Tocqueville as to the influence and example of American Democracy. Responsibilities involved in this view, especially those of American Women.

THERE are some reasons why American women
should feel an interest in the support of the democratic institutions of their Country, which it is important that they should consider. The great maxim,
which is the basis of all our civil and political institutions, is, that "all men are created equal," and that
they are equally entitled to "life, liberty, and the
pursuit of happiness."

But it can readily be seen, that this is only another
mode of expressing the fundamental principle which
the Great Ruler of the Universe has established, as
the law of His eternal government. "Thou shalt
love thy neighbor as thyself;" and "Whatsoever ye
would that men should do to you, do ye even so to

them." These are the Scripture forms, by which the Supreme Lawgiver requires that each individual of our race shall regard the happiness of others, as of the same value as his own ; and which forbids any institution, in private or civil life, which secures advantages to one class, by sacrificing the interests of another.

The principles of democracy, then, are identical with the principles of Christianity.

But, in order that each individual may pursue and secure the highest degree of happiness within his reach, unimpeded by the selfish interests of others, a system of laws must be established, which sustain certain relations and dependencies in social and civil life. What these relations and their attending obligations shall be, are to be determined, not with reference to the wishes and interests of a few, but solely with reference to the general good of all ; so that each individual shall have his own interest, as much as the public benefit, secured by them.

For this purpose, it is needful that certain relations be sustained, that involve the duties of subordination. There must be the magistrate and the subject, one of whom is the superior, and the other the inferior. There must be the relations of husband and wife, parent and child, teacher and pupil, employer and employed, each involving the relative duties of subordination. The superior in certain particulars is to direct, and the inferior is to yield obedience. Society could never go forward, harmoniously, nor could any craft or profession be successfully pursued, unless these superior and subordinate relations be instituted and sustained.

But who shall take the higher, and who the subordinate, stations in social and civil life ? This matter, in the case of parents and children, is decided by the Creator. He has given children to the control of parents, as their superiors, and to them they remain subordinate, to a certain age, or so long as they are members of their household. And parents can delegate such a portion of their authority to teachers and employers, as the interests of their children require.

In most other cases, in a truly democratic state, each individual is allowed to choose for himself, who shall take the position of his superior. No woman is forced to obey any husband but the one she chooses for herself; nor is she obliged to take a husband, if she prefers to remain single. So every domestic, and every artisan or laborer, after passing from parental control, can choose the employer to whom he is to accord obedience, or, if he prefers to relinquish certain advantages, he can remain without taking a subordinate place to any employer.

Each subject, also, has equal power with every other, to decide who shall be his superior as a ruler. The weakest, the poorest, the most illiterate, has the same opportunity to determine this question, as the richest, the most learned, and the most exalted.

And the various privileges that wealth secures, are equally open to all classes. Every man may aim at riches, unimpeded by any law or institution that secures peculiar privileges to a favored class at the expense of another. Every law, and every institution, is tested by examining whether it secures equal advantages to all; and if the people become convinced that any regulation sacrifices the good of the majority to the interests of the smaller number, they have power to abolish it.

The institutions of monarchical and aristocratic nations are based on precisely opposite principles. They secure, to certain small and favored classes, advantages which can be maintained, only by sacrificing the interests of the great mass of the people. Thus, the throne and aristocracy of England are supported by laws and customs, that burden the lower classes with taxes, so enormous, as to deprive them of all the luxuries, and of most of the comforts, of life. Poor dwellings, scanty food, unhealthy employments, excessive labor, and entire destitution of the means and time for education, are appointed for the lower classes, that a few may live in palaces, and riot in every indulgence.

The tendencies of democratic institutions, in reference to the rights and interests of the female sex, have been fully developed in the United States ; and it is in this aspect, that the subject is one of peculiar interest to American women. In this Country, it is established, both by opinion and by practice, that women have an equal interest in all social and civil concerns ; and that no domestic, civil, or political, institution, is right, that sacrifices her interest to promote that of the other sex. But in order to secure her the more firmly in all these privileges, it is decided, that, in the domestic relation, she take a subordinate station, and that, in civil and political concerns, her interests be intrusted to the other sex, without her taking any part in voting, or in making and administering laws. The result of this order of things has been fairly tested, and is thus portrayed by M. De Tocqueville, a writer, who, for intelligence, fidelity, and ability, ranks second to none.*

---

* The work of this author, entitled ' Democracy in America,' secured for him a prize from the National Academy, at Paris. The following extract expresses an opinion, in which most of the best qualified judges would coincide.

" The manner of conducting the inquiry which the Author has instituted ; the intimate acquaintance with all our institutions and relations, every where evinced ; the careful and profound thought ; and, above all, the spirit of truth, which animates and pervades the whole work, will not only commend it to the present generation, but render it a monument of the age in which it is produced." " In Europe, it has already taken its stand with Montesquieu, Bacon, Milton, and Locke. In America, it will be regarded, not only as a classic philosophical treatise of the highest order, but as indispensable in the education of every statesman, and of every citizen who desires thoroughly to comprehend the institutions of his Country."

The following extracts present his views.

"There are people in Europe, who, confounding together the different characteristics of the sexes, would make of man and woman, beings not only equal, but alike. They would give to both the same functions, impose on both the same duties, and grant to both the same rights. They would mix them in all things,—their business, their occupations, their pleasures. It may readily be conceived, that, by *thus* attempting to make one sex equal to the other, both are degraded; and from so preposterous a medley of the works of Nature, nothing could ever result, but weak men and disorderly women.

"It is not thus that the Americans understand the species of democratic equality, which may be established between the sexes. They admit, that, as Nature has appointed such wide differences between the physical and moral constitutions of man and woman, her manifest design was, to give a distinct employment to their various faculties; and they hold, that improvement does not consist in making beings so dissimilar do pretty nearly the same things, but in getting each of them to fulfil their respective tasks, in the best possible manner. The Americans have applied to the sexes the great principle of political economy, which governs the manufactories of our age, by carefully dividing the duties of man from those of woman, in order that the great work of society may be the better carried on.

"In no country has such constant care been taken, as in America, to trace two clearly distinct lines of action for the two sexes, and to make them keep pace one with the other, but in two pathways which are always different. American women never manage the outward concerns of the family, or conduct a business, or take a part in political life; nor are they, on the other hand, ever compelled to perform the rough labor of the fields, or to make any of those laborious exertions, which demand the exertion of physical strength. No families are so poor, as to form an exception to this rule.

" If, on the one hand, an American woman cannot escape from the quiet circle of domestic employments, on the other hand, she is never forced to go beyond it. Hence it is, that the women of America, who often exhibit a masculine strength of understanding, and a manly energy, generally preserve great delicacy of personal appearance, and always retain the manners of women, although they sometimes show that they have the hearts and minds of men.

" Nor have the Americans ever supposed, that one consequence of democratic principles, is, the subversion of marital power, or the confusion of the natural authorities in families. They hold, that every association must have a head, in order to accomplish its object ; and that the natural head of the conjugal association is man. They do not, therefore, deny him the right of directing his partner ; and they maintain, that, in the smaller association of husband and wife, as well as in the great social community, the object of democracy is, to regulate and legalize the powers which are necessary, not to subvert all power.

" This opinion is not peculiar to one sex, and contested by the other. I never observed, that the women of America considered conjugal authority as a fortunate usurpation of their rights, nor that they thought themselves degraded by submitting to it. It appears to me, on the contrary, that they attach a sort of pride to the voluntary surrender of their own will, and make it their boast to bend themselves to the yoke, not to shake it off. Such, at least, is the feeling expressed by the most virtuous of their sex ; the others are silent ; and in the United States, it is not the practice for a guilty wife to clamor for the rights of woman, while she is trampling on her holiest duties."

"Although the travellers, who have visited North America, differ on a great number of points, they agree in remarking, that morals are far more strict, there, than elsewhere. It is evident that, on this point, the Americans are very superior to their progenitors, the English." "In England, as in all other countries of Europe, public malice is constantly attacking the frailties of women. Philosophers and statesmen are heard to deplore, that morals are not sufficiently strict; and the literary productions of the country constantly lead one to suppose so. In America, all books, novels not excepted, suppose women to be chaste; and no one thinks of relating affairs of gallantry."

"It has often been remarked, that, in Europe, a certain degree of contempt lurks, even in the flattery which men lavish upon women. Although a European frequently affects to be the slave of woman, it may be seen, that he never sincerely thinks her his equal. In the United States, men seldom compliment women, but they daily show how much they esteem them. They constantly display an entire confidence in the understanding of a wife, and a profound respect for her freedom. They have decided that her mind is just as fitted as that of a man to discover the plain truth, and her heart as firm to embrace it, and they have never sought to place her virtue, any more than his, under the shelter of prejudice, ignorance, and fear.

"It would seem, that in Europe, where man so easily submits to the despotic sway of woman, they are nevertheless curtailed of some of the greatest qualities of the human species, and considered as seductive, but imperfect beings, and (what may well provoke astonishment) women ultimately look upon themselves in the same light, and almost consider it as a privilege that they are entitled to show themselves futile, feeble, and timid. The women of America claim no such privileges."

".It is true, that the Americans rarely lavish upon women those eager attentions which are commonly paid them in Europe. But their conduct to women always implies, that they suppose them to be virtuous and refined ; and such is the respect entertained for the moral freedom of the sex, that, in the presence of a woman, the most guarded language is used, lest her ear should be offended by an expression. In America, a young unmarried woman may, alone, and without fear, undertake a long journey."

" Thus the Americans do not think that man and woman have either the duty, or the right, to perform the same offices, but they show an equal regard for both their respective parts ; and, though their lot is different, they consider both of them, as beings of equal value. They do not give to the courage of woman the same form, or the same direction, as to that of man ; but they never doubt her courage : and if they hold that man and his partner ought not always to exercise their intellect and understanding in the same manner, they at least believe the understanding of the one to be as sound as that of the other, and her intellect to be as clear. Thus, then, while they have allowed the social inferiority of woman to subsist, they have done all they could to raise her, morally and intellectually, to the level of man ; and, in this respect, they appear to me to have excellently understood the true principle of democratic improvement.

" As for myself, I do not hesitate to avow, that, although the women of the United States are confined within the narrow circle of domestic life, and their situation is, in some respects, one of extreme dependence, I have nowhere seen women occupying a loftier position ; and if I were asked, now I am drawing to the close of this work, in which I have spoken of so many important things done by the Americans, to what the singular prosperity and growing strength of that people ought mainly to be attributed, I should reply,—*to the superiority of their women.*"

This testimony of a foreigner, who has had abundant opportunities of making a comparison, is sanctioned by the assent of all candid and intelligent men, who have enjoyed similar opportunities.

It appears, then, that it is in America, alone, that women are raised to an equality with the other sex; and that, both in theory and practice, their interests are regarded as of equal value. They are made subordinate in station, only where a regard to their best interests demands it, while, as if in compensation for this, by custom and courtesy, they are always treated as superiors. Universally, in this Country, through every class of society, precedence is given to woman, in all the comforts, conveniences, and courtesies, of life.

In civil and political affairs, American women take no interest or concern, except so far as they sympathize with their family and personal friends; but in all cases, in which they do feel a concern, their opinions and feelings have a consideration, equal, or even superior, to that of the other sex.

In matters pertaining to the education of their children, in the selection and support of a clergyman, in all benevolent enterprises, and in all questions relating to morals or manners, they have a superior influence. In all such concerns, it would be impossible to carry a point, contrary to their judgement and feelings; while an enterprise, sustained by them, will seldom fail of success.

If those who are bewailing themselves over the fancied wrongs and injuries of women in this Nation, could only see things as they are, they would know, that, whatever remnants of a barbarous or aristocratic age may remain in our civil institutions, in reference to the interests of women, it is only because they are ignorant of it, or do not use their influence to have them rectified ; for it is very certain that there is nothing reasonable which American women would unite in asking, that would not readily be bestowed.

The preceding remarks, then, illustrate the position, that the democratic institutions of this Country are in reality no other than the principles of Christianity carried into operation, and that they tend to place woman in her true position in society, as having equal rights with the other sex; and that, in fact, they have secured to American women a lofty and fortunate position, which, as yet, has been attained by the women of no other nation.

There is another topic, presented in the work of the above author, which demands the profound attention of American women.

The following is taken from that part of the Introduction to the work, illustrating the position, that, for ages, there has been a constant progress, in all civilized nations, towards the democratic equality attained in this country.

" The various occurrences of national existence have every where turned to the advantage of democracy; all men have aided it by their exertions; those who have intentionally labored in its cause, and those who have served it unwittingly; those who have fought for it, and those who have declared themselves its opponents, have all been driven along in the same track, have all labored to one end ; " " all have been blind instruments in the hands of God."

" The gradual developement of the equality of conditions, is, therefore, a Providential fact ; and it possesses all the characteristics of a Divine decree : it is universal, it is durable, it constantly eludes all human interference, and all events, as well as all men, contribute to its progress."

" The whole book, which is here offered to the public, has been written under the impression of a kind of religious dread, produced in the Author's mind, by the contemplation of so irresistible a revolution, which has advanced for centuries, in spite of such amazing obstacles, and which is still proceeding in the midst of the ruins it has made.

" It is not necessary that God Himself should speak, in order to disclose to us the unquestionable signs of His will. We can discern them in the habitual course of Nature, and in the invariable tendency of events."

" If the men of our time were led, by attentive observation, and by sincere reflection, to acknowledge that the gradual and progressive developement of social equality is at once the past and future of their history, this solitary truth would confer the sacred character of a Divine decree upon the change. To attempt to check democracy, would be, in that case, to resist the will of God ; and the nations would then be constrained to make the best of the social lot awarded to them by Providence."

" It is not, then, merely to satisfy a legitimate curiosity, that I have examined America ; my wish has been to find instruction by which we may ourselves profit." " I have not even affected to discuss whether the social revolution, which I believe to be irresistible, is advantageous or prejudicial to mankind. I have acknowledged this revolution, as a fact already accomplished, or on the eve of its accomplishment ; and I have selected the nation, from among those which have undergone it, in which its developement has been the most peaceful and the most complete, in order to discern its natural consequences, and, if it be possible, to distinguish the means by which it may be rendered profitable. I

confess, that in America I saw more than America ;
I sought the image of democracy itself, with its in-
clinations, its character, its prejudices, and its passions, in order to learn what we have to fear, or to
hope, from its progress."

It thus appears, that the sublime and elevating
anticipations which have filled the mind and heart of
the religious world, have become so far developed,
that philosophers and statesmen perceive the signs
of its approach and are predicting the same grand
consummation.   There is a day advancing, " by
seers predicted, and by poets sung," when the curse
of selfishness shall be removed ; when " scenes sur-
passing fable, and yet true," shall be realized ; when
all nations shall rejoice and be made blessed, under
those benevolent influences which the Messiah came
to establish on earth.

And this is the nation, which the Disposer of
events designs shall go forth as the cynosure of
nations, to guide them to the light and blessedness
of that day.   To us is committed the grand, the
responsible privilege, of exhibiting to the world,
the beneficent influences of Christianity, when
carried into every social, civil, and political institution, and though we have, as yet, made such imperfect advances, already the light is streaming into the
dark prison-house of despotic lands, while startled
kings and sages, philosophers and statesmen, are
watching us with that interest which a career so
illustrious, and so involving their own destiny, is
calculated to excite.   They are studying our institutions, scrutinizing our experience, and watching
for our mistakes, that they may learn whether " a
social revolution, so irresistible, be advantageous or
prejudicial to mankind."

There are persons, who regard these interesting
truths merely as food for national vanity ; but every
reflecting and Christian mind, must consider it as

an occasion for solemn and anxious reflection. Are we, then, a spectacle to the world ? Has the Eternal Lawgiver appointed us to work out a problem involving the destiny of the whole earth? Are such momentous interests to be advanced or retarded, just in proportion as we are faithful to our high trust? "What manner of persons, then, ought we to be," in attempting to sustain so solemn, so glorious a responsibility ?

But the part to be enacted by American women, in this great moral enterprise, is the point to which special attention should here be directed.

The success of democratic institutions, as is conceded by all, depends upon the intellectual and moral character of the mass of the people. If they are intelligent and virtuous, democracy is a blessing ; but if they are ignorant and wicked, it is only a curse, and as much more dreadful than any other form of civil government, as a thousand tyrants are more to be dreaded than one. It is equally conceded, that the formation of the moral and intellectual character of the young is committed mainly to the female hand. The mother writes the character of the future man ; the sister bends the fibres that hereafter are the forest tree ; the wife sways the heart, whose energies may turn for good or for evil the destinies of a nation. Let the women of a country be made virtuous and intelligent, and the men will certainly be the same. The proper education of a man decides the welfare of an individual ; but educate a woman, and the interests of a whole family are secured.

If this be so, as none will deny, then to American women, more than to any others on earth, is committed the exalted privilege of extending over the world those blessed influences, that are to renovate degraded man, and " clothe all climes with beauty."

No American woman, then, has any occasion for

feeling that hers is an humble or insignificant lot. The value of what an individual accomplishes, is to be estimated by the importance of the enterprise achieved, and not by the particular position of the laborer. The drops of heaven that freshen the earth are each of equal value, whether they fall in the lowland meadow, or the princely parterre. The builders of a temple are of equal importance, whether they labor on the foundations, or toil upon the dome.

Thus, also, with those labors that are to be made effectual in the regeneration of the Earth. The woman who is rearing a family of children; the woman who labors in the schoolroom; the woman who, in her retired chamber, earns, with her needle, the mite to contribute for the intellectual and moral elevation of her country; even the humble domestic, whose example and influence may be moulding and forming young minds, while her faithful services sustain a prosperous domestic state;—each and all may be cheered by the consciousness, that they are agents in accomplishing the greatest work that ever was committed to human responsibility. It is the building of a glorious temple, whose base shall be coextensive with the bounds of the earth, whose summit shall pierce the skies, whose splendor shall beam on all lands, and those who hew the lowliest stone, as much as those who carve the highest capital, will be equally honored when its top-stone shall be laid, with new rejoicings of the morning stars, and shoutings of the sons of God.

CHAPTER II.

DIFFICULTIES PECULIAR TO AMERICAN WOMEN.

A Law of Moral Action to be noted. Its Application. Considerations
to be borne in mind, in appreciating peculiar Trials. Application
to American Women. Difference between this and Aristocratic
Countries. How this affects the Interests of American Women.
Effect of Wealth, in this Country, on Domestic Service. Effects
on the Domestic Comfort of Women. Second peculiar Trial of
American Women. Extent of this evil. The Writer's observation on this point. Effects on the anticipations of Mothers and
Daughters. Infrequency of Healthful Women in the Wealthy
Classes. Causes which operate to undermine the Female Constitution. Excitement of Mind. Course of Intellectual Training.
Taxation, in domestic life, of American Mothers and Housekeepers. Exercise and Fresh Air needful to balance Mental Excitement. Defect in American, compared with English, Customs, in
this respect. Difference in the Health and Youthfulness of Appearance between English and American Mothers. Liabilities of
American Women to the uncommon exposures of a New Country.
Remarks of De Tocqueville and the Writer on this point.

In the preceding Chapter, were presented those
views, which are calculated to inspire American women with a sense of their high responsibilities to
their Country, and to the world ; and of the excellence and grandeur of the object to which their energies may be consecrated.

But it will be found to be the law of moral action,
that whatever involves great results and great benefits, is always attended with great hazards and difficulties. And as it has been shown, that American
women have a loftier position, and a more elevated
object of enterprise, than the females of any other
nation, so it will appear, that they have greater trials
and difficulties to overcome, than any other women
are called to encounter.

Properly to appreciate the nature of these trials, it
must be borne in mind, that the estimate of evils and
privations depends, not so much on their positive na-

ture, as on the character and habits of the person
who meets them. A woman, educated in the savage
state, finds it no trial to be destitute of many conveniences, which a woman, even of the lowest condition, in this country, would deem indispensable to
existence. So a woman, educated with the tastes
and habits of the best New England or Virginia
housekeepers, would encounter many deprivations
and trials, that would never occur to one reared in
the log cabin of a new settlement. So, also, a woman, who has been accustomed to carry forward her
arrangements with well-trained domestics, would
meet a thousand trials to her feelings and temper, by
the substitution of ignorant foreigners, or shiftless
slaves, which would be of little account to one who
had never enjoyed any better service.

Now, the great portion of American women are the
descendants of English progenitors, who, as a nation,
are distinguished for systematic housekeeping, and
for a great love of order, cleanliness, and comfort.
And American women, to a greater or less extent,
have inherited similar tastes and habits. But the
prosperity and democratic tendencies of this country
produce results greatly affecting the comfort of
housekeepers, and which the females of monarchical
and aristocratic lands are not called to meet. In
those countries, all ranks and classes are fixed in a
given position, and each person is educated for a
particular sphere and style of living. And the dwellings, conveniences, and customs of life, remain very
nearly the same, from generation to generation. This
secures the preparation of all classes for their particular station, and makes the lower orders more dependent, and more subservient to employers.

But how different is the state of things in this
country. Every thing is moving and changing.
Persons in poverty, are rising to opulence, and persons of wealth, are sinking to poverty. The chil-

dren of common laborers, by their talents and enterprise, are becoming nobles in intellect, or wealth, or station; while the children of the wealthy, enervated by indulgence, are sinking to humbler stations. The sons of the wealthy are leaving the rich mansions of their fathers, to dwell in the log cabins of the forest, where very soon they bear away the daughters of ease and refinement, to share the privations of a new settlement. Meantime, even in the more stationary portions of the community, there is a mingling of all grades of wealth, intellect, and education. There are no distinct classes, as in aristocratic lands, whose bounds are protected by distinct and impassable lines, but all are thrown into promiscuous masses. Thus, the person of humble means is brought into contact with those of vast wealth, while all gradations, between, are placed side by side. Thus, too, there is a constant comparison of conditions, among equals, and a constant temptation presented to imitate the customs, and to strive for the enjoyments, of those who possess larger means.

In addition to this, the flow of wealth, among all classes, is constantly increasing the number of those who live in a style demanding much hired service, while the number of those, who are compelled to go to service, is constantly diminishing. Our manufactories, also, are making increased demands for female labor, and offering larger compensation. In consequence of these things, there is such a disproportion between those who wish to hire, and those who are willing to go to domestic service, that, in the non-slaveholding states, were it not for the supply of poverty-stricken foreigners, there would not be one domestic for each family who demands one. And this resort to foreigners, poor as it is, scarcely meets the demand; while the disproportion must every year increase, especially if our prosperity increases. For, just in proportion as wealth rolls in upon us, the number of those, who will give up their own independent homes to serve strangers, will be diminished.

The difficulties and sufferings that have accrued to American women, from this cause, are almost incalculable. There is nothing, which so much demands system and regularity, as the affairs of a housekeeper, made up as they are of ten thousand desultory and minute items ; and yet, this perpetually fluctuating state of society seems forever to bar any such system and regularity. The anxieties, vexations, perplexities, and even hard labor, that come upon American women, from this state of domestic service, are endless ; and many a woman has, in consequence, been disheartened, discouraged, and ruined in health. The only wonder is, that, amid so many real difficulties, American women are still able to maintain such a character for energy, fortitude, and amiableness, as is universally allowed to be their due.

But the second, and still greater difficulty, peculiar to American women, is a delicacy of constitution, which renders them early victims to disease and decay.

The fact that the women of this Country are unusually subject to disease, and that their beauty and youthfulness is of shorter continuance than that of the women of other nations, is one which always attracts the attention of foreigners, while medical men and philanthropists are constantly giving fearful monitions as to the extent and alarming increase of this evil. Investigations make it evident that a large proportion of young ladies from the wealthier classes have the incipient stages of curvature of the spine, one of the most sure and fruitful causes of future disease and decay. The Writer has heard medical men, who have made extensive inquiries, say, that probably one in every six, of the young women at boarding schools, are affected in this way, while many other indications of disease and debility exist, in cases where this particular evil cannot be detected.

In consequence of this enfeebled state of their constitutions, induced by a neglect of their physical education, as soon as they are called to the responsibilities and trials of domestic life, their constitution fails, and their whole life is rendered a burden. For no person can enjoy existence, when disease throws a dark cloud over the mind, and incapacitates her for the proper discharge of every duty.

The Writer, who for some ten years has had the charge of an institution, consisting of young ladies from almost every state in the Union, since relinquishing that charge, has travelled and visited extensively in most of the non-slaveholding states. In these circuits, she has learned the domestic history, not merely of her pupils, but of many other young wives and mothers, whose sorrowful experience has come to her knowledge. And the impression produced by the dreadful extent of this evil, has at times been almost overwhelming.

It would seem as if the primeval curse, that has written the doom of pain and sorrow on one period of a young mother's life, in this Country had been extended over all; so that the hour never arrives, when " she forgetteth her sorrow for joy that a man is born into the world." Many a mother will testify, with shuddering, that the most exquisite sufferings she ever endured, were not those appointed by Nature, but those, which, for week after week, have worn down health and spirits, when nourishing her child. And medical men teach us, that this, in most cases, results from a debility of constitution, consequent on the mismanagement of early life. And so frequent and so mournful are these, and the other distresses that result from the failure of the female constitution, that the Writer has repeatedly heard mothers say, that they had wept tears of bit-

terness over their infant daughters, at the thought
of the sufferings which they were destined to under-
go; while they cherished the decided wish that
these daughters should never marry. At the same
time, many a reflecting young woman is looking to
her future prospects, with very different feelings and
hopes from those which Providence designed.

A perfectly healthy woman, especially a perfectly
healthy mother, is so unfrequent, in some of the
wealthier classes, that those who are so may be regarded as the exceptions, and not as the general
rule. The Writer has heard some of her friends
declare, that they would ride fifty miles, to see a
perfectly healthy and vigorous woman, out of the
laboring classes. This, although somewhat jocose,
was not an entirely unfair picture of the true state of
female health in the wealthier classes.

There are many causes operating, which tend to
perpetuate and increase this evil. It is a well-known
fact, that mental excitement tends to weaken the
physical system, unless it is counterbalanced by a
corresponding increase of exercise and fresh air.
Now, the people of this Country are under the influence of high commercial, political, and religious
stimulus, altogether greater than was ever known
by any other nation; and in all this, women are
made the sympathizing companions of the other sex.
At the same time, young girls, in pursuing an education, have ten times greater an amount of intellectual taxation demanded, than was ever before
exacted. Let any daughter, educated in our best
schools at this day, compare the course of her study
with that pursued in her mother's early life, and it
will be seen that this estimate of the increase of
mental taxation probably falls below the truth.
Though, in some countries, there are small classes
of females, in the higher circles, who pursue literature and science to a far greater extent than in any

corresponding circles in this Country, yet in no nation in the world, are the advantages of a good intellectual education enjoyed by so large a proportion of the females. And this education has consisted far less of accomplishments and far more of those solid studies that demand the exercise of the various powers of mind, than the education of the women of other lands.

And when the American women are called to the responsibilities of domestic life, the degree in which their minds and feelings are taxed, is altogether greater than in any other nation.

No women on earth have a higher sense of their moral and religious responsibilities, or better understand, not only what is demanded of them, as housekeepers, but all the claims that rest upon them as wives, mothers, and members of a social community. An American woman, who is the mistress of a family, feels her obligations, in reference to her influence over her husband, and a still greater responsibility in rearing and educating her children. She feels, too, the claims the moral interests of her domestics have on her watchful care. In social life, she recognises the claims of hospitality, and the demands of friendly visiting. Her responsibility, in reference to the institutions of benevolence and religion, are deeply realized. The regular worship of the Lord's day, and all the various religious and benevolent societies that place so much dependence on female activity, she feels obligated to sustain, by her influence and example. Add to these multiplied responsibilities, the perplexities and evils that have been pointed out, resulting from the fluctuating state of society, and the deficiency of domestic service, and no one can deny that American women are exposed to a far greater amount of intellectual and moral excitement, than those of any other land. Of course, in order to escape the danger resulting from this, a greater amount of exercise in the fresh air, and all those methods which strengthen the constitution, are imperiously required.

But, instead of this, it will be found, that, owing to the climate and customs of this Nation, there are no women who secure so little of this healthful and protecting regimen. Walking and riding and gardening, in the open air, are practised by the women of other lands, to a far greater extent, than by American females. Most English women, in the wealthier classes, are able to walk six and eight miles on a stretch, without oppressive fatigue; and when they visit this Country, always express their surprise at the inactive habits of American ladies. In England, the regular daily exercise, in the open air, is very commonly required by the mother, as a part of daily duty, and is sought by young women, as an enjoyment. In consequence of a different physical training, English women, in those circles that enjoy competency, present an appearance which always strikes American gentlemen as a contrast to what they see at home. An English mother, at thirty, or thirty-five, is in the full bloom of perfected womanhood; as fresh and healthful as her daughters. But where are the American mothers, who can reach this period unfaded and unworn? In America, young ladies in the wealthier classes, are sent to school from early childhood; and neither parents nor teachers make it a definite object to secure a proper amount of fresh air and exercise, to counterbalance this intellectual taxation. As soon as they pass their school days, dressing, visiting, evening parties, and stimulating amusements, take the place of study, while the most unhealthful modes of dress add to the physical exposures. To make morning calls, or do a little shopping, is all that can be called their exercise in the fresh air; and this, compared to what is needed, is absolutely nothing, and on

some accounts is worse than nothing. In consequence of these, and other evils, that will be pointed
out more at large in the following pages, the young
women of America grow up with such a delicacy of
constitution, that probably eight out of ten become
subjects of disease either before or as soon as they
are called to the responsibilities of domestic life.

But there is one peculiarity of situation, in regard to
American women, that makes this delicacy of constitution still more disastrous. It is the liability to the
exposures and hardships of a newly-settled country.

One more extract from De Tocqueville will give a
view of this part of the subject, which any one,
familiar with western life, will admire for its veri-
similitude.

"The same strength of purpose which the young
wives of America display in bending themselves, at
once, and without repining, to the austere duties of
their new condition, is no less manifest in all the great
trials of their lives. In no country in the world are
private fortunes more precarious, than in the United
States. It is not uncommon for the same man, in the
course of his life, to rise and sink again through all the
grades which lead from opulence to poverty. American women support these vicissitudes with a calm
and unquenchable energy. It would seem that their
desires contract, as easily as they expand, with their
fortunes. The greater part of the adventurers, who
migrate, every year, to people the Western wilds,
belong" "to the old Anglo-American race of the
Northern States. Many of these men, who rush so
boldly onward in pursuit of wealth, were already in
the enjoyment of a competency in their own part of
the country. They take their wives along with
them, and make them share the countless perils and
privations, which always attend the commencement
of these expeditions. I have often met, even on the
verge of the wilderness, with young women, who, after

having been brought up amid all the comforts of the
large towns of New England, had passed, almost
without any intermediate stage, from the wealthy
abode of their parents, to a comfortless hovel in a
forest. Fever, solitude, and a tedious life, had not
broken the springs of their courage. Their features
were impaired and faded, but their looks were firm :
they appeared to be, at once, sad and resolute."

In another passage, he gives this picturesque
sketch : "By the side of the hearth, sits a woman,
with a baby on her lap. She nods to us, without
disturbing herself. Like the pioneer, this woman is
in the prime of life ; her appearance would seem
superior to her condition ; and her apparel even be-
trays a lingering taste for dress. But her delicate
limbs appear shrunken ; her features are drawn in ;
her eye is mild and melancholy ; her whole phys-
iognomy bears marks of a degree of religious res-
ignation, a deep quiet of all passion, and some
sort of natural and tranquil firmness, ready to meet
all the ills of life, without fearing and without
braving them. Her children cluster about her, full
of health, turbulence, and energy ; they are true
children of the wilderness : their mother watches
them, from time to time, with mingled melancholy
and joy. To look at their strength, and her languor,
one might imagine that the life she had given them
had exhausted her own ; and still she regrets not
what they have cost her. The house, inhabited by
these emigrants, has no internal partition or loft. In
the one chamber of which it consists, the whole family is gathered for the night. The dwelling is itself a
little world ; an ark of civilization amid an ocean of
foliage. A hundred steps beyond it, the primeval forest spreads its shades, and solitude resumes its sway."

Such scenes, and such women, the Writer has
met, and few persons realize how many refined
and lovely women are scattered over the broad prai-

ries and deep forests of the West; and none but the Father above appreciates the extent of those sacrifices and sufferings, and the value of that firm faith and religious hope, that lives, in perennial bloom, amid those vast solitudes. If the American women of the East merit the palm, for their skill and success as accomplished housekeepers, still more is due to the heroines of the West, who, with such unyielding fortitude and cheerful endurance, attempt similar duties, amid so many disadvantages and deprivations.

But, though American women have those elevated principles and feelings, which enable them to meet such trials in so exemplary a manner, their physical energies are not equal to the exertions demanded. Though the mind may be bright and firm, the casket is shivered; though the spirit may be willing, the flesh is weak. A woman of firm health, with the hope and elasticity of youth, may be envied rather than pitied, as she shares with her young husband the hopes and enterprises of pioneer life. But, when the body fails, the eye of hope grows dim, the heart sickens, the courage dies, and in solitude, weariness, and suffering, the wanderer pines for the dear voices and the tender sympathies of a far distant home. Then it is, that the darkest shade is presented, that marks the peculiar trials and liabilities of American women, and which exhibits still more forcibly the disastrous results of that delicacy of constitution which has been pointed out. For, though all American women, or even the greater part of them, are not called to encounter such trials, yet no mother, who rears a family of daughters, can say, that such a lot will not fall to one of her flock, nor can she know which will escape. The reverses of fortune, and the chances of matrimony, expose every woman in the Nation to such liabilities, for which they need to be prepared.

CHAPTER III.

REMEDY FOR THESE DIFFICULTIES.

First Remedy suggested. Obligations of Wealthy Ladies on this point. How a dearth of Domestics may prove a blessing. Second Remedy. Third Remedy. Reasons for endowing Colleges and Professional Schools. Similar reasons exist for endowing Female Institutions. Present evils in conducting Female Education. A Sketch of a Model Female Institution. Accommodations provided. Mode of securing exercise to Pupils. Objections to this answered. Calisthenics. Course of Intellectual Discipline adopted. Mode of Division of Labor adopted. Example of Illinois in regard to Female Education. Economy of Health and Time secured by such Institutions. Plan suggested for the Early Education of Young Girls. Last Remedy suggested.

HAVING pointed out the peculiar responsibilities of American women, and the peculiar embarrassments they are called to encounter, the following suggestions are offered, as the remedy for these difficulties.

In the first place, the physical and domestic education of daughters should occupy the principal attention of mothers, in childhood; and the stimulation of the intellect should be very much reduced. As a general rule, daughters should not be sent to school before they are six years old; and when they do go, far more attention should be paid to their physical developement. They should never be confined, at any employment, more than an hour at a time; and this confinement should be followed by sports in the open air. Such accommodations should be secured, that, at all seasons, and in all weathers, the teacher can send out a portion of her school, every half hour, for sports.

In addition to this, much less time should be given to school, and much more to domestic employments, especially in the wealthier classes. A little girl may begin, at five or six years of age, to assist her mother; and, if properly trained, by the time she is ten, she can render essential aid. From this time, until she is fourteen or fifteen, it should be the principal object of her education to secure a strong and healthy constitution, and a thorough practical knowledge of all kinds of domestic employments. During this period, though some attention ought to be paid to intellectual culture, it ought to be made altogether secondary in importance; and such a measure of study and intellectual excitement, as is now demanded in our best female seminaries, ought never to be allowed, until a young lady has passed the most critical period of her youth, and has a vigorous and healthful constitution fully established.

And it is to that class of mothers, who have the most means of securing hired service, and who are the most tempted to allow their daughters to grow up with inactive habits, that their country and the world must look for a reformation, in this respect. Whatever ladies in the wealthier classes decide shall be fashionable, will be followed by all the rest; while, if ladies of this class persist in the aristocratic habits, now so common, and bring up their daughters to feel as if labor was degrading and unbecoming, the evils pointed out will never find a remedy. It is, therefore, the peculiar duty of ladies who have wealth, to set a proper example, in this respect, and make it their first aim to secure a strong and healthful constitution for their daughters, by active domestic employments. All the sweeping, dusting, care of furniture and beds, the clear starching, and the nice cooking, should be done by the daughters of a family, and not by hired service. It may cost the mother more care, and she may find it needful to hire a person for the express purpose of instructing and superintending her daughters in these employments, but it is what should be regarded as indis-

pensable to be secured, either by the mother's agency, or by a substitute.

It is in this point of view, that the dearth of good
domestics in this Country may, in its results, prove
a substantial blessing. If all housekeepers, that have
the means, could secure good service, there would
be little hope that so important a revolution, in the
domestic customs of the wealthy classes, could be
effected. And so great is the *vis inertiæ** of mankind, that the amount of exercise, needful for health,
would never be secured by those who were led to it
by no necessity, but merely from rational considerations. But already the pressure of domestic troubles,
from the want of good domestics, has led many a
mother, in the wealthy classes, to determine to train
her daughters to aid her in domestic service; and
thus necessity is driving mothers to do what abstract
principles of expediency never could secure.

A second method of promoting the same object,
is, to raise the science and practice of domestic
economy to its appropriate place, as a regular study
in female seminaries. The succeeding chapter will
present the reasons for this, more at large. But it is
to the mothers in this Country, that the community
must look for this change. It cannot be expected,
that teachers, who have their attention chiefly absorbed by the intellectual and moral interests of
their pupils, should properly realize the importance
of this department of education. But if mothers
generally become convinced of the importance of
this measure, their judgement and wishes will meet
the respectful consideration they deserve, and the
thing will be done.

The third method for securing a remedy for the
evils pointed out, is by means of endowed female

---

* "The power of inertness." In Natural Philosophy, this term is
applied to the tendency of matter to keep at rest; in morals, it has a
figurative signification, and is another name for sluggishness.

institutions, under the care of suitable trustees, who shall secure a proper course of female education. The importance of this measure cannot be realized by those, who have not turned their attention to this subject; and for such, the following considerations are presented.

The endowment of colleges, and of law, medical, and divinity, schools, for the other sex, is designed to secure a thorough and proper education, for those who have the most important duties of society to perform. The men who are to expound the laws, the men who have the care of the public health, and the men who are to communicate religious instruction, should have well-disciplined and well-informed minds; and it is mainly for this object that collegiate and professional institutions are established. Liberal and wealthy men contribute funds, and the legislatures of the States also lend assistance, so that every State in this Nation has from one to twenty such endowed institutions, supplied with buildings, apparatus, library, and a faculty of learned men to carry forward a superior course of instruction. And the use of all these advantages is secured, in many cases, at an expense no greater than is required to send a boy to a common school and pay his board there. No private school could offer these advantages, without charging such a sum, as would forbid all but the rich from securing its benefits. By furnishing such superior advantages, on low terms, multitudes are properly educated, who would otherwise have remained in ignorance; and thus the professions are supplied, by men properly qualified.

Were there no such institutions, and no regular and appropriate course of study demanded for admission to the bar, pulpit, and medical practice, the education of most professional men would be desultory, imperfect, and deficient. Parents and children would regulate the course of study according to their own crude notions, and instead of having institutions that agree in carrying on a similar course of study, each school would have its own peculiar system, and be competing and conflicting with every other. Meantime, the public would have no means of deciding which was best, nor any opportunity for learning when a professional man was properly qualified for his duties. But as it is, the diploma of a college, and the license of an appointed body of judges, must both be secured, before a young man feels that he has entered the most promising path to success in his profession.

Our Country, then, is most abundantly supplied with endowed institutions, which secure a liberal education, on such low terms as make them accessible to all classes, and in which the interests of education are watched over, sustained, and made permanent, by an appropriate board of trustees.

But are not the most responsible of all duties committed to the care of woman? Is it not her profession to take care of mind, body, and soul? and that, too, at the most critical of all periods of existence? And is it not as much a matter of public concern, that she should be properly qualified for her duties, as that ministers, lawyers, and physicians, should be prepared for theirs? And is it not as important to endow institutions that shall make a superior education accessible to all classes, for females, as much as for the other sex? And is it not equally important, that institutions for females be under the supervision of intelligent and responsible trustees, whose duty it shall be to secure a uniform and appropriate education for one sex as much as for the other? It would seem as if every mind must accord an affirmative reply, as soon as the matter is fairly considered.

As the education of females is now conducted, any man or woman that pleases can establish a female seminary, and secure recommendations that will attract pupils. But whose business is it to see that these young females are not huddled into crowded rooms? or that they do not sleep in ill-ventilated chambers? or that they have healthful food? or that they have the requisite amount of fresh air and exercise? or that they pursue an appropriate and systematic course of study? or that their manners, principles, and morals, are properly regulated? Parents either have not the means, or else are not qualified to judge; or, if they are furnished with means and capacity, they are often restricted to a choice of the best school within reach, even when it is known to be exceedingly objectionable.

If the Writer were to disclose all that could truly be told of boarding-school life, and its influence on health, manners, disposition, intellect, and morals, it would be a tale, which would both astonish and shock every rational mind. And yet she believes that such institutions are far better managed in this Country than in any other; and that the number of those, which are subject to imputations in these respects, is much less than could reasonably be expected. But it is most surely the case, that much remains to be done, in order to supply such institutions as are needed for the proper education of American women.

In attempting a sketch of the kind of institutions which are demanded, it is very fortunate that there is no necessity for presenting a theory, which may, or may not, be approved by experience. It is the greatest honor of one of our newest Western States, that it can boast of such an Institution, and one endowed, too, wholly by the munificence of one individual. A slight sketch of this Institution, which the Writer has examined in all its details, will give an idea of what can be done, by showing what has actually been accomplished.

This Institution* is under the supervision of a Board of Trustees, appointed by the Founder, who hold the property, in trust for the object to which it is devoted, and who have the power to fill their own vacancies. It is furnished with a noble and tasteful building, of stone, so liberal in dimensions and arrangement, that it can accommodate eighty pupils and teachers, giving one room to every two pupils, and all being so arranged, as to admit of thorough ventilation. This building is surrounded by extensive grounds, enclosed with handsome fences, where remains of the primeval forest still offer refreshing shade for juvenile sports.

To secure adequate exercise for the pupils, two methods are adopted. By the first, each young lady is required to spend two hours in domestic employments, either in sweeping, dusting, setting, and clearing tables, washing and ironing, or other household concerns.

Let not the aristocratic mother and daughter express their dislike of such an arrangement, till they can learn how well it succeeds. Let them walk, as the Writer has done, through the large airy halls, kept clean and in order by their fair occupants, to the washing and ironing rooms. There they will see a long hall, conveniently fitted up with some thirty neat looking tubs, with a clean floor, and water conducted so as to save both labor and slopping. Let them see some thirty or forty merry girls, superintended by a motherly lady, chatting and singing, washing and starching, while every convenience is at hand, and every thing around is clean and comfortable. Two hours, thus employed, enables each young lady to wash the articles she used during the previous week, which is all that is demanded, while thus they are all practically initiated into the arts

* The Monticello Female Seminary, endowed by Mr. Godfrey, of Alton, Illinois.

and mysteries of the wash-tub. The Superintend-
ent remarked to the Writer, that, after a few weeks
of probation, her young washers succeeded quite as
well as most of those whom she could hire, and who
made it their business. Adjacent to the washing
room, was the ironing establishment; where another
class were arranged, on the ironing day, around
long extended tables, with heating furnaces, clothes
frames, and all needful appliances.

By a systematic arrangement of school and domestic duties, two hours, each day, from each of the
pupils, accomplished all the domestic labor of a family of eighty, except the cooking, which was done
by two hired domestics. This part of domestic labor it was deemed inexpedient to incorporate as a
part of the business of the pupils, inasmuch as it
could not be accommodated to the arrangements of
the school, and was in other respects objectionable.

Is it asked, how can young ladies paint, play the
piano, and study, when their hands and dresses must
be unfitted by such drudgery? The woman who
asks this question, has yet to learn that a pure and
delicate skin is better secured by healthful exercise,
than by any other method; and that a young lady,
who will spend two hours a day at the wash-tub, or
with a broom, is far more likely to have rosy cheeks,
a finely-moulded form, and a delicate skin, than one
who lolls all day in her parlor or chamber, or only
leaves them, girt in tight dresses, to make fashionable calls. It is true, that long-protracted daily labor hardens the hand, and unfits it for delicate employments; but the amount of labor needful for health
produces no such effect. As to dress, and appearance,
if neat and convenient accommodations are furnished,
there is no occasion for the exposures that demand
shabby dresses. A dark calico, genteelly made, with
an oiled silk apron, and wide cuffs of the same material, secure both good looks and good service. This

plan of domestic employments for the pupils in this institution, not only secures regular healthful exercise, but also reduces the expenses of education, so as to bring it within the reach of many, who otherwise could never gain such advantages.

In addition to this, a system of Calisthenic* exercises is introduced, which secures all the advantages which dancing is supposed to effect, and which is free from the dangerous tendencies of that fascinating fashionable amusement. This system is so combined with music, and constantly varying evolutions, as to serve as an amusement, and also as a mode of curing distortions, particularly all tendencies to curvature of the spine; while, at the same time, it tends to promote grace of movement, and easy manners.

Another advantage of this institution, is, an elevated and invigorating course of mental discipline. Many persons seem to suppose, that the chief object of an intellectual education is the acquisition of knowledge. But it will be found, that this is only a secondary object. It is the formation of habits of investigation, of correct reasoning, of persevering attention, of regular system, of accurate analysis, and of vigorous mental action, that are the primary objects to be sought in preparing American women for their arduous duties, which will demand not only quickness of perception, but steadiness of purpose, regularity of system and perseverance in action.

It is for such purposes, that the discipline of the Mathematics is so important an element in female education; and it is in this aspect, that the mere acquisition of facts, and the attainment of accomplishments, should be made of altogether secondary account.

In the institution here described, a systematic

---

* From two Greek words,—καλος, *kalos*, beauty, and σϑενος, *sthenos*, strength, being the union of both.

course of study is adopted, as in our colleges; designed to occupy three years. The following slight outline of the course of study, will exhibit the liberal plan adopted in this respect.

In Mathematics, the whole of Arithmetic contained in the larger works used in schools, the whole of Euclid, and such portions from Day's Mathematics as are requisite to enable the pupils to demonstrate the various problems in Olmsted's larger work on Natural Philosophy. In Language, besides English Grammar, a short course in Latin is required, sufficient to secure an understanding of the philosophy of the language, and that kind of mental discipline which the exercise of translating affords. In Philosophy, Chemistry, Astronomy, Botany, Geology and Mineralogy, Intellectual and Moral Philosophy, Political Economy, and the Evidences of Christianity, the same textbooks are used as are required at our best colleges. In Geography, the largest work, and most thorough course, is adopted; and in History, a more complete knowledge is secured, by means of charts and textbooks, than most of our colleges offer. To these branches, are added Griscom's Physiology, Bigelow's Technology,* and Jahn's Archæology, together with a course of instruction in polite literature, for which Chalmers's English Literature is employed, as the textbook, each recitation being attended with selections and criticisms, from teacher or pupils, on the various authors brought into notice. Vocal Music, on the plan of the Boston Academy, is a part of the daily instructions. Linear drawing and pencilling are designed also to be a part of the course. Instrumental Music is taught, but not as a part of the regular course of study.

---

* This work, greatly improved, enlarged, brought down to the present time, and illustrated by numerous engravings, now forms vols. xi. and xii. of the larger series of 'The School Library,' issued by the publishers of this volume. Its present title is 'The Useful Arts, considered in connexion with the Applications of Science.'

To secure the proper instruction in all these branches, the division of labor, adopted in colleges, is pursued. Each teacher has distinct branches as her department, for which she is responsible, and in which she is independent. By this method, the teachers have sufficient time, both to prepare themselves, and to impart instruction and illustration in the class-room.

One peculiarity of this Institution demands consideration. By the method adopted there, the exclusive business of educating their own sex is confined to females, as it ever ought to be. The Principal of the Institution, indeed, is a gentleman ; but, while he takes the position of a father of the family, and responsible head of the whole concern, the whole charge of instruction, and all the responsibilities in regard to health, morals, and manners, rest upon the female teachers, in their several departments. The Principal is the chaplain and religious teacher ; and is a member of the board of instructers, so far as to have a voice, and an equal vote, in every question pertaining to the concerns of the Institution : and thus he acts as a sort of regulating mainspring in all the various departments. But no one person in the Institution is loaded with the excessive responsibilities, that rest upon one person where a large institution of this kind has one Principal, who employs and directs all the subordinate assistants. The Writer has never before seen the principle of the division of labor and responsibility so perfectly carried out in any female institution ; and believes that experience will prove that this is the true model for combining, in appropriate proportions, the agency of both sexes in carrying forward such an institution.

One other thing should be noticed, to the credit of the rising State where this Institution is located. A female association has been formed, embracing a large portion of the ladies of standing and wealth, the design of which, is, to educate, gratuitously, at this, and other similar, institutions, such females, as are anxious to obtain a good education, and are destitute of the means. If this enterprise is continued, with the same energy and perseverance as has been manifested the last few years, Illinois will take the lead of her sister States, in well-educated women; and if the views in the preceding pages are correct, this will give her precedence in every intellectual and moral advantage.

Many, who are not aware of the great economy secured by a proper division of labor, will not understand how so extensive a course can be properly completed in three years. But in this Institution, none are received under fourteen, and a certain amount of previous acquisition is required, in order to admission, as is done in our colleges. This secures a diminution of classes, so that but few studies are pursued at one time; while the number of well-qualified teachers is so adequate, that full time is afforded for all needful instruction and illustration. Where teachers have so many classes, that they merely have time to find out what their pupils learn from books, without any aid from their teacher, the acquisitions of the pupils are vague and imperfect, and soon pass away; so that an immense amount of expense, time, and labor, are spent in acquiring what is lost about as fast as it is gained.

Parents are little aware of the immense waste incurred by the present mode of conducting female education. In the wealthy classes, young girls are sent to school, as a matter of course, year after year, confined, six hours a day, to the schoolhouse, and required to add some time out of school to acquiring school exercises. Thus, during the most critical period of life, they are confined, six hours a day, in a room filled with an atmosphere vitiated by many breaths, and are constantly kept under some sort of responsibility in regard to mental effort. Their studies are pursued at random, often changed with changing schools, while one schoolbook after another (heavily taxing the parent's purse) is conned awhile and then supplanted by another. Teachers usually have so many pupils, and such a variety of branches to teach, that little time can be afforded to each pupil, while scholars, at this thoughtless period of life, feeling sure of going to school as long as they please, feel little interest in their pursuits.

The Writer believes that the actual amount of education, permanently secured by most young ladies from the age of ten to fourteen, could all be acquired in one year, at the Institution described, by a young lady at the age of fifteen or sixteen.

Instead of such a course as the common one, if mothers would keep their daughters as their domestic assistants, until they are fourteen, requiring them to study one lesson, and go out, once a day, to recite it to a teacher, it would abundantly prepare them, after their constitution is firmly established, to enter such an institution, where, in three years, they could secure more than almost any young lady in the Country now gains, by giving the whole of her youth to school pursuits.

In the early years of female life, writing, needlework, drawing, and music, should interchange with domestic duties; and one hour a day, being devoted to these pursuits, or to reading, would be all that would be needful to prepare them for a thorough education after they attain their growth. This is the time when young women would feel the value of an education, and pursue their studies with that maturity of mind, and vividness of interest, which would double the perpetuity and value of all their acquisitions.

But the great difficulty which opposes such a plan, is, the want of such institutions as would enable a young lady to complete, in three years,

such a liberal course of study, as the one described.
But if American mothers become convinced of the
importance of such advantages for their daughters,
and will use their influence appropriately and efficiently, they will certainly be furnished. There
are other men of liberality and wealth, besides the
one in Illinois, who can be made to feel that a fortune, expended in securing an appropriate education
to American women, is as wisely bestowed, as in
founding colleges for the other sex, who are already
so abundantly supplied. We ought to have such
institutions, as the one at Monticello, in every part
of this Nation ; and funds should be provided for
educating young women destitute of means : and if
American women think and feel that, by such a
method, their own trials will be lightened, and their
daughters will secure a healthful constitution and a
thorough domestic and intellectual education, the
appropriate expression of their wishes will secure
the necessary means. The tide of charity, which
has been so long flowing from the female hand to
provide a liberal education for young men, will re-
flow with abundant remuneration.

The last method suggested for lessening the evils
peculiar to American women, is, a decided effort to
oppose the aristocratic feeling, that labor is degrading ; and to bring about the impression that it is
refined and lady-like to engage in domestic pursuits.
In past ages, and in aristocratic countries, leisure
and indolence and frivolous pursuits have been
deemed lady-like and refined, because those classes,
which were most refined, patronised such an impression. But as soon as ladies of refinement, as
a general custom, patronise domestic pursuits, then
these pursuits will be deemed lady-like. But it
may be urged, that it is impossible for a woman
who cooks, washes, and sweeps, to appear in the
dress, or acquire the habits and manners, of a lady ;

that the drudgery of the kitchen is dirty work, and
t!iat no one can appear delicate and refined, while
engaged in it.   Now all this depends on circumstances.   If a woman has a house, destitute of neat
and convenient facilities; if she has no habits of
order and system; if she is slack and careless in
person and dress;—then all this may be true.
But, if a woman will make some sacrifices of costly
ornaments in her parlor, in order to make her kitchen
neat and tasteful; if she will sacrifice costly dishes,
in order to secure such conveniences for labor as
protect from exposures; if she will take pains to
have the dresses, in which she works, made of suitable materials, and in good taste; if she will rise
early, and systematize and oversee the work of her
family, so as to have it done thoroughly, neatly, and
in the early part of the day; she will find no necessity for any such apprehensions.   It is because such
work has generally been done by vulgar people, and
in a vulgar way, that we have such associations;
and when ladies manage such things, as ladies
should, then such associations will be removed.
There are pursuits, deemed very refined and genteel,
that involve quite as much exposure as kitchen employments.   For example, to draw a large landscape,
in colored crayons, would be deemed very lady-like;
but the Writer can testify, from sad experience, that
no cooking, washing, sweeping, or any other domestic duty, ever left such deplorable traces on hands,
face, and dress, as this same lady-like pursuit.   Such
things depend entirely on custom and associations;
and every American woman, who values the institutions of her Country, and wishes to lend her influence in extending and perpetuating such blessings, may feel that she is doing this, whenever, by
her example and influence, she destroys the aristocratic association, that would render domestic labor
degrading.

CHAPTER IV.

ON DOMESTIC ECONOMY AS A BRANCH OF STUDY.

Impediment to the Object of this Chapter. First Reason for making
Domestic Economy a Study at School. Second Reason. Examples illustrating. Third Reason. Questions asked. First Objection; how answered. Next Objection; how answered. Next
Objection; how answered. Last Reason.

THE greatest impediment to the object of this
chapter, is, the fact, that neither parents nor teachers
realize, either the importance, or the practicability
of making domestic economy a regular part of school
education.

It is with reference to this, that the first aim will
be, to point out some of the reasons for introducing
Domestic Economy as a branch of female education,
to be studied at school.

The first reason, is, that there is no period, in a
young lady's life, when she will not find such
knowledge useful to herself, and to others. The
state of domestic service, in this country, is so
precarious, that there is scarcely a family, in the
free States, where it can be affirmed, that either
sickness, discontent, or love of change, will not deprive them of all their domestics, so that every female member of the family will be required to lend
some aid in providing food and the conveniences of
living. Every young lady is the member of some
family, which will need her aid in such emergencies, and the better she is qualified to render it, the
happier she will be, herself, and the more she will
contribute to the enjoyment of others.

A second reason, is, that every young lady, at the
close of her schooldays, and even before they are
closed, is liable to be placed in a situation, in which

she will need to do, herself, or to teach others to do, all the various processes and duties detailed in this work. That this may be more fully realized, the Writer will detail some instances, that have come under her own observation.

The eldest daughter of a family returned from school, on a visit, at sixteen years of age. Before her vacation had closed, her mother was laid in the grave ; and such were her father's circumstances, that she was obliged to assume the cares and duties of her lost parent. The care of an infant, the management of young children, the superintendence of domestics, the charge of family expenses, the responsibility of entertaining company, and the many other cares of the family state, all at once came upon this young and inexperienced schoolgirl.

Again ; a young lady went to reside with a married sister, in a distant State. While on this visit, the elder sister died, and there was no one but this young lady to fill the vacant place, and assume all the cares of the nursery, parlor, and kitchen.

Again ; a pupil of the Writer, at the end of her schooldays, married, and removed to the West. She was an entire novice in all domestic matters ; an entire stranger in the place to which she removed. In a year she became a mother, and *her health failed ;* while, for most of the time, she had no domestics, at all, or only Irish or Germans, who scarcely knew even the names, or the uses, of many cooking utensils. She was treated with politeness by her neighbors, and wished to return their civilities ; but how could this young and delicate creature, who had spent all her life at school, or in visiting and amusement, take care of her infant, attend to her cooking, washing, ironing, and baking, take care of her parlor, chambers, kitchen, and cellar, and yet visit and receive company ? If there is any thing that would make a kindly heart ache with sorrow and sympathy, it would be to see so young, so amiable, so helpless a martyr to the mistaken system of female education now prevalent. " I have the kindest of husbands," said the young wife, after her narrative of sufferings, " and I never regretted my marriage ; but, since this babe was born, I have never had a single waking hour of freedom from anxiety and care. O! how little young girls know what is before them, when they enter the married life!" Let the mother or teacher, whose eye may rest on these lines, ask herself, if there is no cause for fear that the young objects of her care may be thrown into similar emergencies, where they may need a kind of preparation, which as yet has been withheld?

Another reason for introducing such a subject, as a distinct branch of school education, is, that, as a general fact, young ladies *will* *not* be taught these things in any other way. In reply to the thousand-times-repeated remark, that girls must be taught their domestic duties by their mothers, at home, it may be inquired, in the first place, What proportion of mothers are qualified to teach a *proper* and *complete* system of Domestic Economy? When this is answered, it may be asked, What proportion of those who are qualified, have that sense of the importance of such instructions, and that energy and perseverance which would enable them actually to teach their daughters, in all the branches of Domestic Economy presented in this work?

When this is answered, it may be asked, How many mothers *actually do* give their daughters instruction in the various branches of Domestic Economy? Is it not the case, that, owing to ill health, deficiency of domestics, and multiplied cares and perplexities, a large portion of the most intelligent mothers, and those, too, who most realize the importance of this instruction, actually cannot find the time, and have not the energy, necessary to properly perform the duty? They are taxed to the full amount of both their mental and physical energies, and cannot attempt any thing more. Almost every woman knows, that it is easier to do the work, herself, than it is to teach an awkward and careless novice; and the great majority of women, in this Country, are obliged to do almost every thing in the shortest and easiest way. This is one reason why the daughters of very energetic and accomplished housekeepers often are the most deficient in these respects; while the daughters of ignorant or inefficient mothers, driven to the exercise of their own energies, often become the most systematic and expert.

It may be objected, that such things cannot be taught by books. This position may fairly be questioned. Do not young ladies learn, from books, how to make hydrogen and oxygen? Do they not have pictures of furnaces, alembics, and the various utensils employed in *cooking* the chemical agents? Do they not study the various processes of mechanics, and learn to understand and to do many as difficult operations as any that belong to housekeeping? All these things are studied, explained, and recited in classes, when every one knows that little practical use can ever be made of this knowledge. Why, then, should not that science and art, which a woman is to practise during her whole life, be studied and recited?

It may be urged, that, even if it is studied, it will soon be forgotten. And so will much of every thing studied at school. But why should that knowledge, most needful for daily comfort, most liable to be in demand, be the only study omitted, because it may be forgotten?

It may also be objected, that young ladies can get such books, and attend to them out of school.

And so they can get books on Chemistry and
Philosophy, and study them out of school ; but *will*
they do it ?   And why ought we not to make sure
the most necessary knowledge, and let the less needful be omitted ?   If young ladies study such a work
as this, in school, they will remember a great part of
it ; and, when they forget, in any emergency, they
will know where to resort for instruction.   But if
such books are not put into schools, probably not
one in twenty will see or hear of them, especially in
those retired places where they are most needed.
So deeply is the Writer impressed with the importance of this, as a branch of female education, at
school, that she would deem it far safer and wiser to
omit any other, rather than this.

Another reason, for introducing such a branch of
study into female schools, is, the influence it would
exert, in leading young ladies more correctly to
estimate the importance and dignity of domestic
knowledge.   It is now often the case, that young
ladies rather pride themselves on their ignorance of
such subjects ; and seem to imagine that it is vulgar
and ungenteel to know how to work.   This is one
of the relics of an aristocratic state of society,
which is fast passing away.   Here the tendency of
every thing is to the equalisation of labor, so that
all classes are feeling, more and more, that indolence
is disreputable.   And there are many mothers,
among the best educated and most wealthy classes,
who are bringing up their daughters, not only to
know how to do, but actually to do, all kinds of
domestic work.   The Writer knows young ladies,
who are daughters of men of wealth and standing,
and who are among the most accomplished in their
sphere, who have for months been sent to work
with a mantuamaker, to acquire a practical knowledge of that occupation, and who have at home
learned to perform all kinds of domestic labor.

And let the young women of this Nation find, that Domestic Economy is placed, in schools, on an equal or superior ground to Chemistry, Philosophy, and Mathematics, and they will blush to be found ignorant of its first principles, as much as they will to hesitate respecting the laws of gravity, or the composition of the atmosphere. But as matters are now conducted, many young ladies, who can tell how to make oxygen and hydrogen, and discuss questions of Philosophy or Political Economy, do not know how properly to make a bed and sweep a room; while they can "construct a diagram" in Geometry with far more skill than they could construct the simplest article of female dress.

It may be urged, that the plan suggested by the Writer, in the previous pages, would make such a book as this needless; for young ladies would learn all these things at home, before they go regularly to school. But it must be remembered, that the plan suggested cannot fully be carried into effect, till such endowed institutions as the one described are universally furnished. This probably will not be done, till at least one generation of young women are educated. It is only on the supposition that a young lady can, at fourteen or fifteen years of age, enter such an institution, and remain three years, that it would be easy to induce her to remain, during all the previous period, at home, in the practice of Domestic Economy, and the limited course of study pointed out. In the present imperfect, desultory, changing mode of female education, where studies are begun, changed, partially learned, and forgotten, it requires nearly all the years of a woman's youth, to acquire the intellectual education now demanded. While this state of things continues, the only remedy is, to introduce Domestic Economy as a study at school.

It is hoped that these considerations will have

weight, not only with parents and teachers, but with young ladies themselves, and that all will unite their influence to introduce this as a popular and universal branch of education in all female schools.

CHAPTER V.

ON THE CARE OF HEALTH.

Importance of a Knowledge of the Laws of Health, and of the Human System, to Females. Construction of the Human Frame. BONES; their Structure, Design, and Use. Engraving, and Description. Exercise of the Bones. Distortions. MUSCLES; their Constitution, Use, and Connection with the Bones. Engraving, and Description. Operation of Muscles. NERVES; their Use. Engraving and Description. BLOOD-VESSELS; their object. Engraving and Description. ORGANS OF DIGESTION AND RESPIRATION. Engraving and Description. Process of Digestion. Circulation of the Blood. Process of Respiration. THE SKIN. Process of Perspiration. Insensible Perspiration. Heat of the Body. Absorbents. Follicles of oily matter in the Skin. Nerves of Feeling.

THERE is no point, where a woman is more liable to suffer from a want of knowledge and experience, than in reference to the health of a family committed to her care. Many a young lady, who never had any charge of the sick ; who never took any care of an infant ; who never obtained information on these subjects, from books, or from the experience of others; in short, with little or no preparation; has found herself the chief attendant in dangerous sickness, the chief nurse of a feeble infant, and the responsible guardian of the health of a whole family.

The care, the fear, the perplexity, of a woman, suddenly called to such unwonted duties, none can realize, till they themselves feel it, or till they see some young and anxious novice first attempting to meet such responsibilities. To a woman of age and experience, such duties often involve a measure of

trial and difficulty, at times deemed almost insup-
portable ; how hard, then, must they press on the
heart of the young and inexperienced !

There is no really efficacious mode of preparing a
woman to take a *rational* care of the health of a
family, except by communicating that knowledge,
in regard to the construction of the body, and the
laws of health, which is the first principle of the
medical profession. Not that a woman should undertake the minute and extensive investigation
requisite for a physician ; but she should gain a
general knowledge of first principles, as a guide to
her judgement in emergencies when she can rely on
no other aid. Therefore, before attempting to give
any specific directions on the subject of this chapter,
a short sketch of the construction of the human
frame will be given, with a notice of some of the
general principles, on which specific rules in regard
to health are based. This description will be arranged under the general head of BONES, MUSCLES,
NERVES, BLOOD-VESSELS, ORGANS OF DIGESTION AND
RESPIRATION, and THE SKIN.

BONES.

The bones are the most solid parts of the body.
They are designed to protect and sustain it, and also
to secure voluntary motion. The annexed engraving, (Fig. 1,) represents the several bones of the body
as they appear when all other parts are removed.

The bones are about two hundred and fifty in
number, being sometimes a few more or less ; and
are fastened together by cartilage, or gristle, a substance like the bones, but softer, and more elastic.
The bones are composed of two substances,—one
animal, and the other mineral. The animal part is
a fine network, called the *cellular membrane ;* in
which is deposited the harder mineral substances,
which consist chiefly of carbonate and phosphate of

lime. In very early life, the bones consist chiefly of the animal part, and are then soft and pliant. As the child advances in age, the bones grow harder, by the gradual deposition of the phosphate of lime, which is supplied by the food, and carried to the bones by the blood. In old age, the hardest material preponderates; making the bones more brittle than in earlier life.

It is the universal law of the human frame, that *exercise* is indispensable to the health of the several parts. Thus, if a blood-vessel is tied up, so as not to be used, it shrinks, and becomes a useless string; if a muscle is condemned to inaction, it shrinks in size, and diminishes in power; and thus it is also with the bones. Inactivity produces softness, debility, and unfitness for the functions they are designed to perform. This is one of the causes of the curvature of the spine, that common and pernicious defect in the females of America. From inactivity, the bones of the spine become soft and yielding; and then, if the person is often placed, for a length of time, in positions that throw the weight of the body unequally on certain portions of the spine, these parts yield to this frequent compression, and a distortion ensues. The positions taken by young persons, when learning to write or draw, and the position of the body when sleeping on one side on high pillows, all tend to produce this effect, by throwing the weight of the body unequally and for a length of time on particular parts of the spine.

In order to convey a more clear and correct idea of the form, relative position, and connection, of the bones constituting the human framework, the engraving (Fig. 1,) on the next page is given.

Fig. 1.

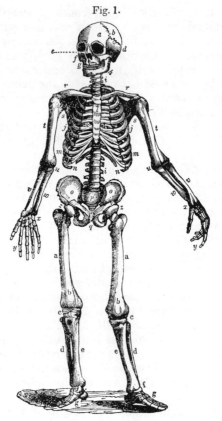

By the preceding engraving, it will be seen, that the *cranium*, or *skull*, consists of several distinct pieces, which are united by sutures, (or seams,) as represented by the zigzag lines in the engraving; *a*, being the *frontal bone;* *b*, the *parietal bone;* *c*, the *temporal bone;* *d*, shows the place of the *occipital bone*, which forms the back part of the head, and therefore is not seen in the engraving; *e*, the *nasal bones*, or bones of the nose; *f*, the *cheek bone;* *g*, the *up-*

per, and *h*, the *lower, jaw bones ; i i*, the *spinal column*, or back bone, consisting of numerous small bones, called *vertebræ ; j j*, are the seven *true ribs*, which are fastened to the spine, behind, and by the *cartilages, k k*, to the *sternum*, or *breast bone, l*, in front ; *m m*, are the first three *false ribs*, which are so called because they are not united directly to the breast bone, but by cartilages to the seventh true rib ; *n n*, are the lower two *false ribs*, which are also called *floating*, because they are not connected with the breast bone, nor the other ribs, in front ; *o o p q*, are the bones of the *pelvis*, which is the foundation on which the spine rests; *r r*, are the *collar bones ; s s*, the *shoulder blade ; t t*, the bones of the *upper arm ; u u*, the *elbow joint*, where the three bones of the arm and fore arm are united in such a way that they can move like a hinge ; *v w v w*, are the bones of the *fore arm ; x x*, the bones of the *wrists ; y y*, those of the *fingers ; z z*, are the round heads of the thigh bones, where they are inserted into the sockets of the bones of the pelvis, giving motion in every direction, and forming the *hip joint ;* a b a b, are the *thigh bones ;* c c, the *knee joint ;* d e d e, the *leg bones ;* f f, the *ankle joint ;* g g, the *bones of the foot*.

MUSCLES.

The muscles are the chief organs of motion, and consist of collections of fine fibres or strings, united in casings of membrane or thin skin. They possess an elastic power, like India rubber, which enables them to extend and contract. The red meat in animals consists of muscles. Every muscle has connected with it nerves, veins, and arteries ; and those designed to move the bones, are fastened to them by tendons at their extremities. The muscles are laid over each other, and are separated by means of membranes and layers of fat, which enable them to move easily, without interfering with each other.

Some idea of the construction and action of the muscles, may be obtained from this engraving.

Fig. 2.

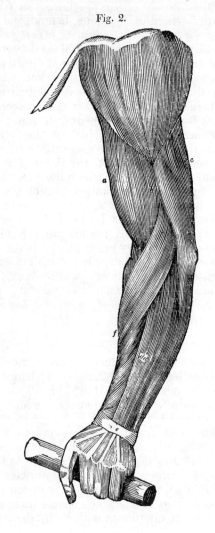

This figure represents the muscles of the arm, as they appear when the skin and fat are removed. The muscles *a* and *b* are attached, at their upper ends, to the bone of the arm, and by their lower ends to the upper part of the fore arm, near the elbow joint. When the fibres of these muscles contract, the middle part of them grows larger, and the arm is bent at the elbow. The muscle *c*, is, in like manner, fastened, by its upper end, to the shoulder blade and the upper part of the arm, and by its lower end to one of the bones of the fore arm, near the elbow. When the arm is bent, and we wish to straighten it, it is done by contracting this muscle. The muscles *d d*, come from the middle of the arm, and on the back of the hand are reduced in size, appearing like strong cords. These cords are called *tendons*. They are employed in straightening the fingers, when the hand is shut, and are attached to the fingers. These tendons are confined by the ligament or band, *e*, which binds them down, around the wrist, and thus enables them to act more efficiently, and secures beauty of form to the limb. The muscles at *f*, are those which enable us to turn the hand and arm outward. Every different motion of the arm has one muscle to produce it, and another to restore the limb to its natural position. Those muscles which bend the body are called *flexors;* those which straighten it, *extensors.* When the arm is thrown up, one set of muscles is used; to pull it down, another set: when it is thrown forward, a still different set is used; when it is thrown back, another, different from the former. When the arm turns in its socket, still another set is used; and thus every different motion of the body is made by a different set of muscles. All these muscles are compactly and skilfully arranged, so as to work with perfect ease. Among them, run the arteries, veins, and nerves, which supply each muscle with blood and nervous power, as will be hereafter described.

The nerves are the organs of sensation. They enable us to see, hear, feel, taste, and smell; and also combine with the bones and muscles in producing motion. The engraving, (Fig. 3,) is a vertical section of the skull, and of the spinal column, or back bone, which supports the head, and through which runs the spinal cord, whence most of the nerves originate. In this engraving, *a*, represents the *cerebrum*, or great brain; *b*, the *cerebellum*, or little brain, which is situated directly under the great brain, at the back and lower part of the head; *c d e*, is the spinal marrow, which is connected with the brain at *c*, and runs through the whole length of the spinal column. This column consists of a large number of small bones, called *vertebræ*, *f f*, laid one above another, and fastened together by *cartilage*, or *gristle*, *g*, between them. The spinal column is perforated through its whole extent; and within the cavity, thus formed, is contained the spinal marrow, *c d e*, as seen in the engraving. Between each two vertebræ, or spinal bones, there issues from the spine, on each side, a pair of nerves. The lower broad part of the spine, (see *p*, Fig. 1,) is called the *sacrum;* in this, are eight holes, through which the lower pairs of nerves pass off.

The nerves, which thus proceed from the spine, branch out, like the limbs and twigs of a tree, till they extend over the whole body; and so minutely are they divided and arranged, that a point, destitute of a nerve, cannot be found on the skin.

Fig. 3.

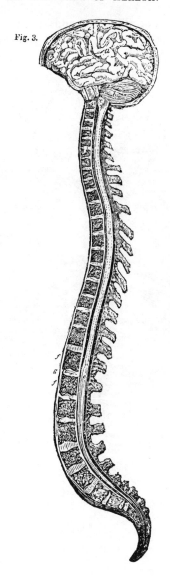

The nerves of the head and lungs run directly from the brain; those of all other parts of the body run from the spine.

Fig. 4.

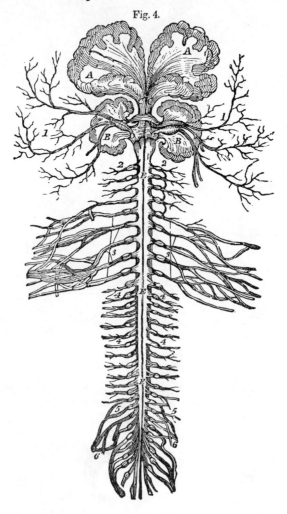

Some idea of the ramifications of the nerves may be obtained from the preceding engraving, (Fig. 4,) in which A A, is the *cerebrum*, or great brain ; B B, the *cerebellum*, or little brain ; (see also *a b*, in Fig. 3 ;) C C, represents the union of the fibres of the cerebrum ; D D, the union of the two sides of the cerebellum ; E E E, the spinal marrow, which passes through the centre of the spine, (as seen at *c d e*, in Fig. 3 ;) 1 2 3 4 5 6, are branches of the nerves going to different parts of the body.

BLOOD-VESSELS.

The blood is the fluid into which our food is changed, and which is employed to minister nourishment to the whole body. For this purpose, it is carried to every part of the body, by the arteries; and, after it has given out its nourishment, returns to the heart, through the veins. Before entering the heart, it receives another fresh supply of nourishment, by a duct which leads from the stomach. The arteries have their origin from the heart, in a great trunk called the *aorta*, which is the parent of all the arteries, as the spine is the parent of the nerves which it sends out. When the arteries have branched out into myriads of minute vessels, the blood which is in them passes into as minute veins; and these run into each other, like the rills and branches of a river, until they are all united in two great veins, which run into the heart. One of these large receivers, called the *vena cava superior*, or *upper vena cava*, brings back the blood from the arms and head, the other, the *vena cava inferior*, or *lower vena cava*, brings back the blood from the body and lower limbs.

Fig. 5.

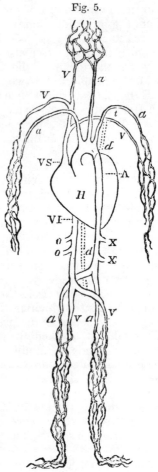

The preceding engraving, (Fig. 5,) which presents a rude outline of the vascular system, will more clearly illustrate this operation. H, is the heart, which is divided into four compartments; two, called *auricles*, used for receiving the blood, and two, called *ventricles,* used for sending out the blood. A, is the *aorta,* or great artery, which sends its branches to every part of the body. In the upper part, at *a a a,* are the main branches of the *aorta,* which go to the head and arms. Below, at *a a,* are the branches which go to the lower limbs. The branches which set off at X X, are those by which the intestines are supplied by vessels from the *aorta.* Every muscle in the whole body, all the organs of the body, and the skin, are supplied by branches sent off from this great *artery.* When the blood is thus dispersed through any organ, in minute vessels, it is received, at their terminations, by numerous minute veins, which gradually unite, forming larger branches, till they all meet in either the upper or lower *vena cava,* which returns the blood to the heart. V I, is the *vena cava inferior,* which receives the blood from the veins of the lower parts of the body, as seen at v v. The branches of these receive the blood sent into the lower limbs from the *aorta:* *o o,* represent the points of entrance of those tributaries of the *vena cava,* which receive that blood from the intestines which is sent out by the *aorta* at X X. In the upper part, V S, is the *vena cava superior,* which receives the blood from the head and arms; v v v, are the tributaries of the upper *vena cava,* which bring the blood back from the head and arms. *d d,* represents the position of the *thoracic duct,* a delicate tube by which the chyle is carried into the circulation, as mentioned on page 65; *t,* shows the place where this duct empties into a branch of the *vena cava.*

It thus appears, that wherever a branch of the *aorta* goes to carry blood, there will be found a tributary of the upper or lower *vena cava,* to bring it back.

The succeeding engravings will enable the reader to form a more definite idea of this important function of the system,—the circulation of the blood.

The heart, in man, and in all warm-blooded animals, is double, having two auricles and two ventricles. In animals with cold blood, (as fishes,) the heart is single, having but one auricle and one ventricle. Fig. 6, represents the double heart as it appears when the two sides are separated, and also the great blood-vessels; those on the left of the figure being on the right side of the body, and *vice versa.* The direction of the blood is represented by the arrows. A, represents the *lower vena cava,* returning the blood from the lower parts of the body, and L, the *upper vena cava,* returning the blood from the head and arms. B, is the *right sinus,* or *auricle,* into which the returned blood is poured. From this cavity of the heart, the blood is carried into the *right ventricle,* C; and from this ventricle, the *pulmonary arteries,* D, convey into the lungs the blood which is returned from the body. These five vessels, A B C D and L, belong to the right side of the heart, and contain the venous or dark-colored blood, which has been through the circulation, and is now unfit for the uses of the system, till it has passed through the lungs. When the blood reaches the lungs, and is exposed to the action of the air which we breathe, it throws off its impurities, becomes bright in color, and is then called arterial blood. It then returns to the left side of the heart, (on the right of the engraving,) by the pulmonary veins, E E, (also seen at *m m,* Fig. 8,) into the left auricle F, whence it is forced into the ventricle, G. From the left ventricle, proceeds the *aorta,* H H, which is the great artery of the body, and conveys the blood to every part of the system. I J K, are branches of the aorta, going to the head and arms.

Fig. 6.

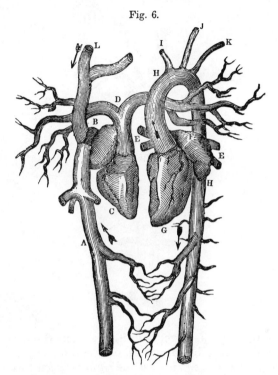

Fig. 7, on the next page, represents the heart, with its two sides united as in nature; and will be understood from the description of Fig. 6.

Fig. 7.

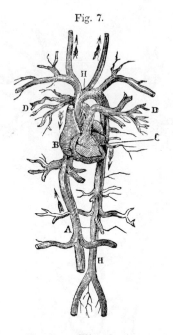

On the opposite page, Fig. 8, represents the heart, with the great blood-vessels, on a still larger scale ; *a*, being the *left ventricle ; b*, the *right ventricle ; c e f*, the *aorta*, or great artery, rising out of the left ventricle ; *g h i*, the branches of the aorta, going to the head and arms ; *k l l*, the *pulmonary artery*, and its branches ; *m m, veins of the lungs ; n, right auricle ; o, vena cava inferior ; p*, veins returning blood from the liver and bowels ; *q*, the *vena cava superior ; r*, the *left auricle ; s*, the left *coronary artery*, which distributes the blood exclusively to the substance of the heart.

Fig. 8.

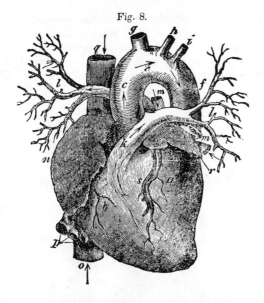

ORGANS OF DIGESTION AND RESPIRATION.

Digestion and respiration are the processes, by
which the food is converted into blood for the nourishment of the body. The engraving (Fig. 9) on
the next page shows the organs by which these operations are performed.

In the lower part of the engraving, is the stomach,
marked S, which receives the food through the *gullet*, marked G. The latter, though in the engraving
it is cut off at G, in reality continues upwards to the
throat. The stomach is a bag composed of muscles,
nerves, and blood-vessels, united by a material similar to that which forms the skin. As soon as food
enters the stomach, its nerves are excited to perform
their proper function of stimulating the muscles. A
muscular (called the *peristaltic*) motion immediately
commences, by which the stomach propels its con-

tents around the whole of its circumference, once in every three minutes. This movement of the muscles attracts the blood from other parts of the system; for the blood always hastens to administer its supplies to any organ which is called to work. The blood-vessels of the stomach are soon distended with

Fig. 9.

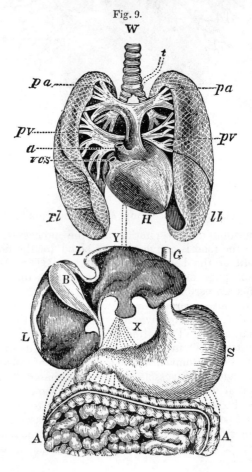

blood, from which, the *gastric juice* is secreted by
minute vessels in the coat of the stomach. This
mixes with the food, and reduces it to a soft pulpy
mass, called chyme. It then passes through the
lower end of the stomach, into the intestines, which
are folded up in the abdomen, and the upper portion,
only, of which is shown in the engraving, at A A.
The organ marked L L, is the liver, which, as the
blood passes through its many vessels, secretes a
substance called *bile*, which accumulates in the gall-
bladder, marked B. After the food passes out of the
stomach, it receives from the liver a portion of bile,
and from the *pancreas* the *pancreatic juice.* The
pancreas does not appear in this drawing, being concealed behind the stomach. These two liquids separate the substance which has passed from the stomach,
into two different portions. One is a light liquid,
resembling cream very much in appearance, and
called *chyle,* of which the blood is formed; the other
is a more solid substance, which contains the refuse
and useless matter, with a smaller portion of nourishment. This, after being further separated from
the nourishing matter which it contains, is thrown
out of the body. As these two mixed substances
pass through the long and winding folds of the intestines in the abdomen, there are multitudes of
small vessels, called *lacteals*, which absorb the chyle
from the intestines, and convey it to the *thoracic
duct*, which runs up close by the spine, and carries
the chyle, thus received, into a branch of the *vena
cava superior*, at *t*, whence it is mingled with the
blood going into the heart. In this engraving, the
lacteals and *thoracic duct* are not shown; but their
position is indicated by the dotted lines, marked
X Y; X, being the lacteals, and Y, the thoracic
duct.

In the upper half of the engraving, H represents
the heart; *a*, the commencement of the *aorta ; v c s,*

the termination of the *vena cava superior*. On each side of the heart, are the lungs ; *l l*, being the left lobe, and *r l*, the right lobe. They are composed of a network of air-vessels, blood-vessels, and nerves. W, represents the *trachea*, or *windpipe*, through which the air we breathe is conducted to the lungs. It branches out into myriads of minute vessels, which are thus filled with air every time we breathe. From the heart, run the *pulmonary arteries*, marked *p a*. These enter the lungs and spread out along side of the branches of the air-vessels, so that every air-vessel has a small artery running side by side with it. When the two *vena cavas* empty the blood into the heart, the latter contracts, and sends this blood, through these pulmonary arteries, into the lungs.

As the air and blood meander, side by side, through the lungs, the superabundant carbon and hydrogen of the blood combine with the oxygen of the air, forming carbonic acid gas, and water, which are thrown out of the lungs at every expiration. This is the process by which the chyle is converted into arterial blood, and the venous blood purified of its excess of carbon and hydrogen. When the blood is thus prepared, in the lungs, for its duties, it is received by the small *pulmonary veins*, which gradually unite, and bring the blood back to the heart, through the large *pulmonary veins*, marked *p v, p v.*

On receiving this purified blood from the lungs, the heart contracts, and sends it out again through the *aorta* to all parts of the body. It then makes another circuit through every part, ministering to the wants of all, and is afterwards again brought back by the veins to receive the fresh chyle from the stomach, and be purified by the lungs.

The throbbing of the heart is caused by its alternate expansion and contraction, as it receives and expels the blood. With one throb, the blood is sent from the right ventricle into the lungs, and from the left ventricle into the aorta.

Every time we inspire air, the process of purifying the blood is going on ; and every time we expire the air, we throw out the redundant carbon and hydrogen, taken from a portion of the blood. If the waist is compressed by tight clothing, a portion of the lungs is compressed, so that the air-vessels cannot be filled. This prevents the perfect purification and preparation of the blood, so that a part returns back to the heart unfitted for its duties. This is a slow, but sure, method, by which many a young lady has her constitution undermined.

OF THE SKIN.

The skin is the covering of the body, and has very important functions to perform. It is more abundantly supplied with nerves and blood-vessels than any other part ; and there is no spot of the skin where the point of the finest needle would not pierce a nerve and blood-vessel. Indeed, it may be considered as composed chiefly of an interlacing of minute nerves and blood-vessels, so that it is supposed there is more nervous matter in the skin, than in all the rest of the body united, and that the greater portion of the blood flows through the skin.

The whole animal system is in a state of continual change and renovation. Food is constantly taken into the stomach, only a portion of which is fitted for the supply of the blood. All the rest has to be thrown out of the system, by various organs designed for this purpose. These organs are, the lungs, which throw off a portion of useless matter when the blood is purified ; the kidneys, which secrete liquids that pass into the bladder and are thrown out from the body by that organ ; and the intestines, which carry off the useless and more solid parts of the food, after the lacteals have drawn off

the chyle. In addition to these organs, the skin has
a similar duty to perform ; and as it has so much
larger a supply of blood, it is the chief organ in relieving the body of the useless and noxious parts of
the materials which are taken for food.

Various experiments show, that not less than a
pound and four ounces of waste matter is thrown off
by the skin every twenty-four hours. This is according to the lowest calculation. Most of those,
who have made experiments to ascertain the quantity, make it much greater; and all agree, that the
skin throws off more redundant matter from the
body than all the other organs together. In the ordinary state of the skin, even when there is no apparent perspiration, it is constantly exhaling waste
matter, in a form which is called *insensible perspiration*, because it cannot be perceived by the senses.
A very cool mirror, brought suddenly near to the
skin, will be covered, in that part, with a moisture,
which is this effluvia thus made visible. When
heat or exercise excite the skin, this perspiration is
increased, so as to be apparent to the senses.

Another office of the skin, is, to regulate the heat
of the body. The action of the internal organs is
constantly generating heat ; and the faster the
blood circulates, the greater is the heat evolved.
The perspiration of the skin serves to reduce and
regulate this heat. For, whenever any liquid
changes to a vapor, it absorbs heat from whatever is
nearest to it. The faster the blood flows, the more
perspiration is evolved. This bedews the skin
with a liquid, which the heat of the body turns
to a vapor ; and in this change, that heat is absorbed. When a fever takes place, this perspiration ceases, and the body is afflicted with heat.
Insensible perspiration is most abundant during
sleep, after eating, and when friction is applied to
the skin. Perspiration is performed by the termina-

tions of minute arteries in every part of the skin, which exude the perspiration from the blood.

The skin also performs another function. It is provided with a set of small vessels, called *absorbents*, which are exceedingly abundant and minute. When particular substances are brought in contact with the skin, these absorbents take up some portions and carry them into the blood. It is owing to this, that opium, applied on the skin, acts in a manner similar to its operation when taken into the stomach. The power of absorption is increased by friction; and this is the reason that liniments are employed, with much rubbing, to bruises and sprains. The substance applied is thus introduced into the injured part, through the absorbents.

The skin is also provided with small follicles, or bags, which are filled with an oily substance. This, by gradually exuding over the skin, prevents water from penetrating and injuring its texture.

The skin is also the organ of touch. This office is performed through the instrumentality of the nerves of feeling, which are spread over all parts of the skin.

This general outline of the construction of the human frame is given, with reference to the practical application of this knowledge in the various cases where a woman will be called upon to exercise her own unaided judgement. The application will be further pointed out, in the chapters on Food, Dress, Cleanliness, the Care of the Sick, and the Care of Little Children.

CHAPTER VI.

ON HEALTHFUL FOOD.

Responsibility of a Housekeeper in regard to Health and Food. The most fruitful Cause of Disease. Gastric Juice ; how proportioned. Hunger the natural Guide as to Quantity of Food. A benevolent provision ; how perverted, and its effects. A morbid Appetite, how caused. Effects of too much Food in the Stomach. Duty of a House-keeper in reference to this. Proper Time for taking Food. Per-istaltic Motion. Need of Rest to the Muscles of the Stomach. Time necessary between each Meal. Exceptions of hard Laborers and active Children. Exercise ; its effect on all parts of the Body. How it produces Hunger. What is to be done by those who have lost the guidance of Hunger in regulating the Amount of Food. On Quality of Food. Difference as to risk from bad Food, between healthy persons who exercise, and those of delicate and sedentary habits. Stimulating Food ; its Effects. Condiments needed only for Medicine, and to be avoided as Food. Difference between An-imal and Vegetable Food. Opinion of some Medical Men. Med-ical Men agree as to the Excess of Animal Food in American Diet. Extracts from Medical Writers on this point. Articles most easily digested. The most unhealthful articles result from bad cook-ing. Caution as to *mode* of eating. Reason why mental and bodily exertions are injurious after a full Meal. Changes in Diet should be gradual ; and why. Drink most needed at Breakfast; and why. Dinner should be the heartiest Meal; and why. Little Drink to be taken while eating ; and why. Extremes of Heat or Cold; why injurious in Food. Fluids immediately absorbed from the Stom-ach. Why Soups are hard of Digestion. Why highly-concentrated Nourishment is not good for Health. Opinion of Dr. Combe as to the selection of Food.

THE person who decides what shall be the food and drink of a family, and the modes of preparation, is the one who decides, to a greater or less extent, what shall be the health of that family. It is the opinion of most medical men, that intemperance in eating is the most fruitful of all causes of disease and death. If this be so, the woman who wisely adapts the food and cooking of her family to the laws of health, removes the greatest risk which threatens the lives of those under her care.

To exhibit this subject clearly, it will be needful

to refer, more minutely, to the organization and operation of the Digestive Organs.

It is found, by experiment, that the supply of gastric juice, furnished from the blood by the arteries,of
the stomach, is proportioned, not to the amount of
food put into the stomach, but to the wants of the
body ; so that it is possible to put much more into
the stomach than can be digested. To guide and
regulate in this matter, the sensation called *hunger*
is provided. In a healthy state of the body, as soon
as the blood has lost its nutritive supplies, the call of
hunger is felt, and then, if the food is suitable, and
is taken in the proper manner, this sensation ceases
as soon as the stomach has received enough to supply the wants of the system. But our benevolent
Creator, in this, as in our other duties, has connected
enjoyment with the operation needful to sustain our
bodies. In addition to the allaying of hunger, there
is the gratification of the palate, secured by the immense variety of food, some articles of which are far
more agreeable than others.

This arrangement of Providence, designed for our
happiness, either through ignorance, or want of self-
control, has become the chief cause of the various
diseases and sufferings that afflict those classes which
have the means of seeking a variety to gratify the
palate. If mankind had only one article of food, and
only water to drink, they would never be tempted to
put any more into the stomach, than the calls of
hunger required. But the customs of society, which
present an incessant change, and a great variety of
food, with those various condiments that stimulate
appetite, lead almost every person very frequently
to eat merely to gratify the palate, after the stomach
has been abundantly supplied, so that hunger has
ceased.

When too great a supply of food is put into the
stomach, the gastric juice dissolves only that portion

which the wants of the system demand. All the rest is ejected from the stomach in an unprepared state, the absorbents take portions of it into the system, and all the various functions of the body, which depend on the ministries of the blood, are thus gradually and imperceptibly injured. Very often, intemperance in eating produces immediate results, such as colic, headaches, pains of indigestion, and vertigo. But the more general result, is, a gradual undermining of all parts of the human frame ; thus imperceptibly shortening life, by a debilitated constitution, which is ready to yield at every point, to any uncommon risk or exposure. Thousands and thousands are passing out of the world, from diseases occasioned by exposures, that a healthy constitution could meet without any danger. It is owing to these considerations, that it becomes the duty of every woman, who has the responsibility of providing food for a family, to avoid a variety of tempting dishes. Only one kind of healthy food, for each meal, is a much safer rule, than the abundant variety which is usually met at the tables of almost all classes in this Country. When there is to be any variety of dishes, they ought not to be successive, but so arranged, as to give the opportunity of selection. How often is it the case, that persons, by the appearance of a favorite article, are tempted to eat, merely to gratify the palate, when the stomach is already adequately supplied. All such intemperance wears on the constitution, and shortens life. It not unfrequently happens, that excess in eating produces a morbid appetite, which must constantly be denied.

But the organization of the digestive organs demands, not only that food be taken in proper quantities, but that it be taken at proper times.

It has before been shown, that, as soon as the food enters the stomach, the muscles are excited by the nerves, and the *peristaltic motion* commences. This is a powerful and constant exercise of the muscles of the stomach, which continues until the process of digestion is complete. During this time, the blood is withdrawn from other parts of the system, to supply the demands of the stomach, which is laboring hard with all its muscles. When this motion ceases, and the digested food has gradually passed out of the stomach, then Nature requires that it should have a period of repose. If fresh food is put into the stomach shortly after eating, it demands a greater muscular effort to carry around this undigested mass, than it would if it had entered at the same time with the other portion, which has now been digested and ejected. And if another meal is eaten, immediately after one is digested, the stomach is set to work again, before it has time to rest, and before a sufficient supply of gastric juice is provided.

The general rule, then, is, that three hours be given to the stomach for labor, and two for rest ; and in obedience to this, five hours at least, ought to elapse between every regular meal. In cases where exercise produces a flow of perspiration, more food is needed to supply the loss ; and strong laboring men may safely eat as often as they feel the want of food. So young and healthy children, who gambol and exercise much, and whose bodies grow fast, may have a more frequent supply of food. But, as a general rule, meals should be five hours apart, and eating between meals avoided. There is nothing more unsafe, and wearing to the constitution, than a habit of eating at any time, merely to gratify the palate. When a tempting article is presented, every person should exercise sufficient self-denial to wait till the proper time for eating arrives.

In deciding as to quantity of food, there is one great difficulty to be met by a large portion of the community. It has been shown, that the exercise of every part of the body is indispensable to its health and perfection. The bones, the muscles, the nerves, the organs of digestion and respiration, and the skin, all demand exercise, in order properly to perform their functions. When the muscles of the body are called into action, all the blood-vessels entwined among them are frequently compressed. As the heart is so contrived, that the blood cannot run back, this compression sends the blood forward towards the heart in the arteries and veins. The heart is immediately put in quicker motion, to send it into the lungs; and they, also, are thus stimulated to quicker motion, which is the cause of that panting which active exercise always occasions. The blood thus courses in quicker streams through the body, and sooner loses its nourishing properties. Then the stomach issues its mandate of hunger, and a new supply of food must be furnished. Thus it appears, as a general rule, that the quantity of food, actually needed by the body, depends on the amount of muscular exercise taken. A laboring man, in the open fields, probably throws off from his skin ten times the amount, which evolves from the skin of a person of sedentary pursuits. In consequence of this he demands ten times the amount of food and drink.

Those persons who keep their bodies in a state of health, by sufficient exercise, can always be guided by the calls of hunger. They can eat when they feel hungry, and stop when hunger ceases; and then they will calculate exactly right. But the difficulty is, that a large part of the community, especially women, are so inactive in their habits, that they seldom feel the calls of hunger. They habitually eat, merely to gratify the palate. This produces such a state of the system, that they have lost the guide which Nature has provided. They are not called to eat, by hunger, nor admonished, by its cessation, when to stop. In consequence of this, such persons eat what pleases the palate, till they feel no more inclination for the article. It is probable that three fourths of the women, in the wealthier circles, sit down to each meal without any feeling of hunger, and eat merely because they find something that gratifies the palate. Such persons find their appetite to depend almost solely on the kind of food on the table. This is not the case with those who take the exercise which Nature demands. They approach their meals in such a state that almost any kind of food will be acceptable.

The question then arises, How are persons, who have lost the guide which Nature has provided, to determine as to the proper amount of food they should take ?

The only rules they can adopt, are of a general nature ; founded on the principles already developed. They should endeavor to proportion their food to the amount of the exercise they ordinarily take. If they take but little exercise, they should eat but little food in comparison with those who are much in the open air and take much exercise ; and their food should be vegetable and not animal. But how often is it seen, that a student, or a man who sits all day in an office, or a lady who spends the day in her parlor and chamber, will sit down to a loaded table, and, by continuing to partake of the tempting varieties, in the end load the stomach with a supply, which a stout farmer could scarcely digest.

But the health of a family depends, not merely on the *quantity* of food taken ; but very much, also, on the *quality*. Some kinds of food are very pernicious in their nature, and some healthful articles are rendered very injurious by the mode of cooking. Persons who have a strong constitution, and take much exercise, may eat almost any thing, with apparent impunity ; but young children, who are forming their constitutions, and persons who are delicate, and who take but little exercise, are very dependent for health, on a proper selection of food.

There are some general principles that aid in regulating the judgement on this subject.

It is found that there are some kinds of food which afford nutriment to the blood, and do not produce any other effect on the system. There are other kinds, which are *stimulating ;* so that they not only furnish nourishment, but quicken the functions of the organs on which they operate. The condiments used in cookery, such as pepper, mustard, and spices, are of this nature. There are certain states of the system, when these stimulants are beneficial ; but it is only in cases where there is some debility. Such cases are to be pointed out by medical men. But persons in perfect health, and especially young children, never receive any benefit from such kind of food ; and just in proportion as condiments operate to quicken the labors of the internal organs, they tend to wear down their powers. A person who thus keeps the body working under an unnatural excitement, *lives faster* than Nature designed, and the sooner his constitution is worn out. A woman, therefore, should provide dishes for her family, which are free from these stimulating condiments, and as much as possible prevent their use. It is found, by experience, also, that animal food is more stimulating than vegetable. This is the reason why, in cases of fevers, or inflammations, medical men forbid the use of meat and butter. Animal food supplies chyle much more abundantly than vegetable food does ; and this chyle is more stimulating in its nature. Of course, a person who lives chiefly on animal food, is under a higher degree of stimulus than if his food was chiefly composed of vegetable substances. His blood will flow faster, and all the functions of his body will be quickened.

This makes it important to secure a proper proportion of animal and vegetable diet. Some medical men suppose that an exclusive vegetable diet is proved by the experience of many individuals to be fully sufficient to nourish the body, and bring, as evidence, the fact, that some of the strongest and most robust men in the world, are those trained, from infancy, exclusively on vegetable food. From this they infer, that life will be shortened, just in proportion as the diet is changed to more stimulating articles; and that, all other things being equal, children will have a better chance of health and long life, if they are brought up solely on vegetable food.

But, though this is not the common opinion of medical men, they all agree, that, in America, far too large a portion of the diet consists of animal food. As a nation, the Americans are proverbial for the gross and luxurious diet with which they load their tables; and there can be no doubt that the general health of the nation would be increased, by a change in our customs in this respect. To take meat but once a day, and this in small quantities, compared with the vegetables eaten, is a rule, the observance of which would probably greatly reduce the amount of fevers, eruptions, headaches, and the many ailments that come from too gross a mode of diet.

The following quaint extract from the work of a physician of Europe, where there is less of gross living among the common people, than in America, expresses the views of most intelligent medical men.

"I must own I never see a fashionable physician mysteriously counting the pulse of a plethoric patient, or, with a silver spoon on his tongue, importunately looking down his red inflamed gullet, but I feel a desire to exclaim, 'Why not tell the poor gentleman, at once,—" Sir, you have eaten too

much, you have drunk too much, and you have not
taken exercise enough!"' These are *the main
causes of almost every one's illness;* there can be no
greater proof, than that those savage nations, who
live actively and temperately, have only one great
disorder,—death. The human frame was not created imperfect; it is we ourselves who have made
it so. There exists no donkey in creation, so over-
laden, as our stomachs; and it is because they groan
under the weight so cruelly imposed upon them,
that we see people driven in herds to drink at some
little watering-place."

The celebrated Roman physician Baglivi, who,
from practising extensively among Roman Catholics,
had ample opportunities to observe, mentions, that,
in Italy, an unusual number of people recover health
in the forty days of Lent, in consequence of the
lower diet which is required as a religious duty.
An American physician remarks, "For every reeling
drunkard that disgraces our country, it contains one
hundred gluttons;—persons, I mean, who eat to
excess, and suffer in consequence." Another distinguished physician remarks, "I believe that every
stomach, not actually impaired by organic disease,
will perform its functions, if it receives reasonable
attention; and when we perceive the manner in
which diet is generally conducted, both in regard to
quantity and *variety* of articles of food and drink,
which are mixed up in one heterogeneous mass,
instead of being astonished at the prevalence of indigestion, our wonder must rather be, that, in such
circumstances, any stomach is capable of digesting
at all."

In regard to articles the most easily digested, only
general rules can be given. Tender meats are
digested more readily than those which are tough,
or than most vegetable food. The farinaceous
articles, such as rice, flour, corn, potatoes, and the

like, are the most nutritious and most easily digested. A perfectly healthy stomach can digest almost any healthful food ; but when the digestive powers are weak, every stomach has its peculiarities, and what is good for one is hurtful to another. In such cases, experiment, alone, can decide, which are the most digestible articles of food. A person, whose food troubles him, must deduct one article after another, till he learns, by experience, which is the best for digestion. Much evil has been done, by assuming that the powers of one stomach are to be made the rule in regulating every other.

The most unhealthful articles of food, are some that result from bad cooking ; such as sour and heavy bread, cakes, pie-crust, and other articles made of fat mixed and cooked with flour, and also high-seasoned articles. The fewer mixtures in cooking, the more healthful is the food likely to be.

There is one caution, as to the *mode* of eating, which it seems Americans peculiarly need. It is indispensable to good digestion, that food be well chewed and taken slowly. It needs to be thoroughly chewed, in order to prepare it for the action of the gastric juice, which, by the *peristaltic motion*, will be thus brought into universal contact with the minute portions. It has been found, that a solid lump of food requires much more time and labor of the stomach, than divided substances. It has also been found, that, as each bolus, or mouthful, enters the stomach, the latter closes until the portion received has had some time to move around and combine with the gastric juice ; and that the orifice of the stomach resists the entrance of any more, till this is accomplished. But, if the eater persists in swallowing fast, the stomach yields ; the food is poured in faster than the organ can perform its duty of digestion ; and evil results are sooner or later developed.

This exhibits the folly of those hasty meals so common to travellers, and to men of business.

After taking a full meal, it is very important to health that no great bodily or mental exertions be made, till the labor of the stomach is over. Intense mental effort draws the blood to the head, and muscular exertions draw it to the muscles; and in consequence of this, the stomach loses the supply which it requires when performing its office. When the blood is thus withdrawn, the adequate supply of gastric juice is not afforded, and indigestion is the result. The heaviness that follows a full meal is the indication which Nature gives of the need of quiet. When the meal is moderate, a sufficient quantity of gastric juice is exuded in an hour, or an hour and a half; after which labor of body and mind may safely be resumed.

When undigested food remains in the stomach, and is at last thrown out into the bowels, it proves an irritating substance, producing an inflamed state in the lining of the stomach and other organs. The same effect is produced by alcoholic drinks.

It is found that the stomach has the power of gradually accommodating its digestive powers to the food it habitually receives. Thus animals, that live on vegetables can gradually become accustomed to animal food; and *vice versa*. Thus, too, the human stomach can eventually accomplish the digestion of some kinds of food, which at first were indigestible.

But any changes of this sort need to be gradual. Any *sudden* changes of diet are trying to the powers of the stomach, as furnishing matter for which its gastric juice is not prepared. Whenever, therefore, a change of diet is resolved upon, it should always be made a gradual process.

In regard to the nature of the meals prepared, the breakfast should furnish a supply of liquids, because the body has been exhausted by the exhalations of the night, and demands them more than at any other period. It should not be the heartiest meal, because the organs of digestion are weakened by long fasting, and the exhalations of sleep. Dinner should be the heartiest meal, because then the powers of digestion are strengthened, by the supplies of the morning meal. After dinner, neither the mind nor body should be heavily taxed ; as the process of digestion would thus be interfered with. Light and amusing employments should occupy mind and body for an hour or more after a full meal.

But little drink should be taken, while eating, as it dilutes the gastric juice which is apportioned to each bolus as it enters the stomach. It is better to take drink after the meal is past.

Extremes of heat or cold are injurious to the process of digestion. Taking hot substances, habitually, tends to debilitate all the organs thus needlessly excited. In regard to cold substances, it is found that a certain degree of warmth is indispensable to digestion ; so that, when the gastric juice is cooled below this temperature, it ceases to act. Taking large quantities of cold drinks, or eating ice creams, after a meal, tend to reduce the temperature of the stomach, and thus to stop digestion. This shows the folly of those refreshments in convivial meetings, where the guests are tempted to load the stomach with a variety, such as would require the stomach of a stout farmer to digest, and then to wind up with ice creams, thus destroying whatever ability might otherwise have existed to digest the heavy load. The fittest temperature for drinks, if taken when the food is in the digesting process, is blood heat. Cool drinks, and even ice, can be safely taken at other times, if not in excessive quantity. When the thirst is excessive, or the body weakened by fatigue, or when in a state of perspiration, cold drinks are injurious. When the body is perspiring freely, taking a large quantity of cold drink has often produced instant death.

Fluids taken into the stomach are not subject to the slow process of digestion, but are immediately absorbed and carried into the blood. This is the reason why drink, more speedily than food, restores from exhaustion. The minute vessels of the stomach inhale or absorb its fluids, which are carried into the blood, just as the minute extremities of the arteries open upon the inner surface of the stomach, and there exude the gastric juice from the blood.

When food is chiefly liquid, (soup, for example,) the fluid part is rapidly absorbed. The solid parts remain to be acted on by the gastric juice. In the case of St. Martin,* in fifty minutes after taking soup, the fluids were absorbed, and the remainder was even thicker than is usual after eating solid food. This is the reason why soups are deemed bad for weak stomachs; as this residuum is more difficult of digestion than ordinary food. In recovering from sickness, beef-tea and broths are good, because the system then demands fluids to supply its loss of blood.

For a similar reason, highly-concentrated food, having much nourishment in a small bulk, is not favorable to digestion, because it cannot be properly acted on by the muscular contractions of the stomach, and is not so minutely divided, as to enable the

---

* The individual here referred to,—Alexis St. Martin,—was a young Canadian, of eighteen years of age, of a good constitution and robust health, who, in 1822, was accidentally wounded by the discharge of a musket, which carried away a part of the ribs, lacerated one of the lobes of the lungs, and perforated the stomach, making a large aperture, which never closed; and which enabled Dr. Beaumont, (a surgeon of the American army, stationed at Michilimackinac, under whose care the patient was placed,) to witness all the processes of digestion and other functions of the body, for several years. The published account of the experiments made by Dr. B. is highly interesting and instructive.

gastric juice to act properly. This is the reason why a certain *bulk* of food is needful to good digestion ; and why those people, who live on whale oil, and other highly nourishing food, in cold climates, mix vegetables and even sawdust with it, to make it more acceptable and digestible. So in civilized lands, bread, potatoes, and vegetables, are mixed with more highly concentrated nourishment. For this reason, soups, gellies, and arrow-root, should have bread or crackers mixed with them.

The following remarks, from Dr. Combe, relate to the *selection* of food. " There are very few articles of diet, which *a person in health, and leading a sufficiently active life,* may not eat with impunity." But "there are some, which ought to be preferred, and others which ought to be avoided, by those *whose digestion is impaired.*" Thus, the coarser " vegetables," like parsnips, beans, &c., " are, generally speaking, slower of digestion than animal and farinaceous aliments," like flour, rice, &c., " and consequently, when digestion is feeble, are liable to remain in the stomach till acetous fermentation takes place, and give rise to acidity and flatulence. Fat and oily meats are nearly in the same predicament, and hence both form unsuitable articles of diet for dyspeptics. Soups and liquid food are also objectionable, both because they are ill adapted for being properly acted upon by the gastric juice and the muscular fibres of the stomach, and because they afford insufficient nourishment. From the former cause, they frequently impair the digestive functions ; and from the latter, they induce diseases of debility."

" Pastry, rich cakes, puddings, and other articles containing much fatty or oily matter in their composition, are perhaps the most generally indigestible of all kinds of food."

" Plain and well-cooked animal food, not too recently killed, and eaten in moderate quantity, with bread, rice, or roasted potatoes, forms one of the most easily digested meals which can be devised for a weak stomach."

Candy and sugar, so much desired by children, are unhealthy, because too highly concentrated. If mixed with other food, and thus diluted, they are harmless, unless eaten in great quantities. Whenever, therefore, candy and sweets are given to children, they should be eaten as a part of a meal, and never taken on an empty stomach.

CHAPTER VII.

ON HEALTHFUL DRINKS.

Responsibility of a Housekeeper in this respect. Stimulating Drinks not required for the Perfection of the Human System. Therefore they are needless. First Evil in using them. Second Evil. Five kinds of Stimulating Articles in use in this Country. First Argument in Favor of Stimulants, and how answered. Second Argument; how answered. The Writer's View of the Effects of Tea and Coffee on American Females. Duty in reference to Children. Black Tea the most harmless Stimulant. Warm Drinks not needful, Hot Drinks injurious. Effect of Hot Drinks on Teeth. Mexican Customs and effects illustrating this. Opinion of Dr. Combe, on this subject. Difference between the Stimulus of Animal Food and the stimulating Drinks used.

ALTHOUGH intemperance in eating is probably the most prolific cause of the diseases of mankind, intemperance in drink has produced more guilt, misery, and crime, than any other one cause. And the responsibilities of a woman, in this particular, are very great; for the habits and liabilities of those under her care will very much depend on her opinions and practice.

It is a point fully established by experience, that the full developement of the human body, and the vigorous exercise of all its functions, can be secured without the use of stimulating drinks. It is, therefore, perfectly safe, to bring up children never to use them; no hazard being incurred by such a course.

It is also found, by experience, that there are two evils incurred by the use of stimulating drinks. The first is, their positive effect on the human system. Their peculiarity consists in exciting the nervous system, in such a way, that all the functions of the body are accelerated, so that they all move quicker than their natural speed. This quickened motion of the animal fluids always produces an agreeable effect on the mind. The intellect is invigorated, the imagination excited, the spirits enlivened; and these effects are so agreeable, that all mankind, after having once experienced them, feel a great desire for a similar result.

But this temporary invigoration of the system, is always followed by a diminution of the powers of the stimulated organs; so that, though in all cases this reaction may not be perceptible, it is invariably the result. It may be set down as the unchangeable rule of physiology, that stimulating drinks (except in cases of disease) deduct from the powers of the constitution, in exactly the proportion in which they operate to produce temporary invigoration.

The second evil, is, the temptation which always attends the use of stimulants. Their effect on the system is so agreeable, and the evils resulting are so imperceptible and distant, that there is a constant tendency to increase such excitement, both in frequency and strength. And the more the system is thus reduced in strength, the more craving is the desire for that which imparts a temporary invigoration. This process of increasing debility and increasing craving for the stimulus that removes it, often go to such an extreme, that the passion is perfectly uncontrollable, and mind and body perish under this baleful habit.

In this Country, there are five forms in which the use of such stimulants is common, namely, *alcoholic drinks, tea and coffee, opium mixtures,* and *tobacco.* These are all alike, in the main peculiarity of imparting that extra stimulus to the system, which tends to exhaust its powers.

Multitudes in this Nation are in the habitual use of some one of these stimulants ; and each person defends the indulgence by these arguments.

First, that the desire for stimulants is a natural propensity, implanted in man's nature, as is manifest from the universal tendency to such indulgences, in every nation.   From this, it is inferred, that it is an innocent desire, which ought to be gratified, to some extent, and that the aim should be to keep it within the limits of temperance, instead of attempting to exterminate a natural propensity.

This is an argument, which, if true, makes it equally proper to use opium, brandy, tea, or tobacco, as stimulating principles, provided they are used temperately.   But, if it be granted that perfect health and strength can be gained and secured without these stimulants, and that their peculiar effect is injurious, then there is no such thing as a temperate use, unless they are so diluted, as to destroy any stimulating power, and in this form, they are seldom desired.

The other argument for their use, is, that they are among the good things provided by the Creator, for our gratification ; that, like all other blessings, they are exposed to abuse and excess ; and that we should rather seek to regulate their use, than to banish them entirely.

This argument is based on the assumption, that they are like healthful foods and drinks, injurious only by excess.   But this is not true ; for, whenever they are used in any such strength as to be a gratification, they operate to a greater or less extent as stimulants ; and, in just such extent, they wear out the powers of the constitution. Such articles are designed for medicine, and not for common use as food and drink. There can be no argument framed to defend the use of one of these articles, which will not equally defend all. That men have a love for being stimulated, after they have once felt the pleasurable excitement, and that Providence has provided the means for securing it, are arguments as much in favor of alcohol, opium, and tobacco, as of coffee and tea. All that can be said in favor of the last-mentioned favorite beverages, is, that the danger in their use is not so great. Let any one, who defends one kind of stimulating drink, remember, then, that he uses an argument, which, if it be allowed that stimulants are not needed, and are injurious, will equally defend all kinds.

The Writer is of opinion, that tea and coffee are a most extensive cause of much of the nervous debility and suffering endured by American women; and that relinquishing such drinks would save an immense amount of nervous suffering. But there is little probability that the present generation will make so decided a change in their habits, as to give up these beverages; and the subject is presented rather in reference to forming the habits of children.

It is a fact, that tea and coffee are, at first, seldom or never agreeable to children. It is the mixture of milk, sugar, and water, that reconciles them to a taste, which in this manner gradually becomes agreeable. Now, suppose that those who provide for a family conclude that it is not *their* duty to give up entirely the use of stimulating drinks, may not the case appear different, in regard to teaching their children to love such drinks? Let the matter be regarded thus:—The experiments of physiologists all prove, that stimulants are not needful to health, and that, as the general rule, they tend to debilitate the constitution. Is it right, then, for a parent to tempt a child to drink what is not needful, when there is a probability that it will prove, to some extent, an undermining drain on the constitution? Some constitutions can bear much less excitement than others; and in every family of children there is usually one, or more, of delicate organization, and consequently peculiarly exposed to dangers from this source. This is the child who ordinarily is the victim to stimulating drinks. The tea and coffee which the parents and the healthier children can use without immediate injury, gradually saps the energies of the feebler child, who proves either an early victim, or a living martyr to all the sufferings that debilitated nerves inflict. Can it be right, when another path is known to be perfectly safe, to lead children where all allow that there is some danger, and where, in many cases, disease and death are met?

Of the stimulating drinks in common use, *black tea* is least injurious, because its flavor is so strong, in comparison with its narcotic principle, that one who uses it, is much less liable to excess. Children can be trained to love milk and water sweetened with sugar, so that it will always be a pleasant beverage; or, if there are exceptions to the rule, they will be few. Water is an unfailing resort. Every one loves it, and it is perfectly healthful.

The impression, common in this Country, that *warm drinks*, especially in Winter, are more healthful than cold, is not warranted by any experience, nor by the laws of the physical system. At dinner, cold drinks are universal, and no one deems them injurious. It is only at the other two meals that they are supposed to be hurtful.

There is no doubt that *warm* drinks are healthful, and more agreeable than cold, at certain times and seasons; but it is equally true that drinks above blood heat are not healthful. If any person should hold a finger in hot water, for a considerable time, twice every day, it would be found that the finger would gradually grow weaker. The frequent application of the stimulus of heat, like all other stimulants, eventually causes debility. If, therefore, a person is in the habit of drinking hot drinks twice a day, the teeth, throat, and stomach, are gradually debilitated. This, most probably, is one of the causes of an early decay of the teeth, which is observed to be much more common among American ladies, than among those in European countries.

It has been stated to the Writer, by an intelligent traveller, who visited Mexico, that it was rare to meet an individual with a good set of teeth ; and that almost every grown person, he met in the street, had only remnants of teeth. On inquiry into the customs of the Country, it was found, that it was the universal practice to take their usual beverage almost at the boiling point ; and this, doubtless, was the chief cause of the almost universal want of teeth in that Country. In the United States, it cannot be doubted that much evil is done, in this way, by hot drinks. Most tea drinkers consider tea as ruined, if it stands until it reaches the healthful temperature for drink.

The following extract from Dr. Combe, presents the opinion of most intelligent medical men, on this subject.

" *Water* is a safe drink for all constitutions, provided it be resorted to in obedience to the dictates of natural thirst, only, and not of habit." " Unless the desire for it is felt, there is no occasion for its use during a meal."

" The primary effect of all distilled and fermented liquors, is, to *stimulate the nervous system and quicken the circulation.*" " In infancy and childhood, the circulation is rapid, and easily excited ; and the nervous system is strongly acted upon, even

by the slightest external impressions. Hence slight
causes of irritation readily excite febrile and convulsive disorders." "In youth, the natural tendency of
the constitution is still to excitement; and consequently, as a general rule, the stimulus of fermented
liquors is injurious."

These remarks show, that parents, who find that
stimulating drinks are not injurious to themselves,
may mistake in inferring, from this, that they will
not be injurious to their children.

Dr. Combe continues thus: "In mature age, when
digestion is good and the system in full vigor, if the
mode of life be not too exhausting, the nervous
functions and general circulation are in their best
condition, and require no stimulus for their support.
The bodily energy is then easily sustained by nutritious food and a regular regimen, and consequently
artificial excitement only increases the wasting of
the natural strength." "In old age, when the
powers of life begin to fail, moderate stimulus may
be used with evident advantage."

"If it be said that this doctrine amounts to a
virtual prohibition of wine and stimulant liquors, I
admit, at once, that, where the whole animal functions go on healthfully and energetically without
them, their use is, in my opinion, adverse to the
continuance of health."

"Many persons imagine that spirits, taken in
moderate quantity, cannot be injurious, *because they
feel no immediate bad effects from their use*." But,
"if all the functions of the system are already vigorously executed *without* their aid, their use can be
followed only by one effect,—*morbid excitement;*
and it is in vain to contend against this obvious
truth."

He then refers to the case of St. Martin,* in which,

* See Note on p. 82.

after using alcoholic drinks, the coat of the stomach became inflamed, and was in a diseased state, and yet St. Martin *felt* no symptom that indicated any injurious effect from such drinks. After describing this diseased appearance of the stomach, Dr. Combe remarks,

"Here we have incontestable proof, that disease of the stomach was induced, and going on from bad to worse, in consequence of indulgence in ardent spirits, although no prominent symptom made its appearance, and St. Martin was in his general habits a healthy and sober man."

"Dr. Beaumont had also frequent occasion to remark, that, when stomachic disorder, attended by febrile action, was present, the mucous coat of the stomach presented distinct appearances of disease. He frequently saw it, for example, red, irritable, and dry; and on the food touching it, *no gastric juice exuded,* and consequently any food taken lay long undigested. But, after the diseased action was subdued by regimen and medicine, the gastric juice again flowed readily, and digestion went on as vigorously as before. Even anger and violent mental emotions sometimes produced these appearances, and gave rise to temporary indigestion. These observations show the futility, not to say mischief, of administering food, during fever and other diseases, by way of supporting the strength, when, from the deficiency of gastric juice, it cannot be digested, and can only add to the existing irritation. In this state, however, bland fluids are appropriate, because they allay irritation, and are almost entirely absorbed without requiring digestion." This "explains, at once, the miserable digestion and impaired appetite of the habitual drunkard."

"If it be asked, whether I go to the length of proscribing all fermented liquors, from tablebeer, upwards, I answer," "that *where the general health is perfect without them, they ought not to be taken, because then their only effect is to produce unnatural excitement.*" He then points out cases of disease or debility when such drinks may be useful ; but of such cases a physician only can be the proper judge.

It may be asked, in this connection, why the stimulus of animal food is not to be regarded in the same light as that of stimulating drinks. In reply, a very essential difference may be pointed out. Animal food furnishes *nourishment* to the organs it stimulates, but stimulating drinks excite the organs to quickened action, without affording any nourishment.

It has been supposed, by some, that tea and coffee have some nourishing power. But it is proved that it is the milk and sugar, and not the main portion of the drink, that imparts the nourishment. Tea has not one particle of nourishing properties ; and what little exists in the coffee-berry, is lost by roasting it in the usual mode. All that these articles do, is simply *to stimulate, without nourishing.*

It is very common, especially in schools, for children to form a habit of drinking freely of cold water. This is a debilitating habit, and should be corrected. Very often, chewing a bit of cracker will stop a craving for drink better than taking water ; and when teachers are troubled with very thirsty scholars, they should direct them to this remedy. A person who exercises but little, requires no drink, between meals, for health ; and the craving for it is unhealthful. Spices, wines, fermented liquors, and all stimulating condiments, produce unhealthful thirst.

CHAPTER VIII.

ON CLOTHING.

London Bills of Mortality; Inference from it. Causes of Infant Mortality. Of the Circulation in Infancy. Warm Dress for Infants, and why. Investigations in France, and Results. Dangers from the opposite extreme. Effects of too much Clothing. Rule of Safety. Featherbeds; why unhealthy in Warm Weather. Best Nightgowns for Young Children. Clothing how to be proportioned. Irrational Dress of Women. Use of Flannel next the Skin. Evils of Tight Dress to Women. False Taste in our Prints of Fashions. Modes in which Tight Dress operates to weaken the Constitution. Rule of Safety as to Looseness of Dress. Extract on the subject of appropriate Dress.

It appears, from the bills of mortality in the city of London, that the health of the people, there, is about the usual average; and consequently that children are as likely to have health and long life, there, as in most places in this Country. And yet it is found, that one quarter of the children, born there, die before completing their second year. From this, it is inferred, that this is about the ordinary mortality of infants. That one quarter of the human race should perish in infancy, is a fact not in accordance with the analogy of Nature. No such mortality prevails among the young of animals; it does not appear to be the design of the Creator; and it must be owing to causes which can be removed. Medical men agree in the opinion, that a great portion of this mortality is owing to mismanagement, in reference to fresh air, food, and clothing.

At birth, the circulation is chiefly in the vessels of the skin; for the liver and stomach, being feeble in action, demand less blood, and it resorts to the surface. If, therefore, an infant is exposed to cold, the blood is driven inward, by the contracting of the blood-vessels in the skin, and the internal organs being thus overstimulated, bowel complaints, croup, convulsions, or some other evil, ensues. This shows the sad mistake of parents, who plunge infants in cold water to strengthen their constitution. And it teaches, also, that infants should be washed in warm water, and in a warm room. Some have constitutions strong enough to bear mismanagement in these respects; but many fail in consequence of it.

This shows the importance of dressing infants warmly, and protecting them from exposure to a cold temperature. It is in reference to this, that mothers, now, very generally, cover the arms and necks of infants, especially in Winter. Fathers and mothers, if they were obliged to go with bare arms and necks, even in moderate weather, would often shiver with cold; and yet they have a power of constitution which would subject them to less hazard and discomfort, than a delicate infant must experience from a similar exposure. This mode of dressing infants, with bare necks and arms, has arisen from the common impression, that they have a power of resisting cold superior to older persons. This is a mistake; for the experiments of medical men have established the fact, that the power of producing heat is least in the period of infancy.

Extensive investigations have been made in France, in reference to this point. It is there required, in some districts, that every infant, at birth, be carried to the office of the *maire*, to be registered. It is found, in these districts, that the death of infants, soon after birth, is much greater in the cold, than in the warm, months; and that a much greater proportion die among those who reside at a distance from the office of the *maire*, than among those in its vicinity. This proves, that exposure to cold has much to do with the continuance of infant life.

But it is as dangerous to go to the other extreme, and keep the body too warm. The skin, when kept at too high a temperature, is relaxed and weakened by too profuse perspiration, and becomes more sensitive, and more readily affected by every change of temperature. This increases the liabilities to sudden colds; so that it frequently happens that the children, who are most carefully guarded from cold, are the ones most liable to take sudden and dangerous chills. The reason is, that, by the too great accumulation of clothing, the skin is too much excited, and the blood is withdrawn from the internal organs, thus weakening them, while the skin itself is debilitated by the same process.

The rule of safety, is, so to cover the body, as to keep it entirely warm, all over, but not so as to induce perspiration in any part. The perspiration induced by exercise is healthful, because it increases the appetite; but the perspiration produced by excess of clothing is debilitating. This shows the importance of adjusting beds and their covering to the season. Featherbeds are unhealthful in warm weather, because they induce perspiration; and in all cases, those who have the care of children should proportion their covering by night to the season of the year. Infants and children should never be so clothed as either to feel chilly, or to induce perspiration.

The greatest trouble, in this respect, to those who have the care of children, is owing to their throwing off their covering in the night. The best guard, against such exposures, is a nightgown, of the warmest and thickest flannel, made like pantaloons at the lower part, and the legs long, so that they can be tied over the feet. This makes less covering needful, and saves the child from excessive cold when it is thrown off.

The clothing ought always to be proportioned to the constitution and habits. A person of strong constitution, who takes much exercise, needs less clothing than one of delicate and sedentary habits. According to this rule, women need much thicker and warmer clothing, when they go out, than men. But how different are our customs, from what sound wisdom dictates! Women go out with thin stockings and thin shoes and open necks, when men are protected by thick woollen hose and boots, and their whole body encased in many folds of flannel and broadcloth.

Flannel, worn next the skin, is useful, for several reasons. It is a bad conductor of heat, so that it protects the body from *sudden* chills when in a state of perspiration. It also produces a kind of friction on the skin, which aids it in its functions, while its texture, being loose, enables it to receive and retain much matter, thrown off from the body, that would otherwise accumulate on its surface. This is the reason why medical men direct that young children wear flannel next the body, and woollen hose, the first two years of life. They are thus protected from sudden exposures. This is the reason, too, why laboring men should wear flannel next the body. Flannels are also considered as preservatives from infection, in unhealthy atmospheres. They give a healthy action to the skin, and thus enable it to resist the operation of unhealthy miasms. For this reason, persons residing in a new country should wear flannel next the skin, to guard them from the noxious miasms caused by extensive vegetable decompositions. It is stated, that the fatal influence of the malaria around Rome, has been much diminished by this practice.

But the practice by which females probably suffer most, is, the use of *tight dresses.* Much has been said against the use of corsets by ladies. But these may be worn with perfect safety, and be left off, and still the injury they often produce be equally felt. It is the *constriction* of dress that is to be feared, and not any particular article that produces it. A frock, or a belt, may be so tight, as to be even worse than a corset, which would more equally divide the compression.

So long as it is the fashion to admire, as models of elegance, the wasp-like figures which are presented at the rooms of mantuamakers and milliners, there will be hundreds of foolish women, who will risk their lives and health to secure some resemblance to these deformities of the human frame. But it is believed that all sensible women, when they fairly understand the evils which result from tight dressing, and learn the *real* model of taste and beauty for a perfect female form, will never risk their own health, or the health of their daughters, in efforts to secure a form, as much at variance with good taste, as it is with good health.

Such female figures as our print-shops present, are made, not by the hand of the Author of all grace and beauty, but by the murderous contrivances of the corset-shop; and the more a woman learns the true rules of grace and beauty for the female form, the more her taste will revolt from such ridiculous distortions. The folly of the Chinese belle, who totters on two useless deformities, is nothing, compared to that of the American belle, who impedes all the internal organs in the discharge of their functions, that she may have a slender waist.

It was shown, in the article on the bones and muscles, that exercise was indispensable to their growth and strength. If any muscles are left unemployed, they diminish in size and strength. The girding of tight dresses operates thus on the muscles of the body. If an article, like corsets, is made to hold up the body, then those muscles which are designed for this purpose are released from duty, and grow weak; so that, after this has been continued for some time, leaving off the unnatural sup-

port produces a feeling of weakness.   Thus a person
will complain of feeling so weak and unsupported,
without corsets, as to be uncomfortable.   This is
entirely owing to the disuse of those muscles which
corsets throw out of employ.

Another, effect of tight dress, is, to stop the office
of the lungs.   Unless the chest can expand, fully,
and with perfect ease, a portion of the lungs are not
filled with air, and thus the full purification of the
blood is prevented.   This movement of the lungs,
when they are fully inflated, increases the peristaltic
movement of the stomach and bowels, and promotes
digestion ; and any constriction of the waist tends
to impede this important operation, and indigestion,
with all its attendant evils, is often the result.

The rule of safety, in regard to the tightness of
dress, is this.   Every person should be dressed so
loosely, that *when sitting in the posture used in
sewing, reading, or study,* THE LUNGS *can be as
fully and as easily inflated, as they are without
clothing.*   Many a woman thinks she dresses loosely, because, when she stands up, her clothing does
not confine her chest.   This is not a fair test.   It is
in the position most used when engaged in common
employments, that we are to judge of the constriction of dress.   Let every woman then bear in mind,
that, just so long as her dress and position oppose
any resistance to her chest, in just such proportion
her blood is unpurified, and her vital organs are
endangered.

The following remark is from the Young Lady's
Friend.

"There is one thing, which is never sufficiently
taken into account, in the fashions of this Country ;
and that is, climate.   Receiving our models from
the more equable temperature of France, they are
often unsuited to the scorching suns of our Summers, and the severe frosts of our Winters.   The

English ladies set us a good example, in this respect." "The most delicately-bred fine lady in the land puts on cotton stockings and thick shoes to walk out for exercise ; and would think it very unladylike not to be so provided ; and on more dressy occasions, when she wears silk hose, she would on no account go out, in cold weather, without warm shoes or boots, either kid, lined with fur, or quilted silk shoes, foxed with leather. To walk out, as our young ladies do, in cold and wet weather, with thin-soled prunella or kid shoes, would seem to them as very vulgar, betraying a want of suitableness, only to be accounted for by supposing the individual unable to provide herself with better."
"All styles of dress, which impede the motions of the wearer ; which do not sufficiently protect the person ; which add unnecessarily to the heat of Summer, or to the cold of Winter ; which do not suit the age and occupation of the wearer ; or which indicate an expenditure unsuited to her means ; are *inappropriate*, and therefore destitute of one of the main essentials of beauty."

CHAPTER IX.

ON CLEANLINESS.

Importance of Cleanliness not realized, without a Knowledge of the Nature of the Skin. Foundation of the Maxim respecting the Healthfulness of Dirt. Office of the Skin. Other Organs that perform similar duties. Amount of matter daily exhaled by the Skin. Effect of a Chill upon the Skin, when perspiring. Illustration of this. Effect of closing the Pores of the Skin, with Dirt or other Matter. The Skin absorbs Matter into the Blood. Reasons for a Daily Ablution of the whole Body. Effects of Fresh Air on Clothing worn next the Skin. Americans compared with other Nations as to care of the Skin. Cautions in regard to a use of the Bath. How to decide when Cold Bathing is useful. Warm Bath tends to prevent Colds; and why. Advantages of general Ablutions to Children. Care of the Teeth.

THE importance of cleanliness, in person and dress, can never be fully realized, by persons who are ignorant of the construction of the skin, and of the influence which its treatment has on the health of the body. Persons deficient in such knowledge, frequently sneer at what they deem the foolish and fidgety particularity of others, whose frequent ablutions and changes of clothing exceed their own measure of importance.

The popular maxim, that "dirt is healthy," has probably arisen from the fact, that playing in the open air is very beneficial to the health of children, who thus get dirt on their persons and clothes. But it is the fresh air and exercise, and not the dirt, which promotes the health.

In a previous article, it was shown, that the lungs, bowels, kidneys, and skin, were the organs employed in throwing off those waste and noxious parts of the food not employed in nourishing the body. Of this, the skin has the largest duty to perform; throwing off, at least, twenty ounces every twenty-four hours, by means of insensible perspiration. When exercise sets the blood in quicker motion, it ministers its supplies faster, and there is consequently a greater residuum to be thrown off by the skin; and then the perspiration becomes so abundant as to be perceptible. In this state, if a sudden chill takes place, the blood-vessels of the skin contract, the blood is driven from the surface, and the internal organs are taxed with a double duty. If the constitution is a strong one, these organs march on and perform the labor exacted. But if any of these organs are debilitated, the weakest one generally gives way, and some disease ensues.

One of the most frequent illustrations of this reciprocated action, is afforded by a convivial meeting in cold weather. The heat of the room, the food, and the excitement, quicken the circulation, and perspiration is evolved. When the company passes into the cold air, a sudden revulsion takes place. The increased circulation continues, for some time after; but the skin being cooled, the blood retreats, and the internal organs are obliged to perform the duties of the skin as well as their own. Then, in case the lungs are the weakest organ, the mucous secretion becomes excessive; so that it would fill up the cells, and stop the breathing, were it not for the spasmodic effort called coughing, by which this substance is thrown out. In case the nerves are the weakest part of the system, such an exposure would result in pains in the head or teeth, or in some other nervous ailment. If the muscles are the weakest part, rheumatic affections will ensue; and if the bowels or kidneys are weakest, some disorder in their functions will result.

But it is found that the closing of the pores of the skin with other substances, tends to a similar result on the internal organs. In this situation, the skin is unable perfectly to perform its functions, and

either the blood remains to a certain extent unpurified, or else the internal organs have an unnatural
duty to perform. Either of these results tends to
produce disease, and the gradual decay of vital
powers.

Moreover, it has been shown, that the skin has
the power of absorbing into the blood particles retained on its surface. In consequence of these
peculiarities, the skin of the whole body needs to
be washed, every day. This process removes from
the pores the matter exhaled from the blood, and
also that collected from the atmosphere and other
bodies. If this process is not often performed, the
pores of the skin fill up with the redundant matter
expelled, and being pressed, by the clothing, to the
surface of the body, the skin is both interrupted in
its exhaling process, and its absorbents take back
into the system portions of the noxious matter.
Thus the blood is not relieved to the extent designed, while it receives back noxious particles,
which are thus carried to the lungs, liver, and every
part of the system.

This is the reason why it is a rule of health that
the whole body should be washed every day, and
that the articles worn next to the skin should often
be changed. This is the reason why it is recommended that persons should not sleep in the article
they wear next the skin through the day. The
alternate change and airing of the articles worn next
the body by day or night is a practice very favorable
to the health of the skin. The fresh air has the
power of removing much of the noxious effluvia
received from the body by the clothing. It is with
reference to this, that, on leaving a bed, its covering
should be thrown open and exposed to the fresh air.

The benefit arising from a proper care of the
skin, is the reason why bathing has been so extensively practised by civilized nations. The Greeks

and Romans considered bathing as indispensable to daily comfort, and as much so, as their meals ; and public baths were provided for all classes. In European countries, this practice is very prevalent, and there is no civilized nation that pays so little regard to the rules of health, on this subject, as our own. The health of a horse is found to depend so much on the care of his skin, that frequent washing and rubbing are deemed indispensable ; but thousands in this land go month after month without paying any such regard to the wants of their own physical system. To wash the face, feet, hands, and neck, is the extent of the ablutions practised by perhaps the majority of our people.

In regard to the use of the bath, there is need of some information, in order to prevent danger from its misuse. Persons in good health, and with strong constitutions, can use the cold bath, and the shower-bath, with entire safety and benefit. Their effect is suddenly to contract the blood-vessels of the skin, and send the blood to the internal organs. Then, if these organs are in health, a reaction takes place as soon as bathing ceases, and the blood is sent in greater supplies to the skin, producing an invigorating and cheerful glow. But if the constitution is feeble, this reaction does not take place, and cold bathing is injurious. But a bath, blood warm, or a little cooler than the skin, is safe for all constitutions, if not protracted over half an hour. After bathing, the body should be rubbed with a brush or coarse towel, to remove the light scales of scarf-skin, which adhere to it, and also to promote a healthful excitement.

When families have no bathing establishment, every member should wash the whole person, on rising or going to bed, either in cold or warm water, according to the constitution. It is especially important, that children have the perspiration and other impurities, which their exercise and sports have occasioned, removed from their skin before going to bed. The hours of sleep are those when the body most freely exhales the waste matter of the system, and all the pores should be properly freed from impediments to this healthful operation. For this purpose, a large tin wash-pan should be kept for children, just large enough, at bottom, for them to stand in, and flaring outward, so as to be very broad at top. A child can then be placed in it, standing, and washed with a sponge, without wetting the floor. It being small at bottom, makes it better than a tub, as lighter, smaller, and not requiring so much water.

A bath should never be taken till three hours after eating, as it interrupts the process of digestion, by withdrawing the blood from the stomach to the surface. Neither should it be taken when the body is weary with exercise, nor be immediately followed by severe exercise. Many suppose that a warm bath exposes a person more readily to take cold; and that it tends to debilitate the system. This is not the case, unless it be protracted too long. If it be used so as to cleanse the skin, and give it a gentle stimulus, it is better able to resist cold than before the process. This is the reason why the Swedes and Russians can rush reeking out of their steam baths and throw themselves into the snow, and not only escape injury, but feel invigorated. It is for a similar reason that we suffer less in going into the cold, from a warm room, with our body entirely warm, than when we go out somewhat chilled. When the skin is warm, the circulation is active on the surface, and the cold does not so reduce its temperature, but that increased exercise will keep up its warmth.

These remarks indicate the wisdom of those parents, who habitually wash their children, all over, before they go to bed. The chance of life and health, to such children, is greatly increased by this practice; and no doubt much of the suffering of childhood, from cutaneous eruptions, weak eyes, earache, colds, and fevers is owing to a neglect of the skin.

The care of the teeth should be made habitual to children, not merely as promoting an agreeable appearance, but as a needful preservative. The following extract from Dr. Combe relates to this point.

"Being constantly moistened with saliva, the teeth have a tendency to become incrusted with the tartar, or earthy matter, which it contains." "As this incrustation not only destroys the beauty of the teeth, but also promotes their decay, it becomes an object of care to remove it as soon as it is formed; and the most effectual mode of doing so, is to brush the teeth regularly twice a day,"—when retiring at night, and on rising in the morning.

"When digestion is impaired, and acidity prevails in the stomach, the mucous secretions in the mouth also become altered in character; and, by their incessant contact, injure and even destroy the teeth. From this cause, we often see the teeth in young people in a state of complete decay."

Intemperance in eating, therefore, by causing indigestion, destroys the teeth, and this is one cause of the defective teeth so common in America.

CHAPTER X.

ON EARLY RISING.

Universal Impression on this Practice. Why it should be regarded as American and Democratic. Practice in Aristocratic Circles in England. Appeal to American Women. First Consideration in Favor of Early Rising. Another Physiological Reason in its Favor. Another Reason. Time necessary for Sleep. Proper Hours for Rising and Retiring. Evils of protracted Sleep. Testimony of Sir John Sinclair. Another Reason for Early Rising. Responsibility of Parents for the Health and Industry of a Family. Early Rising; —its Effects on General Society.

THERE is no practice, which has been more extensively eulogized, in all ages, than early rising; and this universal impression is an indication that it is founded on true philosophy. For it is rarely the case, that the common sense of mankind fastens on a practice as really beneficial, especially one that demands self-denial, without some substantial reason.

This practice, which may justly be called a domestic virtue, is one which has a peculiar claim to be called American and democratic. The distinctive mark of aristocratic nations, is a disregard of the great mass, and a disproportionate regard for the interests of certain privileged orders. All the customs and habits of such a nation are, to a greater or less extent, regulated by this principle. Now the mass of any nation must always consist of persons who labor at occupations which demand the light of day. But in aristocratic countries, especially in England, labor is regarded as the mark of the lower classes, and indolence is considered as one mark of a gentleman. This impression gradually and imperceptibly has, to a great extent, regulated their customs, so that, even in their hours of meals and repose, the higher orders aim at being different and distinct from those, who, by laborious pursuits, are placed below them. In consequence of this, while the lower orders labor by day, and sleep at night, the rich, the noble, and the honored, sleep by day, and follow their pursuits and pleasures by night. It will be found that the aristocracy of London breakfast near mid-day, dine after dark, visit and go to Parliament between ten and twelve, and retire to sleep towards morning. In consequence of this, the subordinate classes, who aim at gentility, gradually fall into the same practice. And the influence of this custom extends across the ocean, and here, in this democratic land, we find many, who measure their grade of gentility by the late hour at which they arrive at a party. And this aristocratic tendency is growing upon us, so that, throughout the Nation, the hours for visiting and retiring are constantly retrograding, while the hours for rising correspond in lateness.

The question, then, is one that appeals to American women, as a matter of patriotism ; as having a bearing on those great principles of democracy, which we claim are equally the principles of Christianity. Shall we form our customs on the principle that labor is degrading, and that indolence is genteel? Shall we assume, by our practice, that the interests of the great mass are to be sacrificed for the pleasures and honors of a privileged few? Shall we ape the customs of aristocratic lands, in those very practices that result from principles and institutions which we condemn? Shall we not rather take the place to which we are entitled, as the leaders, rather than the followers, in the customs of society, turn back the tide of aristocratic inroads, and carry through the whole, not only of civil and political, but of social and domestic life, the true principles of democratic freedom and equality? The following considerations may serve to strengthen an affirmative decision.

The first consideration relates to the health of a family. It is a universal law of physiology, that all living things flourish best in the light. Vegetables, in a dark cellar, grow pale and spindling, and children, brought up in mines, are wan and stinted. This universal law indicates the folly of turning day into night, thus losing the genial influence which the light of day produces on all animated creation.

There is another phenomenon in the physiology of Nature, which equally condemns this practice. It has been shown, that the purification of the blood in the lungs is secured, by the absorption of carbon and hydrogen from the blood by the oxygen of the atmosphere. This combination forms carbonic acid and water, which are expired into the atmosphere from our lungs. Now all the vegetable world undergoes a similar process. In the light of day, all the leaves of vegetables absorb carbon and expire oxygen, thus supplying the air with its vital principle, and withdrawing the more deleterious element. But when the light is withdrawn, this process is reversed, and all vegetables exhale carbonic acid and inspire the oxygen of the air. Thus it appears, that the atmosphere of day is much more healthful than that of the night, especially out of doors.

Moreover, when the body is fatigued, it is much more liable to deleterious influences from noxious particles in the atmosphere, which may be absorbed by the skin or the lungs. In consequence of this, the last hours of daily labor are more likely to be those of risk, especially to delicate constitutions. This is a proper reason for retiring to the house and to slumber, at an early hour, that the body may not be exposed to the most risk, when after the exertions of the day it is least able to bear it.

The observations of medical men, whose inquiries have been directed to this point, have decided, that from six to eight hours is the amount of sleep demanded by persons in health. Some constitutions require as much as eight, and others no more than six, hours of repose. But eight hours is the maximum for all persons in ordinary health, with ordinary occupations. In cases of extra physical exertions, or the debility of disease or a decayed constitution, more than this is required. Let eight hours, then, be regarded as the ordinary period required for sleep, by an industrious people, like the Americans. According to this, the practice of rising between four and five, and retiring between nine and ten, in Summer, would secure most of the sunlight and least of the noxious period of the atmosphere. In Winter, the night air is less deleterious, because the frost binds noxious exhalations, and vegetation ceases its inspiring and expiring process ; and, moreover, as the constitution is more tried in cold than in warm weather, and as in cold weather the body exhales less during the hours of sleep, it is not so injurious to protract our slumbers beyond the period allowed in the warm months. In Winter, therefore, the proper rule would be, to rise as soon as we can see to dress, and retire so as to allow eight hours for sleep.

It thus appears, that the laws of our political condition, the laws of the natural world, and the constitution of our bodies, alike demand that we rise with the light of day to prosecute our employments, and that we retire within doors, when this light is withdrawn.

In regard to the effects of protracting the time spent in repose, many extensive and satisfactory investigations have been made. It has been shown, that during sleep the body perspires most freely, while yet neither food nor exercise are ministering to its wants. Of course, if we continue our slumbers beyond the time required to restore the body to its usual vigor, there is an unperceived undermining of the constitution, by this protracted and debilitating exhalation. This process, in a course of years, renders the body delicate, and less able to withstand disease ; and in the result shortens life. Sir John Sinclair, who has written a large work on the Causes of Longevity, states, as one result of his extensive investigations, that he never has yet heard or read of a single case of great longevity, where the individual was not an early riser. He says that he has found cases, in which the individual has violated some one of all the other laws of health, and yet lived to great age ; but never a single instance in which any constitution has withstood that undermining consequent on protracting the hours of repose beyond the demands of the system.

Another reason for early rising, is, that it is indispensable to a systematic and well-regulated family. At whatever hour the parents retire, children and domestics, wearied by play or labor, must retire early. Children usually awake with the dawn of light, and commence their play, while domestics usually prefer the freshness of morning for their labors. If, then, the parents rise at a late hour, they either induce a habit of protracting sleep in their children and domestics, or else the family is up, and at their pursuits, while their supervisors are in bed. Any woman, who asserts that her children and domestics, in the first hours of day, when their spirits are freshest, will be as well regulated without her presence as with it, confesses that, which surely is little for her credit. It is believed that any candid woman, whatever may be her excuse for late rising, will concede, that, if she could rise early, it would be for the advantage of her family. A late breakfast puts back the work, through the whole day, for every member of a family ; and if the parents thus occasion the loss of an hour or two, to each individual, who but for their delay in the morning would be usefully employed, the parents, alone, are responsible for all this waste of time. Is it said, that those, who wish to rise early, can go to their employments before breakfast? it may be replied, that, in most cases, it is not safe to use the eyes or the muscles in the morning, till the losses of the night have been repaired by food. In addition to this, it may be urged, that, where the parents set an example of the violation of the rules of health and industry, their influence goes in the wrong direction; so that whatever waste of time is induced, by a practice which they thus uphold, must be set down to their account. If, by the early rising of parents, every member of the family would be saved from the wear of constitution consequent on protracted sleep, and would secure an hour of useful industry, the parents are responsible to their consciences and to God for the whole loss.

But the practice of early rising has a relation to the general interests of the social community, as well as to that of each distinct family. All that great portion of the community who are employed in business and labor, find it needful to rise early; and all their hours of meals, and their appointments for business or pleasure, must be accommodated to these arrangements. Now, if a small portion of the community establish very different hours, it makes a kind of jostling in all the concerns and interests of society. The various appointments for the public, such as meetings, schools, and business hours, must be accommodated to the mass, and not to individuals. The few, then, who establish domestic habits at variance with the majority, are either constantly interrupted in their own arrangements, or else are interfering with the rights and interests of others. This is exemplified in the case of schools. In families where late rising is practised, either hurry, irregularity, and neglect, are engendered in the family, or else the interests of the school, and thus of the community, are sacrificed. In this, and many

other concerns, it can be shown, that the interests of
the bulk of the people, to a greater or less extent,
are sacrificed by the aristocratic practice of having
late hours for rising and meals. Let any teacher
select the unpunctual scholars,—a class who most
seriously interfere with the interests of the school;
—and let men of business select those who cause
them most waste of time and vexation, by unpunc-
tuality;—and it will be found, that they are among
the late risers, and rarely among those who rise
early. Thus it is manifest, that late rising not only
injures the person and family which practise it, but
interferes with the rights and convenience of the
community in which they reside.

CHAPTER XI.

ON DOMESTIC EXERCISE.

Remarks from Dr. Combe. Effects of Exercise or a want of it on
the Muscles. Effects of neglecting to use the Muscles of the
Trunk; Effects of excessive use of them. How Female Weakness and Deformity result from a Neglect of these Principles.
Effects of Stays. Effect of School Confinement and Seats. Importance of a Feeling of Interest in taking Exercise. A Walk
merely for Exercise is useful. Morning Exercise most proper for
Young Girls. Extract from the Young Lady's Friend. Madam
Roland. Lady Montague. Daughter of a French Nobleman.

THE following extract from a work of Dr. Combe,
will present the views which all intelligent physicians hold in common, on the subject of exercise.

" Whenever a muscle is called into frequent use,
its fibres increase in thickness, within certain limits, and become capable of acting with greater force
and readiness; and, on the other hand, when a
muscle is little used, its volume and power decrease,
in a corresponding degree. When in a state of

activity, the quantity of blood which muscles receive is considerably increased; and, in consequence, those which are much exercised, become of a deeper red color, than those which are less used."
" To every organ of the body, arterial blood is an indispensable stimulus ; and its supply is, during health, always proportioned to the extent and energy of the action.   When any part, therefore, is stinted of its usual quantity of blood, it very soon becomes weakened, and at last loses its power of action."

" A state of *permanent* contraction is both unnatural and impossible ; and, accordingly, the most fatiguing muscular employment, to which a man can be subjected, is that of remaining immovable in any given attitude."   " We may easily put the fact to the test, by attempting to hold the arm extended at right angles to the body for the short space of ten minutes.   He whose muscles, if indeed capable of the exertion, do not feel sore with fatigue at the end of that time, may think himself peculiarly fortunate in being blessed with a powerful constitution.

" The principle just stated, explains, very obviously, the weariness, debility, and injury to health, which invariably follow forced confinement to one position, or to one limited variety of movement, as is often witnessed in the education of young females."   " Exercise of the muscles which support the trunk of the body are the only means, which, according to the Creator's laws, are conducive to muscular developement, and by which bodily strength and vigor can be secured.   Instead of promoting such exercise, however, the prevailing system of female education places the muscles of the trunk, in particular, under the worst possible circumstances, and renders their exercise nearly impossible.   Left to its own weight, the body would fall to the ground, in obedience to the ordinary law of gravitation : in sitting and standing, therefore, as well as in walking, the position is preserved only by" exertion of the muscles that support the spine and trunk. " But, if we confine ourselves to one attitude, such as that of sitting erect upon a chair, —or, what is still worse, on benches without backs, as is the common practice in schools,—it is obvious that we place the muscles which support the spine and trunk in the very disadvantageous position of permanent, instead of alternate contraction." " Girls, thus restrained daily for many successive hours, invariably suffer, being deprived of the sports and exercise after school hours, which strengthen the muscles of boys, and enable them to withstand the oppression. The muscles, being thus enfeebled, the girls either lean over insensibly to one side, and thus contract curvature of the spine ; or, their weakness being perceived, they are forthwith cased in stiffer and stronger stays ; that support being sought for in steel and whalebone, which Nature intended they should obtain from the bones and muscles of their own bodies." But the " want of varied motion, which was the prime cause of the muscular weakness, is still further aggravated, by the tight pressure of the stays interrupting the play of the muscles, and rendering them, in a few months, more powerless than ever." " During the short time allotted to that nominal exercise,—the formal walk, the body is left almost as motionless as before." " The natural consequences of this treatment are, debility of the body, curvature of the spine, impaired digestion, and, from the diminished tone of all the animal and vital functions, general ill health ; and yet, while we thus set Nature and her laws at defiance, we presume to express surprise at the prevalence of female deformity and disease ! "

" The sedentary and unvaried occupations which follow each other, for hours in succession, in many of our schools, have also been the cause of needless suffering to thousands; and it is high time that a sound physiology should step in, to root out all such erroneous and hurtful practices." "The custom of causing the young to sit on benches without any support to the back, and without any variety of motion, cannot be too soon exploded. If the muscles of the spine were strengthened by the exercise which they require, but which is so generally denied; and if the school employments were varied or interrupted at reasonable intervals, to admit of change of position and of motion; nothing could be better adapted for giving an easy and erect carriage, than seats without backs." "But it is a gross misconception, to suppose that the same good results will follow the absence of support, when the muscles are weakened by constant straining and want of play."

"Instead, therefore, of so many successive hours being devoted to study and to books, the employments of the young ought to be varied or interrupted by proper intervals of cheerful and exhilarating exercise," "which require the cooperation and society of companions. This is infinitely preferable to the solemn processions which are so often substituted for exercise, and which are hurtful, inasmuch as they delude parents and teachers into the notion that they constitute, in reality, that which they only counterfeit and supersede."

"Every body knows how wearisome and disagreeable it is to saunter along, without having some object to attain; and how listless and unprofitable a walk, taken against the inclination, and merely for exercise, is, compared to the same exertion made in pursuit of an object on which we are intent. The difference is, simply, that, in the former case, the muscles are obliged to work without that full nervous impulse which Nature has decreed to be essential to their healthy and energetic action; and that, in the latter, the nervous impulse is in full and harmonious operation." In illustration of this, "the elastic spring, bright eye, and cheerful glow of the beings thus excited, form a perfect contrast to the spiritless and inanimate aspect of many of our boarding-school processions."

"It must not, however, be supposed, that a walk, simply for the sake of exercise, can never be beneficial. If a person be thoroughly satisfied that exercise is requisite, and perfectly *willing* or rather *desirous*, thus to " secure good health, "*the desire* then becomes a sufficient nervous impulse, and one in perfect harmony with the muscular action."

The foregoing principles of physiology enable us to appreciate, more readily, the benefits to health of the various domestic exercise which all young ladies should be trained to practise. In the morning, every young lady should dress herself very loosely, to give full play to all her muscles. She should first throw open her windows, and lay open her bed, that the sheets and bed may be aired. In this way, she fills her room with fresh air. After breakfast, if it is cold, she can shut the windows, and, while making her bed and sweeping and dusting her room, almost every muscle in the body will be called into vigorous activity; and this kind of exercise should be continued two or three hours. Washing, ironing, starching, rubbing furniture, tending infants, and all employments that require stooping, bending, and change of position, are promoting the health of the muscles used, and of all the various organs of the body. Some persons object to sweeping, on account of the dust inhaled. But there is no need of such an impediment. Free ventilation, frequent sweeping, and the use of damp sand, or tea leaves, will prevent any such quantity of dust as can be in the least degree injurious. And the mothers, who will hire domestics to take away all these modes of securing to their daughters health, grace, beauty, and domestic virtues, and the young ladies who consent to be deprived of these advantages, will probably both live to mourn over the languor, discouragement, pain, disappointment, and sorrow, that will come with ill health, as the almost inevitable result.

The following extracts from 'The Young Ladies' Friend,' are given, as most excellent remarks on this topic, with the hope, also, that it will lead to the perusal of the whole of that valuable work.

"Whether rich or poor, young or old, married or single, a woman is always liable to be called to the performance of every kind of domestic duty, as well as to be placed at the head of a family; and nothing short of a *practical* knowledge of the details of housekeeping can ever make those duties easy, or render her competent to direct others in the performance of them.

"All moral writers on female character treat of Domestic Economy as an indispensable part of female education; and this, too, in the old countries of Europe, where an abundant population, and the institutions of society, render it easy to secure the services of faithful domestics. Madam Roland, one of the most remarkable women of the last century, says of herself, 'The same child who read systematic works, who could explain the circles of the celestial sphere, who could handle the crayon and the graver, and who, at eight years of age, was the best dancer in the youthful parties, was frequently called into the kitchen, to make an omelet, pick herbs, and skim the pot.'

"All female characters that are held up to admiration, whether in fiction or biography, will be found to possess these domestic accomplishments; and if they are considered indispensable in the Old World, how much more are they needed in this land of independence, where riches cannot exempt the mistress of a family from the difficulty of procuring efficient aid, and where perpetual change of domestics renders perpetual instruction and superintendence necessary.

"Since, then, the details of good housekeeping must be included in a good female education, it is very desirable that they should be acquired when young, and so practised as to become easy, and to be performed dexterously and expeditiously."

"The elegant and accomplished Lady Mary Wortley Montague, who figured in the fashionable, as well as the literary circles of her time, has said, that 'the most minute details of household economy become elegant and refined, when they are ennobled by sentiment;' and they are truly ennobled, when we do them either from a sense of duty, or consideration for a parent, or love to a husband. 'To furnish a room,' continues this lady, 'is no longer a commonplace affair, shared with upholsterers and cabinet-makers; it is decorating the place where I am to meet a friend or lover. To order dinner is not merely arranging a meal with my cook,—it is preparing refreshment for him whom I love. These necessary occupations, viewed in this light, by a person capable of strong attachment, are so many pleasures, and afford her far more delight than the games and shows which constitute the amusements of the world.'

"Such is the testimony of a titled lady of the last century, to the sentiment that may be made to mingle in the most homely occupations. I will now quote that of a modern female writer and traveller, who, in her pleasant book, called 'Six Weeks on the Loire,' has thus described the housewifery of the daughter of a French nobleman, residing in a superb chateau on that river. The travellers had just arrived, and been introduced, when the following scene took place.

" ' The bill of fare for dinner was discussed in my presence, and settled, *sans façon*, with that delightful frankness and gayety, which, in the French character, gives a charm to the most trifling occurrence. Madamoiselle Louise then begged me to excuse her for half an hour, as she was going to make some creams, and some *pastilles*. I requested that I might accompany her, and also render myself useful; we accordingly went together to the dairy. I made tarts *à l'Anglaise*, whilst she made confections and *bonbons*, and all manner of pretty things, with as much ease as if she had never done any thing else, and as much grace as she displayed in the saloon. I could not help thinking, as I looked at her, with her servants about her, all cheerful, respectful, and anxious to attend upon her, how much better it would be for the young ladies in England, if they would occasionally return to the habits of their grandmammas, and mingle the animated and endearing occupations of domestic life, and the modest manners and social amusements of home, with the perpetual practising on harps and pianos, and the incessant efforts at display, and search after gayety, which, at the present day, render them any thing but what an amiable man, of a reflecting mind and delicate sentiments, would desire in the woman he might wish to select as the companion of his life.' "

CHAPTER XII.

ON DOMESTIC MANNERS.

What are Good-manners. Defect in American Manners. Coldness and Reserve of the Descendants of the Puritans accounted for. Cause of the Want of Courtesy in American Manners. Want of Discrimination. Difference of Principles regulating Aristocratic and Democratic Manners. Rules for regulating the Courtesies founded on Precedence of Age, Office, and Station, in a Democracy. Manners appropriate to Superiors and Subordinates. Peculiar Defect of Americans in this Respect. This to be remedied in the Domestic Circle, alone. Rules of Precedence to be enforced in the Family. Manners and tones towards Superiors to be regulated in the Family. Treatment of grown Brothers and Sisters by Young Children. Acknowledgement of Favors by Children to be required. Children to ask leave or apologize in certain cases. Rules for avoiding Remarks that wound the Feelings of Others. Rules of Hospitality. Conventional Rules. Rules for Table Manners. Caution as to teaching these Rules to Children. Caution as to Allowances to be made for those deficient in Good-manners. Comparison of English and American Manners. America may hope to excel all Nations in Refinement, Taste, and Good-breeding; and why. Effects of Wealth and Equalisation of Labor. Allusion to the Manners of Courts in the past Century.

GOOD-MANNERS are the expressions of benevolence in personal intercourse, by which we endeavor ·to promote the comfort and enjoyment of others, and to avoid all that gives needless pain. It is the exterior exhibition of the Divine precept which requires us to do to others as we would that they should do to us. It is saying, by our deportment, to all around, that we consider their feelings, tastes, and convenience, as equal in value to our own.

Good-manners lead us to avoid all practices that offend the taste of others; all violations of the conventional rules of propriety ; all rude and disrespectful language and deportment; and all remarks that would tend to wound the feelings of another.

There is a defect in the manners of the American people, especially in the free States, which is a serious one, and which can never be efficiently remedied, except in the domestic circle, and in early life. It is a deficiency in the free expression of kindly feelings and sympathetic emotions, and a want of courtesy in deportment. The causes, which have led to this result, may easily be traced.

The forefathers of this Nation, to a wide extent, were men who were driven from their native land, by laws and customs which they believed to be opposed both to civil and religious freedom. The sufferings they were called to endure, the subduing of those gentler feelings which bind us to country, kindred, and home, and the constant subordination of the passions to stern principle, induced characters of great firmness and self-control. They gave up the comforts and refinements of a civilized country, and came as pilgrims to a hard soil, a cold clime, and a heathen shore. They were constantly called to encounter danger, privations, sickness, loneliness, and death ; and all these, their religion taught them to meet with calmness, fortitude, and submission. And thus it became the custom and habit of the whole mass, to repress, rather than to encourage, the expression of feeling.

Persons who are called to constant and protracted suffering and privation, are forced to subdue and conceal emotion; for the free expression of it would double their own suffering, and increase the sufferings of others. Those, only, who are free from care and anxiety, and whose minds are mainly occupied by cheerful emotions, are at full liberty to unveil their feelings.

It was under such stern and rigorous discipline, that the first children in New England were reared ; and the manners and habits of parents are usually, to a great extent, transmitted to children. Thus it comes about, that the descendants of the Puritans, now scattered over every part of the Nation, are predisposed to conceal the gentler emotions, while their manners are calm, decided, and cold, rather than free and impulsive. Of course, there are very many exceptions to these predominating results.

The causes, to which we may attribute a general want of courtesy in manners, are certain incidental results of our democratic institutions. Our ancestors, and their descendants, have constantly been combating the aristocratic principle, which would exalt one class of men at the expense of another. They have had to contend with this principle, not only in civil, but in social, life. Almost every American, in his own person, as well as in behalf of his class, has had to assume and defend the main principle of democracy,—that every man's feelings and interests are equal in value to those of every other man. But, in doing this, there has been some want of clear discrimination. Because claims founded on distinctions of mere birth and position were found to be injurious, many have gone to the extreme of inferring that all distinctions, involving subordination, are useless. Such would regard children as equals to parents, pupils to teachers, domestics to their employers, and subjects to magistrates ; and that, too, in all respects.

The fact, that certain grades of superiority and subordination are needful, both for individual and for public benefit, has not been clearly discerned ; and there has been a gradual tendency to an extreme, which has sensibly affected our manners. All the proprieties and courtesies which depend on the recognition of the relative duties of superior and subordinate, have been warred upon, and thus we see, to an increasing extent, disrespectful treatment of parents from children, of teachers from pupils, of employers from domestics, and of the aged from the young. Children too often address their parents in the same style and manner as they do their companions. Domestics address their employers, and the visiters of the family, as they do their associates ; while, in all classes and circles, there is a gradual decay in courtesy of address.

In cases, too, where kindness is rendered, it is often accompanied with a cold unsympathizing manner, which greatly lessens its value, while kindness or politeness is received in a similar style of *nonchalance*, as if it were but the payment of a just due.

It is owing to these causes, that the American people, especially the inhabitants of New England, do not do themselves justice. For, while those, who are near enough to learn their real character and feelings, can discern the most generous impulses, and the most kindly sympathies, they are so veiled, in a composed and indifferent demeanor, as to be almost entirely concealed from strangers.

These defects in our national manners, it especially falls to the care of mothers, and all who have charge of the young, to rectify ; and if they seriously undertake the matter, and wisely adapt means to ends, these defects will be remedied. With reference to this object, the following ideas are suggested.

The law of Christianity and of democracy, which teaches that all men are born equal, and that their interests and feelings should be regarded as of equal value, seems to be adopted in aristocratic circles, with exclusive reference to the class in which the individual moves. The courtly gentleman addresses all of his own class with politeness and respect, and in all his actions seems to allow that the feelings and convenience of others are to be regarded the same as his own. But his demeanor to those of inferior station is not based on the same rule.

Among those who make up aristocratic circles, such as are above them, are deemed of superior, and such as are below, of inferior, value. Thus, if a young, ignorant, and vicious coxcomb, happens to be born a lord, the aged, the virtuous, the learned, and the well-bred of another class must give his convenience the precedence, and must address him in terms of respect. So when a man of noble birth is thrown among the lower classes, he demeans himself in a style, which, to persons of his own class, would be deemed the height of assumption and rudeness.

Now the principles of democracy require, that the same courtesy, which we accord to our own circle, shall be extended to every class and condition ; and that distinctions of superiority and subordination shall depend, not on accidents of birth, fortune, or occupation, but solely on those relations, which the good of all classes equally require. The distinctions demanded in a democratic state, are simply those, which result from relations that are common to every class, and which are for the benefit of all.

It is for the benefit of all, that children be subordinate to parents, pupils to teachers, the employed to their employers, and subjects to magistrates. In addition to this, it is for the general wellbeing, that the comfort and convenience of the delicate and feeble should be preferred to that of the strong and healthy, who would suffer less by any deprivation.

It is on these principles, that the rules of good-breeding, in a democratic state, must be founded. It is, indeed, assumed, that the value of the happiness of each individual is the same as that of every other ; but as there always must be occasions, where there are advantages which all cannot enjoy, there must be general rules for regulating a selection. Otherwise, there would be constant scrambling among those of equal claims, and brute force must be the final resort, in which case the strongest would have the best of every thing. The democratic rule, then, is, that superiors in age, station, or office, have precedence of subordinates; and that age and feebleness have precedence of youth and strength.

It is on this principle, that the feebler sex has precedence of more vigorous man, while the young and healthy give precedence to age or feebleness.

There is, also, a style of deportment and address, which is appropriate to these different relations. It is suitable for a superior to secure compliance with his wishes from those subordinate to him, by commands; but a subordinate must secure compliance with his wishes, from a superior, by requests. It is suitable for a parent, teacher, or employer, to admonish for neglect of duty; it is not suitable for an inferior to take such a course to a superior. It is suitable for a superior to take precedence of a subordinate, without any remark; but in such cases, an inferior should ask leave, or offer an apology. It is proper for a superior to use the language and manners of freedom and familiarity which would be improper from a subordinate to a superior.

It is a want of proper regard to these proprieties, which occasions the chief defect in American manners. It is very common to see children talking to their parents in a style proper only between equals; so, also, the young address their elders, and those employed their employers, in a style which is inappropriate to their relative positions. It is not merely towards superiors that a respectful address is required; every person likes to be treated with courtesy and respect, and therefore the law of benevolence demands such demeanor towards all whom we meet in the social intercourse of life. "Be ye courteous," is the direction of the Apostle, in reference to our treatment of *all*.

It is in early life, and in the domestic circle, alone, that good-manners can be successfully cultivated. There is nothing that so much depends on *habit*, as

the constantly recurring proprieties of good-breeding;
and if a child grows up without forming such habits,
it is very rarely the case that they can be formed at
a later period. The feeling that it is of little consequence how we behave at home, if we conduct
properly abroad, is a very fallacious one. Persons
who are careless and illbred at home, may imagine
that they can assume good-manners abroad; but
they mistake. Fixed habits of tone, manner, language, and movements, cannot be suddenly altered;
and those who are illbred at home, even when they
try to hide their bad habits, are sure to violate many
of the obvious rules of propriety, and yet be uncon-
scious of it.

And there is nothing which would so effectually
remove prejudice against our democratic institutions,
as the general cultivation of good-breeding in the
domestic circle. Good-manners are the exterior of
benevolence, the minute and often recurring exhibi-
tions of "peace and good-will;" and the nation, as
well as the individual, which most excels in the
exterior, as well as the internal principle, will be
most respected and beloved.

The following are the leading points, which claim
attention from those who have the care of the young.

In the first place, in the family, there should be
required a strict attention to the rules of precedence,
and those modes of address appropriate to the various
relations to be sustained. Children should always
be required to offer their superiors, in age or station,
the precedence, in all comforts and conveniences,
and always address them in a respectful tone and
manner. The custom of adding "Sir," or "Ma'am,"
to "Yes," or "No," is a valuable practice, as a perpetual indication of a respectful recognition of superiority. It is now going out of fashion, even among
the most wellbred people; probably from want of
consideration of its importance. Every remnant of

courtesy in address, in our customs, should be carefully cherished, by all who feel a value for the
proprieties of good-breeding.

If parents allow their children to talk to them,
and to the grown persons in the family, in the same
style in which they address each other, it will be
vain to hope for the courtesy of manner and tone,
which good-breeding demands in the general intercourse of society. In a large family, where the
elder children are grown up and the younger are
small, it is important to require the latter to treat
the elder as superiors. There are none so ready as
young children to assume airs of equality; and if
they are allowed to treat one class of superiors in
age and character disrespectfully, they will soon use
the privilege universally. This is the reason why
the youngest children of a family are most apt to be
pert, forward, and unmannerly.

Another point to be aimed at, is, to require children always to acknowledge every act of kindness
and attention, either by words or manner. If they
are trained always to make grateful acknowledge-
ments, when receiving favors, one of the objectionable features in American manners will be avoided.

Again, children should be required to ask leave,
whenever they wish to gratify curiosity, or use an
article which belongs to another. And if cases
occur, when they cannot comply with the rules of
good-breeding, as, for instance, when they must step
between a person and the fire, or take the chair of
an older person, they should be required either to
ask leave, or offer an apology.

There is another point of good-breeding, which
cannot, in all cases, be applied by children, in its
widest extent. It is that which requires us to avoid
all remarks which tend to embarrass, vex, mortify,
or in any way wound the feelings, of another. To
notice personal defects; to allude to others' faults,

or the faults of their friends ; to speak disparagingly of the sect or party to which a person belongs ; to be inattentive, when addressed in conversation ; to contradict flatly; to speak in contemptuous tones of opinions expressed by another ;—all these are violations of the rules of good-breeding, which children should be taught to regard. Under this head, comes the practice of whispering, and staring about, when a teacher, or lecturer, or clergyman, is addressing a class or audience. Such inattention is practically saying that what the person is uttering is not worth attending to, and persons of real good-breeding always avoid it. Loud talking and laughing, in a large assembly, even when no exercises are going on ; yawning and gaping in company ; and not looking in the face a person who is addressing you, are deemed marks of ill-breeding.

Another branch of good-manners, relates to the duties of hospitality. Politeness requires us to welcome visiters with cordiality ; to offer them the best accommodations ; to address conversation to them ; and to express, by tone and manner, kindness and respect. Offering the hand to all visiters, at one's own house, is a courteous and hospitable custom ; and a cordial shake of the hand, when friends meet, would abate much of the coldness of manner ascribed to Americans.

The last point of good-breeding to be noticed, refers to the conventional rules of propriety and good taste. Of these, the first class relates to the avoidance of all disgusting or offensive personal habits, such as fingering the hair ; cleaning the teeth or nails ; picking the nose ; spitting on carpets ; snuffing, instead of using a handkerchief, or using the article in an offensive manner ; lifting up the boots or shoes, as some men do, to tend them on the knee, or to finger them ;—all these tricks, either at table or in society, children should be taught to avoid.

Another branch under this head, may be called *table manners.* To persons of good-breeding, nothing is more annoying, than violating the conventional proprieties of the table. Reaching over another person's plate ; standing up to reach distant articles, instead of asking to have them passed ; using one's own knife, and spoon, for butter, salt, or sugar, when it is the custom of the family to provide separate utensils for the purpose ; setting cups, with tea dripping from them, on the table-cloth, instead of the mats or small plates provided for the purpose ; using the table-cloth instead of the napkins provided ; eating fast and in a noisy manner ; putting large pieces in the mouth ; looking and eating as if very hungry, or as if anxious to get at certain dishes ; sitting at too great a distance from the table, and dropping food ; laying the knife and fork on the table-cloth, instead of on the bread, or the edge of the plate ;— all these particulars children should be taught to avoid. It is always desirable, too, to require children, when at table with grown persons, to be silent, except when addressed by others; or else their chattering will interrupt the conversation and comfort of their elders. They should always be required, too, to wait *in silence,* till all the older persons are helped.

All these things should be taught to children, gradually, and with great patience and gentleness. Some parents, who make good-manners a great object, are in danger of making their children perpetually uncomfortable, by suddenly surrounding them with so many rules, that they must inevitably violate some one or other a great part of the time. It is much better to begin with a few rules, and be steady and persevering with these till a habit is formed, and then take a few more, thus making the process easy and gradual. Otherwise, the temper of

children will be injured ; or, hopeless of fulfilling
so many requisitions, they will become reckless
and indifferent to all.

But in reference to those who have enjoyed advantages for the cultivation of good-manners, and
who duly estimate its importance, one caution is
important. Those who never have had such habits
formed in youth, are under disadvantages, which no
benevolence of temper can remedy. They may
often violate the taste and feelings of others, not
from a want of proper regard for them, but from
ignorance of custom, or want of habit, or abstraction
of mind, or from other causes, which demand forbearance and sympathy, rather than displeasure.
An ability to bear patiently with defects in manners, and to make candid and considerate allowance
for a want of advantages, or for peculiarities in mental habits, is one mark of the benevolence of real
good-breeding.

The advocates of monarchical and aristocratic institutions have always had great plausibility given
to their views, by the seeming tendencies of our
institutions to insubordination and bad-manners.
And it has been too indiscriminately conceded, by the
defenders of our institutions, that such are these
tendencies, and that the offensive points in American manners, are the necessary result of democratic
principles.

But it i⁻ believed that both facts and reasonings
are in opposition to this opinion. The following
extract from the work of De Tocqueville exhibits
the opinion of an impartial observer, when comparing American manners with those of the English,
who are confessedly the most aristocratic of all
people.

He previously remarks on the tendency of aristocracy to make men more sympathizing with persons of their own peculiar class, and less so towards

those of lower degree ; which he illustrates by the deportment of nobles to their boors, and slaveholders towards slaves. And he claims that the progress in equality of conditions has always been attended with a corresponding refinement of manners and humanity of feeling. " While the English," says he, " retain the bloody traces of the dark ages in their penal legislation, the Americans have almost expunged capital punishments from their codes. North America is, I think, the only country upon earth, in which the life of no one citizen has been taken for political offence in the course of the last fifty years."

He then contrasts American manners with the English, claiming that the Americans are much the most affable, mild, and social. " In America, where the privileges of birth never existed, and where iches confer no peculiar rights on their possessors, nen acquainted with each other are very ready to requent the same places, and find neither peril ior advantage in the free interchange of their houghts. If they meet by accident, they neither seek nor avoid intercourse ; their manner is therefore natural, frank, and open." " If their demeanor is often cold and serious, it is never haughty or con-strained." But an " aristocratic pride is still extremely great among the English ; and as the limits of aristocracy are ill-defined, every body lives in constant dread, lest advantage should be taken of his familiarity. Unable to judge at once of the social position of those he meets, an Englishman prudently avoids all contact with them. Men are afraid lest some slight service rendered should draw them into an unsuitable acquaintance ; they dread civilities, and they avoid the obtrusive gratitude of a stranger as much as his hatred."

Thus *facts* seem to show that when the most aristocratic nation in the world is compared, as to manners, with the most democratic, the judgement of strangers is in favor of the latter.

And if good-manners are the outward exhibition of the democratic fundamental principle of impartial benevolence and equal rights, surely the nation that adopts this rule, both in social and civil life, is the most likely to secure the desirable exterior. The aristocrat, by his principles, extends the exterior of impartial benevolence to his own class only; the democratic principle requires it to be extended *to all.*

There is reason, therefore, to hope and expect more refined and polished manners in America, than in any other land; while all the developements of taste and refinement, such as poetry, music, painting, sculpture, and architecture, it may be expected, will come to a higher state of perfection, here, than in any other nation.

If this Country increases in virtue and intelligence, as it may, there is no end to the wealth that will pour in as the result of our resources of climate, soil, and navigation, and the skill, industry, energy, and enterprise, of our countrymen. This wealth, if used as intelligence and virtue will dictate, will furnish the means for a superior education to all classes, and all the facilities for the refinement of taste, intellect, and feeling.

Moreover, in this Country, labor is ceasing to be the badge of a lower class; so that already it is disreputable for a man to be "a lazy gentleman." And this feeling will increase, till there will be such an equalisation of labor, as will afford all the time needful for every class to improve the many advantages offered to them. Already, in Boston, through the munificence of some of her citizens, there are literary and scientific advantages offered to all classes of the citizens, rarely enjoyed elsewhere. In Cincinnati, too, the advantages of education, now offered to the poorest classes, without charge, surpass what, a few years ago, most wealthy men could purchase, for any price. And it is believed, that a time will come, when the poorest boy in America can secure advantages, which will equal what the heir of the proudest peerage can now command.

The records of the courts of France and Germany, (as detailed by the Duchess of Orleans,) in and succeeding the brilliant reign of Louis the Fourteenth,—a period which was deemed the acme of elegance and refinement,—exhibit a grossness, a vulgarity, and a coarseness, not to be found among the lowest of our respectable poor. And the biography of Beau Nash, who attempted to reform the manners of the gentry in the times of Queen Anne, exhibits violations of the rules of decency, which the commonest yeoman of this Land would feel disgraced in perpetrating.

This shows that our lowest classes, at this period, are more refined than were the highest in aristocratic lands, a hundred years ago ; and another century may show the lowest classes, in wealth, in this Country, attaining as high a polish, as adorns those who now are leaders of good-manners in the courts of kings.

CHAPTER XIII.

ON THE PRESERVATION OF A GOOD TEMPER IN A HOUSEKEEPER.

Influence of a Housekeeper on Domestic Happiness. Contrasts to illustrate. Sympathy. Influence of Tones. Allowances to be made for Housekeepers. Considerations to aid in regulating Temper and Tones. First ; Her Duties to be regarded as Dignified, Important, and Difficult. Second ; She should feel that she really has Great Difficulties to meet and overcome. Third ; She should deliberately calculate upon having her Plans interfered with, and be prepared for the Emergency. Fourth ; All her Plans should be formed consistently with the Means at command. Fifth ; System, Economy, and Neatness only valuable when they tend to promote the Comfort and Well-being of the Family. Sixth ; Government of Tones of Voice. Some Persons think Angry Tones needful. They mistake. Illustration. Scolding, unlady-like, and in Bad Taste. A Forgiving Spirit necessary. Seventh and Last Consideration offered ; Right View of a Superintending Providence. Fretfulness and Complaining sinful.

THERE is nothing, which has a more abiding influence on the happiness of a family, than the preservation of equable and cheerful temper and tones in the housekeeper. A woman who is habitually gentle, sympathizing, forbearing, and cheerful, carries an atmosphere about her, which imparts a soothing and sustaining influence, and renders it easier for all to do right, under her administration, than in any other situation.

The Writer has known families, where the mother's presence seemed the sunshine of the circle around her ; imparting a cheering and vivifying power, scarcely realized, till it was withdrawn. Every one, without thinking of it, or knowing why it was so, experienced a peaceful and invigorating influence, as soon as they entered the sphere illumined by her smile and sustained by her cheering kindness and sympathy. On the contrary, many a good housekeeper, good in every respect but this, by wearing a countenance of anxiety and dissatisfaction, and by indulging in the frequent use of sharp and reprehensive tones, more than destroys all the comfort that otherwise would result from her system, neatness, and economy.

There is a secret, social sympathy, which every mind, to a greater or less degree, experiences with the feelings of those around, as they are manifested by the countenance and voice. A sorrowful, a discontented, or an angry, countenance, produces a silent sympathetic influence, imparting a sombre shade to the mind, while tones of anger or complaint still more effectually jar the spirits.

No person can maintain a quiet and cheerful frame of mind, while tones of discontent and displeasure are sounding on the ear. We may gradually accustom ourselves to the evil, till it is partially diminished ; but it always is an evil, which greatly interferes with the enjoyment of the family state. There are sometimes cases, where the entrance of the mistress of a family seems to awaken a slight apprehension, in every mind around, as if each felt in danger of a reproof, for something either perpetrated or neglected. A woman who should go around her house with a small stinging snapper, which she habitually applied to those she met, would be encountered with feelings very similar to those, experienced by the inmates of a family where the mistress often uses her countenance and voice to inflict similar penalties for duties neglected.

Yet there are many allowances to be made for housekeepers, who sometimes imperceptibly and unconsciously fall into such habits. A woman, who attempts to carry out any plans of system, order, and economy, and who has her feelings and habits conformed to certain rules, is constantly liable to have her plans crossed, and her taste violated, by the in-

experience or inattention of those about her. And
no housekeeper, whatever are her habits, can escape
the frequent recurrence of negligence or mistake,
which interferes with her plans. It is probable
that there is no class of persons, in the world, who
have such incessant trials of temper, and such
temptation to be fretful, as American housekeepers.
For a housekeeper's business is not like that of the
other sex, limited to a particular department, for
which previous preparation is made. It consists of
ten thousand little disconnected items, which can
never be so systematically arranged, that there is no
daily jostling, somewhere. And in the best regulated families, it is not unfrequently the case, that
some act of forgetfulness or carelessness, from some
member, will disarrange the business of the whole
day, so that every hour will bring renewed occasion
for annoyance. And the more strongly a woman
realizes the value of time, and the importance of
system and order, the more will she be tempted to
irritability and complaint.

The following considerations may aid in preparing
a woman to meet such daily crosses with even a
cheerful temper and tones.

In the first place, a woman, who has charge of a
large household, should regard her duties as dignified, important, and difficult. The mind is so made,
as to be elevated and cheered by a sense of far-
reaching influence and usefulness. A woman, who
feels that she is a cipher, and that it makes little
difference how she performs her duties, has far less
to sustain and invigorate her, than one who truly
estimates the importance of her station. A man,
who feels that the destinies of a nation are turning
on the judgement and skill with which he plans and
executes, has a pressure of motive, and an elevation
of feeling, which are great safeguards from all that
is low, trivial, and degrading.

So an American mother and housekeeper, who looks at her position in the aspect presented in the previous pages, and who rightly estimates the long train of influences which will pass down to hundreds, whose destinies, from generation to generation, will be modified by those decisions of her will, which regulated the temper, principles, and habits, of her family, must be elevated above petty temptations which would otherwise assail her.

Again, a housekeeper should feel that she really has great difficulties to meet and overcome. A person, who wrongly thinks that there is little danger, can never maintain so faithful a guard, as one who rightly estimates the temptations which beset her. Nor can one, who thinks that they are trifling difficulties which she has to encounter, and trivial temptations, to which she must yield, so much enjoy the just reward of conscious virtue and self-control, as one who takes an opposite view of the subject.

A third method, is, for a woman deliberately to calculate on having her best-arranged plans interfered with, very often ; and to be in such a state of preparation that the evil will not come unawares. So complicated are the pursuits, and so diverse the habits of the various members of a family, that it is almost impossible for every one to avoid interfering with the plans and taste of a housekeeper, in some one point or another. It is therefore most wise, for a woman to keep the loins of her mind ever girt, to meet such collisions with a cheerful and quiet spirit.

Another important rule, is, to form all plans and arrangements in consistency with the means at command, and the character of those around. A woman who has a heedless husband, and young children, and incompetent domestics, ought not to make such plans, as one may properly form, who will not, in so many directions, meet embarrassment. She **must**

aim at just so much as it is probable she can secure,
and no more ; and thus she will usually escape much
temptation, and much of the irritation of disappointment.

The fifth, and a very important, consideration, is,
that *system, economy,* and *neatness,* are valuable,
only so far as they tend to promote comfort and the
well-being of those affected.   Some women seem to
act under the impression, that these advantages *must*
be secured, at all events, even if the comfort of the
family be the sacrifice.   True, it is very important
that children grow up in habits of system, neatness,
and order ; and it is very desirable that the mother
give them every incentive, both by precept and example : but it is still more important, that they grow
up with amiable tempers, that they learn to meet
the crosses of life with patience and cheerfulness ;
and nothing has a greater influence to secure this,
than a mother's example.   Whenever, therefore, a
woman cannot carry her plans of neatness and order,
without injury to her own temper, or to the temper
of others, she ought to modify and reduce them,
until she can.

The sixth method, relates to the government of
the tones of voice.   In many cases, when a woman's
domestic arrangements are suddenly and seriously
crossed, it is impossible not to feel some irritation.
But it *is* always possible to refrain from angry tones.
A woman can resolve, that, whatever happens, she
will not speak, till she can do it in a calm and gentle
manner.   *Perfect silence* is a safe resort, when such
control cannot be attained as enables a person to
speak calmly ; and this determination, persevered in,
will eventually be crowned with success.

Many persons seem to imagine, that tones of anger
are needful, in order to secure prompt obedience.
But observation has convinced the Writer that they
are *never* necessary ; that *in all cases,* reproof, ad-

ministered in calm tones, would be better. A case will be given in illustration.

A young girl had been repeatedly charged to avoid a certain arrangement in cooking. On one day, when company was invited to dine, the direction was forgotten, and the consequence was an accident, which disarranged every thing, seriously injured the principal dish, and delayed dinner for an hour. The mistress of the family entered the kitchen just as it occurred, and at a glance saw the extent of the mischief. For a moment, her eyes flashed and her cheeks glowed; but she held her peace. After a minute or so she gave directions, in a calm voice, as to the best mode of retrieving the evil, and then left, without a word said to the offender.

After the company left, she sent for the girl, alone, and in a calm and kind manner pointed out the aggravations of the case, and described the trouble which had been caused to her husband, her visiters, and herself. She then portrayed the future evils which would result from such habits of neglect and inattention, and the modes of attempting to overcome the evil; and then offered a reward for the future, if, in a given time, she succeeded in improving in this respect. Not a tone of anger was uttered; and yet the severest scolding of a practised Xantippe could not have secured such contrition, and determination to reform, as was gained by this method.

But similar negligence is often visited by a continuous stream of complaint and reproof, which, in most cases, is met, either by sullen silence, or impertinent retort, while anger prevents any contrition, or any resolution of future amendment.

It is very certain, that some ladies do carry forward a most efficient government, both of children and domestics, without employing tones of anger; and therefore they are not indispensable, nor on any account desirable.

Though some ladies, of intelligence and refinement, do fall unconsciously into such a practice, it is certainly very unlady-like, and in very bad taste, to *scold ;* and the further a woman departs from all approach to it, the more perfectly she sustains her character as a lady.

Another method of securing equanimity, amid the trials of domestic life, is, to cultivate a habit of making allowance for the difficulties, ignorance, or temptations, of those who violate rule or neglect duty. It is vain, and most unreasonable, to expect the consideration and care of a mature mind, in childhood and youth ; or that persons, of such limited advantages as most domestics have enjoyed, should practise proper self-control, and possess proper habits and principles.

Every parent, and every employer, needs daily to cultivate the spirit expressed in the Divine prayer, "forgive us our trespasses, as we forgive those who trespass against us."   The same allowances and forbearance we supplicate from our Heavenly Father, and desire from our fellow-men, in reference to our deficiencies, we should constantly aim to extend to all who cross our feelings and interfere with our plans.

The last, and most important mode of securing placid and cheerful temper and tones, is, by a right view of the doctrine of a superintending Providence. All persons are too much in the habit of regarding the more important events of life as exclusively under the control of Perfect Wisdom.   But the fall of a sparrow, or the loss of a hair, they do not feel to be equally the result of His directing agency.   In consequence of this, Christian persons, who aim at perfect and cheerful submission to heavy afflictions, and who succeed, to the edification of all about them, are sometimes sadly deficient under petty crosses. If a beloved child is laid in the grave, even if its death resulted from the carelessness of a domestic, or a physician, the eye is turned from the subordinate agent, to the Supreme Guardian of all, and to Him they bow without murmur or complaint. But if a pudding is burnt, or a room badly swept, or an errand forgotten, then vexation and complaint are allowed, just as if these events were not appointed by Perfect Wisdom, as much as the sorer chastisement.

A woman, therefore, needs to cultivate the *habitual* feeling, that all the events of her nursery and kitchen are brought about by the permission of our Heavenly Father, and that fretfulness and complaint, in regard to these, is, in fact, complaining and disputing at the appointments of God, and are really as sinful, as unsubmissive murmurs amid the sorer chastisements of His hand. And a woman, who will daily cultivate this habit of referring all the events of her life to the wise and benevolent agency of a Heavenly Parent, will soon find it the perennial spring of abiding peace and content.

CHAPTER XIV.

ON HABITS OF SYSTEM AND ORDER.

Question of the Equality of the Sexes, frivolous and useless. Relative Importance and Difficulty of the Duties a Woman is called
to perform. Her Duties not trivial. More difficult than those of
the Queen of a great Nation. A Habit of System and Order
necessary. Right Apportionment of Time. General Principles.
Christianity to be the Foundation. Intellectual and Social Interests to be preferred to Gratification of Taste or Appetite. The
Latter to be last in our Estimation. No Sacrifice of Health al-
lowable. Neglect of Health a Sin in the Sight of God. Regular
Season of Rest appointed by the Creator. Divisions of Time.
Systematic Arrangement of House Articles, and other Conveniences. *Regular* Employment for each Member of a Family.
Children can be of great Service. Boys should be taught Family
Work. Advantage to them in afterlife. Older Children to take
care of Infants of a Family.

THE discussion of the question of the equality of
the sexes, in intellectual capacity, seems both frivolous and useless, not only because it can never be
decided, but because there would be no possible
advantage in the decision. But one topic, which is
often drawn into this discussion, is of far more consequence; and that is, the relative importance and
difficulty of the duties a woman is called to perform.

It is generally assumed, and almost as generally
conceded, that women's business and cares are con-
tracted and trivial; and that the proper discharge of
her duties demands far less expansion of mind and
vigor of intellect, than the pursuits of the other sex.
This idea has prevailed, because women, as a mass,
have never been educated with reference to their
most important duties; while that portion of their
employments which are of least value, have been
regarded as the chief, if not the sole concern of a
woman. The covering of the body, the conveniences of residences, and the gratification of the

appetite, have been too much regarded as the sole objects on which her intellectual powers are to be exercised.

But as society gradually shakes off the remnants of barbarism, and the intellectual and moral interests of man rise in estimation above the merely sensual, a truer estimate is formed of woman's duties, and of the measure of intellect requisite for the proper discharge of them. Let any man of sense and discernment become the member of a large household, in which a well-educated and pious woman is endeavoring systematically to discharge her multiform duties; let him fully comprehend all her cares, difficulties, and perplexities; and it is probable he would coincide in the opinion, that no statesman, at the head of a nation's affairs, had more frequent calls for wisdom, firmness, tact, discrimination, prudence, and versatility of talent, than such a woman.

She has a husband, whose peculiar tastes and habits she must accommodate; she has children, whose health she must guard, whose physical constitution she must study and develope, whose temper and habits she must regulate, whose principles she must form, whose pursuits she must direct. She has constantly changing domestics, with all varieties of temper and habits, whom she must govern, instruct, and direct; she is required to regulate the finances of the domestic state, and constantly to adapt expenditures to the means and to the relative claims of each department. She has the direction of the kitchen, where ignorance, forgetfulness, and awkwardness are to be so regulated, that the various operations shall each start at the right time, and all be in completeness at the same given hour. She has the claims of society to meet, calls to receive and return, and the duties of hospitality to sustain. She has the poor to relieve; benevolent societies to aid;

the schools of her children to inquire and decide
about; the care of the sick; the nursing of infancy;
and the endless miscellany of odd items constantly
recurring in a large family.

Surely it is a pernicious and mistaken idea, that
the duties which tax a woman's mind are petty,
trivial, or unworthy of the highest grade of intellect
and moral worth. Instead of allowing this feeling,
every woman should imbibe, from early youth, the
impression, that she is training for the discharge of
the most important, the most difficult, and the most
sacred and interesting duties that can possibly employ the highest intellect. She ought to feel that
her station and responsibilities, in the great drama of
life, are second to none, either as viewed by her
Maker, or in the estimation of all minds whose judgement is most worthy of respect.

She, who is the mother and housekeeper in a large
family, is the sovereign of an empire demanding as
varied cares, and involving more difficult duties,
than are really exacted of her, who, while she wears
the crown, and professedly regulates the interests of
the greatest nation on earth, finds abundant leisure
for theatres, balls, horseraces, and every gay pursuit.

There is no one thing, more necessary to a housekeeper, in performing her varied duties, than *a habit
of system and order ;* and yet the peculiarly desultory nature of women's pursuits, and the embarrassments resulting from the state of domestic service
in this Country, render it very difficult to form such
a habit. But it is sometimes the case, that women,
who could and would carry forward a systematic
plan of domestic economy, do not attempt it, simply from a want of knowledge of the various modes
of introducing it. It is with reference to such, that
various modes of securing system and order, which
the Writer has seen adopted, will be pointed out.

A wise economy is nowhere more conspicuous,

than in the right *apportionment of time* to different pursuits. There are duties of a religious, intellectual, social, and domestic, nature, each having different relative claims on attention. Unless a person has some general plan of apportioning these claims, some will intrench on others, and some, it is probable, will be entirely excluded. Thus, some find religious, social, and domestic, duties, so numerous, that no time is given to intellectual improvement. Others, find either social, or benevolent, or religious, interests, excluded by the extent and variety of other engagements.

It is wise, therefore, for all persons to devise a general plan, which they will at least keep in view, and aim to accomplish, and by which, a proper proportion of time shall be secured for all the duties of life.

In forming such a plan, every woman must accommodate herself to the peculiarities of her situation. If she has a large family, and a small income, she must devote far more time to the simple duty of providing food and raiment, than would be right were she in affluence and with a small family. It is impossible, therefore, to draw out any general plan, which all can adopt. But there are some *general principles*, which ought to be the guiding rules, when a woman arranges her domestic employments. These general principles are to be based on Christianity, which teaches us to " seek first the kingdom of God," and to place food, raiment, and the conveniences of life, as of secondary account. Every woman, then, ought to start with the assumption, that religion is of more consequence than any worldly concern, and that whatever else may be sacrificed, this shall be the leading object in all her arrangements, in respect to time, money, and attention. It is also one of the plainest requisitions of Christianity, that we devote some of our time and efforts to the comfort and improvement of others. There is no duty so constantly enforced, both in the Old and New Testament, as the duty of charity, in dispensing to those who are destitute of the blessings we enjoy. In selecting objects of charity, the same rule applies to others, as well as to ourselves; that their moral and religious interests are of the first concern, and that for them, as well as ourselves, we are to "seek first the kingdom of God."

Another general principle, is, that our intellectual and social interests are to be preferred to the mere gratification of taste or appetite. A portion of time, therefore, must be devoted to the cultivation of the intellect and the social affections.

Another general principle, is, that the mere gratification of appetite is to be placed *last* in our estimate, so that, when a question arises as to which shall be sacrificed, some intellectual, moral, or social, advantage, or some gratification of sense, we should invariably sacrifice the last.

Another general principle, is, that, as health is indispensable to the discharge of every duty, nothing that sacrifices that blessing is to be allowed, in order to gain any other advantage or enjoyment. There are emergencies, when it is right to risk health and life, to save ourselves and others from greater evils; but these are exceptions, which do not vacate the general rule. Many persons imagine, that, if they violate the laws of health in performing religious or domestic duties, they are guiltless before God. But such greatly mistake. We as directly violate the law "thou shalt not kill," when we do what tends to risk or shorten our own life, as if we should intentionally run a dagger into a neighbor. True, we may escape any fatal or permanently injurious effects, and so may a dagger or bullet miss the mark, or do only transient injury. But this, in either case, makes the sin none the less. The life and happiness of all His creatures are dear to our Creator; and He is as much displeased, when we injure our own interests, as when we injure others. So that the idea that we are excusable if we harm no one but ourselves, is most false and pernicious. These, then, are the general principles, to guide a woman in systematizing her duties and pursuits.

The Creator of all things is a Being of perfect system and order; and to aid us in our duty, in this respect, he has divided our time, by a regularly returning day of rest from worldly business. In following this example, the intervening six days may be subdivided to secure similar benefits. In doing this, a certain portion of time must be given to procure the means of livelihood, and for preparing food, raiment, and dwellings. To these objects, some must devote more, and others less, attention. The remainder of time not necessarily thus employed, might be divided somewhat in this manner: The leisure of two afternoons and evenings could be devoted to religious and benevolent objects, such as religious meetings, charitable associations, Sunday school visiting, and attention to the sick and poor. The leisure of two other days might be devoted to intellectual improvement, and the pursuits of taste. The leisure of another day might be devoted to social enjoyments, in making or receiving visits; and that of another to miscellaneous domestic pursuits, not included in the other particulars.

It is probable that few persons could carry out such an arrangement, very strictly; but every one can make out a systematic arrangement of time, and at least *aim* at accomplishing it; and they can also compare the time which they actually devote to these different objects, with such a general outline, for the purpose of modifying any mistaken proportions.

Instead of attempting some such systematic employment of time, and carrying it out so far as they can control circumstances, most women are rather driven along by the daily occurrences of life, so that, instead of being the intelligent regulators of their own time, they are the mere sport of circumstances. There is nothing which so distinctly marks the difference between weak and strong minds, as the fact, whether they control circumstances, or circumstances control them.

It is very much to be feared, that the apportionment of time, actually made by a great portion of women, exactly inverts the order required by reason and Christianity. Thus the furnishing a needless variety of food, the conveniences of dwellings, and the adornments of dress, often take a larger portion of time, than is given to any other object. Next after this, comes intellectual improvement ; and last of all, benevolence and religion.

It may be urged, that it is indispensable for most persons to give more time to earn a livelihood, and to prepare food, raiment, and dwellings, than to any other object. But it may be asked, how much time devoted to these objects is employed in preparing varieties of food, not necessary, but rather injurious, and how much is spent for those parts of dress and furniture not indispensable, and merely ornamental? Let a woman subtract from her domestic employments, all the time given to pursuits which are of no use, except as they gratify a taste for ornament, or minister increased varieties to tempt appetite, and she will find, that much, which she calls "domestic duties," and which prevent her attention to intellectual, benevolent, and religious, objects, should be called by a very different name. No woman has a right to give up attention to the higher interests of herself and others, for the ornaments of taste or the gratification of the palate. To a certain extent, these lower objects are lawful and desirable; but, when they intrude on nobler interests, they become selfish and degrading.

Some persons endeavor to systematize their pursuits, by apportioning them to particular hours of each day. For example, a certain period before breakfast, is given to devotional duties; after breakfast, certain hours are devoted to exercise and domestic employments; other hours to sewing, or reading, or visiting; and others to benevolent duties. But, in most cases, it is more difficult to systematize the hours of each day, than it is to sustain some regular division of the week.

In regard to the minutiæ of domestic arrangements, the Writer has known the following methods adopted. *Monday*, with some of the best housekeepers, is devoted to preparing for the labors of the week. Any extra cooking, the purchasing of articles to be used during the week, and the assorting of clothes for the wash, and mending such as would be injured without;—these and similar items belong to this day. *Tuesday* is devoted to washing, and *Wednesday* to ironing. On *Thursday*, the ironing is finished off, the clothes folded and put away, and all articles which need mending put in the mending basket, and attended to. *Friday* is devoted to sweeping and housecleaning. On *Saturday*, and especially the last Saturday of every month, every department is put in order; the castors and table furniture are regulated, the pantry and cellar inspected, the trunks, drawers, and closets arranged, and every thing about the house put in order for *Sunday*. All the cooking needed for Sunday is also prepared. By this regular recurrence of a particular time for inspecting every thing, nothing is forgotten till ruined by neglect.

Another mode of systematizing, relates to providing proper supplies of conveniences, and proper

places in which to keep them. Thus, some ladies
keep a large closet, in which are placed the tubs,
pails, dippers, soap-dishes, starch, bluing, clothes-
line, clothes-pins, and every other article used in
washing; and in the same or another place are kept
every convenience for ironing. In the sewing department, a trunk, with suitable partitions, is provided, in which are placed, each in its proper place,
white thread of all sizes, colored thread, yarns for
mending, colored and black sewing-silks and twist,
tapes and bobbins of all sizes, white and colored
welting-cords, silk braids and cords, needles of all
sizes, papers of pins, remnants of linen and colored
cambric, a supply of all kinds of buttons used in the
family, black and white hooks and eyes, a yard
measure, and all the patterns used in cutting and
fitting. These are done up in separate parcels and
labelled. In another trunk, are kept all pieces used
in mending, arranged in order, so that any article
can be found without loss of time. A trunk like
the first mentioned, will save many steps, and often
much time and perplexity; while purchasing thus
by the quantity makes them come much cheaper
than if bought in little portions as they are wanted. Such a trunk should be kept locked, and a
smaller supply, for current use, be kept in a workbasket.

The full supply of all conveniences in the kitchen
and cellar, and a place appointed for each article,
very much facilitates domestic labor. For want of
this, much vexation and loss of time is occasioned,
while seeking vessels in use, or in cleansing those
used by different persons for various purposes. It
would be far better for a lady to give up some expensive article in the parlor, and apply the money,
thus saved, for kitchen conveniences, than to have a
stinted supply where the most labor is to be performed. If our Countrywomen would devote more

to comfort and convenience, and less to show, it would be a great improvement. Mirrors and pier-tables in the parlor, and an unpainted, gloomy, ill-furnished kitchen, not unfrequently are found under the same roof.

Another important item, in systematic economy, is the apportioning of *regular* employment to the various members of a family. If a housekeeper can secure the cooperation of *all* her family, she will find that "many hands make light work." There is no greater mistake, than in bringing up children to feel that they must be taken care of, and waited on, by others, without any corresponding obligations on their part. The extent to which young children can be made useful in a family, would seem surprising to those who have never seen a *systematic* and *regular* plan for securing their services. The Writer has been in a family, where a little girl of eight or nine washed and dressed herself and little brother, and made their little beds before breakfast, set and cleared all the tables at meals, with a little help from a grown person in moving tables and spreading cloths, while all the dusting of parlors and chambers was also neatly performed by her. A little brother of ten, brought in and piled all the wood used in the kitchen and parlor, brushed the boots and shoes neatly, went on errands, and took all the care of the poultry. They were children whose parents could afford to hire this service, but who chose to have their children grow up healthy and industrious, while proper instructions, system, and encouragement, made these services rather a pleasure than otherwise to the children.

Some parents pay their children for such services; but this is hazardous, as tending to make them feel that they are not bound to be helpful without pay, and also as tending to produce a hoarding, money-making spirit. But where children have no hoarding propensities, and need to acquire a sense of the value of property, it may be well to let them earn money for some extra services, rather as a favor. When this is done, they should be taught to spend it for others, as well as for themselves; and in this way, a generous and liberal spirit will be cultivated.

There are some mothers, who take pains to teach their boys most of the domestic arts which their sisters learn. The Writer has seen boys mending their own garments, and aiding their mother or sisters in the kitchen, with great skill and adroitness; and at an early age they usually very much relish joining in such occupations. The sons of such mothers, in their college life, or in roaming about the world, or in nursing a sick wife or infant, find occasion to bless the forethought and kindness which prepared them for such emergencies. Few things are in worse taste, than for a man needlessly to busy himself in women's work; and yet a man never appears in a more interesting attitude, than when, by skill in such matters, he can save a mother or wife from care and suffering. The more a boy is taught to use his hands in every variety of domestic employment, the more his faculties, both of mind and body, are developed; for mechanical pursuits exercise the intellect, as well as the hands. The early training of New England boys, in which they turn their hand to almost every thing, is one great reason of the quick perceptions, versatility of mind, and mechanical skill, for which that portion of our Countrymen are distinguished.

The Writer has known one mode of systematizing the aid of the older children in a family, which, in some cases of very large families, it may be well to imitate. In the case referred to, when the oldest daughter was eight or nine years old, an infant sister was given to her as her special charge. She tended it, made and mended its clothes, taught it to read, and was its nurse and guardian through all its childhood. Another infant was given to the next daughter, and thus the children were all paired in this interesting relation. In addition to the relief thus afforded to the mother, the elder children were thus qualified for their future domestic relations, and both older and younger bound to each other by peculiar ties of tenderness and gratitude.

In offering these examples of various modes of systematizing, one suggestion may be worthy of attention. It is not unfrequently the case, that ladies, who find themselves cumbered with oppressive cares, after reading remarks on the benefits of system, immediately commence the task of arranging their pursuits, with great vigor and hope. They divide the day into regular periods, and give each hour its duty ; they systematize their work, and endeavor to bring every thing into a regular routine. But in a short time, they find themselves baffled, discouraged, and disheartened, and finally relapse into their former desultory ways, with a sort of resigned despair. The difficulty, in such cases, is, that they attempt too much at a time. There is nothing which so much depends upon *habit*, as a systematic mode of performing duty ; and where no such habit has been formed, it is impossible for a novice to start at once into a universal mode of systematizing, which none but an adept could carry through. The only way for such persons, is, to begin with a little at a time. Let them select some three or four things, and resolutely attempt to conquer at these points. In time, a habit will be formed of doing a few things at regular periods, and in a systematic way. Then it will be easy to add a few more ; and thus, by a gradual process, the object can be secured, which it would be vain to attempt by a more summary course. Early rising is almost a *sine qua non* to

success, in such an effort ; but where a woman
lacks either the health or the energy to secure a
period for devotional duties before breakfast, let her
select that hour of the day in which she will be
least liable to interruption, and let her then seek
strength and wisdom from the only true Source.
At this time, let her take a pen and make a list of
all the things which she considers as duties.   Then
let a calculation be made, whether there is time
enough in the day or the week for all these duties.
If there is not, let the least important be stricken
from the list, as what are not duties and must be
omitted.   In doing this, let a woman remember,
that, though " what we shall eat, and what we shall
drink, and wherewithal we shall be clothed," are
matters requiring due attention, they are very apt to
take a wrong relative importance, while social, intellectual, and moral, interests, receive too little regard.

In this Country, eating, dressing, and household furniture and ornaments, take far too large a
place in the estimate of relative importance ; and it is
probable that most women could modify their views
and practice, so as to come nearer to the Saviour's
requirements.   No woman has a right to put a stitch
of ornament on any article of dress or furniture, or
to provide one superfluity in food, until she is sure
she can secure time for all her social, intellectual,
benevolent, and religious, duties.   If a woman will
take the trouble to make such a calculation as this,
she will usually find that she has time enough to
perform all her duties easily and well.

It is impossible for a conscientious woman to
secure that peaceful mind, and cheerful enjoyment
of life, which all should seek, who is constantly
finding her duties jarring with each other, and much
remaining undone, which she feels that she ought to
do.   In consequence of this, there will be a secret

uneasiness, which will throw a shade over the whole
current of life, never to be removed, till she so efficiently defines and regulates her duties, that she can
fulfil them all.

And here the Writer would urge upon young
ladies the importance of forming habits of system,
while unembarrassed with multiplied cares which
will make the task so much more difficult and hopeless. Every young lady can systematize her pursuits, to a certain extent. She can have a particular
day for mending her wardrobe, and for arranging
her trunks, closets, and drawers. She can keep her
workbasket, her desk at school, and all her conveniences in proper places, and in regular order.
She can have regular periods for reading, walking,
visiting, study, and domestic pursuits. And by following this method, in youth, she will form a taste
for regularity, and a habit of system, which will
prove a blessing to her through life.

CHAPTER XV.

ON GIVING IN CHARITY.

No Point of Duty more difficult to fix by Rule, than Charity. First Consideration ;—Object for which we are placed in this World. How to be perfectly happy. Self-denying Benevolence. Important Distinction. Second Consideration;—Natural Principles not to be exterminated, but regulated and controlled. All Constitutional Propensities good, and designed to be gratified. Their Abuses to be guarded against. Third Consideration;—Superfluities sometimes proper, and sometimes not. Fourth Consideration ;—No Rule of Duty right for One and not for All. The Opposite of this Principle tested. Some Use of Superfluities necessary. Physical Gratifications should always be subordinate to Social, Intellectual, and Moral Advantages. Difficulties in the Way. Remarks upon them. Plan for Keeping an Account of Necessaries and Superfluities. Untoward Results of our Actions do not always prove that We deserve Blame. Examples of Conformity to the Rules here laid down. General Principles to guide in deciding upon Objects of Charity. Parable of Good Samaritan. Who are our Neighbors. Those most in Need to be first relieved. Intellectual and Moral Wants more necessary to be supplied than Physical. Not much need of Charity in supplying Physical Wants in this Country. System of Associated Charities, in which many small sums are combined. Indiscriminate Charity. Very injurious to Society, as a General Rule. Exceptions. Impropriety of judging of the Charities of others.

It is probable that there is no point of duty, where conscientious persons differ more in opinion, or where they find it more difficult to form discriminating and decided views, than on the matter of charity. That we are bound to give *some* of our time, money, and efforts, to relieve the destitute, all allow. But, as to how much we are to give, and on whom our charities shall be bestowed, many a reflecting mind has been at a loss. Yet it seems very desirable, that, in reference to a duty so constantly and so strenuously urged by the Supreme Ruler, we should be able so to fix metes and bounds, as to keep a conscience void of offence, and to free the mind from disquieting fears of deficiency.

The Writer has found no other topic of investigation so beset with difficulty, so absolutely without
the range of definite rules which can apply to all in
all circumstances. But on this, as on a previous
topic, there seem to be *general principles,* by the aid
of which, any candid mind, sincerely desirous of
obeying the commands of Christ however much
self-denial may be involved, can arrive at definite
conclusions as to its own individual obligations, so
that, when these are fulfilled, the mind may be at
peace.

But for a mind that is worldly, living mainly to
seek its own pleasures, instead of living to please
God, no principles can be so fixed, as not to leave a
ready escape from all obligation. Such minds, either
by indolence (and consequent ignorance) or by
sophistry, will convince themselves that a life of
engrossing self-indulgence, with perhaps the gift of
a few dollars and a few hours of time, may so suf-
fice to fulfil the requisitions of the Eternal Judge,
that they can safely meet Him at the final day.

For such minds, no reasonings will avail, till the
heart is so changed, that, to learn the will and follow the example of Jesus Christ, becomes the leading object of interest and effort. It is to aid those
who profess to possess this temper of mind, that the
following suggestions are offered.

The first consideration, which gives definiteness
to this subject, is, a correct view of the object for
which we are placed in this world. A great portion,
even of professed Christians, seem to be acting on
the supposition, that the object of life is to secure
as much as possible of all the various enjoyments
placed within reach. Not so teaches reason or reve-
lation. From these, we learn, that, though the
happiness of His creatures is the end for which God
created and sustains them, yet that this happiness
depends, not on the various modes of gratification

put within our reach, but mainly on *character*. A man may possess all the resources for enjoyment which this world can afford, and yet feel that "all is vanity and vexation of spirit," and that he is supremely wretched. Another may be in want of all things, and yet possess that living spring of benevolence, faith, and hope, which will make an Eden of the darkest prison.

In order to be perfectly happy, man must attain that character, which Christ exhibited; and the nearer he approaches it, the more will happiness reign in his breast.

But what was the grand peculiarity of the character of Christ? It was *self-denying benevolence.* He came "not to seek His own;" He "went about doing good," and this was His "meat and drink;" that is, it was this that sustained the health and life of His mind, as food and drink sustain the health and life of the body. Now, the mind of man is so made, that it can gradually be transformed into the same likeness. A selfish being, who for a whole life has been nourishing habits of indolent self-indulgence, can, by taking Christ as his example, by communion with Him, and by daily striving to imitate His character and conduct, form such a temper of mind, that "doing good" will become the chief and highest source of enjoyment. And this heavenly principle will grow stronger and stronger, until self-denial loses the more painful part of its character, and then, *living to make happiness*, will be so delightful and absorbing a pursuit, that all exertions, regarded as the means to this end, will be like the joyous efforts of men when they strive for a prize or a crown with the full hope of success.

In this view of the subject, efforts and self-denial for the good of others are to be regarded, not merely as duties enjoined for the benefit of others, but as the moral training indispensable to the formation of that character, on which depends our own happiness both for time and eternity. This view exhibits the full meaning of the Saviour's declaration, "how hardly shall they that have riches enter the kingdom of Heaven!" He had before taught, that the kingdom of Heaven consisted not in such enjoyments as the worldly seek, but in the temper of self-denying benevolence like His own ; and, as the rich have far greater temptations to indolent self-indulgence, they are far less likely to acquire this temper, than those, who, by limited means, are inured to some degree of self-denial.

But on this point, one important distinction needs to be made, and that is, between the self-denial which has no other aim than mere self-mortification, and that which is exercised to secure greater good to ourselves and others. The first is the foundation of monasticism, penances, and all other forms of asceticism ; the latter, only, is that which Christianity requires.

A second consideration, which may give definiteness to this subject, is, that the formation of a perfect character involves, not the extermination of any principles of our nature, but rather the regulating of them, according to the rules of reason and religion ; so that the lower propensities shall always be kept subordinate to nobler principles. Thus we are not to aim at destroying our appetites, or at needlessly denying them, but rather so to regulate them, that they shall best secure the objects for which they were implanted. We are not to annihilate the love of praise and admiration ; but so to control it, that the favor of God shall be regarded more than the estimation of men. We are not to extirpate the principle of curiosity, which leads us to acquire knowledge ; but so to direct it, that all our acquisitions shall be useful and not frivolous or injurious. And thus with all the principles of the mind, God has implanted no desires in our constitution, which are evil and pernicious. On the contrary, all our constitutional propensities, either of mind or body, he designed we should gratify, whenever no evils would thence result, either to ourselves or others. Such principles as envy, ambition, pride, revenge, and hate, are to be exterminated ; for they are either excesses or excrescences : not created by God, but rather the result of our own neglect to form habits of benevolence and self-control.

In deciding the rules of our conduct, therefore, we are ever to bear in mind, that the developement of the nobler principles, and the subjugation of inferior propensities to them, is to be the main object of effort, both for ourselves and for others. And in conformity with this, in all our plans, we are to place religious and moral interests as first in estimation, our social and intellectual interests next, and our physical gratifications, as subordinate to all.

A third consideration, is, that, though the means for sustaining life and health are to be regarded as necessaries, without which no other duties can be performed, yet that a very large portion of the time spent by most persons in easy circumstances, for food, raiment, and dwellings, are for mere *superfluities*, which *are right when they do not involve the sacrifice of higher interests*, and *wrong when they do*. Life and health can be sustained in the humblest dwellings, with the plainest dress, and the simplest food, and after taking from our means what is necessary for life and health, the remainder is to be so divided, that the larger portion shall be given to supply the moral and intellectual wants of ourselves and others, and the smaller share to procure those additional gratifications, of taste and appetite, not indispensable. Mankind, as yet, have never made this apportionment of their means; but, just as fast as they have risen from a savage state, mere

physical wants have been made subordinate to
higher objects.

Another very important consideration, is, that in
urging the duty of charity, and the prior claims of
moral and religious objects, no rule of duty should
be maintained, that it would not be right and wise
for all to follow. And we are to test the wisdom
of any general rule, by inquiring what would be
the result, if all mankind should practise according
to it. In view of this, we are enabled to judge of
the correctness of those who maintain, that, to be
consistent, men who hold to the eternal destruction
of all those of our race who are not brought under
the influence of the Christian system, should give
up, not merely the elegances, but all the superfluities, of life, and devote the whole of their means,
not indispensable to life and health, for the propagation of Christianity. But, if this is the duty of
any, it is the duty of all ; and we are to inquire
what would be the result, if all conscientious persons gave up the use of all superfluities. Suppose
that two millions of the people in the United States
were conscientious persons, and relinquished the use
of every thing not absolutely necessary to life and
health. It would instantly throw out of employment one half of the whole community. The man-
ufacturers, mechanics, merchants, agriculturists, and
all the agencies they employ, would be beggared,
and one half of the community not reduced to poverty, would be obliged to spend all their extra means
in simply supplying necessaries to the other half.
The use of superfluities, therefore, to a certain extent, is as indispensable to promote industry, virtue,
and religion, as any direct giving of money or time :
and it is owing entirely to a want of reflection, and
of comprehensive views, that any men ever make
so great a mistake, as is here exhibited.

Instead, then, of urging a rule of duty which is

at once irrational and impracticable, there is another
course, which commends itself to the understand-
ings of all. For whatever may be the *practice* of
intelligent men, they universally concede the *principle*, that our physical gratifications should always
be made subordinate to social, intellectual, and
moral advantages. And all that is required, for the
advancement of our whole race to the most perfect
state of society, is, simply, that men should act in
agreement with this principle. And if only a very
small portion of the most intelligent of our race
should act according to this rule, under the control
of Christian benevolence, the immense supplies,
that would be furnished for the general good, is far
beyond what any would imagine, who had never
made any calculations on the subject. In this Nation, alone, suppose the one million and more of
professed followers of Christ should give a larger
portion of their means for the social, intellectual,
and moral, wants of mankind, than for the superfluities that minister to taste, convenience, and appetite ;
it would be enough to furnish all the schools, colleges, Bibles, ministers, and missionaries, that the
whole world could demand ; or at least, it would be
far more than properly qualified agents to administer
it could employ.

But it may be objected, that, though this view is
one, which, in the abstract, looks plausible and
rational, not one in a thousand can practically adopt
it. How few keep any account at all of their current expenses ? How impossible it is to determine
exactly what are necessaries, and what are superfluities ! And in regard to women, how few have
the control of an income, so as not to be bound
by the wishes of a parent or a husband !

In reference to these difficulties, the first remark
is, that we are never under obligations to do what is
entirely out of our power, so that those persons who

have no power to regulate their expenses or their
charities, are under no sort of obligation to attempt
it. The second remark is, that when a rule of duty
is discovered, we are bound to *aim* at it and to fulfil
it, just so far as we can. The third remark is, that
no person can tell how much can be done, till a
faithful attempt has been made. If a woman never
did keep any accounts, nor attempt to regulate her
expenditures by the right rule, nor use her influence
with those that control her plans, to secure this object, she has no right to say how much she can, or
cannot, do, till after a fair trial has been made.

In attempting such a trial, the following method
can be taken. Let a woman keep an account of all
she spends for herself and her family, for a year,
arranging the items under three general heads.
Under the first, put all articles for food, raiment,
rent, wages, and all conveniences. Under the second, place all sums paid in securing an education and books and all intellectual advantages.
Under the third head, place all that is spent for
benevolence and religion. At the end of the year,
the first and largest account will show the mixed
items of necessaries and superfluities, which can be
arranged so as to gain some sort of idea how much
has been spent for superfluities, and how much for
necessaries. Then, by comparing what is spent for
superfluities with what is spent for intellectual and
moral advantages, data will be gained for judging of
the past, and regulating the future.

Does a woman say she cannot do this? let her inquire, whether the offer of a thousand dollars, as a
reward for attempting it one year, would not make
her undertake to do it; and if so, let her decide, in
her own mind, which is most valuable, a clear conscience, and the approbation of God, in this effort to
do His will, or one thousand dollars. And let her
do it with this warning of the Saviour before her

eyes,—"No man can serve two masters." "Ye cannot serve God and Mammon."

Is it objected, How can we decide between superfluities and necessaries in this list ? it is replied, we are not required to judge exactly, in all cases. Our duty is, to use the means in our power to aid us in forming a correct judgement ; to seek the Divine aid in freeing our minds from indolence and selfishness ; and then to judge as well as we can, in our endeavors rightly to apportion and regulate our expenses. Many persons seem to feel that they are bound to do better than they know how. But God is not so hard a Master; and after we have used all proper means to learn the right way, if we then follow it according to our ability, we do wrong to feel misgivings, or to blame ourselves, if results come out differently from what seems desirable. The results of our actions, alone, can never prove that we deserve blame. For it is often the case, that, by lack of intellect or means, men are so placed, that it is impossible for them to decide correctly. To use all the means of knowledge within our reach, and then to judge with a candid and conscientious spirit, is all that God requires; and when we have done this, and the event seems to come out wrong, we should never wish that we had decided otherwise. For it is the same as wishing that we had not followed the dictates of judgement and conscience. As this is a world designed for discipline and trial, untoward events are never to be construed as indications of the rectitude of our past decisions.

In order to act in accordance with the rule here presented, it is true, that many would be obliged to give up the idea of conforming to the notions and customs of those with whom they associate, and compelled to adopt the maxim, "be not conformed to this world." In many cases, it would involve an entire change in the style of living. And the Writer has the happiness of knowing more cases than one, where men, who have come to similar views on this subject, have given up large and expensive establishments, disposed of their carriages, dismissed a portion of their domestics, and modified all their expenditures, that they might keep a pure conscience, and regulate their charities more according to the requirements of Christianity. And there are persons, well known in the religious world, who save themselves all labor of minute calculation, by giving so large a portion of their means to benevolent objects, that they find no difficulty in knowing that they give more for religious, benevolent, and intellectual, than for any inferior objects.

In deciding what particular objects shall receive our benefactions, there are also general principles to guide us. The first, is that presented by our Saviour, when, after urging the great law of benevolence, He was asked, "and who is my neighbor?" His reply, in the parable of the Good Samaritan, teaches us, that any human being, whose wants are brought to our knowledge, is our neighbor. The wounded man was not only a stranger, but he belonged to a foreign nation peculiarly hated ; and he had no claim, except that his wants were brought to the knowledge of the wayfaring man. From this, we learn that the destitute, of all nations, become our neighbors, as soon as their wants are brought to our knowledge.

Another general principle, is this, that those who are most in need, must be relieved, in preference to those who are less destitute. On this principle, it is, that the followers of Christ should give more to supply those who are suffering for want of the bread of eternal life, than for those who are deprived of physical enjoyments. And another reason for this preference, is, the fact that many, who give in charity, have made such imperfect advances in civilization and Christianity, that the intellectual and moral wants of our race make but a feeble impression on the mind. Relate a pitiful tale of a family reduced to live for weeks on potatoes, only, and many a mind would awake to deep sympathy, and stretch forth the hand of charity. But describe cases where the immortal mind is pining in stupidity and ignorance, or racked with the fever of baleful passions, and how small the number so elevated in sentiment, and so enlarged in their views, as to appreciate and sympathize in these far greater misfortunes! The intellectual and moral wants of our fellow-men, therefore, should claim the first place in our attention, both because they are most important, and because they are most neglected.

Another consideration to be borne in mind, is, that, in this Country, there is much less real need of charity in supplying physical necessities, than is generally supposed by those who have not learned the more excellent way. This Land is so abundant in supplies, and labor is in such demand, that every healthy person can earn a comfortable support. And if all the poor were instantly made virtuous, it is probable that there would be no physical wants which could not readily be supplied by the immediate friends of each sufferer. The sick, the aged, and the orphan, would be the only objects of charity. In this view of the case, the primary effort in relieving the poor should be, to furnish them the means of earning their own support, and to supply them with those moral influences which are most effectual in securing virtue and industry.

Another point to be attended to, is, the importance of maintaining a system of *associated* charities. There is no point, in which the economy of charity has more improved, than in the present mode of combining many small contributions for sustaining enlarged and systematic plans of charity. If all the half-dollars, which are now contributed to aid in organized systems of charity, were returned to the donors, to be applied by the agency and discretion of each, thousands and thousands of the treasures, now employed to promote the moral and intellectual wants of mankind, would become entirely useless. In a democracy, like ours, where few are very rich, and the majority are in comfortable circumstances, this collecting and dispensing of drops and rills is the mode by which, in imitation of Nature, the dews and showers are to distil on parched and desert lands. And every person, while earning a pittance to unite with many more, may be cheered with the consciousness of sustaining a grand system of operations, which must have the most decided influence in raising all mankind to that perfect state of society, which Christianity is designed to secure.

Another consideration relates to the indiscriminate bestowal of charity. Persons who have taken pains to inform themselves, and who devote their whole time to dispensing charities, unite in declaring, that this is one of the most fruitful sources of indolence, vice, and poverty. From several of these, the Writer has learned, that, by their own personal investigations, they have ascertained, that there are large establishments of idle and wicked persons in most of our cities, who associate together to support themselves by every species of imposition. They hire large houses, and live in constant rioting on the means thus obtained. Among them, are women who have, or who hire the use of, infant children; others, who are blind, or maimed, or deformed, or who can adroitly feign such infirmities, and by these means of exciting pity, and by artful tales of wo, they collect alms, both in city and country, to spend in all manner of gross and guilty indulgences. Meantime, many persons, finding themselves often duped by impostors, refuse to give at all; and thus

many benefactions are withdrawn, which a wise
economy in charity would have secured. For this,
and other reasons, it is wise and merciful, to adopt
the general rule, never to give alms, till some knowledge is gained, of knowing how they will be spent.
There are exceptions to this, as to every general rule,
which a person of discretion can determine. But
the practice, so common among benevolent persons,
of giving at least a trifle to all who ask, lest, per-
chance, they may turn away some who are really
sufferers, is one which causes more sin and misery
than it cures.

The Writer has never known any system for dispensing charity, so successful, as the one which, in
many places, has been adopted in connection with
the distribution of tracts. By this method, a town
or city is divided into districts; and each district is
committed to the care of two ladies, whose duty it
is to call on each family and leave a tract, and make
that the occasion for entering into conversation, and
learning the situation of all residents in the district.
By this method, the ignorant, the vicious, and the
poor, are discovered, and their physical, intellectual,
and moral, wants, are investigated. In some places,
where the Writer has resided or visited, each lady
retained the same district, year after year, so that
every poor family in the place was under the watch
and care of some intelligent and benevolent lady,
who used all her influence to secure a proper education for the children, to furnish them with suitable
reading, to encourage habits of industry and economy,
and to secure regular attendance on public religious
instruction. Thus, the rich and the poor were
brought in contact, in a way advantageous to both
parties; and if such a system could be universally
adopted, more would be done for the prevention of
poverty and vice, than all the wealth of the Nation
could avail for their relief. In one of these places,

the Writer heard a resident reply to some remarks about the danger of having her fruit stolen, "No ; the boys never steal fruit here. The people never take any pains to protect it, and have it in great abundance ; but it is seldom if ever taken without leave." This was in a city of twenty thousand inhabitants, where the plan above described had been in efficient operation for several years. But this plan cannot be successfully carried out, in this manner, unless there is a large proportion of intelligent, benevolent, and self-denying, persons ; and the mere distribution of tracts, without the other parts of the plan, is of very little avail.

But there is one species of charity, which needs especial consideration. It is that, which leads a person to refrain from judging of the means and the relative charities of other persons. There have been such indistinct notions, and so many different standards of duty, on this subject, that it is rare for two persons to think exactly alike, in regard to the measure of duty. Each person is bound to inquire and judge for himself, as to his own duty or deficiencies ; but as both the resources, and the amount of actual charities of other men are beyond our ken, it is as indecorous, as it is uncharitable, to set in judgement on their decisions.

CHAPTER XVI.

ON ECONOMY OF TIME AND EXPENSES.

Economy of Time. Value of Time. Right Apportionment of Time. Laws appointed by God for the Jews. Proportions of Property and Time the Jews were required to devote to Intellectual, Benevolent, and Religious Purposes. The Levites. The weekly Sabbath. The Sabbatical Year. Three sevenths of the Time of the Jews devoted to God's Service. Christianity removes the Restrictions laid on the Jews, but demands all our Time to be devoted to our own best Interests and the Good of our Fellow-men. Some Practical Good to be the Ultimate End of all our Pursuits. Enjoyment connected with the Performance of every Duty. Great Mistake of Mankind. A Final Account to be given of the Apportionment of our Time. Various Modes of economizing Time. System and Order. Uniting several Objects in one Employment. Employment of Odd Intervals of Time. We are bound to aid Others in economizing Time. ECONOMY OF EXPENSES. Necessity of Information on this Point. Contradictory Notions. General Principles in which all agree. Knowledge of Income and Expenses. Every One bound to do as much as she can to secure System and Order. Examples. Evils of Want of System and Forethought. Young Ladies should early learn to be systematic and economical. Articles of Dress and Furniture should be in keeping with each other, and with the Circumstances of the Family. Mistaken Economy. Education of Daughters away from Home injudicious. Nice Sewing should be done at Home. Cheap Articles not always most economical. Buying by wholesale economical only in special cases. Penurious Savings made by getting the Poor to work cheap. Relative Obligations of the Poor and the Rich in regard to Economy. Economy of Providence in the Unequal Distribution of Property. Carelessness of Expense not a Mark of Gentility. Beating down Prices improper in Wealthy People. Inconsistency in American would-be Fashionables.

ON ECONOMY OF TIME.

THE value of time, and our obligation to spend every hour for some useful end, are what few minds properly realize. And those, who have the highest sense of their obligations in this respect, sometimes greatly misjudge in their estimate of what are useful and proper modes of employing time. This arises from limited views of the importance of some pursuits, which they would deem frivolous and useless, but which are, in reality, necessary to preserve the health of body and mind, and those social affections, which it is very important to cherish. Christianity teaches, that, for all the time afforded us, we must give account to God; and that we have no right to waste a single hour. But time which is spent in rest or amusement, is often as usefully employed, as if it were devoted to labor or devotion. In employing our time, we are to make suitable allowance for sleep, for preparing and taking food, for securing the means of a livelihood, for intellectual improvement, for exercise and amusement, for social enjoyments, and for benevolent and religious duties. And it is the *right apportionment* of time to these various duties, which constitutes its true economy.

In making this apportionment, we are bound by the same rules as relate to the use of property. We are to employ whatever portion is necessary to sustain life and health, as the first duty; and the remainder we are so to apportion, that our highest interests shall receive the greatest allotment, and our physical gratifications the least.

The laws of the Supreme Ruler, when He became the civil as well as the religious Head of the Jewish theocracy, is an example which it would be well for all attentively to consider, when forming plans for the apportionment of time and property. To estimate this properly, it must be borne in mind, that the main object of God was to preserve His religion among the Jewish nation, and that they were not required to take any means to propagate it among other nations, as is now required by Christianity. So low were they in the scale of civilization and mental developement, that a system, which confined them to one spot, as an agricultural people, and prevented their growing very rich, or having extensive commerce with other nations, was indispensable to prevent their relapsing into the low idolatries and vices of the nations around them.

The proportion of time and property, which every Jew was required to devote to intellectual, benevolent, and religious purposes, were as follows.

In regard to property, they were required to give one tenth of all their yearly income, to support the Levites and the priests and religious service. Next, they were required to give the first fruits of all their corn, wine, oil, and fruits, and the first-born of all their cattle, for the Lord's treasury, to be employed for the priests, the widow, the fatherless, and the stranger. The first-born, also, of their children, were the Lord's, and were to be redeemed by a specified sum, paid into the sacred treasury. Besides this, they were required to bring a freewill offering to God, every time they went up to the three great yearly festivals. In addition to this, regular yearly sacrifices, of cattle and fowls, were required of each family, and occasional sacrifices for certain sins or ceremonial impurities. In reaping their fields, they were required to leave the corners for the poor, unreaped, and not to glean their fields, or olive and vineyards; and if a sheaf was left, by mistake, they were not to return for it, but leave it for the poor. When a man sent away a servant, he was thus charged : " Furnish him liberally out of thy flock, and out of thy floor, and out of thy winepress." When a poor man came to borrow money, they were forbidden to deny him, or to take any interest; and if, at the sabbatical, or seventh, year, he could not pay, the debt was to be cancelled. And to this command, is added the significant caution, " Beware that there be not a thought in thy wicked heart, saying, the seventh year, the year of release, is at hand; and thine eye be evil against thy poor brother, and thou givest him nought; and he cry unto the Lord against thee, and it be sin unto thee. Thou shalt surely give him," " because that for this thing the Lord thy God shall bless thee in all thy works, and in all that thou puttest thine hand unto." Besides this, the Levites were distributed through the land, with the intention that they should be instructers and priests in every part of the nation. Thus, one twelfth of the people were set apart, having no landed property, to be priests and teachers; and the other tribes were required to support them liberally.

In regard to the time taken from secular pursuits, for the support of religion, an equally liberal amount was demanded. In the first place, one seventh part of their time was taken for the weekly sabbath, when no kind of work was to be done. Then the whole nation were required to meet at the appointed place, three times a year, which, including their journeys, and stay there, occupied eight weeks, which was another seventh of their time. Then the sabbatical year, when no agricultural labor was to be done, took another seventh of their time from their regular pursuits, as they were an agricultural people. This was the amount of time and property demanded by God, simply to sustain religion and morality within the bounds of that nation. Christianity demands the spread of its blessings to all mankind, and so the restrictions laid on the Jews are withheld, and all our wealth and time, not needful for our own best interest, is to be employed in improving the condition of our fellow-men.

In deciding respecting the rectitude of our pursuits, we are bound to aim at some practical good, as the ultimate object. With every duty of this life, our benevolent Creator has connected some species of enjoyment, to draw us to perform it. Thus the palate is gratified, by performing the duty of nourishing our bodies; the principle of curiosity is gratified, in pursuing useful knowledge; the desire of approbation

is gratified, when we perform benevolent and social
duties; and every other duty has an alluring enjoyment connected with it. But the great mistake
of mankind has consisted in seeking the pleasures,
connected with these duties, as the sole aim, without
reference to the main end that should be held in view,
and to which the enjoyment should be made subservient. Thus, men seek to gratify the palate, without
reference to the question whether the body is properly
nourished; and follow after knowledge, without inquiring whether it ministers to good or evil.

But, in gratifying the implanted desires of our nature, we are bound so to restrain ourselves, by reason
and conscience, as always to seek the main objects
of existence,—the highest good of ourselves and
others; and never to sacrifice this, for the mere
gratification of our sensual desires. We are to gratify
appetite, just so far as is consistent with health and
usefulness, and no further. We are to gratify the
desire for knowledge, just so far as will enable us to
do most good by our influence and efforts; and no
further. We are to seek social intercourse, to that
extent, which will best promote domestic enjoyment
and kindly feelings among neighbors and friends.
And we are to pursue exercise and amusement, only
so far as will best sustain the vigor of body and
mind. And for the right apportionment of time, to
these and various other duties, we are to give an account at the final day.

Instead of attempting to give any very specific
rules on this subject, some modes of economizing time
will be suggested. The most powerful of all agencies,
in this matter, is, that habit of system and order, in all
our pursuits, which has been already pointed out. It
is probable, that a person, who is regular and systematic in employing time, will accomplish thrice the
amount, that could otherwise be secured.

Another mode of economizing time, is, by uniting

several objects in one employment. Thus, exercise, or charitable efforts, can be united with social enjoyments, as is done in associations for sewing or visiting the poor. Instruction and amusement can also be combined. Pursuits like music, gardening, drawing, botany, and the like, unite intellectual improvement with amusement, social enjoyment, and exercise.

With housekeepers, and others whose employments are various and desultory, much time can be saved by preparing employments for little odd intervals. Thus, some ladies prepare, and keep in the parlor, light work, to take up when detained there; some keep a book at hand, in the nursery, to read while holding or sitting by a sleeping infant. One of the most popular poetesses of our Country very often shows her friends, at their calls, that the thread of the knitting never need interfere with the thread of agreeable discourse.

It would be astonishing, to one who had never tried the experiment, how much can be accomplished, by a little planning and forethought, in thus finding employment for odd intervals of time.

But besides economizing our own time, we are bound to use our influence and example to promote the discharge of the same duty by others. A woman is under obligations so to arrange the hours and pursuits of her family, as to promote systematic and habitual industry; and if, by late breakfasts, irregular hours for meals, and other hinderances of this kind, she interferes with, or refrains from promoting regular industry in, others, she is accountable to God for all the waste of time consequent on her negligence. The mere example of a systematic and industrious housekeeper, has a wonderful influence in promoting the same virtuous habit in others.

ON ECONOMY IN EXPENSES.

It is impossible for a woman to practise a wise economy in expenditures, unless she is taught how to do it, either by a course of experiments, or by the instruction of those who have had experience. It is amusing to notice the various, and oftentimes contradictory, notions of economy, among judicious and experienced housekeepers; for there is probably no economist, who would not be deemed lavish or wasteful, in some respects, by another equally experienced and judicious person, who, in some other points, would herself be equally condemned by the other. These diversities are occasioned by different early habits, and by the different relative value given by each to the different modes of enjoyment, for which money is expended.*

But, though there may be much disagreement in minor matters, there are certain general principles, which all unite in sanctioning. The first, is, that care be taken to know the amount of income and of current expenses, so that the proper relative proportion be preserved, and the expenditures never exceed the means. Few women can do this, thoroughly, without keeping regular accounts. The habits of this Nation, especially among business-men, are so desultory, and the current expenses of a family, in many points, are so much more under the control of the man than of the woman, that many women, who are disposed to be systematic in this matter, cannot follow their wishes. But there are often cases, when much is left undone in this particular,

* The Writer, not long since, met an amusing illustration of this. "Anna," said a wealthy lady, to her daughter, who had returned from an expensive boarding-school, and was playing on the piano, "where is *the* fine needle?" "I have broken it," was the reply. "Where is the coarse one, then?" "Ellen is using it." "Then just step over, and ask Mrs. C. to lend me her fine needle." The daughter went, and returned, saying, "Mrs. C. says she has lost hers, and has not had time to get another." A visiter, present, sent off for her wellstocked workbasket; and the remarks afterwards made, by the lady, in regard to its supplies, showed that she deemed her visiter lavish and extravagant in this matter. The wealthy lady hired out most of her plain sewing, and all her tailoring and mantuamaking. The visiter cut and made all the garments for her family, and each thought the other uneconomical.

simply because no effort is made. Yet every woman
is bound to do as much as is in her power, to accomplish a systematic mode of expenditure, and the
regulation of it by Christian principles.

The following are examples of different methods
which have been adopted, for securing a proper ad-
justment of expenses to the means.

The first, is that of a lady, who kept a large
boarding-house, in one of our cities. Every evening,
before retiring, she made an account of the expenses
of the day ; and this usually occupied her not more
than fifteen minutes, at a time. On each Saturday,
she took an inventory of the stores on hand, and of
the daily expenses, and also of what was due to
her ; and then made an exact estimate of her expenditures and profits. This, after the first two or
three weeks, never took more than an hour, at the
close of the week. Thus, by a very little time,
regularly devoted to this object, she knew, accurate-
ly, her income, expenditures, and profits.

Another friend of the Writer lives on a regular
salary. The method adopted, in this case, is to
calculate to what the salary amounts, each week.
Then an account is kept of what is paid out, each
week, for rent, fuel, wages, and food. This amount
of each week is deducted from the weekly income.
The remainders of each week are added, at the
close of a month, as the stock from which is to be
taken, the dress, furniture, books, travelling expenses,
charities, and all other expenditures.

Another lady, whose husband is a lawyer, divides
the year into four quarters, and the income into four
equal parts. She then makes her plans, so that the
expenses of one quarter shall never infringe on the
income of another. So resolute is she, in carrying
out this determination, that if, by any mischance,
she is in want of articles before the close of a quarter,
for which she has not the means, she will subject

herself to temporary inconvenience, by waiting, rather than violate her rule.

Another lady, whose husband is in a business, which he thinks makes it impossible for him to know what his yearly income will be, took this method. She kept an account of all her disbursements, for one year. This she submitted to her husband, and obtained his consent that the same sum should be under her control, the coming year, for similar purposes, with the understanding that she might modify future apportionments, in any way her judgement and conscience might approve.

A great deal of uneasiness and discomfort is caused to both husband and wife, in many cases, by an entire want of system and forethought, in arranging expenses. Both keep buying what they think they need, without any calculation as to how matters are coming out, and with a sort of dread of running in debt, all the time harassing them. Such never know the comfort of independence. But, if a man or woman will only calculate what the income is, and then plan so as to know that all the time they live within it, they secure one of the greatest comforts, which wealth ever bestows, and what many of the rich, who live in a loose and careless way, never enjoy. It is not so much the amount of income, as the regular and correct apportionment of expenses, that makes a family truly comfortable. A man, with ten thousand a year, is often more harassed, for want of money, than the systematic economist, who supports a family on only six hundred a year.

As it is very important that young ladies should learn systematic economy in expenses, it will be a great benefit for every young girl to begin, at twelve or thirteen, to make her own purchases, under the guidance of her mother or some other friend. And if parents would ascertain the actual expense of a daughter's clothing, for a year, and give the sum to her, in quarterly payments, requiring a regular account, it would be of great benefit in preparing her for future duties. How else are young ladies to learn properly to make purchases, and to be systematic and economical? The art of system and economy can no more come by intuition, than the art of watchmaking or bookkeeping; and how strange it appears, that so many young ladies take charge of a husband's establishment, without having had either instruction or experience in the leading duty of their station!

The second general principle of economy, is, that, in apportioning an income, among various objects, the most important should receive the largest supply, and that all retrenchments be made in matters of less importance. In a previous chapter, some general principles have been presented, to guide in this duty. Some additional hints will here be added, on the same topic.

In regard to dress and furniture, much want of judgement and good taste is often seen, in purchasing some expensive article, which is not at all in keeping with the other articles connected with it. Thus, a large sideboard, or elegant mirror, or sofa, which would be suitable only for a large establishment, with other rich furniture, is crowded into too small a room, with coarse and cheap articles around it. So, also, sometimes a parlor, and company-chamber, will be furnished in a style suitable only for the wealthy, while the table will be supplied with shabby linen, and imperfect crockery, and every other part of the house will look, in comparison with these fine rooms, mean and niggardly. It is not at all uncommon, to find very showy and expensive articles in the part of the house visible to strangers, when the children's rooms, kitchen, and other back portions, are on an entirely different scale.

So in regard to dress, a lady will sometimes purchase an elegant and expensive article, which, instead of attracting admiration from the eye of taste, will merely serve as a decoy to the painful contrast of all other parts of the dress. A woman of real good taste and discretion, will strive to maintain a relative consistency between all departments, and not, in one quarter, live on a scale fitted only to the rich, and in another, on one appropriate only to the poor.

Another mistake in economy is often made, by some of the best-educated and most intelligent of mothers. Such will often be found spending day after day at the needle, when, with a comparatively small sum, this labor could be obtained of those who need such earnings. Meantime, the daughters of the family, whom the mother is qualified to educate, or so nearly, that she could readily keep ahead of her children, are sent to expensive boarding-schools, where their delicate frames, their plastic minds, and their moral and religious interests, are relinquished to the hands of strangers. And the expense, thus incurred, would serve to pay the hire of every thing the mother can do in sewing, four or five times over. The same want of economy is shown in communities, where, instead of establishing a good female school in their vicinity, the men of wealth send their daughters abroad, at double the expense, to be either educated or spoiled, as the case may be.

Another species of poor economy, is manifested in neglecting to acquire and apply mechanical skill, which, in consequence, has to be hired from others. Thus, all the plain sewing will be done by the mother and daughters, while all that requires skill will be hired. Instead of this, others take pains to have their daughters instructed in mantuamaking, and the simpler parts of millinery, so that the plain work is given to the poor, who need it, and the more expensive and tasteful operations are performed in the family. The Writer knows ladies, who not only make their own dresses, but also their caps, bonnets, and artificial flowers.

Some persons make miscalculations in economy, by habitually looking up cheap articles, while others go to the opposite extreme, and always buy the best of every thing. Those ladies, who are considered the best economists, do not adopt either method. In regard to cheap goods, the fading colors, the damages discovered in use, the poorness of material, and the extra sewing demanded to replace articles lost by such causes, usually render such bargains very dear, in the end. On the other hand, though some articles, of the most expensive kind, wear longest and best, yet, as a general rule, articles at medium prices do the best service. This is true of table and bed linens, broadcloths, shirtings, and the like; though, in these cases, it is often found that the coarsest and cheapest last the longest.

Buying by wholesale, and keeping a large supply on hand, is economical only in large families, where the mistress is careful; but in other cases, the hazards of accident, and the temptation to a lavish use. will make the loss outrun the profits.

There is one mode of economizing, which, it is hoped, will every year grow more rare; and that is, making penurious savings by getting the poor to work as cheap as possible. Many amiable and benevolent women have done this, on principle, without reflecting on the want of Christian charity thus displayed. Let every woman, in making bargains with the poor, conceive herself placed in the same circumstances, toiling hour after hour, and day after day, for a small sum, and then deal with others as she would be dealt by in such a situation. *Liberal prices*, and *prompt payment*, should be an unfailing maxim in dealing with the poor.

The third general principle of economy, is, that all articles should be so used, and taken care of, as to secure the longest service with the least waste. Under this head, come many particulars in regard to the use and preservation of articles, which will be found more in detail in succeeding chapters. It may be proper, however, here to refer to one very common impression, as to the relative obligation of the poor and the rich in regard to economy. Many seem to suppose, that those who are wealthy, have a right to be lavish and negligent in the care of expenses. But this surely is a great mistake. Property is a talent, given by God, to spend for the welfare of mankind; and the needless waste of it, is as wrong in the rich, as it is in the poor. The rich are under obligations to apportion their income, to the various objects demanding attention, by the same rule as all others; and if this will allow them to spend more for superfluities than those of smaller means, it never makes it right to misuse or waste any of the bounties of Providence. Whatever is no longer wanted for their own enjoyment, should be carefully saved, to add to the enjoyment of others.

It is not always that men understand the economy of Providence, in that unequal distribution of property, which, even under the most perfect form of government, will always exist. Many, looking at the present state of things, imagine that the rich, if they acted in strict conformity to the law of benevolence, would share all their property with their suffering fellow-men. But such do not take into account the inspired declaration, that a man's life consisteth not in the abundance of that which he possesseth, or, in other words, life is made valuable, not by great possessions, but by such a character as prepares a man to enjoy what he holds. God perceives that human character can be most improved by that kind of discipline which exists, when there is something valuable to be gained by industrious efforts. This stimulus to industry, never could exist in a community where all are just alike, as it does in a state of society where every man sees enjoyments possessed by others, which he desires and may secure by effort and industry. So in a community where all are alike as to property, there would be no chance to gain that noblest of all attainments, a habit of self-denying benevolence, which toils for the good of others, and takes from one's own store to increase the enjoyments of another.

Instead, then, of the stagnation both of industry and of benevolence, which would follow the universal and equable distribution of property, one class of men, by superior advantages of birth, or intellect, or patronage, come into possession of a great amount of capital. With these means, they are enabled, by study, reading, and travel, to secure expansion of mind, and just views of the relative advantages of moral, intellectual, and physical enjoyments. At the same time, Christianity imposes obligations corresponding with the increase of advantages and means. The rich are not at liberty to spend their treasures for themselves, alone. Their wealth is given, by God, to be employed for the best good of mankind ; and their intellectual advantages are designed, primarily, to enable them to judge correctly, in employing their means most wisely for the general good.

Now, suppose a man of wealth inherits ten thousand acres of real estate : it is not his duty to divide it among his poor neighbors and tenants. It is probable, that, if he took this course, most of them would spend all in thriftless waste and indolence, or in mere physical enjoyments. Instead of thus putting his capital out of his hands, he is bound to retain it, and so employ it, as to raise his neighbors and tenants to such a state of virtue and intelligence, that they could secure far more, by their own efforts and industry, than he could bestow by dividing his capital.

In this view of the subject, it is manifest, that the unequal distribution of property is no evil. The great difficulty is, that so large a portion of those who hold great capital, instead of using their various advantages for the common good, employ the chief of them for mere selfish indulgences; thus inflicting as much mischief on their own souls, as results to others from their culpable neglect. A great portion of the rich seem to be acting on the principle, that the more God bestows on them, the less are their obligations to practise any self-denial, in fulfilling his benevolent plan of raising our race to intelligence and holiness.

There are not a few, who seem to imagine that it is a mark of gentility to be careless of expenses. But this notion is owing to a want of knowledge of the world. As a general fact, it will be found, that persons of rank, and wealth, abroad, are much more likely to be systematic and economical, than persons of inferior standing in these respects. Even the most frivolous, among the rich and great, are often found practising a rigid economy, in certain respects, in order to secure gratifications in another direction. And it will be found so common, among persons of vulgar minds and little education and less sense, to make a display of profusion and indifference to expense, as a mark of their claims to gentility, that the really genteel look upon it rather as a mark of low breeding. So that the sort of feeling which some persons cherish, as if it were mean to be careful of small sums, and to be attentive to relative prices, in making purchases, is founded on mistaken notions of gentility and propriety.

But one caution is needful, in regard to another extreme. When a lady of wealth is seen roaming about in search of cheaper articles, or trying to beat down a shopkeeper, or making a close bargain with those she employs, the impropriety is glaring to all minds. A person of wealth has no occasion to spend time in looking for extra cheap articles; her time could be more profitably employed in distributing to the wants of others. And the practice of beating down tradespeople, is vulgar and degrading, in any one. A woman, after a little inquiry, can ascertain what is the fair and common price of things; and if she is charged an exorbitant sum, she can decline taking the article. If the price be a fair one, it is inappropriate to search for another article which is below the regular charge. If a woman finds that she is in a store where they charge high prices, expecting to be beat down, she can simply mention, that she wishes to know the lowest price, as it is contrary to her principles to beat down charges.

There is one inconsistency, found among that class who are ambitious of being ranked among the aristocracy of society, which is worthy of notice. It has been remarked, that, in the real aristocracy of other lands, it is much more common than with us, to practice systematic economy. And such do not hesitate to say so, when they cannot afford certain indulgences. This practice descends to subordinate grades; so that foreign ladies, when they come to reside in this Country, seldom hesitate in assigning the true reason, when they cannot afford any gratification.

But in this Country, it will be found, that many, most fond of copying aristocratic examples, are on this point rather with the vulgar. Not a few of those young persons, beginning life with parlors and dresses in a style fitting only to established wealth, go into expenses which they can ill afford, and are ashamed even to allow that they are restrained from any expense by motives of economy. Such a con-

fession is never extorted, except by some call of
benevolence, and then they are very ready to declare
that they cannot afford to bestow even a pittance.
In such cases, it would seem as if the direct opposite of Christianity had gained possession of their
tastes and opinions. They are ashamed to appear
to deny themselves; but very far from any shame
in denying the calls of benevolence.

CHAPTER XVII.

ON HEALTH OF MIND.

Intimate Connection between the Body and Mind. Brain excited by
improper Stimulants taken into the Stomach. Mental Faculties
then affected. Example of a Person having lost a Portion of his
Skull. Causes of Mental Diseases. Want of oxygenized Blood.
Fresh Air absolutely necessary. Excessive Exercise of the Intellect or Feelings a Cause of Derangement. Such Attention to
Religion, as prevents the Performance of other Duties, wrong.
Teachers and Parents should look to this. Unusual Precocity in
Children usually the Result of a Diseased Brain. Parents generally add Fuel to this Fever. Idiocy often the Result, or the Pre-
cocious Child sinks below the Average of Mankind. This Evil
yet prevalent in Colleges and other Seminaries. A Medical Man
necessary in every Seminary. Some Pupils always needing Re-
straint in regard to Study. A Third Cause of Mental Disease,
the Want of Appropriate Exercise of the Various Faculties of the
Mind. Extract from Dr. Combe. Examples of Wealthy Ladies.
Beneficial Results of active Intellectual Employments. Indications of a Diseased Mind.

THERE is such an intimate connection between
the body and mind, that the health of one cannot
be preserved, without a proper care of the other.
And it is from a neglect of this principle, that some
of the most exemplary and conscientious persons in
the world, suffer a thousand agonies, from a diseased
state of body, while others ruin the health of the
body, by neglecting the proper care of the mind.
When the brain is excited, by stimulating drinks

taken into the stomach, it produces a corresponding excitement of the mental faculties. The reason, the imagination, and all the powers, are stimulated to preternatural vigor and activity. In like manner, when the mind is excited by earnest intellectual effort, or by strong passions, the brain is equally excited, and the blood rushes into the head. Sir Astley Cooper records, that, in examining the brain of a young man who had lost a portion of his skull, whenever "he was agitated, by some opposition to his wishes," "the blood was sent, with increased force, to his brain," and the pulsations "became frequent and violent." The same effect was produced by any intellectual effort; and the flushed countenance which attends earnest study, or strong emotions of fear, shame,·or anger, are external indications of the suffused state of the brain from such causes.

In exhibiting the causes which injure the health of the mind, they will be found to be partly physical, partly intellectual, and partly moral.

The first cause of mental disease and suffering, is not unfrequently found in the want of a proper supply of duly oxygenized blood. It has been shown, how the blood, in passing through the lungs, is purified, by the oxygen of the air combining with the superabundant hydrogen and carbon of the venous blood, thus forming carbonic acid and water, which are expired into the atmosphere. Every pair of lungs is constantly withdrawing from the surrounding atmosphere its healthful principle, and returning an injurious one.

When, by confinement, and this process, the atmosphere is deprived of its appropriate supply of oxygen, the purification of the blood is interrupted, and it passes unprepared into the brain, producing languor, restlessness, and inability to exercise the intellect and feelings. Whenever, therefore, per-

sons sleep in a close apartment, or remain for a
length of time in a crowded ill-ventilated room, a
most pernicious influence is exerted on the brain,
and, through this on the mind. A person often exposed to such influences, can never enjoy that elasticity and vigor of mind, which is one of the chief
indications of its health. This is the reason why
all rooms for religious meetings, and all schoolrooms,
and sleeping apartments, should be so contrived, as
to secure a constant supply of fresh air from without. The minister, who speaks in a crowded and
ill-ventilated apartment, loses much of his ability to
feel and to speak, while the audience are equally reduced, in their ability to attend and to feel. The
teacher, who confines children in a close apartment,
diminishes their ability to study, or to attend to his
instructions. And the person who habitually sleeps
in a close room, diminishes his mental energies in a
similar degree. It is not unfrequently the case, that
depression of spirits, and stupor of intellect, are
occasioned solely by this neglect.

Another cause of mental disease, is, the excessive
exercise of the intellect or feelings. If the eye is
taxed beyond its strength, by protracted use, its
blood-vessels become engorged, and the bloodshot
appearance warns of the excess and the need of
rest.

The brain is affected, in a similar manner, by excessive use, though the suffering and inflamed organ
cannot make its appeal to the eye. But there are
some indications, which ought never to be misun-
derstood or disregarded. In cases of pupils, at
school or at college, a diseased state, from over
action, is often manifested by increased clearness of
mind, and ease and vigor of mental action. In one
instance, known to the Writer, a most exemplary
and industrious pupil, anxious to improve every
hour, and ignorant or unmindful of the laws of

health, first manifested the diseased state of her brain and mind, by demands for more studies, and a sudden and earnest activity in planning modes of improvement for herself and others. When warned of her danger, she protested that she never was better, in her life ; that she took regular exercise in the open air, went to bed in season, slept soundly, and felt perfectly well ; that her mind was never before so bright and clear, and study never so easy and delightful. And at this time, she was on the verge of derangement, from which she was saved only by an entire cessation of all her intellectual efforts.

A similar case occurred, under the eye of the Writer, from over-excited feelings. It was during a time of unusual religious interest in the community, and the danger was first manifested by the pupil bringing her Hymn-book or Bible to the class-room, and making them her constant resort in every interval of school duty. It finally became impossible to convince her that it was her duty to attend to any thing else ; her conscience became morbidly sensitive, her perceptions indistinct, her deductions unreasonable, and nothing but entire change of scene, exercise, and amusement, saved her. When the health of the brain was restored, she found that she could attend to the " one thing needful," not only without interruption of duty, or injury of health, but rather so as to promote both. This is a danger, which clergymen and teachers need most carefully to notice and guard against.

Any such attention to religion, as prevents the performance of daily duties and needful relaxation, is dangerous, as tending to produce such a state of the brain as makes it impossible to feel or judge correctly. And when any morbid and unreasonable pertinacity appears, much exercise and engagement in other interesting pursuits should be urged, as the only mode of securing the religious benefits aimed at. And whenever any mind is oppressed with care, anxiety, or sorrow, the amount of active exercise in the fresh air should be greatly increased, that the action of the muscles may withdraw the blood, which, in such seasons, is constantly tending too much to the brain.

There has been a most appalling amount of suffering, derangement, disease, and death, occasioned by a want of attention to this subject, in teachers and parents. Unusual precocity in children, is usually the result of an unhealthful state of the brain; and in such cases, medical men would now direct, that the wonderful child should be deprived of all books and study, and turned to play or work in the fresh air. Instead of this, parents frequently add fuel to the fever of the brain, by supplying constant mental stimulus, until the victim finds refuge in idiocy or an early grave. Where such fatal results do not occur, the brain, in many cases, is so weakened, that the genius of infancy sinks below the medium of intellectual powers in afterlife. In our colleges, too, many of the most promising minds sink to an early grave, or drag out a miserable existence, from this same cause. And it is an evil, as yet little alleviated by the increase of physiological knowledge. Every college and professional school, and every seminary for young ladies, needs a medical man, not only to lecture on physiology and the laws of health, but empowered, in his official capacity, to investigate the case of every pupil, and, by authority, to restrain him to such a course of study, exercise, and repose, as his physical system requires. The Writer has found, by experience, that, in a large institution, there is one class of pupils who need to be restrained, by penalties, from late hours and excessive study, as much as another class need stimulus to industry.

A third cause of mental disease, is, the want of

the appropriate exercise of the various faculties of the mind. On this point, Dr. Combe remarks, " We have seen, that, by disuse, muscle becomes emaciated, bone softens, blood-vessels are obliterated, and nerves lose their characteristic structure. The brain is no exception to this general rule. Of it, also, the tone is impaired by permanent inactivity, and it becomes less fit to manifest the mental powers with readiness and energy." It is "the withdrawal of the stimulus necessary for its healthy exercise, which renders solitary confinement so severe a punishment, even to the most daring minds. It is a lower degree of the same cause, which renders continuous seclusion from society so injurious, to both mental and bodily health."

" *Inactivity of intellect and of feeling* is a very frequent predisposing cause of every form of nervous disease. For demonstrative evidence of this position, we have only to look at the numerous victims to be found among " persons " who have no call to exertion in gaining the means of subsistence, and no objects of interest on which to exercise their mental faculties, and who consequently sink into a state of mental sloth and nervous weakness." " If we look abroad upon society, we shall find innumerable examples of mental and nervous debility from this cause. When a person of some mental capacity is confined, for a long time, to an unvarying round of employment, which affords neither scope nor stimulus for one half of his faculties, and, from want of education or society, has no external resources ; his mental powers, for want of exercise," " become blunted, and his perceptions slow and dull." " The intellect and feelings, not being provided with interests external to themselves, must either become inactive and weak, or work upon themselves and become diseased."

" The most frequent victims of this kind of pre-

disposition, are females of the middle and higher
ranks, especially those of a nervous constitution, and
good natural abilities ; but who, from an ill-directed
education, possess nothing more solid than mere
accomplishments, and have no materials of thought,"
and no " occupation to excite interest or *demand* attention." " The liability of such persons to melancholy, hysteria, hypochondriasis, and other varieties
of mental distress, really depends on a state of irritability of brain, induced by imperfect exercise."

These remarks, of a medical man, illustrate the
principles before indicated ;—namely, that the demand of Christianity, that we live to promote the
general happiness, and not merely for selfish indulgence, has for its aim, not merely the general good,
but the highest happiness, of the individual of whom
it is required.

A person possessed of wealth, who has nothing
more noble to engage his attention, than seeking his
own personal enjoyment, subjects his mental powers
and moral feelings to a degree of inactivity, utterly
at war with health of mind. And the greater the
capacities, the greater are the sufferings which result
from this cause. Any one, who has read the misanthropic wailings of Lord Byron, has seen the necessary result of great and noble powers bereft of their
appropriate exercise, and, in consequence, becoming
sources of the keenest suffering.

It is this view of the subject, which has often
awakened feelings of sorrow and anxiety in the
mind of the Writer, while aiding in the developement and education of superior female minds, in the
wealthier circles. Not because there are not noble
objects for interest and effort, abundant, and within
reach of such minds; but because long-established
custom has made it seem so Quixotic, to the majority, even of the professed followers of Christ, for a
woman of wealth to practise any great self-denial,

that few have independence of mind and Christian principle sufficient to overcome such an influence. The more a mind has its powers developed, the more does it aspire and pine after some object worthy of its energies and affections; they are commonplace and phlegmatic characters, who are most free from such deep-seated wants. Many a young woman, of fine genius and elevated sentiment, finds a charm in Lord Byron's writings, because they present a glowing picture of what, to a certain extent, must be felt by every well-developed mind, which has no nobler object in life, than the pursuit of its own gratification.

If young ladies of wealth and standing could pursue their education under the full conviction that the increase of their powers and advantages increased their obligations to use all for the good of society, and with some plan of benevolent enterprise in view, what new motives of interest would be added to their daily pursuits! And what blessed results would follow to our beloved Country, if all well-educated females carried out the principles of Christianity in the exercise of their developed powers!

It is cheering to know that there are women, among the most intelligent and wealthy, who can be presented as examples of what may be done, when there is a heart to do. A pupil of the Writer is among this number, who, though a rich heiress, on the close of her school life immediately commenced a course of self-denying benevolence in the cause of education. She determined to secure a superior female institution in her native place, which should extend the benefits of the best education to all in that vicinity, at a moderate charge. Finding no teacher on the ground, prepared to take the lead, and though herself a timid and retiring character, she began, with the aid of the governess in her mother's family, a daily school, superintending all, and teaching six hours a day. The liberal-minded and intelligent mother cooperated, and the result is a flourishing female seminary, with a large and beautiful and well-furnished building ; the greater part of the means being supplied by the mother, and almost all by the members of that family connection. And both these ladies will testify, that no time or money, spent for any other object, has ever secured to them more real and abiding enjoyment, than witnessing the results of this successful and benevolent enterprise, which, for years to come, will pour forth blessings on society.

Another lady could be pointed out, who, possessing some property, went into a new western village, built and furnished her schoolhouse, and established herself there, to aid in raising a community from ignorance and gross worldliness, to intelligence and virtue. And in repeated instances, among the friends and pupils of the Writer, young ladies have left wealthy homes, and affectionate friends, to find nobler enjoyments in benevolent and active exertions to extend intelligence and virtue where such disinterested laborers were needed. In other cases, where it was not practicable to leave home, well-educated young ladies have interested themselves in common schools in the vicinity, aiding the teachers, by their sympathy, counsel, and personal assistance.

Other ladies, of property and standing, having families to educate, and being well qualified for such duties, have relinquished a large portion of domestic labor and superintendence, which humbler minds could be hired to perform, and received other less fortunate children, to share with their own these superior advantages. But, so long as the feeling widely exists, that the increase of God's bounties diminishes the obligations of self-denying service for the good of mankind, so long well-educated women, in easy circumstances, will shrink from such confinement and exertion.

It is believed, however, that there are many most benevolent and intelligent women in this Country, who would gladly engage in such enterprises, were there any appropriate way within their reach. And it is a question, well deserving consideration among those who guide the public mind in benevolent enterprises, whether some organization is not demanded, which shall bring the religious community to act systematically, in voluntary associations to extend a proper education to every child in this Nation, and to bring into activity all the female enterprise and benevolence now lying dormant, for want of proper facilities to exercise them. There are hundreds of villages, which need teachers, and that would support them, if they were on the spot, but which never will send for them. And there are hundreds of females, now unemployed, who would teach, if a proper place and home and support and escort were provided for them. And there needs to be some enlarged and systematic plan, conducted by wise and efficient men, to secure these objects.

Could such a plan as this be carried out, it is believed that many female minds, now suffering from diseases occasioned by want of appropriate objects for their energies, would be relieved. The duties of a teacher exercise every intellectual faculty, to its full extent; while, in this benevolent service, all the social, moral, and benevolent, emotions, are kept in full play. The happiest persons the Writer has ever known,—those who could say that they were as happy as they wished to be in this world, (and she has seen such,)—were persons engaged in this employment.

The indications of a diseased mind, owing to a want of the proper exercise of its powers, are apathy, discontent, a restless longing for excitement, a crav-

ing for unattainable good, a diseased and morbid
action of the imagination, dissatisfaction with the
world, and factitious interest in trifles which the
mind feels to be unworthy of its powers.   Such
minds sometimes seek alleviation in exciting amusements ; others resort to the grosser enjoyments of
sense.   Oppressed with the extremes of languor, or
over-excitement, or apathy, the body fails under the
wearing process, and adds new causes of suffering
to the mind.   It is to such that the compassionate
Saviour calls to his service in such appropriate terms,
"Come unto Me, all ye that labor and are heavy
laden, and I will give you rest.   Take my yoke
upon you, and learn of Me," "and ye shall find rest
unto your souls."

CHAPTER XVIII.

ON THE CARE OF DOMESTICS.

No Subject on which American Women need more Wisdom, Patience, Principle, and Self-control. Its Difficulties. Necessary
Evils. Miseries of Aristocratic Lands. Wisdom of Conforming
to Actual Circumstances. How to judge correctly respecting Domestics. They should be treated as we would expect to be under
similar Circumstances. When Labor is scarce, its Value is increased. Instability of Domestics ; how it may be remedied. Pride
and Insubordination ; how remedied. Abhorrence of Servitude a
National Trait of Character. Domestics easily convinced of the
Appropriateness of different Degrees of Subordination. Example.
Domestics may be easily induced to be respectful in their Deportment, and appropriate in their Dress. Deficiences of Qualifications
for the Performance of their Duties ; how remedied. Forewarning,
better than Chiding. Preventing, better than finding Fault. Faults
should be pointed out in a Kind Manner. Some Employers think it
their Office and Duty to find Fault. Domestics should be regarded
with Sympathy and Forbearance.

THERE is no point, where the women of this
Country need more wisdom, patience, principle, and

self-control, than in relation to those whom they employ in domestic service. The subject is attended with many difficulties, which powerfully influence the happiness of families; and the following suggestions are offered, to aid in securing right opinions and practice.

One consideration, which it would be well to bear in mind, on this subject, is, that a large portion of the peculiar trials, which American women suffer from this source, are the necessary evils connected with our most valuable civil blessings. Every blessing of this life involves some attendant liability to evil, from the same source; and, in this case, while we rejoice at a state of society which so much raises the condition and advantages of our sex, the evils involved should be regarded as more than repaid, by the compensating advantages. If we cannot secure the cringing, submissive, well-trained, servants of aristocratic lands, let us be consoled that we thus escape from the untold miseries and oppression which always attend that state of society.

Instead, then, of complaining that we cannot have our own peculiar advantages, and those of other nations, too; or imagining how much better off we should be, if things were different from what they are, it is much wiser and more Christianlike to strive cheerfully to conform to actual circumstances; and, after remedying all that we can control, patiently submit to what is beyond our power. If domestics are found to be incompetent, unstable, and unconformed to their station, it is Perfect Wisdom which appoints these trials, to teach us patience, fortitude, and self-control; and if the discipline is met in a proper spirit, it will prove a blessing, rather than an evil.

But, to judge correctly in regard to some of the evils involved in the state of domestic service, in this Country, we should endeavor to conceive ourselves placed in the situation of those, of whom complaint is made, that we may not expect, from them, any more than it would seem right should be exacted from us, in similar circumstances.

It is sometimes urged, against domestics, that they exact exorbitant wages. But what is the rule of rectitude, on this subject? Is it not the universal law, of labor and of trade, that an article is to be valued according to its scarcity and the demand? When wheat is scarce, the farmer raises his price; and when a mechanic offers services, difficult to be obtained, he has a corresponding increase of price. And why is it not right for domestics to act according to a rule allowed to be correct in reference to all other trades and professions? It is a fact, that really good domestic service must continue to increase in value, just in proportion as this Country waxes rich and prosperous; thus making the proportion of those, who wish to hire labor, relatively greater, and the number of those, willing to go to service, less.

Money enables the rich to gain many advantages, which those of more limited circumstances cannot secure; and one of these, is, securing good domestics, by offering high wages: and this, as the scarcity of this class increases, will serve constantly to raise the price of service. It is right for domestics to charge the market value, and this value is always decided by the scarcity of the article and the amount of demand. Right views of this subject, will sometimes serve to diminish hard feelings towards those, who would otherwise be wrongfully regarded as unreasonable and exacting.

Another complaint against domestics, is, that of instability and discontent, leading to perpetual change. But in reference to this, let a mother or daughter conceive of their own circumstances as so changed, that the daughter must go out to service. Suppose a place is engaged, and it is then found that she must sleep in a comfortless garret; and that, when a new domestic comes, perhaps a coarse and dirty foreigner, she must share her bed with her. Another place is offered, where she can have a comfortable room, and an agreeable room-mate : in such a case, would not both mother and daughter think it right to change ?

Or, suppose, on trial, it was found that the lady of the house was fretful, or exacting and hard to please ; or, that her children were so ungoverned, as to be perpetual vexations; or, that the work was so heavy that no time was allowed for relaxation and the care of a wardrobe ;—and another place offers, where these evils can be escaped : would not mother and daughter here think it right to change ? And is it not right for domestics, as well as their employers, to seek places where they can be most comfortable ?

In some cases, this instability and love of change would be remedied, if employers would take more pains to make a residence with them agreeable ; and to attach domestics to the family, by feelings of gratitude and affection. There are ladies, even where such domestics are most rare, who seldom find any trouble in keeping good and steady ones. And the reason is, that their domestics know they cannot better their condition, by any change within reach. It is not merely by giving them comfortable rooms, and good food, and presents, and privileges, that the attachment of domestics is secured ; it is by the manifestation of a friendly and benevolent interest in their comfort and improvement. This is exhibited, in bearing patiently with their faults ; in kindly teaching them how to improve; in showing them how to make and take proper care of their clothes; in guarding their health ; in teaching them to read, if necessary, and supplying them with proper books ; and, in short, by endeavoring, so far as may be, to supply the place of a parent. It is seldom that such a course would not secure steady service, and such affection and gratitude, that even higher wages would not tempt them away. There would probably be some cases of ungrateful returns; but there is no doubt that the course indicated, if generally pursued, would very much lessen the evil in question.

Another subject of complaint, in regard to domestics, is, their pride, insubordination, and a spirit not conformed to their condition. They are not willing to be called *servants;* in some places, they claim a seat, at meals, with the family; they imitate a style of dress unbecoming their condition; and their manners and address are rude and disrespectful. That these evils are very common, among this class of persons, cannot be denied; the only question is, how can they best be met and remedied.

In regard to the common feeling among domestics, which is pained and offended by being called "servants," there is need of some consideration and allowance. It should be remembered, that, in this Country, children, from their earliest years, are trained to abhor servitude, in reference to themselves, as the greatest of all possible shame and degradation. They are perpetually hearing orations, songs, and compositions of all sorts, which set forth the honor and dignity of freemen, and heap scorn and contempt on all who would be so mean as to be slaves. Now the term servant, and the duties it involves, are, in the minds of many persons, nearly the same as those of the slave. And there are few minds, entirely free from associations which make servitude a degradation. It is not always pride, then, which makes this term so offensive. It is a consequence of that noble and generous spirit of freedom, which every American draws from his mother's breast, and which ought to be respected, rather than despised. In order to be respected by others, we must respect ourselves; and sometimes the ruder classes of society make claims, deemed forward and offensive, when, with their views, such a position seems indispensable to preserve a proper self-respect.

Where an excessive sensibility on this subject exists, and forward and disrespectful manners result from it, the best remedy is, a kind attempt to give correct views, such as better-educated minds are best able to attain. It should be shown to them, that, in this Country, labor has ceased to be degrading, in any class; that, in all classes, different grades of subordination must exist; and that it is no more degrading for a domestic to regard the heads of a family as superiors in station, and treat them with becoming respect, than it is for children to do the same, or for men to treat their rulers with respect and deference. They should be taught, that domestics use a different entrance to the house, and sit at a distinct table, not because they are inferior beings, but because this is the best method of securing neatness and order and convenience. They can be shown, if it is attempted in a proper spirit and manner, that these very regulations really tend to their own ease and comfort, as well as to that of the family.

The Writer has known cases, where the lady of the family, for the sake of convincing her domestic of the truth of these views, allowed her to follow her own notions, for a short time, and join the family at meals. It was merely required, as a condition, that she should always dress her hair as the other ladies did, and appear in a clean dress, and abide by all the rules of propriety at table, which the rest were required to practise, and which were duly detailed. The experiment was tried, two or three times; and, although the domestic was treated with studious politeness and kindness, she soon felt that she should be much more comfortable in the kitchen, where she could talk, eat, and dress, as she pleased.

A reasonable person can also be made to feel the propriety of allowing a family opportunity to talk freely of their private affairs, when they meet at meals, as they never could do, if restrained by the constant presence of a stranger. Such views, presented in a kind and considerate manner, will often entirely change the views of a domestic who is sensitive on such subjects.

When a domestic is forward and bold in manners, and disrespectful in address, a similar course can be pursued. It can be shown, that those, who are among the best-bred and genteel, have courteous and respectful manners and language to all they meet, while many, who have wealth, are regarded as vulgar, because they exhibit rude and disrespectful manners. The very term, *gentle*man, indicates the refinement and delicacy of address, which distinguishes the high-bred from the coarse and vulgar.

In regard to appropriate dress, in most cases it is difficult for an employer to interfere *directly* with comments or advice. The most successful mode, is, to offer some service in mending or making a wardrobe, and when a confidence in the kindness of feeling is thus gained, remarks and suggestions will generally be properly received, and new views of propriety and economy can be imparted. In some cases, it may be well for an employer,—who, from appearances, anticipates difficulty of this kind,—in making the agreement, to state that she wishes to have the room, person, and dress of her domestics kept neat, and in order, and that she expects to remind them of their duty, in this particular, if it is neglected. Domestics are very apt to neglect the care of their own chambers and clothing ; and such habits have a most pernicious influence on their wellbeing, and on that of their children in future domestic life. An employer, then, is bound to exercise a parental care over them, in these respects.

In regard to the great deficiencies of domestics, in qualifications for their duties, much patience and benevolence are required. Multitudes have never been taught to do their work properly; and, in such cases, how unreasonable it would be to expect it of them! Most persons, of this class, depend for their knowledge, in domestic affairs, not on their parents, who usually are not qualified to instruct them, but on their employers; and if they live in a family where nothing is done neatly and properly, they have no chance to learn how to perform their duties well. When a lady finds that she must employ a domestic who is ignorant, awkward, and careless, her first effort should be, to make all proper allowance for past want of instruction, and the next, to remedy the evil, by kind and patient teaching. In doing this, it should ever be borne in mind, that nothing is more difficult, than to change old habits, and to learn to be thoughtful and considerate. And a woman must make up her mind to tell the same thing "over and over again," and yet not lose her patience. It will often save much vexation, if, on the arrival of a new domestic, the mistress of the family, or a daughter, for two or three days, will go round with the novice, and show the exact manner in which it is expected the work will be done. And this, also, it may be well to specify in the agreement, as some domestics would otherwise resent such a supervision.

But it is often remarked, that, after a woman has taken all this pains to instruct a domestic, and make her a good one, some other person will offer higher wages, and she will leave. This, doubtless, is a sore trial; but still, if such efforts were made in the true spirit of benevolence, the lady will still have her reward, in the consciousness that she has contributed to the welfare of society, by making one more good domestic, and one more comfortable family where that domestic is employed; and if the latter becomes the mother of a family, a whole circle of children share in the benefit.

There is one great mistake, not unfrequently made, in the management both of domestics and of children; and that is, in supposing that the way to cure defects, is by finding fault as each failing occurs. But, instead of this being true, in many cases the directly opposite course is the best; while, in all instances, much good judgement is required, in order to decide when to notice faults, and when to let them pass unnoticed. There are some minds, very sensitive, easily discouraged, and infirm of purpose. Such persons, when they have formed habits of negligence, haste, and awkwardness, often need expressions of sympathy and encouragement, rather than reproof. They usually have been found fault with, so much, that they have become either hardened or desponding; and it is often the case, that a few words of commendation will awaken fresh efforts and renewed hope. In almost every case, words of kindness, hope, and encouragement, should be mingled with the needful admonitions or reproof.

It is a good rule, in reference to this point, to *forewarn*, instead of finding fault. Thus, when a thing has been done wrong, let it pass unnoticed, till it is to be done again; and then, a simple request, to have it done in the right way, will secure quite as much, and probably more, willing effort, than a reproof administered for neglect. Some persons seem to take it for granted, that young and inexperienced minds are bound to have all the forethought and discretion of mature persons; and freely express wonder and disgust, when mishaps occur for want of these traits. But it would be far better to save from mistake or forgetfulness, by previous caution and care on the part of those who have gained experience and forethought; and thus many occasions of complaint and ill humor will be avoided.

Grown persons, who fill the places of heads of families, are very apt to forget how painful it is to be chided for neglect of duty, or for faults of character. If they would sometimes, in imagination, put themselves in the place of those whom they control, and conceive of some person as daily administering reproof to them, and pointing out their faults, in the same tone and style as they employ to those under their control, it might serve as a useful check. It is often the case, that persons, who are most strict and exacting, and least able to make allowances and receive palliations, are themselves peculiarly sensitive to any thing which implies that they are in fault. By such, the spirit implied in the Divine petition, "forgive us our trespasses as we forgive those who trespass against us," especially needs to be cherished.

One other consideration is very important. There is no duty, more binding on Christians, than that of patience and meekness under provocations and disappointment. Now the tendency of every sensitive mind, when thwarted in its wishes, is to complain and find fault, and often in tones of fretfulness or anger. But there are few domestics, who have not heard enough of the Bible, to know that angry or fretful fault-finding, from the mistress of a family, when her work is not done to suit her, is not in agreement with the precepts of Christ. They notice and feel the inconsistency; and every woman, when she gives way to feelings of anger and impatience at the faults of those around her, lowers herself in their respect, while her own conscience, unless very much blinded, cannot but suffer a wound.

There are some women, who, in the main, are amiable, who seem to feel that it is their office and duty to find fault with their domestics, whenever any thing is not exactly right, and follow their fancied calling without the least appearance of ten-

derness or sympathy, as if the objects of their discipline were stocks or stones, without human feelings.
The writer once heard a domestic, describing her
situation in a family which she had left, make this
remark of her past employer: "She was a very
good housekeeper, allowed good wages, and gave
us many privileges and presents; but if we ever did
any thing wrong, she always *talked to us just as if
she thought we had no feelings,* and I never was so
unhappy in my life as while living with her." And
this was said of a kind-hearted and conscientious
woman, by a very reasonable and amiable domestic.

Every woman, who has the care of domestics,
should cultivate a habit of regarding them with that
sympathy and forbearance, which she would wish
for herself or her daughters, if deprived of parents,
fortune, and home. The fewer advantages they
have enjoyed, and the greater difficulties of temper
or of habit they have to contend with, the more
claims they have on compassionate forbearance.
They ought ever to be looked upon, not as the mere
ministers to our comfort and convenience, but as the
humbler and more neglected children of our Heavenly Father, whom he has sent to claim our sympathy
and aid.*

* The excellent little work of Miss Sedgwick, entitled, ' Live, and
Let Live,' contains many valuable and useful hints, conveyed in a
most pleasing narrative form, which every housekeeper would do
well to read. And her ' Means and Ends,' forming the third volume
of the Juvenile Series of ' THE SCHOOL LIBRARY ' issued by the Publishers of this Volume, is equally worthy of notice.

CHAPTER XIX.

ON THE CARE OF INFANTS.

Necessity of a Knowledge of this Subject, to every Young Lady. Examples. Extracts from Dr. Combe. Half the Deaths of Infants owing to Mismanagement, and Errors in Diet. Errors of Parents and Nurses. Eating regarded as a Sovereign Panacea. Other Common Mistakes. Animal Food. Remark of Dr. Clark. Opinion of other Medical Men. Many Popular Notions relating to Animal Food for Children, erroneous. It does not contain so much Nourishment as Vegetable Food. The Formation of the Human Teeth and Stomach do not indicate that Man was designed to live on Flesh. Opinions of Linnæus, Cuvier, Thomas Bell, Professor Lawrence, Sir John Sinclair. Examples of Men who lived to a great age. Albany Orphan Asylum. Animal Diet not necessary in Cold Climates. Russia. Siberia. Scarcity of Wheat, during William Pitt's Administration. Beneficial Effects of using unbolted Flour. Dr. Franklin's Testimony. Sir Isaac Newton and others. Extracts from Dr. Combe and Dr. Bell. Empiricism and Quackery. Necessity of Fresh Air. Bathing. Cholera Infantum not cured by Nostrums. Fashionable Dress injurious. Milk sometimes injured by the Food of the Cow. Rules for Management of Children at Weaning.

EVERY young lady ought to learn how to take proper care of an infant; for, even if she never becomes the responsible nurse in the care of one, she will always be mingling with those who have: and such knowledge and experience will often be of great value, in enabling her to render benevolent aid to others.

To illustrate this, a case will be mentioned, which fell under the notice of the Writer. An inexperienced young mother was travelling with her infant, in a steamboat, without any attendant to aid her. For want of proper care, the infant became restless and sick, while its cries annoyed the mother and the passengers. To prevent this, she was constantly administering doses of paregoric; but this finally failed to quiet the child. At last, the mother lost all patience and energy; and seemed to fall into a

sort of stupor of indifference and weariness. A young
lady on board, who had been instructed in the care of
infants, at this point volunteered to take charge of the
child, if the mother would give it up entirely to her
discretion. The offer was accepted; and the young
lady then proceeded to cleanse the head and skin of
the little sufferer, which were in a shocking state,
from long neglect. She put on dry and warm
clothing, and prepared suitable medicine and food.
The child was speedily quieted and restored, by this
judicious management, and the young nurse was
more than repaid, by the smiles of the little sufferer,
and the gratitude of the mother and the other
voyagers.

In another instance, while visiting in one of the
newest western States, the Writer had occasion to
realize the importance of knowledge, and experience
in these matters, to young mothers. A lady in the
neighborhood became the mother of her firstborn;
and, though in a town containing fifteen hundred
inhabitants, there was not, so far as was known, in
the place, a nurse, for such emergencies, and the
service was performed by the ladies of the neighborhood. With no attendant, but an inexperienced
young husband, and with no domestic, but a girl of
twelve, all the care of an infant, and all the responsibility of directing about its management, came
upon the mother, in this anxious and feeble state.
What mother can be sure that her daughter is not
destined to meet similar trials and anxieties?

The following extracts from Dr. Combe's Physiology of Digestion,* contain information with which
every woman should be familiar.

"Those whose opportunities of observation have
been extensive, will agree with me in opinion, that
nearly one half of the deaths occurring during the

---

* Issued by the Publishers of this Work.

first two years of existence, are ascribable to mismanagement, and to errors in diet. At birth, the
stomach is feeble, and as yet unaccustomed to food.
Its cravings are consequently easily satisfied, and
frequently renewed." "At that early age, there
ought to be no fixed time for giving nourishment.
The stomach cannot be thus satisfied. In one child,
digestion may be slow, and the interval be consequently too short; in another, it may be quick, and
the interval too long. But the active call of the
infant is a sign, which needs never be mistaken,
and none else ought to be listened to.

"Many mothers consider every expression of uneasiness as an indication of appetite," and offer it
food, "although ten minutes may not have elapsed
since its preceding repast. Nothing can be more
injurious than this custom. It overloads and op-
presses the stomach; excites griping and bowel
complaints, restlessness, and fever; and not unfrequently leads to fatal diseases in the brain."

"It is astonishing, indeed, with what exclusive-
ness of understanding *eating* is regarded, even by
intelligent parents, as the grand *solatium*, or *panacea*
for all the pains and troubles which afflict the young."
"Because the mouth is open, when the child is
crying," "parents jump to the conclusion, that it is
open for the purpose of being filled." "Let appetite, then, be the only rule;" "and do not attempt
to provoke it." "The lower animals instinctively
avoid this error," and "rather allow themselves to
be strongly solicited, before yielding to the wishes
of their young." "When the system has become
more developed, and the stomach accustomed to the
exercise of its functions, regularity in the distribution
of its meals may be gradually and beneficially introduced."

"Through pure ignorance, and mistaken kindness,
many nurses, imagining themselves wiser than Na-

ture, and conceiving that the newly-born infant must of necessity be starving," "hasten to fill its stomach." "Not unfrequently severe indigestion is thus induced." "At birth" "the stomach and bowels, never having been used," "contain a quantity of mucous secretion," "which requires to be removed." "To effect this object, Nature has rendered the first portions of the mother's milk purposely watery and laxative; and, on the part of the infant, nothing further is required, than to allow it to follow its natural instinct." "Nurses, however, distrusting Nature, often hasten to administer castor oil, or some other active purgative;" and the consequence is, "irritation in the stomach and bowels, which is not always easily subdued." "In early infancy, when no teeth exist," milk is "the only food intended by Nature." If "the mother's milk is scanty," "cow's milk, diluted with one third of water, and slightly sweetened" may be given. This is "more suitable than any preparation of milk and flour or arrow-root."

"It is a common mistake, to suppose, that, because a woman is nursing, she ought to live very fully, and to add an allowance of wine, porter, or other fermented liquor, to her usual diet. The only result of this plan, is, to cause an unnatural degree of fulness in the system, which places the nurse on the brink of disease," and retards, rather than increases, the food of the infant. "More will be gained by the observance of the ordinary laws of health, on the part of the nurse, than by any foolish deviation, founded on ignorance." "After a child has been weaned, panado, gruel, thin arrow-root, tapioca, sago, rusk, or crust of bread," fruit, "fresh milk and water and sugar," may be given.

On the subject of giving animal food to young children, the following opinion of Dr. Clark, Physician in Ordinary to the Queen of England, expresses the views of most of the celebrated physicians.

" There is no greater error in the management of children, than that of giving them animal diet very early." " By persevering in the use of an over-stimulating diet, the digestive organs become irritated, and the various secretions, immediately connected with, and necessary to, digestion, are diminished, especially the *biliary secretion ;*" and " constipation of the bowels, and congestion of the abdominal circulation succeed." " Children so fed, become, moreover, very liable to attacks of fever and of inflammation, affecting, particularly, the mucous membranes ; and measles, and the other diseases incident to childhood, are generally severe in their attack."

In reference to this last remark, a distinguished medical gentleman mentioned to the Writer, that, in families where children lived on simple diet, without tea and coffee, if they were seized with measles, whooping cough, mumps, and similar diseases, he never called but once, as he knew there was no danger ; but that in families where an opposite course was pursued, he always expected trouble.

In regard to the importance of giving animal food to children, at all, there are many popular notions, which are very incorrect. Many seem to think that animal food is more nourishing than vegetable, and, when a child is weak and thin, will for this reason give it meat. This is an entire mistake. Experiments, repeatedly made by chemists, prove the contrary ; and tables are made out, showing the relative amount of nourishment in each kind of food. From these tables, it appears, that, while beef contains thirty-five per cent. of nutritious matter, rice and wheat contain from eighty to ninety-five per cent. One pound of rice, then, contains as much nourishment as two pounds and a half of beef. The reason why meat has been supposed to be more nourishing, is that, on account of its stimulating property, the stomach works faster, and digests it quicker; while the withdrawal of a meat diet produces a temporary loss of strength, just as the withdrawal of other stimulants are followed by consequent languor.

Another mistake, is, the common supposition, that the formation of the human teeth and stomach indicate that man was designed to feed on flesh. But this is contrary to the testimony of all the most distinguished naturalists. Linnæus says, that the organization of man, when compared with other animals, shows, that "fruits and esculent vegetables constitute his most suitable food." Baron Cuvier, the highest authority on comparative anatomy, says, "the natural food of man, judging from his structure, appears to consist of fruits, roots, and other succulent parts of vegetables."

Mr. Thomas Bell, Lecturer in Guy's Hospital, in a work on the natural and proper food for man, as deducible from the construction of his teeth and stomach, says, "*every* fact, connected with human organization, goes to prove, that man was originally formed a frugivorous animal;" and, "if analogy be allowed to have any weight," "those animals, whose teeth and digestive apparatus most nearly resemble our own, namely, the apes and monkeys, are undoubtedly frugivorous."

Another common mistake, is, that the stimulus of animal food is necessary for the full developement of the physical and intellectual powers. On this subject, Professor Lawrence, a distinguished writer, says, "that animal food renders man strong and courageous, is fully disproved, by the inhabitants of Lapland, Kamschatka, and Patagonia, who, living solely on animal food, are among the smallest, weakest, and most timid of races." On the contrary, the Scotch Highlanders, who, in a very cold latitude, live, most of them, exclusively on vegetable diet, are among the stoutest, largest, and most athletic of men. The South-Sea Islanders, in a tropical clime, feed almost exclusively on fruits and vegetables; and yet it is testified, that "the stoutest and most expert English sailors had no chance with them in wrestling and boxing." In Africa, the stoutest and largest races live exclusively on vegetables; and the bright and active Arabs live entirely on milk and vegetables.

The greatest portion of those, who have lived to a remarkable and robust old age, have been persons of abstemious habits, whose diet was almost exclusively vegetables. Sir John Sinclair, an eminent British surgeon, says, "I have wandered a good deal about the world; my health has been tried in all ways; and, by the aid of temperance and hard work, I have worn out two armies, in two wars, and probably could wear out another." "I eat no animal food, drink no wine," "or spirits of any kind." Henry Jenkins lived to the age of one hundred and sixty-nine years, on a low coarse simple diet. Thomas Parr died at the age of one hundred and fifty-two years, and his diet was coarse bread, milk, cheese, whey, and small beer. The early Christians, who fled to the deserts to escape persecution, lived exclusively on vegetables, to a great age. James the Hermit lived to the age of one hundred and four years, Arsenius to one hundred and twenty, St. Epiphanius to one hundred and fifty, and Romaldus to one hundred and twenty. It is stated, too, as a wellknown and undisputed fact, that the pulse of a hardy, robust man, who lives on simple vegetable diet, is from ten to thirty beats less in a minute than that of men who live on a mixed diet. The teeth, also, of those nations who live on such simple diet, are white and enduring, and extreme contrasts to those of people who live on more stimulating food.

The result of the treatment of young children in the

Orphan Asylum, at Albany, New York, is one upon which all who have the care of young children, should deeply ponder. This institution was established in 1829–1830 ; and, during the six succeeding years, its average number of children was eighty. For the first three years, their diet was meat once a day, fine bread, rice, Indian puddings, vegetables, fruits, and milk. Considerable attention was given to clothing, fresh air, and exercise ; and they were bathed once in three weeks. During these three years, from four to six children were continually on the sick list, and sometimes more ; one or two assistant nurses were necessary ; a physician was called two or three times a week ; and in this time there were between thirty and forty deaths. At the end of this time, the management was changed, in these respects. Daily ablutions of the whole body were practised ; bread of unbolted flour was substituted for that of fine wheat; and all animal food was banished. More attention was also paid to clothing, bedding, fresh air, and exercise. The result was, that the nursery was vacated, the nurse and physician no longer needed, and for two years not a single case of sickness or death occurred. The third year, also, there were no deaths, except those of two idiots, and one other child, all of whom were new inmates, who had not been subjected to this treatment. Their teachers also testified that there was a very manifest increase of intellectual vigor and activity, while there was much less irritability of temper.

Many persons suppose, that meat diet is more needful in a cold than in a warm climate ; but in some of the coldest portions of Russia, a hardy and vigorous peasantry subsist wholly on vegetable diet ; and a very intelligent gentleman, who spent many months in Siberia, testifies, that no exiles endure the climate better than those, who have all their lives been accustomed to a simple vegetable diet.

There is another fact, in relation to coarse bread, worthy of notice. Under the administration of William Pitt, for two years or more, there was such a scarcity of wheat, that Parliament passed a law, that, to make it hold out longer, the army should have all their bread made of unbolted flour. The result was, that the health of the soldiers improved so much, as to be a subject of surprise to themselves, the officers, and the physicians. These last came out publicly, and declared, that the soldiers never before were so robust and healthy; and that disease had nearly disappeared from the army. The civic physicians joined and pronounced it the healthiest bread; and, for a time, schools, families, and public institutions, used it almost exclusively. Even the nobility, convinced by these facts, adopted it for their common diet; and the fashion continued a long time after the scarcity ceased, until more luxurious habits resumed their sway.

In regard to the intellect, Dr. Franklin asserted, from his own experience, that an exclusive vegetable diet "promotes clearness of ideas and quickness of perception; and is to be preferred by all who labor with the mind." The mightiest efforts of Sir Isaac Newton were performed while he was nourished only by bread and water; and many others, of the greatest genius and intellect, carried on their intellectual labors, sustained only by this simple diet. These facts, to say the least, prove that animal food is not necessary either to the physical or intellectual perfection of our race.

The following extracts from a late Treatise by Dr. Combe, relate to other topics of infant management.

"Of all the defects which a nurse can have, none is more directly destructive of infant life, than that in which many mothers, as well as nurses, indulge, of administering, of their own accord, strong and dangerous medicines to children."' "It appears, from a late return, printed by order of the House of Commons, of all inquests held in England and Wales, in 1837 and 1838, in cases of death from poison, that" "nearly *one seventh of the whole* number resulted from the carelessness of mothers and nurses, in administering medicines, with the properties of which they were not acquainted, in doses far beyond those in which they are ever prescribed by medical men." For example, in one year, fifty-two infants were killed by giving preparations containing opium, and twenty were destroyed by other powerful agents. The Coroner of Nottingham reported, that great numbers in that borough were destroyed, every year, by taking Godfrey's Cordial; but he remarks, "as they die off gradually," they do not come into his report, as coroner.

"In addition to cases of absolute poisoning, of the above description, it is well known to practitioners, that much havoc is made among infants, by the abuse of calomel and other medicines, which procure momentary relief, but end by producing incurable disease; and it has often excited my astonishment, to see how recklessly remedies of this kind are had recourse to, on the most trifling occasions, by mothers and nurses, who would be horrified, if they knew the nature of the power they are wielding, and the extent of injury they are inflicting. Whenever a child shows any symptom of uneasiness, instead of inquiring whether it may not have been caused by some error of regimen, which only requires to be avoided in future, to remove the suffering, many mothers act as if it were indispensably necessary to interfere immediately and forcibly with the operations of Nature, by giving some powerful medicine to counteract its effects; and if relief does not ensue, within an hour or two, the dose must be repeated. In this way, it is not uncommon for a medical man to be sent for, in alarm, and told, that the child began to complain at such a time; that, *notwithstanding* that a large dose of calomel, or laudanum, or tincture of rhubarb, was immediately given, and repeated every hour or two, it is still very ill, or becoming hourly worse; and that, if he cannot *do something*, instantly, it will soon be beyond recovery. Whereas, it may appear, on examination, that there was, at first, only a slight indisposition, which required no active treatment, at all, and that the urgent symptoms are those caused solely by the intended remedies.

"That there are cases of diseases, in which very active means must be promptly used, to save the child, is perfectly true. But it is not less certain, that these are cases, of which no mother or nurse ought to attempt the treatment. As a general rule, indeed, where the child is well managed, medicine, of any kind, is very rarely required; and if disease were more generally regarded in its true light, not as a something thrust into the system, which requires to be expelled by force, but as an aberration from a natural mode of action, produced by some external cause, we should be in less haste to attack it by medicine, and more watchful, and therefore more successful, in our management, and in its prevention. Accordingly, where a constant demand for medicine exists in a nursery, the mother may rest assured, that there is something essentially wrong in the treatment of her children."

Dr. Combe further remarks, "All women are not destined, in the course of Nature, to become mothers; but how very small is the number of those, who are unconnected, by family ties, friendship, or sympathy, with the children of others! How very few are there, who, at some time or other of their lives,

would not find their usefulness and happiness increased, by the possession of a kind of knowledge
so intimately allied to their best feelings and affections! And how important is it, to the mother herself, that her efforts should be seconded by intelligent, instead of ignorant, assistants!" "In all
points of view, *every* right-minded woman has an
interest" "in removing the ignorance, in which this
subject has been involved," from her own mind, and
the minds of others.

"It may, indeed, be alleged, that mothers require
no knowledge of the laws of the infant constitution,
or of the principles of infant management, because
medical aid is always at hand, to correct their errors." But "professional men are rarely consulted,
till the evil is done, and health is broken ; and even
if they were, it requires intelligence and information
in the mother," properly to obey their directions.
Dr. Bell remarks, "Physicians would confer an essential service on the community, if they were to
take more pains to divert the curiosity of their pa-
tients and invalids from medical matters to questions
relating to the health and vigor of the functions of
the organs, and to the means of avoiding disease."

The Writer, in reference to the above remark,
would inquire, whether the prevalence of empiricism, and of quack medicines, would not be most
effectually stopped, by giving the common people,
in all possible ways, a knowledge of the wonderful
and delicate construction of the several organs of
life, and of the causes which operate to produce their
diseased action? Such views would instantly convince any mind of common sense, that ignorant men
cannot be qualified to administer medicine ; and that
medical drugs, given without a knowledge of their
nature, must, in a vast majority of cases, produce
and increase disease, instead of curing it.

Dr. Combe further remarks, "I have seen" "a

nursery," that was "like a paradise on earth, compared to one under the more ordinary guidance. In one of the latter kind, I lately saw a strong, and naturally healthy, infant, literally gasping for breath, and in a state bordering on convulsions, from extreme anxiety on the part of the parent, to exclude every breath of air, from a nursery overheated by a large fire, as a precaution against cold, which she supposed to have been the chief cause of the death of a former child." "When I insisted on the admission of fresh air," "she remonstrated, with all the earnestness of the most tender affection. With difficulty I carried the point, and remained to prevent the too speedy termination of the experiment. In a few minutes, the uneasy twitching and contortion of the features ceased; and, in a quarter of an hour, a smile of contentment and cheerfulness took their place, and encouraged the mother to allow the continued entrance of some small portion of the air." "The child took no cold, and required only fresh air, moderate diet, and exercise, to restore it to perfect health."

Dr. Bell observes, "the necessity of a continued supply of fresh air is manifested, in the construction of some of the rooms in many houses. These rooms have no fireplaces, and consequently, during night, if they are used for sleeping in, the doors and windows being shut, there is no channel, either for the introduction of air from the atmosphere without, or for the escape of the impure air, within, which latter is made in the processes of breathing and exhalation from the lungs and skin." "The sufferings of" children of feeble constitutions, and of invalids, "are increased, beyond measure, by such lodgings as these. *An action, brought by the Commonwealth,* ought to lie against those persons, who build houses for sale or rent, in which rooms are so constructed as not to allow of free ventilation; and *a writ of lunacy* taken out against those, who, with the knowledge of the common elements of natural philosophy, or, indeed, with the common-sense experience which all have on this head, should spend any portion of their time, still more, should sleep, in rooms thus nearly air-tight."

" Parents," in cities, " who are desirous that their children should avoid bowel complaints, under various names, must contrive to change the air which their children breathe, by taking them into the country." " The indispensable condition, in a vast number of cases, for the avoidance of disease, as well as for its cure, is the access of fresh and somewhat cooler air, both to the lungs and skin." This, also, is a condition " for restoration from the irritation, and feebleness, and fever, which harass so often in the Summer months, a child during the process of teething." Those who cannot go into the country, should " so manage, that their children shall enjoy, early in the morning, the air of some of the public squares of a city," or " the still fresher air on the water," in some ferry or steamboat. The money spent in giving a child fresh and cool air, every day, is well laid out ; and " these little excursions will be much cheaper, than the cost of medicine, to say nothing of professional attendance, and the necessary interruption of the domestic and other duties of the mother." " It is desirable to allow the free access of the outer air, during the night, to bed-rooms," in hot weather. " If the inmates do not gain a cooler, they at any rate breathe a fresher, a more elastic, air, and suffer less." The bed " should always be a mattrass, and a hard feather or hair pillow. A child, tossing about, in feverish heat, in a featherbed, or buried under a load of clothes, will often be revived, at once, and restored to sound and refreshing sleep, by putting it on a folded sheet, which again rests simply on a piece of matting or floor-cloth, and by throwing a light coverlet or sheet over it."

"Another, and a valuable resource, is afforded to all classes, in the use of a bath. Water, and a wash-tub, are the only conditions required for this purpose." In cases of delicacy of constitution, "it is proper to raise a little the temperature of the water for the bath, so as to render it tepid, or slightly warm." "After the morning bath, the child is better able to bear, without suffering, the great heat and close air of its lodging, should it unhappily be thus restricted. Friction, assiduously practised, on the whole skin, especially along the spine, and on the abdomen, and chest, and lower limbs, ought to follow the bath." "When the stomach is peculiarly irritable," (from teething,) "it is of paramount necessity and duty to withhold all the nostrums, which have been so boast-ingly and so falsely lauded "as sovereign cures for *cholera infantum.*" "The true restoratives to a child threatened with disease, at this season, are, cool air, cool bathing, and cool drinks of simple water, in addition to its proper food, taken at stated intervals." As cool weather approaches, the cloth-ing must "be of a thicker substance and warmer texture : the feet particularly will require protection against sudden changes of temperature, as well as against moisture."

"Dr. Eberle," says Dr. Combe, "has very properly called attention to a glaring inconsistency in infant clothing, which ought to be immediately reme-died, and which consists in leaving the neck, shoul-ders, and arms, quite bare, while the rest of the body is kept abundantly warm." "'It has been supposed,' he says, 'that this custom is one of the principal reasons why inflammatory affections of the respiratory organs are so much more common during the period of childhood, than at a more advanced age.'" On this, Dr. Bell remarks, "Many are, we fear, influenced to this," "by a desire to imitate others," and by "a love of exposing their beautiful breasts and round arms." But what "has fashion to do with children, or they with fashion? It is enough for mothers and grown daughters to be the victims to fashion, as when they parade with bare shoulders and. tightly-corsetted waists, and paper-soled shoes, without inflicting punishment on young beings, who, insensible to admiration," "find no compensation for their sufferings in gratified vanity."

"The head," says Dr. Combe, "is commonly kept too warm, in infancy;" but Dr. Bell says, "a better practice is now getting into fashion. It is for the infant not to wear caps, at all." "Colds," continues Dr. Combe, are often induced by "the infant being laid to sleep with the head immersed in a very soft warm pillow." "This plan has the double disadvantage of" having one part of the head overheated, and the other entirely uncovered. "When the head is kept very warm, the nervous excitability is greatly increased, so that every change makes an impression on the infant, and any accidental irritation is more likely to be followed by spasmodic or convulsive fits."

The preceding general views of medical writers, furnish the ground for several more minute directions. An infant should be washed all over, every morning, with warm water, and, in cool weather, in a warm room. The head should be thoroughly washed, and brushed clean with a soft brush. If, by neglect, a covering of dirt forms at the roots of the hair, the yolk of an egg, rubbed in and combed out while damp, will remove it without trouble. After washing, fine starch should be sprinkled, from a muslin bag, in creases of fat, under the knees and in the groins.

A wrapper, high in the neck, with long sleeves, put on over the frock, and left open in front, is now very fashionable. This is to cover the neck and arms. It is safest to fasten the clothing of infants with strings and buttons. Woollen socks should be kept on the feet. In sleep, the child's head should be uncovered, and its eyes shaded. An infant should not sleep on its mother's arm, as it will be kept too warm, and from the fresh air. It should be daily carried or drawn in a wagon, in the fresh air; but great pains should be taken, to protect the eyes from too much light. Blindness is very common, among children, in countries where mothers labor in the open air, on account of want of care in this respect.

When an infant lives on cow's milk, if it is sick, inquiry should be made respecting the cow, and its food; as the health of the animal, and the nature of its food, very much affects the child. In cities, cows fed on still slops never give healthy milk; and city cows are very apt to be diseased, from want of proper food and care. The milk of a new-milch cow is best for an infant, as other milk is too old.

In changing the food of children, at weaning, the following are safe and important rules.

Do not give any stimulating food or drinks, such as tea, coffee, spices, pepper, mustard, and the like; and the less animal food given, the better. The Writer knows a family of eleven children, all but one born with robust constitutions, and reared in the country, through early childhood, in fine health. But they were allowed to eat meat, twice a day, with butter and gravy; and every one, in afterlife, suffered severely, either from chronic cutaneous eruptions, or from dyspepsy, or from liver complaints, or from excessive nervous excitability. Not one escaped.

Always give a large supply of fruit, or some coarse vegetable food, such as bread of unbolted flour, potatoes, and the like, to keep up a regular daily action of the bowels, by a due admixture of innutritious matter with that which is more nourishing.

Avoid highly-concentrated nourishment, unmixed, such as sugar, sweetmeats, gellies, candy, and the like. Such are healthy only when eaten with a large mixture of other food.

Do not give either food or drinks at a temperature exceeding blood heat.

Give food at regular hours, and do not provoke the appetite by a variety.

When a child seems ill, first try the effect of fasting and free perspiration, that the system may rest and throw off the evil probably resulting from too much, or from improper food. If this does not succeed, apply to a physician.

Avoid giving to children, fat, or any cooking combined with grease, as it tends to weaken the powers of digestion, and to affect injuriously the biliary secretions.

CHAPTER XX.

ON THE MANAGEMENT OF YOUNG CHILDREN.

Submission to the Will of Superiors, Self-denial, and Benevolence, the three most important Habits to be formed in Early Life. Extremes to be guarded against. Medium Course. Adults sometimes forget the Value which Children set on Trifles. Example. Impossible to govern Children, properly, without appreciating the Value they attach to their Pursuits and Enjoyments. Those who govern Children should join in their Sports. This the best way to gain their Confidence and Affection. But Older Persons should never lose the Attitude of Superiors. Unsteadiness in Government. Illustrations. Punishment from unsteady Governors, does little Good. Over-Government. Want of Patience and Self-Control in Parents and Governors. Formation of Habits of Self-denial in Early Life. Denying Ourselves to promote the Happiness of Others. Example of Parents more effectual than their Precepts. Habits of Honesty and Veracity. In what Lying and Stealing consist. Habits of Modesty. Delicacy studiously to be cherished. Licentious and impure Books to be banished. Bulwer a Licentious Writer, and to be discountenanced. Intellectual Education. Hours of School. Inquiries of Secretary of Massachusetts Board of Education, and Answers of Distinguished Physicians.

IF the happiness of our race depend on the formation of habits of self-denying benevolence, then this ought to be the prominent object, in the minds of those who have the control of young children. As the commands of the Supreme Ruler are the only sure guide to a right course of benevolent action, *submission of the will,* to the will of a superior, is the best preparative for such a course of benevolent action. Submission of the will, self-denial, and benevolence, then, are the three most important habits to form in early life.

In regard to habits of obedience, there have been two extremes, both of which need to be shunned. One is, a stern, unsympathizing maintenance of parental authority, demanding perfect and constant obedience, without any attempt to convince a child of the propriety and benevolence of the requisitions, and without any manifestation of sympathy and tenderness for the pain and difficulty with which it has to meet, under this discipline. Children, under such discipline, grow up to fear their parents, rather than to love and confide in them, and some of the most valuable and happy-making principles of character are chilled or forever blasted.

In shunning this danger, others pass to the other extreme, and put themselves on the footing of equals with their children, as if nothing were due to superiority of age and relation. Nothing is exacted, without the implied concession, that the child is to be the judge of the propriety of the requisition; and reason and persuasion are employed, as if the parent had no right to command. This system produces a most pernicious influence. Children very soon perceive the position which they are thus allowed to occupy, and they take every advantage of it. They soon acquire habits of forwardness and self-conceit, assume disrespectful manners and address, maintain their views with incessant disputes, and yield with ill-humor and resentment, as if their rights were infringed.

The medium course, is, for the parent to take the attitude of a superior in age, knowledge, and relation; who has a perfect right to control every action of the child, and to exact respectful language and manners; and, whenever an express command is given, to demand prompt obedience, without hesitation or dispute. But at the same time, care should be taken to make the child perceive that the requisitions are reasonable and benevolent; designed both for the good of the child, and for the good of all.

Grown persons are very apt to forget the value which children attach to things which a mature mind, having higher resources, regards as trifles. A lady, of great strength of mind and sensibility, once told the Author, that one of the most acute periods of suffering she could remember, was occasioned by her mother's burning up some milkweed-silk. The child had found, for the first time, this shining and beautiful substance, was filled with delight at her discovery, and was planning its future uses, and her pleasure in showing it to her companions; when her mother, finding the carpet all strewed with it, hastily brushed it into the fire, and, with so careless and indifferent an air, that the child fled away, almost distracted with grief and disappointment. The mother little realized the pain she had inflicted, but the child felt the unkindness so severely, that, for some time, her mother was an object almost of aversion.

It is impossible to govern children, properly, especially those of strong and sensitive feelings, without a constant effort to appreciate the value they attach to their pursuits and enjoyments. And with this, should be maintained a habit of carefully explaining the necessity of all requisitions that try their feelings, and of expressing tender sympathy for their grief and disappointment.

There is no way, in which those who govern children can gain so powerful and pleasing an influence over them, as by joining in their sports. By this method, a grown person learns to understand the feelings and interests of childhood, and to detect peculiarities of intellect or temper; and, at the same time, secures a degree of confidence and affection, which can be gained so easily in no other way. Those who help children along in their sports, with kindness and sympathy, are always favorites with them; and, if qualified and disposed so to do, can exert more influence over them, than any other person. It is a great misfortune, to the children of this Nation, that so many fathers are absorbed in making money, for mere show or physical enjoyments, and so many mothers engaged in using it for the same ignoble ends, that they find no time to share in the sports or pursuits of their children, and relinquish this most powerful mode of influence to domestics and playmates, who often use it for the most pernicious purposes.

In sharing the sports of childhood, older persons never should relinquish the attitude of Superiors, or allow disrespectful manners or address. If a superior demand such deportment, it is never more cheerfully accorded, than in seasons when young hearts are pleased, and made grateful, by having their tastes and enjoyments so efficiently promoted. The Writer has often seen parents and teachers, engaged with children in the most boisterous sports, without a single violation of such proprieties.

Next to the entire want of all government, the two most fruitful sources of mischief, in the management of children, are *unsteadiness* in government, and *over-government*. Most of those cases, in which the children of sensible and conscientious persons turn out badly, will be found to result from one or the other of these causes.

Children are exposed to the evils of unsteady government, when those, who control them, are sometimes very strict and decided, in exacting obedience, and, at other times, let disobedience go unrebuked and unpunished. In such cases, the children, never knowing exactly when they can escape with impunity, are constantly tempted to make a trial. The bad effect of this system, on the temper, can be better appreciated, by reference to one important principle of mind. It is found to be universally true, that objects of desire, put beyond the reach of hope, do not agitate the mind with anxious wishes, nor produce regret, at being deprived of what is not hoped for. A child is never harassed with longings for any object, which he knows can never be obtained.   It is in reference to objects which awaken desire, with some hope of attainment, that the mind suffers from regret and disappointment. And all the time the mind is aiming at some supposed good, and using efforts to gain it, opposition excites irritable feelings ; but the moment it is put beyond the reach of hope, such irritation ceases.   In consequence of this principle, whenever a thing is denied or forbidden to children, who are under the control of persons of steady and decided government, they know that it is entirely out of their reach. The agitation of hope and desire of course ceases, and the mind turns to other objects.

But children under the control of weak and indulgent parents, or of unsteady and undecided persons, never enjoy this preserving aid.   When a thing is denied, they do not know but that either coaxing may win it, or disobedience gain it, without any penalty ; and so they are kept in just that state of hope and uncertainty, which produces irritation, and tempts to insubordination.   Such children are very apt to become irritable and fractious, while a constant warfare is kept up with those who govern them, destructive to the peace and harmony so important in domestic life.   The Writer has heard parents, of such unsteady government, lamenting, that, while they punished their children more than most parents, it seemed to do little or no good !

Another class of persons, in aiming to avoid this evil, go to another extreme, and are very strict and pertinacious, in regard to every requisition.   Such, keep the young mind in a state of constant apprehension, lest some of the multiplied requisitions be omitted, and a penalty be inflicted.   The result of such management, is, that children gradually acquire, either obtuseness of conscience and an indifference to rebukes, or else they become excessively irritable or misanthropic.   It is the merciful provision of our

Creator, that the constant repetition of an evil gradually hardens the mind, till eventually it is borne with comparative indifference. This principle, designed for good, is sadly abused, when children become so inured to rebuke, that it produces little grief or contrition.

To avoid these evils, it is a wise precaution, for those who govern children, in their ordinary intercourse to *advise* and *request*, rather than to command. The most important duties of life should be enforced by commands ; but all the little acts of heedlessness, or awkwardness, or ill-manners, so frequently occurring with children, should pass as instances of forgetfulness, and not as acts of direct disobedience. Whenever a child deliberately disobeys an express command, the penalty should always follow, as sure as the laws of Nature. This will be the most infallible preservative from voluntary and known disobedience.

Children of active, heedless temperament, or those who are odd, awkward, or *mal apropos* in remarks and deportment, are often essentially injured, by a want of patience and self-control in those who govern them. Such children often possess a morbid sensibility, which they strive to conceal, or a desire of love and approbation that preys like a famine on the soul. And yet, they become objects of ridicule and rebuke to almost every member of the family, until their sensibilities are tortured into obtuseness or misanthropy. Such children, above all others, need tenderness and sympathy. A thousand instances of mistake or forgetfulness should be passed over, in silence, while opportunities for commendation and encouragement should be diligently sought.

In regard to the formation of habits of self-denial, tender and affectionate parents seem to forget the importance of inuring them to this duty, in early life. Instead of this, they seem to be constantly aiming, by seeking to gratify every wish, to remove every chance for forming so important a habit. Some parents, under this mistaken feeling, will maintain, that nothing shall be put on their table, which their children may not join them in eating. But where can a parent, so effectually as at the daily meal, teach that government of the appetites, which is a lesson that children must learn or be ruined? The food which is proper for grown persons, is often not suitable for children; and this is a sufficient reason for accustoming them to see others partake of delicacies, which they must not share. Requiring children to wait till others are helped, and to refrain from conversation at table, except when addressed by their elders, is another mode of forming habits of self-denial and self-control. Requiring them to help others, first, and to offer the best to others, has a similar influence.

The still more difficult duty of denying themselves, to promote the enjoyment of others, is a lesson which needs to be assiduously taught. But how few parents make this a definite object of interest and effort, although they will allow that it is the most important as well as the most difficult duty! Instead of this, a course is often followed, which tends rather to cultivate selfishness. Thus, almost all motive, offered to stimulate children, are those which refer to mere self-gratification. How few are the parents, who excite their children by the hope of good which others will secure! And yet, very much might be done, to awaken the love of benevolent activity, if it were habitually and systematically attempted. Many parents have succeeded in leading their children to deny their appetites, for some benevolent object, with entire success. By similar efforts, they can be trained to give up their time, their property, or their sports, to add to the comforts, or relieve the wants of others. Let a parent make this a distinct and important object of effort, and much will be accomplished.

Habits of honesty and veracity very much depend on the character, and example of parents. Children are creatures of sympathy and imitation; and when they see that their parents and older friends are particular in respecting rights of property, and always exact in stating truth, they are led to similar uprightness. In inculcating these duties, it is important for older people to form exact and definite ideas, themselves, or they will often perplex children with inconsistencies. For example, when children are taught, that lying is saying what is not true, how often will they hear their parents or other older friends, either jocosely, or in other ways, say what is not strictly true! So, if stealing is said to consist in taking or using what belongs to others, how often is this done by parents, and guardians, and for sufficient reasons!

Instead of this, children should be taught that *intentional deceit* is wrong; and that lying is *telling what is false, with an intention to deceive.* So, stealing is *taking or using the property of others, without proper evidence that the owner is willing.* By these simple definitions, children can be shown, that sometimes people may say what is not true, without intending to deceive, and that this is not lying; and that they may sometimes deceive, when it is not their intention so to do : and that, in such cases, they may not do wrong.

So there are cases, when we may know that persons are willing we should use their property, even without asking; and in such cases, it is not stealing. Parents and teachers, also, have certain rights over the property of children, which should be explained. The effect of sympathy and example is very manifest, in some families, where the parents have very strict notions respecting truth and honesty. From early infancy, the children hear lying, deceit, and dishonesty, spoken of as mean, vulgar, cowardly, and wicked, and feeling a sympathy with those around, avoid these practices, very readily, and are never known to lie, or practise any deceitful or dishonest tricks. In other families, children will see their parents deceiving others, and practising many little artful or dishonest measures. Of course, such parents never can impart an admiration for virtues they do not possess, nor great disgust for vices which they daily practise.

There is no more important duty, devolving upon a mother, than the cultivation of habits of modesty and propriety in young children. All indecorous words or deportment, should be carefully restrained ; and delicacy and reserve studiously cherished. It is a common notion, that it is important to secure these virtues to one sex more than to the other ; and, by a strange inconsistency, the sex most exposed to danger, is the one selected as least needing care. But a wise mother will be especially careful that her sons are trained to modesty and purity of mind.

But few mothers are sufficiently aware of the dreadful penalties that often result from indulged impurity of thought. If children, in future life, can be preserved from licentious associates, it is supposed that their safety is secured. But the records of our insane retreats, and the pages of medical writers, teach, that even in solitude, and without being aware of the sin or the danger, children may inflict evils on themselves, which not unfrequently terminate in disease, delirium, and death. Every mother and every teacher, therefore, carefully avoiding all explanation of the mystery, should teach the young, that the indulgence of impure thoughts and actions is visited by the most awful and terrific penalties. Disclosing the details of vice, in order

234 MANAGEMENT OF YOUNG CHILDREN.

to awaken dread of its penalties, is a most dangerous experiment, and often leads to the very evils feared. The safest course, is, to cultivate habits of modesty and delicacy, and to teach that all impure thoughts, words, and actions, are forbidden by God, and are often visited by the most dreadful punishment. At the same time, it is important for mothers to protect the young mind from false notions of delicacy. It should be shown, that whatever is necessary, to save from suffering or danger, must be met, without shame or aversion; and that all which God has instituted, is wise and right and pure.

It is in reference to these dangers, that mothers and teachers should carefully guard the young from those highly-wrought fictions, which lead the imagination astray; and especially from that class of licentious works, made interesting by genius and taste, which have flooded this Country, and which are often found on the parlor table, even of moral and Christian people. Of this class, the writings of Bulwer stand conspicuous. The only difference, between some of his works and the obscene prints, for vending which men suffer the penalties of law, is, that the last are so gross, as to revolt the taste and startle the mind to resistance, while Bulwer presents the same ideas so clothed in the fascinations of taste and genius, as most insidiously to seduce the unwary. It seems to be the chief aim of this licentious writer, to make thieves, murderers, and adulterers appear beautiful, refined, talented, and interesting. It is time that all virtuous persons in the community should rise in indignation, not only against the writers, but the venders of such poison.

In conducting the intellectual education of children, some modifications have already been pointed out, as desirable, with reference to their physical well-being. Very recently, the Secretary of the Massachusetts Board of Education addressed letters to three of the most distinguished medical men in this Country, requesting their opinion as to the number of hours in which children under eight years of age might safely be kept at school. They were unanimous in limiting the time to *four* hours devoted to school employments that tax the mind. And this period, they maintain, should not be continuous, but divided by long recesses, so that no child should be confined to one pursuit, for more than half an hour at a time.

Of the six hours usually devoted to school, then, two should be given to exercise and sports, and only four to the duties of school. It is very important, to the comfort of most mothers, that their children should be removed from their care, during the six hours of school. And there are many advantages in subjecting young children to the discipline and regularity of a school, and to intercourse with other children, of their own age. If, then, a parent can secure a suitable teacher, it is no matter how early they are sent to school, provided their health is not endangered by confinement and mental stimulus. But a decided effort is demanded, to change the customs of schools, so that two thirds of the time shall be allowed for relaxation and sports. And the vigor of mind, and physical comfort, thus secured, would make children learn even faster than by the ordinary method.

CHAPTER XXI.

ON THE CARE OF THE SICK.

Women frequently called upon to direct in Cases of Indisposition. Extremes to be avoided. Grand Cause of most Diseases, Excess in Eating and Drinking. Fasting useful. Want of Reflection and Good Sense displayed by Many, in dosing. Pernicious Results. Necessity of a Woman's Understanding the Nature and Operation of Common Medicines. Cough Mixtures. Opium. Mucilaginous Mixtures. Calomel. Discretion required. Child bleeding to Death. Sulphur the safest Cathartic in ordinary cases. Remarks of Dr. Combe on keeping the Bowels in good order. Tempting Delicacies injurious in Sickness. Fresh Air absolutely necessary. Frequent Ablutions important. Arrangements to be made beforehand, when practicable, Importance of Cleanliness; nothing more annoying to the Sick, than a want of it. Necessity of a proper Preparation of Food, for the Sick. Every Woman should strive to prepare herself to be a good Nurse. How to drop Medicines. Physicians' Directions to be well understood and implicitly followed. Kindness, Patience, and Sympathy, towards the Sick, important. Impositions of Apothecaries. Drugs to be locked up from the Access of Children.

Such is the state of health, in this Nation, that a woman, with the care of a large family, seldom passes a week without being called on to know what shall be done for some one who is indisposed. In this situation, two extremes are to be avoided; one is, neglecting to do any thing until the person becomes quite sick, the other is, excessive dosing. In regard to the first, many would be saved from long and dangerous illness, if proper attention were paid to the first symptoms; whereas, by neglect, the case, which at first would yield readily, becomes a long and distressing disease.

But the other extreme is much more common, and involves far greater danger. All medical men unite in the declaration, that the grand cause of most diseases, is, excess in eating and drinking, united with too sedentary habits. Without the exercise which aids to throw off redundant matter, through the

pores of the skin and the lungs, and stimulated by
various condiments, an excessive quantity is put
into the stomach, when either digestion must fail,
or, if all is absorbed, the system becomes too full,
and inflammatory attacks follow. For this reason,
it is, that most medical men would, in all slight
cases of illness, recommend fasting over two meals,
that the overloaded system may have a chance to
relieve itself. Another chief cause of disease, is,
sudden chills, closing the pores of the skin, and thus
causing inflammation of the throat, lungs, and nostrils. The best remedy for these attacks, is, warm
aperient drinks, bathing the feet, and warm covering,
to promote perspiration. After such a process, the
skin is more susceptible than before, and should be
carefully guarded.

It is astonishing to see what want of reflection
and good sense is displayed, by persons when sick,
in pouring doses into the stomach, without knowing
anything of their properties, simply because some
one tells them it is good for such a complaint. It
does not come to mind, that all which goes into the
stomach is either dissolved and carried into the
blood, or expelled as redundant matter. Thus,
when the lungs, for example, are inflamed, doses
will be taken, as if under the apparent impression
that the cooling or healing article was somehow
going to be poured into the lungs, instead of the
stomach. In this way, sometimes one article will
be taken, calculated to produce one effect, and another, exactly calculated to counteract it; or something will be taken, calculated to open the pores,
and promote perspiration, just as a person is going to
be most exposed to cold. The frequent result of
such dosing, is, that the stomach, being loaded with
a variety of contradictory principles, is debilitated,
and interrupted in its natural operations, and the
whole system, and especially the diseased part, sym-

pathizes in the evil. It is very important, therefore, that a woman should understand something of the nature and operation of the most common articles given in a family, that some discretion may be used, in adapting means to ends, and in avoiding the excessive or the wrong use of them. Most of the cough mixtures contain some narcotic, generally opium, to quiet the irritability of the nervous system, and thus act on the nerves of the lungs and diminish coughing. To this principle, is usually added, something of the nature of ipecac, to promote a slight nausea, and thus open the pores. To this, sometimes, is added, some cathartic, to remedy the binding tendency of the narcotic principle. Of course, such mixtures should be used sparingly, and with reference to these objects. Opium, in all forms, tends to produce constipation of the bowels. It also powerfully affects the nervous system, and should be used as little as possible. Balsams, and mucilaginous mixtures, such as flaxseed tea, slippery-elm-bark, and the like, are useful, when the membrane of the throat, and the parts connected with it, are affected; but have little effect, when a cold affects the lungs. Whenever any article is taken, to promote perspiration, the body should be kept very warm.

Calomel is a very dangerous medicine; and should seldom be used, without advice from a physician. Even when prescribed by a medical man, discretion is often needed. The Writer knew a case, where the physician left several small papers of calomel, and told the mother to give them so often, *till an operation was produced.* Something peculiar in the case prevented their acting as a cathartic; the mother, having no knowledge of the nature of the medicine, kept on giving the powders, till all were used up. The result was, the blood-vessels of the mouth and other parts were so affected, that, after drenching sheet after sheet with blood, the child actually bled to death.

The most common cathartics, used in a family, are rhubarb, salts, castor oil, and calomel. Salts should be given, when the system needs reducing; and never in a weak and low state of the system. One of the most distinguished practitioners in the Nation, observed to the Writer, that he considered sulphur as the safest cathartic, for family use, in ordinary cases.

Dr. Combe remarks, on this subject, "In the natural and healthy state, under a proper system of diet, and with sufficient exercise, the bowels are relieved regularly, once every day." *Habit* "is powerful in modifying the result, and in sustaining healthy action when once fairly established. Hence the obvious advantage of observing as much regularity, in relieving the system, as in taking our meals." It is often the case, that soliciting Nature at a regular period, each day, will remedy constipation, without medicine, and induce a regular and healthy state of the bowels. "When, however, as most frequently happens, the constipation arises" "from the absence of all assistance from the abdominal and respiratory muscles, the first step to be taken, is, again to solicit their aid;—first, by removing all impediments to free respiration, such as stays, waistbands, and belts; and, secondly, by resorting to such active exercises, as shall call the muscles into full and regular action:" and lastly, "to proportion the quantity of food to the wants of the system, and to the condition of the digestive organs. If we employ these means, systematically and perseveringly, we shall rarely fail in at last restoring the healthy action of the bowels, with little aid from medicine. But if we" neglect these modes, "we may go on, for years, adding pill to pill, and dose to dose, without ever attaining the end at which we aim."

It is not unfrequently the case, that, when appetite ceases, from some disarrangement of the system, the first effort of friends, is, to seek some tempting delicacy, to stimulate the palate. But a knowledge of the organization of the stomach, would prevent this pernicious practice. The cessation of appetite is ordinarily the signal, that the system is in such a state that food is not needed, and cannot be digested. Of course, as there will be little or no gastric juice, what is thus urged into the stomach, cannot be properly digested, and disease is increased.

In nursing the sick, too much attention cannot be given to securing a proper supply of fresh air. The fact, that persons in the debility of sickness cannot bear exposure to sudden chills, has led to the pernicious practice, of keeping sick-rooms not only warm, but close. But there is nothing, which more contributes to the restoration of a diseased body, than a plentiful supply of the pure air, which is appointed to draw off from the lungs the unhealthful portions of the system. The purer the air, the faster this restoring process is carried on. It should, therefore, be a primary object, to keep a sick-room well ventilated: this can be done, and still keep it warm. A sick person should always be put in a room with an open fireplace, through which the fresh air, from without, gains access, and impure air passes off. At least twice in the twenty-four hours, the patient should be entirely covered in bed, and a window opened in an adjoining room, into which the door of the sick-room opens. No air in a house, can be so pure, as that which comes from without. After this airing, the patient should remain in bed, till the room is restored to the proper temperature, by the aid of a fire, if need be.

Frequent changes of clothing and bedding, are needful in sickness; as the exhalations from the skin are then more abundant and more noxious.

Frequent ablutions, also, are very important, and greatly promote the comfort of the patient. If the room be kept warm, and warm water be used, there is not the least danger in performing this operation. If the whole body cannot be sponged with water, at least the face, neck, and limbs, should be washed, once or twice a day.

It greatly promotes the comfort of the sick, to have their room, and the articles used about them, kept clean and in order. In doing this, care should be used, to avoid bustle, haste, or noise. If, when a person is taken sick, there are indications that the disease will continue several days, the following arrangements are suggested, to secure quiet, neatness, and order.

If it is Winter, let a supply of fuel be put in a large box in the room, and let it be filled, once or twice a day. It would be well to have the following articles provided, to keep in the room or adjacent closet, to prevent constant passing to obtain them from without:—a small teakettle, a saucepan, a large pail of water, for ablutions, and other water, for drink, in a pitcher, a covered porringer, to warm food and drinks, two pint bowls, two tumblers, two cups and saucers, two wine-glasses, two large and two small spoons, a bowl and towel, to use in washing these articles, a supply of white towels, and also of dish towels. A slop bucket should be in an adjacent room or closet, to receive the wash of the room.

Whenever medicine or food is given, a clean towel should be spread over the person or bed-clothing, as nothing is more annoying, to a weak stomach, than the stickiness and soiling produced by medicine and food. It is also very desirable, that every thing about a sick-room be kept clean and in order. The fireplace should be often cleansed of ashes and coals, and the carpet or floor be kept neat. All the articles

used should be immediately after washed, and set in
a proper place; and every implement be put in good
order.   A sick person has nothing to do, but look
about, and when everything is neat, quiet, and in
order, a feeling of comfort is induced, while disorder,
filth, and neglect, are constant objects of annoyance,
which, if not complained of, are yet felt.   An air of
cheerfulness is given to a sick-room, by covering the
table and stand with a clean napkin, and placing
flowers and fruit on them.   Oranges and lemons give
an agreeable look and perfume to any apartment.
Pains should be taken to keep flies out of a sick-
room ; and for this purpose, all articles which attract
them should be covered.

There is nothing, more important to the comfort
of the sick, than to have their food prepared in a
neat and proper manner.   It is at such times, that
the sense of smell and taste are most susceptible of
annoyance ; and defects, that would scarcely be
noticed in health, will often seem so revolting, as to
take away all appetite.   And the sick have so few
sources of enjoyment and comfort, that the minds,
even of the most rational, will sometimes fix on
some article of food, with great earnestness, and
when disappointed, by neglect or mistake in the
preparation, will sometimes feel it so keenly, as to
shed tears.   Perhaps, too, the disappointment will
be enhanced, by a feeling that the nurse has little
care and interest for the comfort of her patient.

It is very important, therefore, that every woman
strive to prepare herself to be a neat, quiet, and
skilful nurse ; and especially, that she learn to prepare articles for the sick with care and accuracy.
For this purpose, all the articles, used in cooking
for the sick, should be carefully washed, and then
scalded, that every disagreeable smell and taste may
be removed.   In boiling articles, great care should
be taken, by having a slow fire, and constant stir-

ring, to prevent the bitter taste acquired by the adherence of the food to the bottom. Articles can seldom be cooked over a blaze, without acquiring a smoky taste; therefore be sure never to stir anything, that is boiling, over a blaze or smoke. Strain out lumps, through a strainer or small colander, and put the article in a bowl standing in a plate or saucer, and set them on a waiter. Beside them, place the sugar or salt, or other articles to be added; and first consult the patient as to the quantity, being careful to put in too little, rather than too much.

Keep a clean handkerchief, and a clean towel, to present with food, as nausea is often produced by such articles, used when taking medicine, and all appetite is thus lost, and sometimes, too, without knowing the reason. When a person is feverish, cooling the pillows, and changing them, is a comfort; also, sponging the hands with water having a little milk in it. Frequent swabbing the mouth, with a clean rag tied on the end of a stick, is often a great comfort. When a sick person is raised in bed, a shawl should always be thrown over the shoulders; and, if weak, a chair put behind the pillows.

In dropping medicine, first, wet the lip of the vial, to make it run smooth, and always drop it into a teaspoon, first, lest some mistake be made. Be careful to understand the physician's directions, and to follow them, exactly. Do not yield to the folly of thinking that persons, who have never studied the complicated system of the human body, nor the nature of medicines, are qualified to modify a physician's advice. If another person is supposed to know better about the case, than the physician, the only rational way is to dismiss the physician, and secure the services of the more competent person.

It is always best to write down the directions of the physician, if he does not do it; and not trust to

memory.   The nurse should be sure she knows
how to properly perform all the directions given.
The Writer knows the mother of several children,
who was nursing a sick infant, and, when the physician directed her to dress a large blister on its chest,
she asked, how it was to be done.   "With cabbage-
leaves, as usual," was the reply.   The mother,
never having had experience, took large cabbage-
leaves, and put them, cold, unbruised, and unwilted,
on the raw flesh of the little sufferer.   This was
done by an educated woman, and one who would
be called a discreet and sensible person.   It shows,
that every nurse should be sure to learn, *exactly*,
from the physician, the proper mode of obeying his
directions.

In nursing the sick, always speak kindly and
bear patiently their hasty murmurs and ill-humors.
In nursing a child, though it is hard to do so, it is
better to secure proper conduct, and the taking of
medicine, by penalties, than to allow rebellion and
disobedience.   The child will suffer much less, in
the end, than if it finds that sickness is a preservative from all penalties for disobedience and ill-humor.
Many children, of delicate health, are ruined in their
disposition and tempers, by the indulgence and false
tenderness of those who nurse them.

Always sympathize with the sufferings of the
sick, and yet strive to induce them to bear pain
with patience, fortitude, and submission, to Him
who appoints it.   In nursing the sick, offer to read
the Bible, at proper times, and use all discreet means
to lead their minds to proper thoughts and feelings,
on a subject, of all others most appropriate in hours
of confinement and suffering.

One caution is very important, in regard to medicines.   Physicians say that there are constant impositions and mistakes practised, by many apothecaries,
who need to be carefully watched.   Some adulterate

their medicines; some mix them in wrong proportions, to make a little more profit; and some buy old and useless drugs, for a trifle, and sell them for good ones. It is always best to consult your physician, in regard to the selection of an apothecary; and, if possible, in all cases you should show him the medicines, before using them. Sometimes, mistakes are made, and poisonous articles are sent, instead of the ones ordered. Many medicines, kept by a family, lose all their virtues, after a time, and are of no use. Always put labels on vials of medicine, and very large and distinct ones on dangerous drugs, which should be kept locked up from the access of children.

CHAPTER XXII.

ON ACCIDENTS AND ANTIDOTES.

Medical Aid should be promptly resorted to. Suffocation, from Substances in the Throat. Common Cuts. Wounds of Arteries, and other severe Cuts. Bruises. Sprains. Broken Limbs. Falls. Blows on the Head. Burns. Drowning. Poisons:—Corrosive Sublimate; Arsenic; Opium; Acids; Alkalies. Stupefaction from Fumes of Charcoal; Suffocation from entering a Well, Limekiln, or Coalmine. Hemorrhage of the Lungs, Stomach, or Throat. Bleeding of the Nose. Dangers from Lightning. Mad Dogs. Insects. Local Inflammations.

WHEN serious accidents occur, medical aid should be immediately procured. Till that can be done, the following directions may be useful.

When a child has any thing in its throat, first try, with the finger, to get the article up. If it is beyond reach, push it down into the stomach, with some elastic stick. If the article be a pin, sharp bone, glass, or other cutting substance, vomiting should be promptly produced.

If the choking be occasioned by something getting into the windpipe, it is very dangerous; but a surgeon can usually save life, if immediately applied to.

In the case of a common cut, bind the lips of the wound together with rags. If the cut is large, and rags will not press it well together, a sticking plaster must be used for the purpose. Sometimes, it is necessary to take a stitch in the skin, on each lip of the wound, and draw them together with a needle and thread.

If an artery is cut, it must immediately be tied up, or the person will bleed to death. The blood of an artery spirts out, in regular jets, with the beating of the heart; and the blood is of a bright red color. Take up the bleeding end of the artery, and hold it; or tie a string around it, till a surgeon arrives. When the artery cannot be found, and in all cases of bad cuts, apply compression; and, where it can be done, tie a very tight bandage *above* the wound, if it is below the heart, and *below*, if the wound is above the heart. Put a stick into the band and twist it as tight as can be borne, till surgical aid is obtained.

Bad bruises are best cured by bathing in hot water, or hot spirits, or a decoction of bitter herbs. Sprains are cured, by *entire rest* from use, and by bathing in warm water or warm whiskey. If a sprained limb is immediately put to rest, and not used, at all, it will heal twice as quick, as if not so treated; and for want of this rest, what would often prove very slight, in the end result in very bad, sprains. A sprained leg should be kept in a horizontal position, on a bed or sofa.

When a leg is broken, tie it to the other leg, to keep it still; and get a surgeon, if possible, before the limb swells. Bind a broken arm to a piece of shingle, to keep it still.

In case of a fall, or blow on the head, causing insensibility, use a mustard paste on the back of the neck and pit of the stomach, and apply spirits, with friction. After the circulation is restored, bleeding is often necessary; but it is dangerous to attempt it before.

In case of bad burns, when the skin is taken off, apply an ointment made of linseed oil and limewater in equal quantities; and cover this with cotton. But never put raw cotton on a burn with the skin off, as is often done. To some skins, cotton is almost poisonous. Sweet oil on cotton is good. For burns when the skin is not taken off, soft soap, or scraped potato, are very alleviating.

In case of drowning, the person should be laid upon his right side, with his head a little elevated, and gently inclined forward; he should as soon as possible be placed in a moderately-warmed bed, or wrapped in blankets to preserve the vital heat which may yet remain. The mouth should be cleared of phlegm, water, or other foreign substance, by carefully introducing the fingers into it. Spirits of hartshorn may be cautiously applied to the nostrils, or rather occasionally held near the nose. The warmth of the body should be slowly restored or increased, by applying a bladder of warm water to the pit of the stomach, bottles of the same, or hot bricks, or bags filled with hot ashes, to the armpits, groins, and soles of the feet. Brisk frictions of the whole body, first with a dry brush, flannel, or the bare hand, and afterwards with cloths wet with spirits of camphor, should be diligently employed. Gentle pressure should be applied, alternately to the breast and belly, and the lungs should be inflated, in imitation of natural respiration. This may be done, by introducing the nose of a bellows into one nostril and closing the other; or by closing both nostrils, applying the mouth to that of the drowned person, and gently blowing in air; in either case closing the gullet, by pressure on the throat. The case should not be abandoned too hastily, as hopeless; for resuscitation has taken place, after *eight or ten hours* persevering use of *proper* means. I say proper means, for highly improper and injurious ones are often, through ignorance, had recourse to; such, for example, as the rolling of the body on a barrel, the suspending of it by the heels, the administering of injections of tobacco, or tobacco smoke, &c. After the person begins to revive, he may take, at short intervals, and in small quantities, wine or spirit and water, diluted spirits of camphor, or Cologne water, &c.

In case of poisoning, from corrosive sublimate, whites of eggs, beaten up with water, should be given. The proportions are ten or twelve eggs, to two quarts of water. Of this mixture, a tumblerful should be administered every two or three minutes, in order to produce vomiting. Where eggs cannot be obtained, give wheat-flour and water, or milk and water, freely; if these are not at command, use gum and water, flaxseed tea, slippery-elm tea, or sugar and water; or, time being precious, if none of these be at hand, give copious draughts of water alone.

In case of poisoning from arsenic, or any of its preparations, let the individual poisoned drink large quantities of *sugared water*, of *warm*, or even of cold, water, or of flaxseed tea, so as to distend the stomach and produce vomiting, if possible, and thereby eject the poison. A mixture of equal quantities of lime-water and sugared water will also prove beneficial.

If opium, or any of its preparations has been taken, in poisonous quantities, induce vomiting, without a moment's unnecessary delay, by giving, in a *small quantity* of water, ten grains of ipecac, and ten grains of sulphate of zinc or white vitriol, (the latter of which is the most prompt emetic known,) and repeating the dose every fifteen minutes, if the desired effect be not produced. The operation may be sometimes expedited, by introducing the fingers into the mouth, or tickling the throat with a feather. If white vitriol cannot be obtained, substitute three or four grains of blue vitriol, (or sulphate of copper.) The soporific influence of the poison should be counteracted, by keeping the person in motion. After the stomach has been thoroughly emptied, but *not previously*, give, every five or ten minutes, alternately, a cup of water made acid with vinegar, cream of tartar, or lemon juice, and a cup of coffee, (without sugar or milk,) prepared by pouring a pint of boiling water upon a quarter of a pound of ground burnt coffee, letting it stand ten minutes, and then straining it. The drinks should be continued, so long as any danger is to be apprehended. Dashing cold water upon the head and body, and friction of the extremities, with a brush or coarse towel, are useful.

If any kind of acid is taken, in too large quantity, give strong pearlash water. If ley, or pearlash, or any alkali, is taken, give vinegar.

In case of stupefaction from fumes of charcoal, or suffocation from entering a well, limekiln, or coalmine, expose the person freely to cold air, on his back ; dash cold water or vinegar, on the head, face, and breast ; rub the body with the same, or spirits of camphor, or Cologne. Apply mustard paste to the pit of the stomach, and use friction to the soles of the feet, the palms of the hands, and the whole length of the back bone. Vinegar and water or lemonade should be given as drink. When the person revives, he should be laid in a warm bed, in a well-ventilated room, and given small quantities of wine and water. Whatever is done must be done promptly and perseveringly.

In case of bleeding at the lungs, or stomach, or throat, take a teaspoonful of dry salt, and repeat it often. For bleeding of the nose, pour cold water on the back of the neck, keeping the head elevated.

If a person is struck with lightning, throw bucketsfull of cold water on the head and over the body, and apply mustard poultices on the stomach, with friction of the whole body, especially the extremities, and inflation of the lungs.

If a person is bitten by a mad dog, or a rattlesnake, sucking the wound, and cutting out the flesh, around the bite, are the immediate preventives. Meantime call medical advice. For bites of insects, spirits of hartshorn, or salt and water, are good. Poultices, kept wet and warm, are good for most cases of local inflammation; but they must be kept constantly warm, to be useful.

CHAPTER XXIII.

ON DOMESTIC AMUSEMENTS.

Indefiniteness of Opinion on this Subject. Every Person needs some Recreation. General Rules. How much Time to be given. What Amusements proper. Those should always be avoided, which cause Pain, or injure the Health, or endanger Life, or interfere with important Duties, or are pernicious in their Tendency. Horse-racing, Circus-riding, Theatres, and Gambling. Dancing, as now conducted, does not conduce to Health of Body or Mind, but the contrary. Dancing in the Open Air beneficial. Social Benefits of Dancing considered. Ease and Grace of Manners better secured by a System of Calisthenics. The Writer's Experience. Balls going out of Fashion, among the more refined Circles. Novel-reading. Necessity for Discrimination. Young Persons should be guarded from Novels. Proper Amusements for Young Persons. Cultivation of Flowers and Fruits. Benefits of the Practice. Music. Children enjoy it. Collections of Shells, Plants, Minerals, &c. Children's Games and Sports. Parents should join in them. Mechanical Skill of Children to be encouraged. Other Enjoyments.

THERE is much indefiniteness of opinion, in many minds, on the subject of amusements, which needs to be removed. All persons perceive that children, at least, must spend much time in pursuits which are mere amusements. Many persons think that grown people are at liberty to spend some portion of their time in this way; while others suppose, that all time, spent by mature minds, for mere amusement, is utterly wasted.

But it is believed, that, where the laws of body and mind are fully understood, it will be allowed, by all, that every person needs some kind of recreation; and that, by securing it, the body is strengthened, the mind invigorated, and all our duties more cheerfully and successfully performed. There are general rules for our guidance, on this subject, also. Children, whose bodies are growing fast, and whose nervous system is tender and excitable, need much more amusement, than mature minds; and any great degree of physical confinement or mental taxation, are dangerous. Persons, also, who have very great duties and cares, or who are subjected to any continuous intellectual or moral excitement, need recreations to secure physical exercise, and to draw off the mind from absorbing interests. But, unfortunately, it is this class of persons, who have least to do with amusement, while the light, gay, and unemployed, seek amusements which are entirely needless, and for which useful occupation would be most beneficial substitutes.

In deciding how much time it is right to give to mere amusement, it surely is clearly our duty to take just so much as, and no more than, is needful to invigorate mind and body, and thus prepare for the serious duties of life. Any protracting of amusement, which induces excessive fatigue, exhausts the mind, or invades the hours of regular repose, cannot be allowed to be right, by those, who concede that we are bound to spend every hour usefully, and that, at the last day, we are to give an account of the use of all our time.

In deciding which amusements should be selected, and which avoided, the following general rules are binding. In the first place, no amusements, which inflict needless pain, should ever be allowed. All tricks, which cause fright or vexation, and all sports, which involve sufferings to animals, should be utterly forbidden. Hunting and fishing, for mere amusement, can never be justified. If a man can convince his children that these are pursued mainly to gain food and health, and not that the wounding and killing of animals is sought for amusement, his example may not be very injurious. But children, who see grown persons killing or frightening animals, for amusement, receive lessons which tend little towards forming habits of benevolence and tenderness, and much to an opposite result.

Another rule, to guide in selecting amusements, is, that we are to choose none which injure the health, endanger life, or interfere with important duties. As the only legitimate object of amusements, is, to promote health, and prepare for more serious duties, of course, selecting what has a directly opposite tendency, cannot be justified.

A third rule, is, to avoid those amusements, which experience has shown to be so exciting, and connected with so many temptations, as to be pernicious in tendency, both to the individual and to the community. It is on this ground, that horseracing and circus-riding are excluded. Not because there is any thing positively wrong, in having men and horses run, and perform feats of agility, or in persons looking on for the amusement; but because experience has shown so many evils connected with these amusements, that they should be relinquished. So with theatres. The enacting of characters, and the amusement thus afforded, in itself may be harmless; and possibly, in certain cases, might be useful: but experience has shown so many evils to result from this source, that it is deemed wrong to patronize it. So with those exciting games of chance, which are employed in gambling.

Under the same head, comes *dancing*, in the estimation of the great majority of the religious world. Still, there are many intelligent, excellent, and conscientious persons, who hold a contrary opinion. Such maintain, that it is an innocent and healthful amusement, tending to promote ease of manners, cheerfulness, social affection, and health of mind and body; that evils are involved only in its excess; and that, like food, study, or religious excitement, it is only wrong, when not properly regulated. Such maintain, that, if serious and intelligent people would strive to regulate, instead of striving to banish, this amusement, much more good would be secured. On the other side, it is objected, not that dancing is a sin, in itself considered, for it was once a part of sacred worship; not that it would be objectionable, if it were properly regulated; not that it does not tend, when used in a proper manner, to health of body and mind, to grace of manners and to social enjoyment: all these things are conceded.

But it is objected to, on the same ground as horse-racing, card-playing, and theatres; that we are to look at amusements as they *are*, and not as they *might* be. Horseracing might be so conducted, as not to involve cruelty, gambling, drunkenness, and every other vice. And so might theatres and card-playing. And if serious and intelligent persons undertook to patronize these amusements, in order to regulate them, perhaps they would be somewhat raised from the depths to which they are now sunk. But serious and intelligent men know, that, with the weak sense of moral obligation in the mass of society, and the imperfect ideas men have of the proper use of amusements, and the little self-control men, or women, or children, practise, such amusements, as a fact, will not be thus regulated. And they believe dancing to be in the same condemnation.

As this amusement is actually conducted, it does not tend to produce health of body or mind, but

directly the contrary.   If young and old went out
to dance together, in the open air, as the French
peasants do, it would be a very different sort of
amusement, from what is seen, when, in a room
furnished with many lights, and filled with guests,
both expending the healthful part of the atmosphere,
the young collect, in their tightest dresses, to protract
a kind of physical exertion, not habitual, for several
hours.   During this process, the blood is made to
circulate more swiftly, in circumstances where it is
less perfectly oxygenized than health requires ; the
pores of the skin are excited by heat and exercise ;
the stomach is loaded with indigestible articles, and
the quiet, needful to digestion, withheld ; the amusement is protracted beyond the usual hour for repose ;
and then, when the skin is made the most highly
susceptible to damps and miasms, the company pass
from a warm room to the cold night air.   It is probable, that there is no single thing that can be pointed
out, which combines so many injurious particulars,
as this amusement, so often defended, as so healthful.   Even if parents, who train their children to
dance, can keep them from public balls, (which is
seldom the case,) dancing in private parlors unites
the same mischievous influences.

As to the claim of social benefits,—when a dancing-
party occupies the centre of parlors, and the music
begins, most of the conversation ceases, while the
young prepare themselves for future sickness, and
the old look smilingly on.

As to the claim for ease and grace of manners,—
all that is gained, by this practice, can be better
secured, by having masters teach the system of Calisthenics, which, in all its parts, embraces a much
more perfect system, both of healthful exercise,
graceful movement, and pleasing carriage.

The Writer was once inclined to the common
opinion, that dancing was harmless, and might be

regulated; and she allowed a fair trial to be made under her auspices, by its advocates. The result was, a full conviction that the amusement secured no good, which could not be better gained another way; that it involved the most pernicious evils to health, character, and happiness; and that those parents were wise, who brought up their children with the full understanding that they were neither to learn nor to practise the art. In the fifteen years, during which she has had the care of young ladies, she has never known any case, where learning this art, and following the amusement, did not have a bad effect, either on the habits, the intellect, the feelings, or the health. Those young ladies, who are brought up to less exciting amusements, are uniformly likely to be the most contented and most useful, while those, who enter the path to which this amusement leads, acquire a relish and desire for high excitement, which makes the more steady and quiet pursuits and enjoyments of home comparatively tasteless. This, the Writer believes to be generally the case, though not invariably so; for there are exceptions to all general rules.

In regard to these exciting amusements, so liable to danger and excess, parents are bound to regard the principle involved in the petition, "lead us not into temptation." Would it not be inconsistent to teach the lisping tongue of childhood this prayer, and then send it to the dancing-master, to acquire a love for an amusement which leads to constant temptations that so few find strength to resist?

It is encouraging, to those who take this view of the subject, to find how fast the most serious and intelligent portion of the community are coming to a similar result. Twenty-five years ago, in every part of the Nation, the young, as a matter of course, universally practised this amusement. Now, in those parts of the Country, where religion and intelligence are most extensively diffused, it is almost impossible to get up a ball among the more refined class of the community. The amusement is fast leaving this rank in society, to remain as a resource for those, whose grade of intelligence and refinement does not relish more elevated amusements. Still, as there is great diversity of opinion, among persons of equal worth and intelligence, a spirit of candor and courtesy should be practised, on both sides. The sneer at bigotry and narrowness of views, on one side, and the uncharitable implication of want of piety, or sense, on the other, are equally illbred and unchristian. Truth, on this subject, is best promoted, not by illnatured crimination and rebuke, but by calm reason and generous candor, forbearance, and kindness.

There is another species of amusement, which a large portion of the religious world have been accustomed to put under the same condemnation as the preceding. This is novel-reading. The indistinctness and difference of opinion on this subject, have arisen from a want of clear and definite distinctions. Now, as it is impossible to define what are novels and what are not, so as to include one class of fictitious writings and exclude every other, it is impossible to lay down any rule respecting them. The discussion, in fact, turns on the use of those works of imagination, which embrace fictitious narrative. That this species of reading is not only lawful, but necessary and useful, is settled by Divine examples in the parables and allegories of Scripture. Of course, the question must be, what kind of fictitious narratives must be avoided, and what allowed. In deciding this, no specific rules can be given ; but it must be a matter to be regulated by the nature and circumstances of each case. No fictitious writings, which tend to throw the allurements of taste and genius around vice and crime, should ever be tolerated ;

and all that tend to give false views of life and duty, should also be banished. Of those which are written for mere amusement, presenting scenes and events that are interesting and exciting, and having no bad moral influence, much must depend on character and circumstances. Some minds are torpid and phlegmatic, and need to have the imagination stimulated ; and such would be benefitted by this kind of reading : others have quick and active imaginations, and would be as much injured. Some persons are often so engaged in absorbing interests, that any thing innocent, which for a short time will draw off the mind, is of the nature of a medicine ; and, in such cases, this kind of reading is useful.

There is need, also, that some men should keep a supervision of the current literature of the day, as guardians to warn others of danger. For this purpose, it is more suitable for *editors, clergymen,* and *teachers,* to read indiscriminately, than for any other class of persons ; for they are the guardians of the public weal, in matters of literature, and should be prepared to advise parents and young persons of the evils in one direction and the good in another. In doing this, however, they are bound to go on the same principles that regulate physicians, when they visit infected districts,—using every precaution to prevent injury to themselves ; having as little to do with pernicious exposures, as a benevolent regard to others will allow ; and faithfully employing all the knowledge and opportunities, thus gained, for warning and preserving others. There is much danger, in taking this course, that men will seek the excitement of the imagination, for the mere pleasure it affords, under the plea of preparing to serve the public, when this is neither the aim nor the result.

In regard to the use of such works, by the young, as a general rule, they ought not to be allowed to any, except those of dull and phlegmatic tempera-

ment, until the solid parts of education are secured,
and a taste for more elevated reading acquired. If
these stimulating condiments in literature are freely
used in youth, in a majority of cases all relish for
more solid reading will be destroyed. If parents
succeed in securing habits of cheerful and implicit
obedience, it will be very easy to regulate this matter, by an express command, that no story book shall
ever be read, until the consent of the parent is obtained.

It is not unfrequently the case, that advocates for
dancing, and the other more exciting amusements,
speak as if those, who were more strict in these
matters, were aiming to deprive the young of all
amusements; just as if, when card-playing, theatres,
and dancing, were cut off, nothing remains but serious and severe duties. Perhaps there has been
some just ground of objection to the course often
pursued by parents, in neglecting to provide agreeable and suitable substitutes, for the amusements denied; but, that there is not a great abundance of
safe, healthful, and delightful, amusements, which
all parents may secure for their children, cannot be
maintained. Some of these will here be pointed out.

One of the most useful and important, is, the cultivation of flowers and fruits. This, especially for
the daughters of a family, is greatly promotive of
health and amusement. It is with the hope, that
many young ladies, whose habits are now so formed,
that they never can be induced to a course of active
domestic exercise, while their parents can hire domestics, may yet be led to an employment which
will tend to secure health and vigor of constitution,
that so much space is given, in this work, to directions for the cultivation of fruits and flowers. It
would be a most desirable improvement, if all female
schools could be furnished with suitable grounds and
instruments for the cultivation of fruits and flowers,

and every inducement offered to engage the young ladies in this pursuit. And every father, who wishes to have his daughters grow up to be healthful women, cannot take a surer method to secure this end. Let him set apart a portion of his yard and garden, for fruits and flowers, and see that the soil is well prepared and dug over, and all the rest may be committed to the care of the children. These would need to be provided with a light hoe and rake, a dibble or garden trowel, a watering-pot, and means and opportunities for securing seeds, roots, buds, and grafts, all which might be done at a trifling expense. Then, with proper encouragement, and by the aid of such directions as are contained in this work, every man, who has even half an acre, could secure a small Eden around his premises.

In pursuing this amusement, children can also be led to acquire many useful habits. Early rising would, in many cases, be thus secured ; and, if required to keep their walks and borders free from weeds and rubbish, habits of order and neatness would be induced. Benevolent and social feelings could also be cultivated, by influencing children to share their fruits and flowers with friends and neighbors, as well as to distribute roots and seeds to those who have not the means of procuring them. A woman or a child, by giving seeds and slips and roots to a washerwoman, or a farmer's boy, thus exciting them to love and cultivate fruits and flowers, awakens a new and refining source of enjoyment in minds, that have few resources, more elevated than mere physical enjoyments. Our Saviour directs, in making feasts, to call, not the rich, who can recompense again, but the poor, who can make no returns. So children should be taught to dispense their little treasures, not alone to companions and friends, who will probably return similar favors ; but to those who have no means of making any return. If the rich, who acquire a love for the enjoyments of taste, and have the means to gratify it, would aim to extend the cheap and simple enjoyment of fruits and flowers among the poor, our Country would soon literally blossom as the rose.

If the ladies of a neighborhood would unite small contributions, and send a list of flower-seeds and roots to some respectable and honest florist, who would not be likely to turn them off with trash, they could divide these among themselves, so as to secure an abundant variety, at a very small expense. A bag of flower-seeds, which can be obtained, at wholesale, at the rate of four cents, would abundantly supply a whole neighborhood; and, by the gathering of seeds in the Autumn, could be perpetuated.

Another very elevating and delightful recreation for the young, is found in *music*. Here, the Writer would protest against the common practice, in wealthy families, of having the daughters learn to play on the piano, whether they have taste and ear for music, or not. No young lady, who cannot sing, and has no great fondness for music, does any thing but waste time, money, and patience, in learning to play on the piano. But all children can be taught to sing, in early childhood, if the scientific mode of teaching music in schools could be introduced, as it is in Prussia, Germany, and Switzerland. Then, young children could read and sing music, as easily as they can read language; and might take any tune, dividing themselves into bands, and sing off, at sight, the endless variety of music that is prepared. And if parents of wealth would take pains to have teachers qualified, as they may be at the Boston Academy, and other similar institutions, for this purpose, who shall teach all the young children in the community, much would be done for the happiness and elevation of the rising generation. This is an amusement, which children enjoy in the highest degree; and it is one that they can enjoy both in the dark weather at home, and in fields and visits abroad.

Another resource for domestic amusement, is, the collection of shells, plants, and specimens in geology and mineralogy, for the formation of cabinets. If intelligent parents would get the simpler works prepared for the young, and study these things, with their children, a *taste* for such amusements would soon be developed. The Writer has seen young boys, of eight and ten years of age, gathering and cleaning shells from rivers, and collecting plants and mineralogical specimens, with a delight bordering on ecstasy; and there are few, if any, who, by proper influences, would not find this a source of ceaseless amusement and improvement.

Another resource for family amusement, is, the various games that are played by children, and in which the joining of older members of the family is always a great advantage to both parties. All medical men unite in declaring, that nothing is more beneficial to health than hearty laughter; and surely our benevolent Creator would not have provided risibles, and made it a source of health and enjoyment to use them, and then have made it a sin so to do. There has been a tendency to asceticism, on this subject, which needs to be removed. Such commands as forbid *foolish* laughing and jesting, "*which are not convenient;*" and which forbid all idle words, and vain conversation, cannot apply to any thing but what is foolish, vain, and useless. But jokes, laughter, and sports, when used in such a degree as tends only to promote health, social feelings, and happiness, are neither vain, foolish, nor "not convenient." It is the excess of these things, and not the moderate use of them, that Scripture forbids. The prevailing temper of the mind, should be cheerful, yet serious; but there are times, when

relaxation and laughter are proper for all.   There is
nothing better for this end, than that parents and
older persons should join in the sports of childhood.
Mature minds can always make such sports more
entertaining to children, and can exert a healthful
moral influence over their minds; and, at the same
time, can gain exercise and amusement for themselves.   How.lamentable, that so many fathers, who
could be thus useful and happy with their children,
throw away such opportunities, and wear out soul
and body in the pursuit of gain or fame!

Another resource for children, is, in the exercise
of mechanical skill.   Fathers, by providing tools for
their boys, and showing them how to make wheel-
barrows, carts, sleds, and various other articles, contribute both to the physical, moral, and social, improvement of their children.   And in regard to little
daughters, much more can be done, in this way,
than many would imagine.   The Writer, blessed
with the example of a most ingenious and industrious mother, had not only learned, before the age of
twelve, to make dolls, of various sorts and sizes, but
to cut and fit and sew every article that belongs to
a doll's wardrobe.   This, which was for mere
amusement, secured such a facility in mechanical
pursuits, that, ever afterward, the cutting and fitting
of any article of dress, for either sex, was accomplished with entire ease.

When a little girl first begins to sew, her mother
can promise her a small bed and pillows, as soon as
she has sewed a patch quilt for them; and then a
bedstead, as soon as she has sewed the sheets and
cases for pillows; and then a large doll to dress, as
soon as she has made the under garments; and thus
go on, till the whole baby-house is earned by the
needle and skill of its little owner.   Thus, the task
of learning to sew will become a pleasure; and every
new toy will be earned by useful exertion.   A little

girl can be taught, by the aid of patterns prepared for the purpose, to cut and fit all articles for her doll. She can also be provided with a little wash-tub, and irons, to wash and iron, and thus keep in proper order a complete little domestic establishment.

Besides these amusements, there are the enjoyments secured in walking, riding, visiting, and many others, which need not be recounted. Children, if trained to be healthful and industrious, will never fail to discover resources for amusement; while their guardians should lend their aid to guide and restrain them from excess.

CHAPTER XXIV.

ON SOCIAL DUTIES.

Social Enjoyments not always considered in the List of Duties. Main Object of Life to form Character. Kindness to Strangers. Hospitality. Change of Character of Communities in Relation to Hospitality. Resolving large Communities into small Circles. Hospitality should be prompt. Strangers should be made to feel at their ease. Family Friendship should be preserved. Plan adopted by Families of the Writer's Acquaintance.

IT is not unfrequently the case, that the social enjoyments of life, with many, are never placed in the list of duties. Many men allow their professional employments, and many mothers the cares of their families, to occupy their whole time, and never imagine, when they confess their neglect of visiting, writing letters, and the various modes of social hospitality, that they are confessing omissions of sacred duties.

If the main object of this life were to make money, and secure those various gratifications of appetite and taste which money purchases, such a course might, to some extent, be justified. But, if the main object of life, for ourselves and for others, is *to form character*, then the neglect of appropriate means to develope the social, domestic, and benevolent, feelings, must be regarded in a very different light. In this view of the subject, every man and every woman are under obligation to devote some portion of time to perpetuating and increasing family and neighborhood friendships, and to sustaining the various claims of domestic hospitality.

There is no social duty, which the Supreme Lawgiver has more strenuously urged, than hospitality and kindness to strangers. The widow, the fatherless, and the stranger, are classed together, as the special objects of Divine tenderness ; and the neglect of their feelings and interests is viewed with particular displeasure. There are some reasons, why this duty peculiarly demands attention from the American people. Reverses of fortune are, in this land, so frequent and sudden, and the habits of the people are so migratory, that there are strangers in every part of the Country, many of whom have been suddenly bereft of wonted comforts, and are pining, in a strange land, without friends, and without the sympathy and society so necessary to sustain the spirits. Such, too frequently, pass along unnoticed, and with no comforter but Him who " knoweth the heart of a stranger."

In a new country, where visiters are few, and in those states where residences are on dissevered plantations, a generous hospitality may thrive, more as the result of personal wants, than as the offspring of benevolent principle. It is when population becomes so dense, that men feel no such personal wants, that the sacred name and claims of " the stranger " are most likely to be neglected. And those, who on this subject are accustomed to act on principles of Christian benevolence, rather than from impulse, are most likely to fulfil such obligations.

It not unfrequently is found, that communities, which, in their earliest history, were most remarkable for a free and ever ready hospitality, as the rush of population pours in, pass to the opposite extreme. They find that the habits of attention to the stranger, which existed in a limited circle, cannot be extended to all who make this claim ; and, finding themselves too severely taxed, instead of modifying, they give up, almost entirely, the practice of this duty.

The increase of population in a community, often involves another evil, in the multiplication of a large circle of acquaintances, so that, keeping up any degree of intimacy with all, makes burdensome demands upon time. It is probable, that, in most large places, the visiting circle of each family is far too large to secure the most useful and agreeable mode of social enjoyment.

The only remedy for this evil, is, attempting to resolve a large community into small circles. A few families, united by similarity of character and pursuits, may perpetuate a degree of intimacy and friendship, which can never be secured by the not uncommon method of keeping up "a calling acquaintance," with some forty or fifty families, and occasionally making a large party to entertain them all. Such a subdivision of society, as the one suggested, cannot suddenly be effected ; but, if systematically aimed at, it can eventually be secured. The Writer has been in circles, where this object was effected, and witnessed most delightful results. The parents mingled in unrestrained modes, with the easy cordiality of affectionate friends ; the children of the families thus associated, grew up together, more like brothers and sisters, than like common acquaintances ; while the joys and sorrows of each family were shared by a common sympathy. When a community is thus subdivided, the claims of the stranger are much more likely to be properly regarded. A person, entering any one of these minor circles, is much more likely to be met by that kind of attention and kindness which is most agreeable, because each member feels some degree of hospitable responsibility; whereas, strangers, having claims only on the community, in general, are very apt to find that they are met by no one in particular.

It is impossible, in large communities, to carry out the practice of each one paying civilities to every stranger. But it is the duty of all to learn whether such attentions are bestowed; and, in cases where there is any neglect, to supply the deficiency.

If a stranger is allowed to remain in a place, day after day, and week after week, unnoticed and unknown, there must be a great want of correct views and feelings in regard to the duty of hospitality. And it should ever be remembered, that the first days of a stranger's sojourn are the most dreary; and that procrastinating hospitable attentions, often destroys half their value. A person who intends to offer civility to a stranger, doubles the kindness, by conferring it at an early period.

In social gatherings, the claims of the stranger are too apt to be forgotten. If the person is handsome, or rich, or distinguished by other adventitious advantages, there is no want of proffered civilities or affable discourse; but a stranger, possessing no such advantages, may often pass a whole evening in society, claiming to be the best, and meet scarcely a word or an act of politeness. When a community learn to act from principle, and not from mere feeling, in this matter, then the mere fact that a person has the claims of a stranger, will ever secure kindness and polite attentions.

The most agreeable hospitality, to strangers who become inmates of a family, is that which puts them entirely at ease. This can never be done, when the guest perceives that the order of family arrangements is altered, and that time, comfort, and convenience are sacrificed.

Offering the best to the stranger, a polite regard to every wish expressed, and giving precedence in all matters of comfort and convenience, can still be combined with the easy freedom which makes the stranger feel at home; and this is the perfection of hospitable entertainment.

It is to be feared, that, in this migratory and business Nation, there is far too little attention given to the preservation of family friendships. There can be no friends, like those reared by the same parents, who have enjoyed together the pleasures of childhood and youth. And yet, such friends scatter abroad, and, taking little or no pains to preserve any social intercourse, they soon become almost as strangers; and some of the dearest ties of life are suffered to untwine, for want of a little care. If a very little of the time and money spent for the luxuries of food, dress, and furniture, were devoted to perpetuating family friendships, how much more elevated and purer enjoyments would be secured! There are families, who make it a definite object of effort to perpetuate the ties of kindred by frequent personal intercourse and correspondence, and who secure the means for doing this, by economizing in other less important particulars. Such will testify that the effort has secured to them some of the purest enjoyments of this life. A practice, which, in some cases, has been adopted by the scattered members of a large family, may be worthy of imitation. The method is this. The first day of each month some member of each family, at the two extreme points of dispersion, take a folio sheet, and, filling a part of one page, send it on, by mail, to the next family, who, after reading it, add another contribution, and remail it to the next. Thus the family circular passes from

each extreme, through, to all the members of a large
and widely dispersed family ; and each member
becomes a sharer in the joys and sorrows, plans,
pursuits, and hopes, of all the rest.   At the same
time, frequent family meetings are sought ; and the
expense, thus incurred, is cheerfully met by retrenchments in other directions.   The sacrifice of
tea and coffee, or of some other useless physical
indulgence, would often purchase many social and
domestic enjoyments, of this kind, a thousand times
more elevating and delightful.

CHAPTER XXV.

ON THE CONSTRUCTION OF HOUSES.

Importance to Family Comfort of well-constructed Houses. Rules
for constructing them. Often disregarded. When. *Economy of
Labor*. Large Houses. Arrangement of Rooms.   Staircases.
Wells and Cisterns. Ornaments and Furniture. *Economy of
Money*. Shape and Arrangement of Houses. Porticos, Piazzas,
and other Ornaments. Simplicity to be preferred. Fireplaces.
Economy of Health. Outdoor Conveniences. Doors and Windows.
Ventilation. *Economy of Comfort*. Domestics. Spare Chambers.
Good Taste. Proportions. Color and Ornaments. PLANS OF
HOUSES AND DOMESTIC CONVENIENCES. Receipts for Whitewash.

THERE is no matter of domestic economy, which
more seriously involves the health and daily comfort
of American women, than the proper construction of
houses.   There are five particulars, to which attention should be given, in building a house ; namely,
economy of labor, economy of money, economy of
health, economy of comfort, and good taste.

The Writer will first point out some particulars,
in which these rules may be disregarded.

The first, respects *economy of labor*.   In deciding
upon the size and style of a house, the probabilities

in regard to hired service, and the health and capacity of the housekeeper, should be the very first consideration.

If a man has a reasonable assurance of an income that will enable him to hire the service which a large house demands, and if he is in those sections of the country where money will secure competent domestics, it is proper to build a large house and live in a style suitable to it. But if a man is uncertain as to his means, or if qualified domestics are scarce, it is poor economy to build a large house. Every room added to a house increases the amount of sweeping, dusting, cleaning of floor, paint, and windows, and the expense and care of the furniture pertaining to it. A house of half the size, requires only just half the labor to take care of it; and so *vice versa.* There is a great disregard of economy, in this particular, in this Country. Multitudes are living in houses so large, as to demand an amount of service which the means of the owners cannot supply; so that the extra rooms must either be neglected, or the labor must fall on the housekeeper herself.

The arrangement of rooms, and the proper supply of conveniences, is another item, in which the economy of labor and comfort are often violated. A great amount of labor is saved, by having rooms and conveniences so arranged, as to avoid walking and carrying. To exhibit these points, more distinctly, some minutiæ will be pointed out, where the rules of economy, in regard to labor and comfort, are violated.

A front entry and staircase, in most houses, occupy a large space, above and below, and are so open to inspection, as to demand daily care, while a back staircase is added for more common uses. This creates the expense involved in building two staircases, and the labor of keeping them in order; the front one occupying the most conspicuous position, and demanding much space.

But a house can be so arranged, that one staircase shall answer all the purposes of two, and save much, both in space, expense, and labor. This will be shown in the engravings on subsequent pages. (See Fig. 11, &c.)

Another violation of economy of labor, may be seen in the position of kitchens. Nothing is more laborious, to a woman of delicate health, than the care of her kitchen, when access to it is gained only by going down one or two flights of stairs. And yet, how often is it the case, that the mother's nursery is in the second story, and her kitchen in the basement! This, in cities, seems to be inevitable; but it is very needless in the country, where land enough can be secured for extending the circuit of a house. A house should be so arranged, that the mother and housekeeper, when she is in feeble health, or is without domestics, can have access to her nursery and kitchen, with the fewest steps and least effort.

Another particular, in which economy in labor is neglected, is in the position of wells and cisterns, and in the methods of drawing the water. These can be so placed, that, by simply turning a cock, or working a small pump, the water will flow directly into the place where it is needed for use. This will be illustrated in the engravings on subsequent pages. But how often is it the case, that wells and cisterns are located out of doors, and at a distance from the place where the water is to be used; while the mode of drawing and carrying it is excessively laborious! To draw and carry a couple of pails of water, will often demand an amount of muscular energy, which would be equal to an hour of additional exertion in common modes, if this needless wear and tear were subtracted.

A want of economy in labor, is often seen in the style, ornaments, and furniture, of a house, such as brasses demanding labor, in place of other materials demanding little or none ; filigree ornaments to the casings and mantelpieces; kitchen floors without paint or oil-cloth, which double the labor in keeping them in order ; and many other items of this sort.

A want of *economy in money* is often seen in the *shape and arrangement* of houses. A *perfect square* encloses more rooms, at a less expense, than any other shape ; while it has least surface exposed to external cold, and is most easily warmed and ventilated. And the further a house departs from this shape, the more is the expense increased, both as to construction and methods of warming it in cold weather. Wings and kitchens built out, behind, add to the expense of a building, and require more fuel to warm them. Piazzas and porticos are very expensive appendages, and would secure far more comfort, if turned into additional accommodations, such as closets, drawers, shelves, and kitchen conveniences. The money demanded for the cheapest kind of portico, would pay for enlarging the house, so as to admit another room of convenient size.

In the subsequent engravings, it will be shown how all the advantages of a portico or piazza may be secured, for a much less sum than is ordinarily bestowed on these expensive appendages.

Much money is often worse than wasted in finical ornaments about porticos, doors, windows, and fireplaces, which, to the eye of taste, really diminish, rather than increase, the beauty of appearance. Ornaments are not suitable for any but large and expensive houses, and even in these, it is every year becoming more fashionable to have simple mouldings and carvings, and but little ornamental filigree work.

A want of economy is sometimes shown, in the

position of fireplaces. When a chimney is in the outer wall of a house, one fourth of the heat passes off, through the wall, and is lost. When the chimney is in the centre, all the heat generated, passes into the house, and tempers its whole atmosphere. A house, so constructed that a stove can be placed in a central room, surrounded by other rooms, can be warmed with less fuel than by any other contrivance. Some of the plans subsequently given, will illustrate this.

In regard to the *economy of health*, it will be allowed, that, considering the cost of medicine, attendance of physicians, loss of labor, and the interruption of domestic plans, nothing is so expensive as sickness. Every arrangement, therefore, which tends to injure the health, is a serious violation of economy. It sacrifices not only health, but also comfort, time, and money. There is much bad economy, in this respect, in constructing houses. One of the most pernicious instances, is found in the position of wells and privies, so that persons in the perspiration of labor, or in the debility of ill health, are obliged to go out of doors, in all weathers. Many an invalid has been thrown back upon a sick-bed, and many a woman, engaged in domestic labor, has been made sick, by this cause. In a subsequent engraving, (Fig. 28, page 294,) the proper arrangement and position of these conveniences is exhibited.

Another cause of sickness, is furnished by outside doors opening into sitting-rooms; an arrangement very common at the South and West. In such cases, children, and persons in delicate health, are very liable to suffer from sudden chills. The warmth of a fire, or the exercise of labor or sport, induces a perspiration. In this state, the door is thrown open, whatever be the temperature abroad; and the frequent result is, fever, bowel complaints, or the many other evils which follow from a sudden chill, when the body is in a state of perspiration. This arrangement, which is so agreeable in warm weather, can be secured without risk, by having a small entry for the outer door, and the windows made long, down to the floor, the lower part on hinges like a door. These can be closed tight, in Winter, and opened only in temperate weather.

Another point, where economy of health is neglected, is, in regard to the construction and ventilation of sleeping-rooms. The family, especially children and domestics, are often placed in small chambers, without fireplaces, and with no contrivance for the proper ventilation of the room. Thus they have only a small quantity of air provided for the hours of slumber; and, before morning, it has been inhaled and expired, until it is loaded with the noxious effluvia from the lungs, and almost deprived of its vital principle. In this way, by a slow, but certain, process, the constitution of childhood and youth is gradually undermined, and life shortened. Every chamber, if not large and airy in dimensions, should have a current of air made to pass through it, by an opening over the door and by a chimney. This will keep up a constant supply of fresh air. When this cannot be secured, a door should be left ajar, and a small opening made in the window, while the bed should be placed out of the immediate current of air.

A disregard of *economy of comfort*, is sometimes seen in the provisions made for the convenience of domestics. A woman, who has large and airy parlors, with a dark and comfortless kitchen, and a small ill-furnished room for her domestics, will often be left to much labor and perplexity, which she would never have felt, had she taken pains to make her house comfortable to her domestics, as well as to herself and her company.

There are persons, so wise and economical, as to

select the largest and pleasantest rooms in the house
for common use, while those designed only for occasional occupancy, though genteel and comfortable,
are selected from those parts least desirable.   Spare
chambers, and spare parlors, are generally used in
the evening, when position makes little difference
in the enjoyment of visiters, while the enjoyment of
a family, through every hour of the day, depends,
in some degree, on the agreeableness of their accommodations.   But multitudes of persons will cramp
their bedrooms, kitchens, and closets, to secure a
large parlor and spare chamber, to be shut up most
of the time, and opened only for transient visiters.
This is poor economy of comfort.

The construction of houses with reference *to taste*,
is a desirable, though the least important, item.   It
is not realized, by persons who have not attended to
the subject, how much the beauty of a house depends
on propriety of *proportions*.   It is always the case,
that a house in good proportions is as cheap as, and
generally cheaper than, one in which the rules of
taste are violated ; and such a house always pleases
the eye, even of one unacquainted with the rules of
proportion.   So the *color* and *ornaments* of a house,
when properly adapted to its situation, style, and use,
have much influence in producing a pleasing effect.

PLANS OF HOUSES AND DOMESTIC CONVENIENCES.

The following plans are drawn on the assumption,
that the present changing state of society, in America, makes it peculiarly important that dwelling-
houses be constructed with reference to *economy
of labor*.   There will always be persons, who can
build large houses, and find means to secure the service, which a corresponding style of living demands.
But any person, who takes general views of the
present tendencies of things in this Country, must be
convinced, that those who demand hired service, will

every year increase, while the relative number of properly-qualified domestics will constantly decrease. The housekeepers in this Nation, to a very wide extent, must either depend on the service of foreigners, who must be both taught and superintended, or mothers and daughters must themselves perform most of the domestic labor. Either alternative demands, that, in constructing a house, the first object of attention should be, economy of labor.

The plans in this work are chiefly designed for persons of moderate circumstances, especially for young housekeepers, who are making their first essays in domestic affairs.

In the three or four first years of married life, the young mothers of this Country are called, suddenly, and, in a great majority of cases, without suitable preparation, to superintend or to perform all the various business of domestic economy ; to nurse children, to manage domestics, to entertain company, to attend the sick, and to multiplied other domestic cares. At the same time, so large a portion of them have delicate health, and suffer so much from the discouragement and depression consequent on disease and the accumulation of harassing cares, that every man, in forming plans for a future residence, ought to make these probabilities the first consideration. And every woman, who has any influence in deciding questions of this sort, ought to regard these liabilities as the foundation of her plans. Especially is this needful, in those newer portions of this Nation, where qualified domestics are most rare.

The plan exhibited on the accompanying engravings, (Fig. 10, and 11,) is, that of a cottage, which will accommodate six grown persons, and one or two children to sleep in the room with the parents. The elevation, or outside front view, (Fig. 10,) is drawn in fine proportions, which is its chief beauty ; and it should be painted white.

Fig. 10.

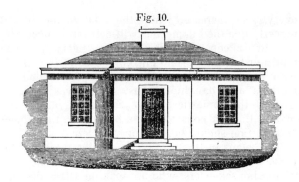

Fig. 11.
Ground Plan.

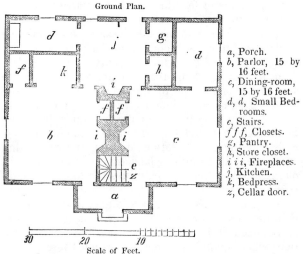

a, Porch.
b, Parlor, 15 by
16 feet.
c, Dining-room,
15 by 16 feet.
d, d, Small Bed-
rooms.
e, Stairs.
f f f, Closets.
g, Pantry.
h, Store closet.
i i i, Fireplaces.
j, Kitchen.
k, Bedpress.
z, Cellar door.

Scale of Feet.

Fig. 11, is the plan of the interior of the same
building. The central part (or porch, a) projects just
enough to afford an entrance to the two adjacent
rooms. This is to avoid having an outer door in
any family sitting-room, the evils of which have
been pointed out. The front, or side windows, or

both, might be made down to the floor, the lower part opening like doors. These could be made tight in Winter, and be opened in Summer.

This house has a parlor, eating-room, and kitchen, of convenient size for a family of six or eight. The parlor, *b*, has the closet, *f*, and the bedpress, *k*, adjoining it.

Fig. 12.

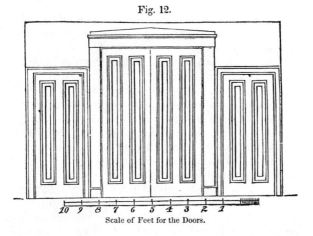

Scale of Feet for the Doors.

Fig. 12, represents the doors on that side of the room. The large central doors open to the bedpress, the smaller side doors open, those on the left into the closet, *f*, and those on the right into the kitchen, *j*. When these large doors are closed, the room looks like a common parlor, with folding-doors opening into another parlor, as is common in most city houses. This makes it a genteel room for receiving company. When these large doors are thrown open, the room becomes a spacious and airy bedroom ; while the two closets, *f, f,* furnish accommodations for concealing all pertaining to a bedroom that cannot appropriately appear in a parlor. The bedpress is just large enough to receive a bed ; and under it can be placed a trucklebed for young children. Thus, the mother can have her parlor, nursery, and kitchen, all under her eye at once. The dining-room, *c*, (Fig. 11,) has the small bedroom, *d*, adjoining it, large enough for a bed, washstand, bureau, and chair. Leaving the door open, at night, will make it sufficiently airy for a sleeping-room.

The kitchen, *j*, has a smaller bedroom, *d*, attached to it. This will contain a narrow single bed for a domestic. If it be necessary to find accommodations there for two persons, a narrow trucklebed can be put under the single bed.

The pantry is at *g*, and store closet, at *h*. The chimney is in the middle, thus economizing fuel. The staircase, is designed to give access to the garret, above, and the cellar, below ; one door being at *e*, and the other at *z*. A plan for back accommodations is shown in Fig. 28, (see page 293.) These should be placed in the rear of the kitchen.

In a plan on so limited a scale, some economy and contrivance will be demanded, in storing away articles of dress and bedclothing. For this end, in the bedpress (*k*) of the parlor, *b*, (Fig. 11,) a wide shelf may be placed about two feet from the ceiling, and a curtain be hung from the wall above in front of it. On this shelf, Winter bedding and clothing can be stowed, and the curtain will protect them from dust. Under this shelf, at the foot of the bed, pegs can be placed, to hold garments. From the edge of the shelf, above, a curtain can be suspended, to conceal these articles, and protect them from dust. This contrivance answers the purpose of a wardrobe, though it is not quite so convenient. One or both of the closets, *f f*, should be also fitted up with shelves and drawers.

Fig. 13.

Fig. 13, represents a fireplace and mantelpiece, in a style which corresponds with the doors and other parts of the building.

In these plans of rooms, an entire vacancy in a wall or partition represents a door; a vacancy with a single line across it, represents a window. A × by a door, shows the place where the door should be hung, and the room into which it should swing. The comfort of a room, in Winter, depends very much on the way in which the doors are hung.

Fig. 14, 15, are plans of another cottage, which contains rooms rather more agreeably arranged, having a bedpress attached to each room, and more space for closets. The disadvantage is, that the chimney is not central; each fireplace having a flue in the side of the house.

Fig. 14.

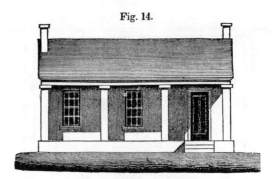

Fig. 15.

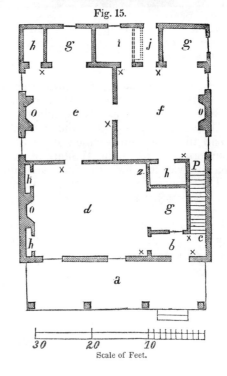

Scale of Feet.

The elevation (Fig. 14) is drawn with a piazza or porch in front, which would probably cost two hundred dollars. For this sum, another story might be added. The two-story house, *without* a piazza, (Fig. 16, 17,) could be built for the same sum as this cottage *with* one. But whoever likes this interior plan better than the preceding one, and prefers to dispense with the piazza, can put the front of the first cottage to this plan. The only alteration required, would be, to make the windows down to the floor, in order to preserve uniformity with the door, which is to be placed at the side, instead of in the middle. In place of the projection for an entry, the slight projection of the width of one brick would preserve the same general appearance on the outside. The folding doors and side doors shown in Fig. 12, are designed only for a room intended to be used for company. They give a genteel look and symmetry to a room, but cost more. In this cottage, (Fig. 15,) they may be put in the front room, and more common doors in the two back ones. In the front room, at *z*, a door is not needed ; a false one is put there to secure the beauty of symmetry. The bedpresses should all be fitted up with shelves, pegs, and curtains, as previously described. Windows are put in the bedpresses, in order to secure proper ventilation. They ought to be left open, every morning, to air the bedclothing. The window, opening from the entry, *b*, to the bedpress, *g*, is designed simply for this purpose.

Explanation of Fig. 15.

a, Porch.	*g g g,* Bedpresses.
b, Entry.	*h h h h,* Closets.
c, Stairs.	*i,* Store closet.
d, Parlor, 16 by 20 feet.	*j,* Back entry and Sink.
e, Dining-room, 16 by 16 feet.	*p,* Cellar stairs.
f, Kitchen.	*o o o,* Fireplaces.

Fig. 16.
Ground Plan.

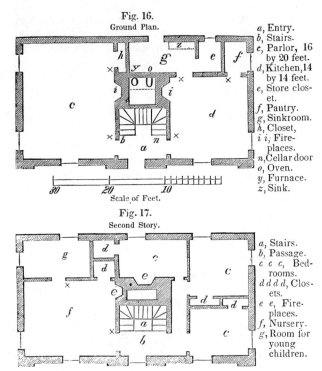

a, Entry.
b, Stairs.
c, Parlor, 16
  by 20 feet.
d, Kitchen, 14
  by 14 feet.
e, Store clos-
  et.
f, Pantry.
g, Sinkroom.
h, Closet,
i i, Fire-
  places.
n, Cellar door
o, Oven.
y, Furnace.
z, Sink.

Scale of Feet.

Fig. 17.
Second Story.

a, Stairs.
b, Passage.
c c c, Bed-
  rooms.
d d d d, Clos-
  ets.
e e, Fire-
  places.
f, Nursery.
g, Room for
  young
  children.

The plans shown in Fig. 16, 17, are designed for a family where most of the domestic labor is to be performed by the ladies of the family. In Fig. 16, the parlor, c, is designed for a sitting-room, and for company. The room d, is designed partly for an eating-room, and partly for a kitchen. Adjacent to it, is the room g, where, at y and o may be placed an oven and large boiler, or a small fireplace. In this room, the washing, baking, and sink-work may be done; so as to withdraw all the most soiling employments from the room d. This room may be furnished with a carpet, having a wide oil-cloth around the fireplace. Here most of the cooking for ordinary meals, and the ironing can be done, and yet the room be made agreeable for an eating-room. The fumes of cooking can be removed by a temporary current of fresh air; and they will be no greater than in many houses where a cooking-stove is used, even in a distant kitchen.

The nursery is in the second story, at f, (Fig. 17,) with the small adjoining room, g, for young children. The nursery, and also the back chamber, have a fireplace, both of which may be needed in case of sickness. The elevation, Fig. 22, is designed for the exterior of this plan.

Fig. 18, 19, are plans of a two-story house, on a larger scale. It has three convenient rooms on the ground story, and four chambers above. The lettering and explanation on the drawing make further description needless. This plan can have either of the elevations, Fig. 20, or 21, for its exterior. In this plan, a concealed staircase is made to serve for front and back use.

Fig. 20, 21, are other plans, for a larger house, which also can have either of the elevations, Fig. 22 or 23, adapted to it. The two parlors, c e, (Fig. 20,) can either be used as parlors, or one of them can be taken for a nursery. In this latter case, the two closets, i i, will be very convenient. The room d, is for an eating-room, and the closets, and store-room, are placed between that and the kitchen, f. It is a great convenience to have the dish-closet between the dining-room and kitchen; and if a small stone or marble sink be placed here, it will also be a great convenience. Small cupboards and drawers should be placed in this closet, for table linen and articles that need to be locked up.

This is an example of the position of a staircase which is concealed from public view, and answers for both front and back stairs. At p, is a place for hanging overgarments out of sight.

Fig. 18.
Ground Plan.

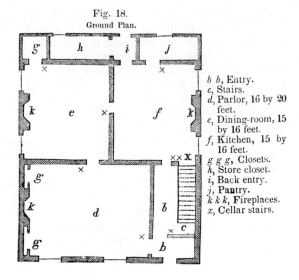

b b, Entry.
c, Stairs.
d, Parlor, 16 by 20 feet.
e, Dining-room, 15 by 16 feet.
f, Kitchen, 15 by 16 feet.
g g g, Closets.
h, Store closet.
i, Back entry.
j, Pantry.
k k k, Fireplaces.
x, Cellar stairs.

Fig. 19.
Second Story.

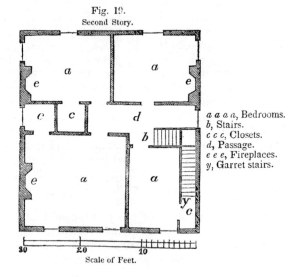

a a a a, Bedrooms.
b, Stairs.
c c c, Closets.
d, Passage.
e e e, Fireplaces.
y, Garret stairs.

Scale of Feet.

Fig. 20.
Ground Floor.

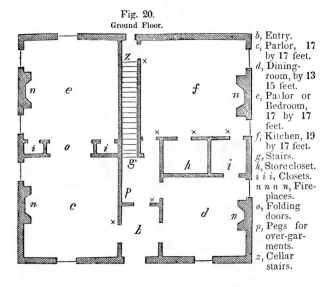

b, Entry.
c, Parlor, 17 by 17 feet.
d, Dining-room, by 13 15 feet.
e, Parlor or Bedroom, 17 by 17 feet.
f, Kitchen, 19 by 17 feet.
g, Stairs.
h, Store closet.
i i i, Closets.
n n n n, Fire-places.
o, Folding doors.
p, Pegs for over-garments.
z, Cellar stairs.

Fig. 21.
Second Story.

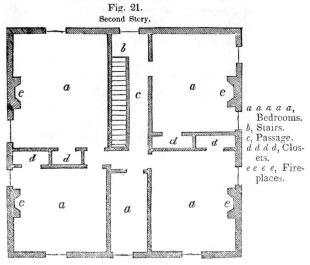

a a a a a, Bedrooms.
b, Stairs.
c, Passage.
d d d d, Closets.
e e e e, Fire-places.

Fig. 22.

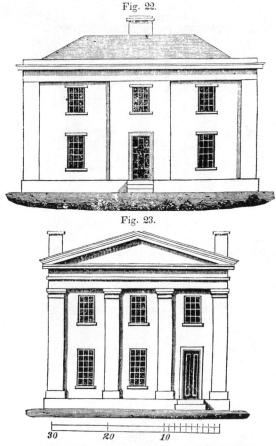

Fig. 23.

Fig. 24 and 25, present a plan, which, for a large
and genteel house, secures the most conveniences, at
the smallest expense of *labor* in housekeeping, of
any the Writer has ever seen.   The elevation (Fig.
24) is of the simplest Gothic style, having a recess
to the central part, which serves as a sort of piazza,
both front and back.

Fig. 24.

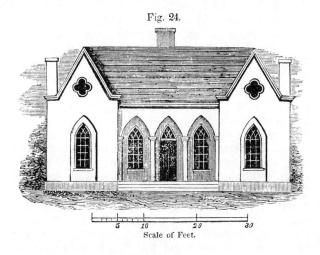

Scale of Feet.

Fig. 25.

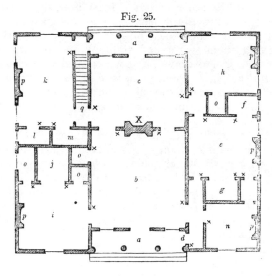

Between these two piazzas, occupying the centre of the house, are the two parlors, (*b* and *c*,) the back one (*c*) to be used for an eating-room. The chimney (X) is here represented as between them ; but in the residence similar to this, which the Writer visited, folding-doors were placed there, near which was set a large *Nott's stove*, to be used in Winter, the pipe of which went through the ceiling, and entered one of the side chimneys. This stove served to warm, not only these, but three or four other large rooms which adjoined ; so that nearly the whole house was thus warmed with one fire. Two windows and a door opened on one side to the north piazza, and the same on the other side to the south, so that, in Summer, when the folding-doors were open, it formed a large and airy saloon, with a piazza at each end ; and the Writer never saw so delightful Summer parlors. In Winter, the outside doors, opening to the piazzas, were fastened up and calked, and the side entrance, *d*, was used, thus making them warm and tight Winter rooms. As the plan is here drawn, a door is placed on each side of the fireplace, directly opposite to the windows, so that, in Summer, by opening the windows and these doors, the rooms are almost as pleasant as with fold-ing-doors.

In the right wing, at *e*, is the nursery, with the small adjoining room, *f*, for children to sleep in, and a bedpress, *g*, which, being closed by day, makes the room a retired parlor for the mother. By this arrangement, the children's rooms are as much shut out from the parlors, as if they were above stairs ; and the mother at once has easy access to nursery, parlor, kitchen, and her own sleeping-room, *h*. A passage is secured, both back and front, so as to go out of doors, or into the kitchen, without entering the parlors. The library, *i*, is a room which can be kept as a spare chamber for visiters, and by day, the bedpress (*j*) can be closed, thus making it a sitting-room. This, the gentleman of the house can use for his library. The kitchen, *k*, has *l*, *m*, for pantry and store-room. Another bedroom, *n*, is adjacent to the nursery; and comfortable chambers for domestics can be finished in the attic. Closets are marked *o*, and fireplaces, *p*. The stairs are at *q*.

The Writer has repeatedly heard ladies, who have kept house where parlor, kitchen, and nursery, were on the same floor, say that it saves nearly one half the fatigue that housekeeping demands, when the nursery is in one story, the parlor in another, and the kitchen in the basement.

Fig. 26, is the representation of a cottage, built by Daniel Wadsworth, Esq., in the vicinity of Hartford, Connecticut. It was for some time the residence of a friend of the Writer, who always spoke of it as one of the most comfortable and agreeable residences she ever entered.

It is arranged on a plan similar to the preceding, but is on a smaller scale. This drawing exhibits the manner in which the *roofs* of the previous plan are to be arranged, which here are seen in perspective, while the other drawing shows the front view only.

The ground plan of this, has the following dimensions. It is forty feet square. The recess for the portico is five feet deep. The wings, on each side of the central rooms, are twelve feet wide. These wings can be divided into a kitchen and sleeping-rooms. Height, from sill to eaves, ten feet; from sill to ridge-pole, eighteen feet; wings, twelve feet front; centre building, sixteen feet front; windows, in the front of the wings, nine feet and nine inches, from the bottom to the highest point; width three feet and four inches. The upper part of these windows is false. Width of windows, in front of the main building, two feet and nine inches.

Fig. 26.

Recess for piazza, five feet deep. The house is of wood, covered with narrow boards, planed and matched, and painted stone color. The columns are nine inches at the base, being trunks of trees, with the bark taken off, and their knots projecting a little, but smoothed, and painted the same color as the house, or a little lighter.

The barn makes a very picturesque appearance. It is thirty feet, on the side toward the street, and forty feet deep. The wings on each side, are sheds for cattle, and a carriage-house. These wings are fifteen feet front, toward the street, and twelve feet deep. Height of sheds, from sill to battlement, twelve feet. Height of barn, from sill to eaves, eighteen feet; from sill to ridge, twenty-nine feet. The barn is covered with boards, planed and capped, and painted to represent blocks. The windows are false. The small building is a model for a Summer-house, or any small out-building.

Both this, and the preceding cottage, require a woodhouse, and the conveniences connected with it. Such are represented in Fig. 28, page 293. A building for this purpose, projecting from the kitchen, with battlements like the wings of the barn, (without the block-work,) and with windows like those in the small Summer-house, would appear in good keeping with the rest. The ornaments of the front, and the pillars of the portico, of this cottage, made simply of trunks of small trees, give a beautiful rural finish to the building, and are trifling in expense. The fence is painted stone color. The interior has two central rooms, and small rooms on each side, in the wings. It has also a cellar kitchen.

In arranging the yard and grounds for such residences, the house should be set back, as in the drawing. The custom of planting shade trees, in straight rows, in yards, is in very bad taste. It is much more beautiful to have them put in clumps, at two or three different points. By this method, a dense shade is secured, for some places, and a clear opening for green grass and flowers, which never flourish well, when shade trees are scattered over the premises. The mode of arranging the front yard, as represented in the drawing, is in much better taste than to have the front gate directly before the front door, and a straight walk from one to the other.

A clump of trees, each side of the gate, a clump at one front corner, and another at one of the back corners of the cottage, and a clump on the circular piece of turf between the barn and house, are what would appear the best. Flowers should be put close to the cottage, and shrubbery on the circle in front, and along the path.

Fig. 27, represents the accommodations for securing water with the least labor. It is designed for a well or cistern under ground. The reservoir, **R**, may be a half hogshead, or something larger, which may be filled once a day, from the pump, by a man, or boy.

Fig. 27.

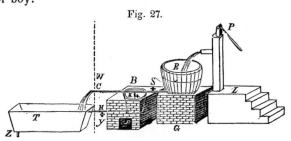

P, Pump. *L*, Steps to use when pumping. *R*, Reservoir. *G*, Brickwork to raise the Reservoir. *B*, A large Boiler. *F*, Furnace, beneath the Boiler. *C*, Conductor of cold water. *H*, Conductor of hot water. *K*, Cock for letting cold water into the Boiler. *S*, Pipe to conduct cold water to a cock over the kitchen sink. *T*, Bathing-tub, which receives cold water from the Conductor *C*, and hot water from the Conductor *H*. *W*, Partition separating the Bathing-room from the Wash-room. *Y*, Cock to draw off hot water. *Z*, Plug to let off the water from the Bathing-tub into a drain.

The conductor, C, should be a lead pipe, which, instead of going over the boiler, should be bent along behind it. From S, a branch sets off, which conducts the cold water to the sink in the kitchen, where it discharges with a cock. H, is a conductor from the lower part of the boiler, made of copper, or some metal not melted by great heat; and at Y, a cock is placed, to draw off hot water. Then the conductor passes to the bathing-tub, where is another cock. At Z, the water is let off from the bathing-tub. By this arrangement, great quantities of hot and cold water can be used, with no labor in carrying, and with very little labor in raising it.

In case a cistern is built above ground, it can be placed as the reservoir is, and then all the labor of pumping is saved.

Fig. 28.

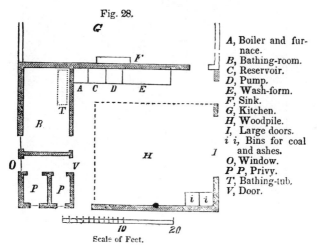

A, Boiler and furnace.
B, Bathing-room.
C, Reservoir.
D, Pump.
E, Wash-form.
F, Sink.
G, Kitchen.
H, Woodpile.
I, Large doors.
i i, Bins for coal and ashes.
O, Window.
P P, Privy.
T, Bathing-tub.
V, Door.

Scale of Feet.

Fig. 28, is the plan of a building for back-door accommodations. At *A C D E*, are accommodations shown in Fig. 27. The bathing-room is adjacent to the boiler and reservoir, to receive the water.

The privy, *P P*, should have two apartments, as indispensable to healthful habits in a family. A window should be placed at *O*, and a door, with springs or a weight to keep it shut, should be at *V*. Keeping the window open, and the door shut, will prevent any disagreeable effects in the house. *G*, is the kitchen, and at *F*, is the sink, which should have a conductor and cock from the reservoir. *H*, is the place for wood, where it should in Summer be stored for Winter. A bin for coal, and also a brick receiver for ashes, should be in this part. Every woman should use her influence to secure all these conveniences; even if it involves the sacrifice of the piazza, or " the best parlor."

Fig. 29.

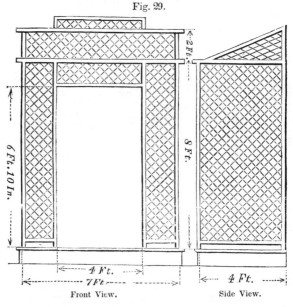

Front View.   Side View.

Fig. 29, is a latticed portico, which is cheap, and answers all the purposes of a more expensive one.

It should be solid, overhead, to shed the rain, and creepers should be trained over it.   A simple latticed arch, over a door, covered with creepers, is very cheap, and serves instead of a portico.

Fig. 30.

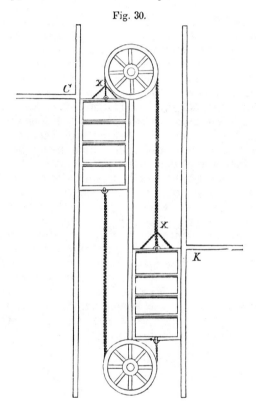

C, Parlor ceiling.   *K*, Kitchen ceiling.

Fig. 30, represents a *sliding closet*, or *dumb waiter*, a convenience which saves much labor, when the kitchen is in the basement.   The two closets should be made wide, and broad enough to receive a common waiter. The chain or rope, which passes over the wheels, should branch at X, so as to keep the closet from rubbing in its movements, when the dishes are not set exactly in the middle, or are of unequal weights.   By this method, almost every thing needed to pass between the kitchen and parlor can be sent up and down, without any steps.   If the kitchen is not directly under the eating-room, the sliding closet can be placed in the vicinity of one or both.   Where the place is not wide enough for two closets like these, they can be made wider than they are long, say one foot and six inches long, and three feet wide.   A strip of wood, an inch broad, should be fastened on the front and back of the shelves, to prevent the dishes from being broken when they are set on carelessly.

There is nothing which so much improves the appearance of a house and the premises, as painting or whitewashing the tenements and fences.   The following receipts for whitewashing, have been found, by experience, to answer the same purpose for wood, brick, and stone, as oil-paint, and are much cheaper.   The first is the receipt used for the President's house at Washington, improved by further experiments.   The second, is a simpler and cheaper one, which the Writer has known to succeed, in a variety of cases, lasting as long, and looking as well, as white oil-paint.

Receipt.

Take half a bushel of unslacked lime, and slack it with boiling water, covering it during the process. Strain it, and add a peck of salt, dissolved in warm water; three pounds of ground rice, boiled to a thin paste, put in boiling hot; half a pound of powdered Spanish whiting; and a pound of clear glue, dissolved in warm water.   Mix, and let it stand several days.   Then keep it in a kettle, on a portable furnace, and put it on as hot as possible, with a painter's or whitewash brush.

Another.

Make whitewash, in the usual way, except that the water used should have two double-handfuls of salt dissolved in each pailful of the hot water used. Then stir in a double-handful of fine sand, to make it thick like cream. This is better to be put on hot. Coloring matter can be added to both, making a light stone color, a cream color, or a light buff, which are most suitable for buildings.

CHAPTER XXVI.

ON FIRES AND LIGHTS.

Wood Fires. Construction of Fireplaces. Firesets. Building a Fire. Wood. Cautions. *Wood Stoves.* Advantages of, and Objections to, them. Remedies for the Objections. Cautions. Stovepipes. Franklin Stoves. *Anthracite Coal Fires.* How to kindle them. Proper Grates and Furniture. *Bituminous Coal Fires.* Proper Grates. How to make the Fires. *Coke Fires. Coal Stoves.* Various Kinds. ON LIGHTS. Oil. Candles. Lard. Pearlash and Water for cleansing Lamps. *Care of Lamps.* Difficulty. Articles needed in trimming Lamps. Astral Lamps. Wicks. Shades. Weak Eyes. Dipping Wicks in Vinegar. Entry Lamps. Night Lamps. Tapers; How made. Sealing Wax. *To make Candles.* Moulds. Dipping. Rush-lights.

Wood Fires.

IN constructing chimneys, the fireplace should be made shallow ; as this secures more heat and a better current of air. When already made too deep, a false back, of brick, is an improvement. If the jambs are not of stone, it is best to paint them black. If the hearth is made of bricks, those nearest the fire should be washed over, every day, with redding mixed with milk. The bricks not reached by ashes should be painted ; or, what is better, covered over with a *zinc sheet* hearth, which can be fitted down by a tinman. This looks very neat and handsome. The hearth, and the lower part of the shovel and tongs, should be washed, every morning. Hooks, for holding up tongs and shovel, and a square block of stone, with crossing creases in it, should be provided for every fireplace. Also, a bellows, and a hearth-brush, and brass nails or knobs, on which to hang them. A fireplace cannot well be kept in proper order, without all these conveniences.

Steel furniture, for a fireplace, is more genteel than brass, and is much less trouble to keep clean. An iron bar, to lay across the andirons, keeps the fire in much better order than it can be without it.

In building a fire, if logs are used, green wood should be employed, as they consume more slowly, and give out more heat. A mixture of green and dry wood makes a cheaper and hotter fire, than dry wood alone. In kindling a fire, in a fireplace not recently used, it is best to burn a newspaper in it, first, to warm the chimney, and insure a good current of air.

Walnut, hickory, and oak, are the best fuel. Chestnut is very bad, as it snaps, and endangers clothing and carpeting. It is wise for a woman to learn to distinguish the different kinds of wood ; for she may be called to make purchases, when such knowledge will be useful. Almost any man can give this information.

Wood that is small and crooked, is unprofitable. The larger and straighter the wood, the better. In laying up fuel, for Winter, it is best to have it all split, before piling. Then it should be piled in separate parcels, one consisting of logs, another of green wood, and another of dry ; with another pile of chips, and kindling stuff. There should also be a supply of oven-wood, in a separate pile. Fagots, and any light, dry wood, are suitable for oven-wood. A bin of charcoal, also, for heating irons, and broiling meat, and a brick bin, for holding ashes, should be provided. Keeping ashes in wooden vessels, or throwing them out near combustibles, is a frequent cause of fires.

When fires are covered, at night, care should be taken that no coal of fire adheres to a broom, or brush used for sweeping the hearth ; as this has often set fire to houses. All combustible articles should be removed to a distance from the fireplace, lest a spark should fly out and set them on fire.

Wood Stoves.

Stoves are used on account of the great economy of fuel thus secured. A common large box-stove, set in a hall, with a long pipe, and a drum in a distant room, will warm the hall and three or four other rooms. The chief objections to stoves, are, the dryness of air which they induce ; the disagreeable smell of the iron ; and the coldness of the lower stratum of air, producing cold feet in those who are subject to this difficulty.

The dryness of the atmosphere can be remedied, most delightfully, by keeping a large number of plants in a room. The common mode, is, by keeping water, in an iron or block-tin vessel, on the stove. Some method of this kind should always be adopted, or else the eyes and lungs will be exposed to injury.

The disagreeable smell is occasioned by the burning, on the surface of the hot iron, of the dust floating in the atmosphere. If stoves are large, so as not to require a very fierce fire, this effect is not produced, as it is only when the iron is nearly red hot, that it takes place. Small sheet-iron stoves almost always produce this effect.

The remedy for cold feet, is to place the stove as

low as possible. This can be done, by putting a shallow box of sand under the stove, and covering it with a sheet of iron, having its edges rest on bricks, so as not to touch the box of sand. It can be bent down, so as to conceal its supporters, and thus look neater, but must not touch the floor. By this method, a current of air passes between the sheet-iron and the sand, and the stove can be brought so low as to warm the stratum of air next the floor without danger.

When the pipe of a stove passes through a wooden partition, the opening should be larger than the pipe, and a sheet of tin be fastened over the opening, with an aperture of about the size of the pipe. When the draught of a stove is poor, it can be increased by lengthening the pipe. Pipes running out of windows, do not have so good a draught, as when they pass into chimneys; nor will they draw as well, when run through a fireboard, as when raised higher. Sometimes, a double elbow, at the end of a pipe which runs through a window, will make the stove draw better, by preventing the access of wind, and by giving two directions to the smoke.

Franklin-stoves are most agreeable for parlors, as they combine the advantages of stoves and open fireplaces.

Anthracite Coal Fires.

Anthracite coal is principally burned east of the Alleghany mountains. Its advantages are, that it makes a very clean and a very hot fire, and that it seldom needs replenishing. In selecting coal, that which has a soft, porous appearance, and is covered with damp dust, is not good. That which is bright, hard, and clear, is the best. The broken or *screened* coal is best for grates, and the nut-coal for small stoves. Three tons are enough for one fire, through the Winter, in the Middle States, and four tons in the

Northern States. With every ton of anthracite coal, two barrels of charcoal may be used for kindling; or the fire may be kept constantly alive, by throwing on, at night, a few coals, to cover up the fire. The grates for anthracite coal must have a very good draught; and, for this purpose, there should be only one opening into the chimney, and this only two and a half inches wide. An aperture for carrying off dust and ashes, diminishes the draught. The grate should also be made deep, as shallow grates make it difficult to keep the fire ignited. If the grate is large, and well made, the fire needs to be replenished, after it is made in the morning, only twice; once at eleven, and once at six, o'clock. In kindling a fire, in the morning, first remove all the coal and ashes, and once a week wash the grate out clean. Then lay on one tier of coal, and on this place the fire, then the kindling stuff, and then the charcoal. Then pile on the coal, which should be of the size of eggs and oranges, laying the largest pieces back. Fill the grate full, then raise the coal still higher against the back, and then put up the blower. This kind of fire should never be poked, except when replenished, and then, not till after the blower has been put up, and the fire kindled by it. The blower should always be taken down before it becomes red hot, or it will soon be burned out. The fire should not be allowed to sink lower than the second bar from the top, or it will go out.

When the fire is to be replenished, put up the blower, to keep off the ashes, and then poke the coal, to bring it to a more compact state. Then fill the grate, as before. When the fire is too hot, it can be diminished by throwing ashes on the top. The dryness of the air can be remedied by hooking a long and narrow iron pan in front of the grate, and keeping it filled with water. A large number of plants in a room, is also a remedy for this evil.

A coal fire, should be furnished with shovel, tongs, and poker, a blower, a coal scuttle, a brush, and a holder for the blower, made of woollen covered with old silk. The ashes of anthracite coal, it is said, serves the same purpose for manure, as plaster of Paris.

Bituminous Coal Fires.

Bituminous coal is burned west of the Mountains, and to some extent at the East. Grates for this kind of fire, should have a flue nearly as deep as the grate ; and the bars should be round, and not near together. The bars which are square and close, do not make so bright and clear a fire as the others. It burns best in large pieces ; though the fine can be burnt with a mixture of chips and fine wood : but if put in alone, it packs so tight as to prevent a draught. The quantity of dust and ashes from a coal fire, depends very much on the construction of the grate. If it has a good draught, much less dust and ashes will be made, and the most of this will be drawn up the chimney. But if the draught is poor, the coal dust will fly about, soiling every thing in the room. It would be a saving of much labor and expense, if a grate is a bad one, to have it replaced by a better one. This kind of fire is improved by poking, when it has burned some time. It may be kept burning slowly all night in a grate, by covering the top with ashes. When the fire is to be kindled anew, in the morning, all the coal and ashes must be removed, and the grate made clear ; then put some small pieces of sticks and coal at the bottom, and on this put the fire and kindling stuff. After they have begun to burn, fill the grate with coal.

Coke Fires.

Coke is the coal which has had the bituminous part extracted from it. It makes a quick bright fire,

but burns out faster than coal, and is best for Spring
and Fall.

Coal-Stoves.

There are various kinds of stoves, for burning coal.
Anthracite, when burnt in stoves, should be as small
as eggs. What is called *nut-coal* is best. Stoves
for coal should be carefully put up, as, if the pipe
gapes, the coal gas may occasion death, especially if
it escapes into a sleeping-room. If a person is apparently lifeless, from the effects of coal smoke,
fresh air, friction, poultices on the feet, stimulants to
the nostrils, and hot drinks, such as pepper and gin-
ger, should be administered with much perseverance.

ON LIGHTS.

Oil is most commonly used, as lamps afford a
clearer and steadier light, and do not scatter grease
like common tallow candles. Oil is much cheaper
than candles of wax and spermaceti. The best oil
is clear, and nearly colorless. Winter-strained oil
should be bought for Winter, as the other kinds will
not burn so well in cold weather. Where lard is
very cheap, as it often is in places where pork
abounds, it will be found a less expensive and more
agreeable material than oil, for astral and other large
lamps. Those who use it, keep it in a coarse
pitcher, and set it to melt every morning, just before
filling their lamps. It will not answer for small
lamps. Oil grows thick, and does not burn well,
when it has been kept long. It is not, therefore,
good economy to buy large quantities. It should
not be left standing, in astral or other lamps not in
steady use, as this spoils the oil. It should be
emptied out, as soon as the lamp is out of use, even
if only a few days intervene before it is used again.
The inside of lamps and oil-cans should often be
cleansed, with pearlash water. In doing this, be care-

ful not to let any of the pearlash get on the gilding
or bronze, as it would do injury.   Also take care to
drain it thoroughly out of the lamps, or it will combine with the oil and form soap, and injure the oil.
Mix one tablespoonful of pearlash with one quart of
water.

On the Care of Lamps.

There is no work intrusted to domestics, which it
is so difficult to have properly attended to, as the care
of lamps.   They forget to screw them on properly,
and the oil is spilt ; or, the oil runs over and soils the
hand that takes the lamp ; or, the wicks are not
properly trimmed ; or, some other thing is neglected,
or done amiss.   For this reason, many ladies, who
keep a full supply of domestics, choose to do this
work themselves.   To do it neatly and properly,
the following articles should be provided :—An old
waiter, on which should be placed all the articles
used ; a lamp-filler, with a spout small at the end
and turning up to prevent oil from dripping ; a ball
of wickyarn, and a small basket to keep it in ; a
lamp-trimmer, made for the purpose, or a pair of
sharp common scissors ; a small soap-cup, and some
pearlash corked in a broad-mouthed bottle ; two
small soft cloths, to wash the lamps with, and several
soft coarse towels to wipe them.   After cleaning and
filling the lamps, the waiter, and every article used,
should be thoroughly cleansed from oil, with soap
suds.   If all these articles are kept neatly, it will not
be so unpleasant a job, as it is, in the manner in
which it is usually done by domestics.   If the lady
of the house chooses to have her domestics do it,
it is very important that she should provide all conveniences, and insist on cleanliness, and the frequent
change of cloths and towels.   In taking care of an
astral lamp, the shade should be washed once a week,
and the glass chimney whenever it is dimmed by

smoke. The whole lamp should be taken apart, and cleansed with pearlash water, once a month, if it is in constant use. In trimming lamps, the fingers should be perfectly dry. The way to raise an astral lamp wick, is, to turn it to the *right;* to lower it, turn it to the left. It should be trimmed, before using it, and raised to the proper height, as near as can be, before lighting. If it is allowed to burn awhile, before raising it to the proper height, it forms a crust, which dims the light. The wick should be renewed, when it is only an inch and a half long. The close-woven wicks burn better than those which are loose. Plain shades are better than cut, for astral lamps, as they give a steady light, and do not injure weak eyes as figured shades do. They also make prints and paintings appear better. An astral lamp should be lighted by a strip of rolled or folded paper, after the shade and chimney are removed. Adjust the lamp, after putting on the chimney, before putting on the shade. Low lights are bad for weak eyes, as the light shines more directly into the eye. Weak eyes should always be shaded from bright lights, by a small screen, set on the table. A person who has weak eyes, can often use them, without much injury, in the evening, if the light is clear and steady, and is shaded from the eyes. Dipping the wick in vinegar, makes a light more steady, and prevents the disagreeable smell, when extinguished. Entry lamps should be trimmed every night, and the lamps in lanterns should be cleansed and filled twice a week, and oftener if much used. Small lamps are best to carry about, and broad-bottomed tin lamps are best for kitchen use, not being easily upset.

The best and simplest kind of night-lamp, is a common small lamp, with a tin cover to set over it. The cover can be made so as to set an article over the lamp to heat water. A common roll of tin, with a few holes in the bottom, made smaller at top than the bottom, and having a handle, is all that is required.

Where a light is to be kept every night, it is cheaper to use the floating tapers, which can be bought at stores, or easily made. To make them, melt some beeswax in water, and run very coarse thread repeatedly through it, until it is as large as the largest sized darning needle. Cut this in pieces, an inch long. Then cut a large cork into thin pieces, and make a hole in the centre. Get some round pieces of tin, about the size of the cork, with a small hole in the centre. Put the tins on the top of the cork, and then draw the waxed thread through. This wick must be made of the size of the holes, or it will slip out. Put some oil in a small tin cup, place one of these with the cork side down in the oil, light it, and it will burn all night. A strip of wick-yarn drawn through melted white wax, till stiff and smooth, makes a good article for sealing letters. It can be rolled in a fanciful form, to be kept on the writing table. The wax must be melted in hot water. It will rise on the top, and then the wick can be repeatedly drawn through it.

To make Candles.

Nice candles are made in moulds. To do this, melt the materials together, in this proportion : one quarter of a pound of white wax, one quarter of an ounce of camphor, and two ounces of alum, to every ten ounces of suet or mutton tallow. Soak the wicks in lime-water and saltpetre ; fix them in the moulds, and pour in the melted tallow. When they have remained one night, for cooling, warm them a little, to melt the tallow, and then draw them out ; and when hard, put them in a box, in a dry place.

Dipped candles are cheaper, and more easily made. To make them, cut the wicks into strips, and double them over a rod, twisting them slightly. They should first be dipped in vinegar, or lime-water, and thoroughly dried. Then melt the tallow in a large kettle of water, having as much water as tallow. Wax, and powdered alum, improve them. Let this stand on a portable furnace, or coals, to keep the water hot. Lay two strips of wood, about three fourths of a yard apart, and about as high from the floor. Under this, put boards, or pans, to catch the drippings. Then take all the rods, dip the wicks once, and suspend them on this frame. Then take each rod separately, and when cold straighten and smooth the wicks, and put them at proper distances. Then continue to dip them, (two rods at a time,) till the candles are of the size wanted. Keep filling the kettle with hot water, so as to keep the tallow near the top. In dipping, do not plunge them perpendicularly, but in a slanting direction, and do it quickly. When the bottom part of the candles grows too large for the upper part, hold them in the hot tallow, till a part melts off. Let them hang one night; then cut off the bottoms, square, and keep them in a dry cool place. Lights, made of rushes dipped in tallow, are very cheap.

CHAPTER XXVII.

ON WASHING.

Good Washers rare. All needful Accommodations should be provid-
ed. Plenty of Water, easily accessible, necessary. Apparatus for
heating Water. Articles to be provided for Washing. Substitutes
for Soft Water. Washerwoman. Common Mode of Washing.
Assorting clothes. To wash Blankets and other Bedding. Feathers.
Soda Washing. Soda Soap. Mode of Soda Washing. Lime-water.
Cautions in regard to Colored Clothes. Bran-water. Potato-water.
To wash Brown Linen, Muslins, Nankeen, Furniture Chintz,
Curtains, &c., Woollen Table Covers and Shawls, Woollen Yarn,
Painted Muslins. To cleanse Gentlemen's cloth Coats and Panta-
loons. To wash Merinos, Bombazines, and Challys. To Manu-
facture Soap-Starch, and other Articles used in Washing. To
make Ley. Soft Soap. Hard Soap. Fine White Soap. Starch.

It is a common complaint, in all parts of the
Country, that *good* washers are very rare. And yet
there are few things, more trying to a neat housekeeper, than to put nice articles into the wash, and
have them returned yellow, streaked, and spotted.
There is nothing, which tends so effectually to diminish this evil, as to secure an abundant supply of
all accommodations and facilities for doing this work
properly. If the washerwoman has to draw water,
at a distance from her place of work, or, if she ob-
tains it only by a laborious process, she will be very
apt to stint her measure of it ; whereas, if it is easily
obtained, and readily heated, she will be much more
likely to make her clothes clean and white, by an
abundance and frequent change of water. The
apparatus for the convenience and heating of water,
spoken of on page 292, (Fig. 27,) can be secured, at
no very great expense ; and will greatly increase the
probabilities of securing good washing. There are
other accommodations, a full supply of which, will
also greatly promote the same object. For persons

who have large washes, all of the following articles will be desirable.

Articles to be provided for Washing.

Soft water is a very important item. When this cannot be obtained, soda or ley, put in the hard water, softens it. But great care is required, lest, by putting in too large a quantity, the clothes, as well as the skin of the person washing, be injured. Two washforms are needful; one for the two tubs in which the suds is put, and the other for the blueing water and starch-tub. Four tubs, of different sizes; two or three pails; a large wooden dipper; a grooved wash-board; a clothes-line, (sea-grass, or horse-hair, is best;) a long wash-stick to move the clothes in boiling; and a wooden fork to take them out;—these are all useful, and prevent loss of time. It is also very desirable to have soap-dishes made of wood, with hooks of wire or wood, so that they can be hooked to the sides of the tubs. This prevents waste, both of time and soap. In addition to these, are needed, a clothes-bag, in which to boil the clothes; an indigo-bag, made of double flannel; a bottle of ox-gall, to use for calicos; a supply of starch; a starch-strainer, of coarse unbleached cotton, made into a bag, tapering down to a point; and six or eight dozen clothes-pins, which are cleft sticks, made to fasten the clothes on the line. A junk bottle of dissolved gum Arabic is also often useful. A brass or copper kettle is best for boiling clothes, as iron is apt to stain them with its rust. Tubs and pails, after having been used, should be put in a cool place, to prevent their shrinking and falling to pieces. A closet, for keeping all these articles at hand, and in proper order for the washer, is a very great convenience. It should be made four feet wide, three feet deep, and six or seven feet in height, with a wooden bottom. In the lower part, are to be placed the tubs, one within another, turned on their sides. A short distance above them, is to be placed a shelf, on which is to be put a basket holding the clothes-pins, the clothes-fork and line, soap-dishes, and dipper. Above this, is to be placed another shelf, upon which may be set the jug of ox-gall, a bottle of dissolved glue, a bottle of gum Arabic, a large box of starch, and a small box of indigo. These shelves should extend to only half the depth of the closet. On one side of the closet, should be four nails, on which to hang the starch-bag, the bag in which the clothes are boiled, the blueing-bag, and the wash-stick. The ironing implements might also be kept in this closet, by making the lower shelf a foot and a half higher, and putting a deep drawer under it. In this drawer, could be kept the ironing sheets and holders, and the irons might be placed on one of the shelves. A lock and key should be put on this closet, so that, if necessary, it may be kept locked. When a washerwoman finds all the conveniences amply provided and neatly arranged, it always will have an effect in leading her to be more particular than she would be, if every thing is at loose ends, and many conveniences are lacking. If the lady of the house requires the washerwoman to see her before leaving, and then inquires if each of these articles are properly cleansed and put in their places, it will be more certainly done.

Common Mode of Washing.

It saves considerable labor, to assort the clothes, and put the white ones to soak, the night before, in warm water. Do not allow *hot* water to be poured on them, as it makes it more difficult to wash out the dirt. In assorting clothes, the flannels are to be put in one lot, the colored clothes in another, the coarser white clothes in a third, and the fine clothes in a fourth lot. Wash the fine clothes first, in suds,

and throw them, when wrung, into another tub of
suds. Then wash them in the second suds, turning
them wrong side out. Then put them into the
boiling bag, and let them boil, in strong soapsuds,
for half an hour, (not more,) moving them about,
with the wash-stick, to keep them from getting
yellow in spots. Take them out of the boiling
water, into a tub, and rub the dirtiest spots. Then
rinse them, throwing them, when wrung, into a tub
of blueing water. Wring them hard the last time,
or they will be liable to dry in streaks. Put the
articles to be stiffened, by themselves, and dip them
in starch just before hanging out. Hang white
clothes, if possible, in the sun, and colored clothes
in the shade. They should be fastened on the line
with wooden clothes-pins, which are safer and more
convenient than any other mode. After the fine
clothes, wash the coarser articles in the above manner. Then wash the colored clothes, which must
not be boiled, nor have ley or soda put in the water.
A tablespoonful of beef-gall, added to the suds, improves the appearance of nice prints, and preserves
their colors. Lastly, wash the flannels. In washing white flannels, make suds as hot as the hand
can bear. It shrinks flannels, in spots, to have soap
rubbed on. Very nice flannels should have a suds
of white soap. After washing through the first suds,
they should be thrown into another tub of hot suds,
and in this last be turned wrong side out. They
should then be thrown into clear hot blueing water,
as suds will not combine well with indigo, and
makes specks in the flannel. Flannels should never
be left long in water, nor ever be put in any but hot
water. After washing, shake them and pull them
into proper shape, before hanging them out. Nothing is so much injured by bad washing, as white
flannel. Colored flannel, and woollen hose, should
be washed after the white. Some persons keep

stocking boards, shaped like a foot and leg, on which they draw woollen hose, when drying. This keeps them from shrinking, and makes them look better than to iron them. Unbleached cotton hose should be dipped in coffee water, unless it is wished to whiten them.

To wash Blankets.

Select a warm and long day, and begin at an early hour. Pound the blankets in a barrel, with hot suds, mixing the soap thoroughly with the water, before putting them in. Rinse in hot suds, not wringing them much. If not dry by night, fold them and hang them out the next morning.

To wash other Bedding.

Bedquilts should be pounded in a barrel, with warm suds. After rinsing, wring as dry as possible. Bolsters and pillows can be washed, without emptying the feathers, by pounding them in warm suds, and rinsing them in fair water. It takes several days to dry them. Usually it is better to take out the feathers from good articles; more common ones can be washed without. Cotton comforters can be washed without taking out the cotton; but it is better to wash the covers only, and then put them together again. To wash beds, the feathers must be taken out, and washed, and laid to dry, on some floor not in use. The ticks must be washed like other articles.

Soda Washing.

A very great improvement in economy of labor has become common, namely, soda washing. Much prejudice has been excited against the method, because, if it is not done with proper care, it injures the texture of the cloth. This evil is done either by boiling in the mixture too long, or by putting in too much soda. To prevent a risk of the last, some ladies make a composition, called *soda soap*, which they keep on hand for the purpose. The following method has been pursued by several friends of the Writer, for successive years, and though they have employed all sorts of washers, no injurious results have ever followed. They calculate that it saves one half the labor of common washing. In preparing for it, it is necessary first to make the soap.

Soda Soap for Washing.

Take twenty-four pounds of common bar-soap; twenty-four pounds of sub-carbonate of soda, (or coarse washing-soda;) and five gallons of soft water. Boil the above for two hours, and keep it on hand for use. Also make a barrel of lime-water, by putting one peck of quicklime to a barrel of soft water. This is to be kept for use.

Mode of Soda-Washing.

Put two pounds of the above soap to two large pailfuls of soft water, and add one pint of lime-water. In this mixture, first put the nicer white clothes. They must be soaked the previous night in warm (not hot) water. Let them boil *just one hour and no more.* If they boil longer, it injures the clothes. Take them out into clear water, (draining them so as not to waste the material.) Turn them wrong side out, and rub the spots that look most soiled. If very dirty, rub on a little soap. Wring them hard, and throw them into the blueing-water. Wring them hard out of the blueing, and hang them out. It will be seen that this saves all the labor of the two first washings in suds in the common mode of washing, and yet it usually makes clothes look whiter than any other method. After the fine clothes are boiled, put in the coarser ones, and proceed as above. The colored clothes, and flannels, must not, of course, be boiled in this. These can be washed while the white clothes are boiling.

The Writer has friends who omit the lime-water, and say that it makes no difference, except that it saves the trouble of making and keeping the lime-water. Another rinsing-water, before the blueing-water, is an improvement.

Cautions in Regard to Colored Clothes.

Neither calico, nor prints, ought to be left lying in water. The water in which they are washed, ought not to be very warm; and when the suds looks dark and dirty, it should be changed, before another article is added: otherwise the succeeding pieces will be streaked or dingy. Soap ought not to be rubbed on; the grease should be removed by a paste of magnesia, or starch, or by French chalk, or Wilmington clay. It is better to make starch for dark calico, with water mixed with cold coffee, as it prevents a whitish appearance. Common glue stiffening, also, is good for dark calico clothes. They should be dried wrong side out, in the shade. Freezing in drying injures the colors of calico. When laid aside from use, all the stiffening should be taken out, or their texture will be injured. Some persons wash calicos in bran-water, without soap. For this purpose, boil four quarts of wheat bran in two pailfuls of water; strain it, and when lukewarm divide it into two parts. Wash the calico first in one and then in the other water. Then rinse, wring hard, and hang out to dry. Potato-water is equally good. For this, grate eight large potatoes to one gallon of water; divide the water into three portions. Wash in the two first, and rinse in the last.

To wash Brown Linen, or Muslins, of Tea, Drab, or Olive Colors.

Boil a bunch of common hay in sufficient soft water to wash and rinse the articles. The water should be the color of new brown linen. If darker, add more water. If the clothes are not very dirty, it is best to wash the first time in lukewarm clear water, without soap. Then wash and rinse in the hay-water, stiffening with glue-water. Put a teaspoonful of oil of vitriol or pyroligneous acid in the rinsing-water. Dry in the shade, and sprinkle and roll three hours before ironing. Ladies' linen travelling dresses, gentlemen's roundabouts, and linen aprons, by the above process can be made to look as when new.

To wash Nankeen.

New Nankeen, if soaked in ley one night, and dried without rinsing, retains its color, perfectly. Wash, after it is worn, in two portions of warm suds, the first having a teacupful of ley added to it. Rinse in two waters, with a very little suds added. Iron on the wrong side.

To wash Furniture Chintz, Curtains, and Spreads.

The Writer has never seen the following tried. It is given on Miss Leslie's authority.

Boil two pounds of rice in two gallons of water, till the rice is perfectly soft. Strain the water, and use one half for washing ; and, where soap is needed, rub on some of the rice tied up in a muslin rag. Put half the boiled rice in a bag, and place it in a tub of clean water; and in this wash the chintz, using the rice-bag for soap. Then put three teaspoonfuls of pyroligneous acid in the last half of the rice-water, and rinse the chintz. Dry, stretch, fold, and press. Then rub it, on the right side, with a smooth stone, or a bit of polished marble, instead of ironing it.

To wash Woollen Table Covers, or Woollen Shawls.

Take out the grease spots, either with starch, French chalk, magnesia, or Wilmington clay-ball.

Take out the stains with spirits of hartshorn.   Wash
in two portions of hot suds made of white soap.
Do not wring, but fold and press the water out,
catching it in a tub under the table.   Shake, stretch,
and dry it, not in the sun, and not by a fire.
Do not let it freeze in drying.   Sprinkle with
warm water three hours before ironing, and fold and
roll it tight.   Iron on the wrong side, pressing very
heavily.

To wash Woollen Yarn.

Wash in hot water, putting in a teacupful of ley to
half a pail of water, and no soap.   Rinse till the
water comes off clear.

To wash Black Worsted or Woollen Hose.

If new, soak all night ; then wash in hot suds,
with beef's gall, a tablespoonful to half a pail of
water.   Rinse till no color comes out.   Then stretch
on stocking-frames, or iron them, when damp, on the
wrong side.

To wash Painted Muslins.

Wash in one or two portions of lukewarm suds,
made with white soap.   Rinse twice, in cold water,
putting in the last rinsing-water a teaspoonful of oil
of vitriol, or pyroligneous acid.   Stiffen with rice-
water made by boiling a pint and a half of rice, one
hour, in a gallon and a half of soft water, and strained.
Stretch and dry in the shade, wrong side out.   Then
sprinkle and roll one hour before ironing.

To-cleanse Gentlemen's Cloth Coats and Panta-loons.

The Writer has tried, and seen others try, the
following method, with remarkable success, on all
sorts of broadcloth articles of dress.   Take one
beef's gall, half a pound of salæratus, and four gal-

lons of warm water. With a clothes-brush dipped in this mixture, scour the article, laying it on a table, for the purpose. The collar of a coat and the grease spots (previously marked by a stitch or two of white thread) must be brushed with this mixture repeatedly. After this, take the article and rinse it up and down in the mixture. Then rinse it up and down in the same way in soft cold water. Then, without any wringing or pressing, hang it up to drain and dry. When dry, dampen with a sponge, and iron on the wrong side, or else spread something between the cloth and iron, ironing till perfectly dry. It is best to rip out pockets and linings, if the articles are worth the trouble. Also brush the article before washing. It is often best to iron no part but the skirt, and press the lappets and cuffs.

Another Mode of washing Broadcloths.

Shake and brush the article. Rip out pockets and linings. Wash in two portions of strong suds, putting a teacupful of ley in the first. Do not wring, but roll them tight, and press the water out. When entirely dry, sprinkle them, and let them lie all night. Iron on the wrong side, or with an intervening cloth, *till perfectly dry.* For light woollens, white soap must be used. Iron on the right side with an intervening cloth.

To wash Merinos. Bombazines, and Challys.

Take out all gathers and plaits. Free the article from dust. Make a suds of warm (not hot) water and white soap, adding a spoonful of ox-gall. Then wash in a weaker suds, adding, for dark things, a handful of salt, and for light things, a teaspoonful of oil of vitriol. Do not wring, but fold and press the water out on a table, catching it in a tub beneath. When nearly dry, roll in a damp towel, and let it lie an hour. Iron on the wrong side. Do not let

them remain damp very long. For black bombazines, put in ley instead of ox-gall.

To manufacture Soap-Starch, and other Articles used in Washing.

To make Ley.

Provide a large ash-tub, small at bottom and large
at top. Set it on a form, so high that a large tub
may stand under it. Make a hole, an inch in diameter, on one side, at the bottom of the tub. Lay
bricks within this tub, about the hole, and put straw
over them. To seven bushels of ashes, put three
pailfuls of boiling water, two gallons of slacked lime,
and one gallon of unslacked lime. Put the lime
into the water, and let it stand some time, and then
pour it in. After this, add one pailful of cold soft
water, once an hour, for ten hours. Set a large tub
under the ash-tub, to catch the drippings, and try
the strength by an egg. If this rises so as to show
a circle of the size of a ten-cent-piece, the ley is right.
If the egg rises higher, the ley must be weakened
with water; if it does not rise so high, the ley is too
weak, and there is no remedy but to go over the
whole process. Much depends on the kind of ashes.
Hickory ashes make the strongest ley; and one fourth
less of this kind is needed, than of most other kinds.
Quick ley is made by pouring one gallon of boiling
soft water on three quarts of ashes, and straining it.

To make Soft Soap.

The grease for this purpose may be secured by saving all drippings and fat not used in a family. This
can be melted up, and poured into weak ley, and when
cold set away. Some persons keep a barrel, or half
barrel, for soap-grease. Weak ley should be kept in
this barrel, and a cover over it. To make soft soap,
take in the proportion of one pailful of ley to three

pounds of fat. Melt the fat, and pour in the ley by degrees. Let it boil steadily, all day, till it is ropy. If it is not boiled enough, when cold it will turn to ley and sediment. While boiling, there should always be a little oil on the surface. If this does not appear, add more grease. If there is too much, it can be skimmed off, when the soap is cold. Try it, by cooling a small quantity. When it appears like gelly, on becoming cold, it is done. It must then be put in a cool place, and stirred often, for several days.

To make Hard Soap.

Take in the proportion of a pound and a half of fat to two gallons of ley, and a piece of quicklime as large as an egg. Boil four hours, stirring often. When it appears like gelly, on cooling, put in one quart of fine salt, boil ten minutes, and then cool it. Next day, melt it, run it in moulds, and put it in a dry place, to harden. Before putting the salt in, if it is too liquid, add a little water, as the ley is too strong. Adding more lime, makes the soap harder.

To make fine White Soap.

Take fifteen pounds of lard or suet. When boiling, add, by dipping slowly, five gallons of ley. Skim it, and then add a gallon of ley mixed with a gallon of water. Cool a small portion, and if no grease rise, it is done; if grease does rise, add ley and boil it till no more grease appears. Then add three quarts of fine salt. If this does not harden it sufficiently, add more salt. Cool it, and if it is to be perfumed, and put in moulds, melt it the next day, for this purpose.

To manufacture Starch.

Cleanse a peck of unground wheat, and soak it, several days, in soft water. When quite soft, remove the husks, with the hand, and the soft part will settle. Pour off the water, and put in fresh, every day, stirring it well. When, after stirring and settling, the water is clear, it is done. Then strain off the water, and dry it several days in the sun.

CHAPTER XXVIII.

ON STARCHING, IRONING, AND CLEANSING.

To Prepare Starch. Glue Starch. Glue for Cementing Furniture. To Prepare Gum Arabic, Beef's or Ox-Gall. Starching Thick Clothes. To Wash and Prepare Thread and Bobbinet Laces. To Cleanse or Whiten Silk Lace, or Blond, and White Lace Veils. On Ironing. Articles to be provided for Ironing. Sprinkling, Folding, and Ironing.

To prepare Starch.

TAKE four tablespoonfuls of starch, and wet it in about as much cold water, rubbing it till all lumps are removed, and then add half a teacupful of cold water. Have ready a quart of boiling water, and into it slowly pour the starch, stirring the water briskly. Some prefer pouring the boiling water into the starch. Boil it for half an hour, and just before taking it up, stir in a bit of spermaceti, as large as a hazelnut. This prevents the starch from sticking to the irons. Loaf sugar, or salt, thrown in, produce a similar effect, but are not quite so good. Strain the starch through the starch-bag, and then add a very little blueing. If the starch is to be made thinner, hot water should be used. For dark calicos, starch, thinned with coffee, prevents the whitish appearance of common starch.

Glue Starch.

Glue stiffening is often better for linen, calicos, and some other articles, than common starch. It is prepared thus:—Put a piece of glue, six inches square, into four quarts of water, having first broken it up. Boil it, and then keep it corked in a jug, to use on washing-days. It must be mixed with the rinsing-water, according to the discretion of the washer. Millinet, and any other article, can be made stiffer, by adding glue to common starch. To prepare glue for cementing furniture, put it in a tin cup with very little water, and set the cup in boiling water until the glue is melted.

To prepare Gum Arabic.

Put one quart of hot water to four ounces of clean gum Arabic. Cork it in a bottle, and set it away for use. It is very good, when doing up lawns, book muslins, and laces. It must be mixed with the starch, at the discretion of the user.

To prepare Beef's-Gall, or Ox-Gall.

Send a bottle or jug to the butcher, and request that it may be filled with beef's-gall. Perfume it with any strong essence that is agreeable. Keep it corked, and in a cool place. If eventually it smells disagreeably, the smell will be removed by drying the articles in the fresh air.

Directions for Starching Thick Clothes.

In starching wristbands, collars, and the like, be careful that the starch is strained, so as to be free from lumps. If the starch is thinned, after it gets cold, the whole should be run through the starch-bag, to make it even. Dip the articles, and squeeze them till the starch is equally distributed. They should be starched just before hanging out.

Directions for Clear Starching.

Many ladies clap their muslins till clear, and then dry them entirely. After this, they sprinkle and roll, and when thoroughly damp, pull them into shape, and iron them. This method saves some time and labor, and is thought, by those who practise it, to be the best way. Others prefer to clap and pull them till nearly dry, then fold them and lay them between two plates to keep them from drying any more, and when all are thus prepared, they are ironed. Wrought muslins should always be ironed on the wrong side, and plain ones on the right side. Wrought work appears much better when ironed on soft flannel.

To wash and prepare Thread and Bobbinet Laces.

Sew a white cloth on a large bottle. Wind the lace around, with much care, pulling out the purl, and rolling it so as not to leave the purl and scollops outside, but covering it, as you proceed in rolling. Cover the lace with white muslin, and then fill the bottle with water, and put it into a kettle of cold suds made of white soap. It will be well to tie it with a string to the handle, to keep it from swaying about. Boil it for one hour, and then rinse it in fair water, squeezing it with the hand. Set it in the sun, and, when perfectly dry, fold it carefully, and press it between white papers, in a large book. If any stiffening is wished, put a very little gum Arabic, or a little thin starch, or rice-water, in the rinsing-water. It makes the lace look more like new, to wet it with sweet oil, after it is rolled on the bottle, before it is put in to boil. The oil can be applied with a sponge or rag.

To cleanse or whiten Silk Lace, or Blond.

Roll it on a bottle, as before directed, and set the bottle upright, in cold suds, and wet it all over with the hand, and set it in the sun. Renew the suds, every day, for a week, wetting and squeezing the lace lightly. Meantime keep it in the sun, as much as possible. Take off the lace when wet, and without rinsing, and pin it back and forth on a pillow or large sheet, making the edge and scollops even, and leave it, till dry, in the sun. Lay it away in loose folds. Instead of rolling on a bottle, common articles can be laid in a flat dish, in suds, and set in the sun ten days, often renewing the suds.

To wash a White Lace Veil.

Boil it, for fifteen minutes, in a strong suds of white soap, putting it in while cold. Squeeze it in the suds, but do not rub it. Rinse in two waters, the last a little blued, and with a little gum Arabic or rice-water added. Pin it on a sheet, to dry, fastening the scollops with care. Iron it on the wrong side, with a piece of muslin between the veil and iron. Any lace may be washed thus.

ON IRONING.

Articles to be provided for Ironing.

A very convenient article, for kitchen use, is a *settee,* or *settle,* made to serve also as an ironing-table. It can be made of pine, and stained of a cherry color. The dimensions are as follows. Length, five feet and six inches; width of the seat, one foot and eight inches; height of the seat, one foot and three inches; height of sides, (or arms of the seat,) two feet and four inches; height of back, five feet and three inches. The back is made with hinges of the height of the sides or arms, so that it can be turned down, and rest on the arms, and thus become an excellent ironing-table. The seat has two lids, opening into two boxes or partitions, in one of which is kept the ironing-sheets, in the other, the other ironing-apparatus. It can be put on casters, to move easily, and have cushions, stuffed with hay and covered with dark covers. It thus serves, in Winter, to set before the fire, and is a comfortable seat, protecting the back from cold; besides serving for the other purposes. The back, when down, rests on the sides, and is fastened, when up, by long hooks behind. Instead of this, a large ironing-board is often used, which can be put on a small table, and should be used for no other purpose. The following articles are also needed, in ironing :—A woollen ironing-blanket, and a linen or cotton one, to put over it; a large fire, of solid wood and charcoal, (unless stoves or furnaces are used;) a hearth, free from cinders and ashes, and a piece of sheet-iron, in front of the fire, on which to set the irons; (this last precaution, saves many black spots from careless ironers;) three or four old holders, made of woollen, and covered with old silk, as these do not take fire like cotton or linen; a ring, or iron-stand, on which to set the irons, and a piece of board to put under it, to prevent very hot irons from scorching the sheet; a linen or cotton wiper, one for each ironer, and a piece of beeswax, to rub on the irons when smoked. There should be, at least, three irons for each person ironing. There should also be one or two large clothes-frames, on which to hang the clothes, when ironed; and a small one for the smaller articles. If the housekeeper will see that all these articles are provided, that the fires are fixed properly, the clothes-frames dusted, and the ironing-sheets spread smoothly and pinned well at each corner, she will be much more sure of securing good ironing, than if she does not.

The following articles will also be found very convenient. A *bosom-board*, for ironing shirt-bosoms. This is made, by covering, with flannel, a board, one foot and six inches long, and one foot wide. It should have two over-cases, made to fit it, like pillow-cases, to be changed and washed. A *skirt-board*. This is a board five feet long, two feet wide at one end, tapering to one foot and four inches wide at the other. This, also, should be covered with

flannel, and have two over-cases provided.   It saves
much trouble, in ironing the skirts of dresses, and
enables the ironer to do them quicker and better.
The large end should be put on the table, and the
small end on a chair.   Both these boards are convenient, when ironing muslins, or when wishing to
press some little articles in the parlor or chamber.
A fluting-iron, called also a patent Italian iron, is
very convenient in ironing ruffles.   It is made with
a tapering hollow tube, fixed to a stand, and provided with two heaters, to run into the tube.   The
ruffles are taken, when damp, and drawn over this
tube.   When persons have practised awhile, they
can iron very quickly, and very beautifully, in this
mode.   And the expense is trifling.   Another article,
called a crimping-iron, is equally useful.   It is made
of two grooved brass rollers, which, when turned,
work into each other.   There is some danger of cutting muslins, in crimping them.   To prevent this,
the iron must be screwed to the right degree of
tightness, and this can be discovered only by trying
it on old muslins.   When it is adjusted right, care
should be taken to have it remain so.   They are
more expensive than the fluting-irons.   They cost
four or five dollars in New York or Boston.

On Sprinkling, Folding, and Ironing.

Wipe the dust from the ironing-board.   Take the
clearest water, (warm water penetrates soonest,) and
laying the articles successively on the board, sprinkle them all, laying them in separate piles, one of colored, one of flannels, one of common, and one of fine,
articles.   Shake, fold, and roll the fine things, wrap-
ping them in a towel ; then shake and fold the rest,
turning them all right side outward.   The colored
clothes ought not to lie long wet or damp, as this injures colors.   The sheets and table-linen must be
stretched, shaken, and folded, by two persons.   The

colored clothes should be separated from the rest, by a towel. Iron all lace and needle-work on the wrong side. Iron calicos with an iron not very hot, (as a hot iron will make them fade,) and generally on the wrong side. In ironing frocks, first do the waist, then the sleeves, then the skirt. Keep the skirt rolled, while ironing the waist and sleeves. Set a chair to hold the waist and sleeves while ironing the skirt. In ironing a shirt, first do the back, then the sleeves, then the collar and bosom, then the front. Laces and muslins should be laid in a basket, and carried away as soon as dry.

Iron silk on the wrong side, when it is quite damp. The iron must not be very hot. Pink, blue, green, and yellow, change color in ironing. Black and other dark colors are less affected.

Velvet can be ironed, only by turning up the face of an iron, and after dampening the velvet, on the wrong side, draw it over the iron.

Black silk should be washed in suds, with ox-gall, and stiffened very little, with glue or gum Arabic. It looks better to wash it, by sponging it, on both sides on a table, and not squeezing or wringing it. It can be stiffened, by applying the gum or glue on the wrong side, when a little damp. Sleeves changed by perspiration, and yellow spots, can be restored, by sponging with spirits of hartshorn mixed with an equal quantity of water.

CHAPTER XXIX.

ON WHITENING, CLEANSING, AND DYEING.

To Whiten and Remove Stains from Cloths and Muslins. Mixtures useful to keep on Hand, to remove Stains and Grease. To cleanse Silk Handkerchiefs and Ribands; Silk Hose and Gloves. Soot Stains and Stove-Pipe Stains. Grease in Wall Paper. To cleanse Gloves, Down, and Feathers; Straw and Leghorn Hats. Stains on Silk and Worsted Dresses. Grease and Oil on Silk and Worsted Dresses. Tar, Pitch, and Turpentine, on Dresses. Lamp-Oil on Carpets and Floors. Oil-Paint. Wax,'and Spermaceti. Ink on Carpets and Colored Table-cloths. Stains on Mahogany, and Other Wood. ON COLORING. Pink, Red, Yellow, Blue, Green, Salmon and Buff, Dove and Slate, Black, Brown, and Olive Colors.

To Whiten, and Remove Stains from Cloths and Muslins.

LAY white clothes for two or three days on the ground, where the sun shines, bringing them in after the sun sets, to prevent mildewing. They will whiten faster, to wet them in soapsuds, every time they are spread. Muslins are best whitened, by first washing them, and then laying them in strong suds, in a flat dish, and setting them in the sun for two or three days. This is much safer and neater, than to lay them on the grass. Any small articles can be whitened thus. When articles are scorched, in ironing, if the stain does not wash out, it can often be remedied, by whitening. Boiling in white soap and milk, in the proportion of one pound of soap to one gallon of milk, will often remove the stain of scorching from linen. Miss Leslie also recommends the juice of two onions, (extracted by chopping and squeezing,) one ounce of white soap, two ounces of fuller's earth, and half a pint of vinegar. These to be mixed, boiled, and, when cooled, spread and dried on the scorched part. When clothes are mildewed, the stain can often be readily removed, by

whitening. Dipping in sour buttermilk, before laying out, hastens the process. This must be washed
out, in *cold* water. Soap and chalk also hasten the
process. Also, soap and starch, adding half as much
salt, as there is of starch, and also the juice of a
lemon. These articles should be applied on *both*
sides. Stains in linen can often be removed, by
first rubbing on soft soap, and then covering it with
starch paste, drying in the sun, and renewing the
application several times. Wash it off, with cold
water.

Mixtures useful to keep on hand to remove Stains and Grease.

Stain Mixture. One ounce of sal ammoniac, one
ounce of salt of tartar, and one pint of soft water,
mixed. These can be kept, corked in a bottle, for
use, with the articles used in washing.

Another Stain Mixture. Half an ounce of oxalic
acid in a pint of soft water. This is very poisonous,
and should be kept with much care. It is infallible in removing ink stains and iron rust. The arti-
ticle must be spread over hot water and often wet
with a sponge or rag.

To remove Grease. Four ounces of fuller's earth,
in powder, half an ounce of pearlash, wet into a
stiff paste, with lemon juice, and dried into balls by
the sun, or in an oven just warm. When grease is
to be removed from *white* clothes, wet the spot with
cold water, and rub on the ball ; then dry it, and
wash it off with cold water. Grease can be removed by a paste of starch, or magnesia, on both
sides, dried and renewed, till the spot is gone.
French chalk scraped on, and left several days, will
remove grease from the nicest silks, without injuring
the texture or color. The apothecaries keep it for
sale. Scrape it in a thin powder, on both sides.
Pin paper over it, to keep it from scattering on other

parts. The harder kind of French chalk is not the best. That which looks white and scrapes easily, is most serviceable.

Wilmington clay-balls are also very useful, for this purpose. They can be obtained from Philadelphia and New York.

Ink spots can often be removed, simply by rubbing on common tallow, and leaving it for a day or two. It will then wash out.

Chloride of lime and warm water, and also oxalic acid and water, will remove indelible or marking-ink stains from white clothes. The articles must be washed immediately, or the application injures the cloth.

To cleanse Silk Handkerchiefs and Ribands.

If there are any spots of grease, scrape French chalk on them. Let them lie two days, and renew the chalk, if needful. Brush the chalk thoroughly off, sponge both sides, on a perfectly clean board, or table, with lukewarm soft water. If very dirty, warm suds of white soap must be used, and afterwards clean water. Stretch and fold them, pressing out the water, after they are folded. Stretch them out to dry, on a board or sheet, in the house. Then stiffen them. A weak solution of isinglass, put on the wrong side, with a sponge, is best. Gum Arabic will answer. When nearly dry, iron them between white papers, with an iron not very hot. Putting a tablespoonful of spirits of wine to one gallon of water is an improvement when washing them.

To cleanse Silk Hose and Gloves.

Wash them in warm suds of white soap. Rinse in cold water. When nearly dry, stretch them into shape, and pinning them to a sheet, rub them, till dry, with flannel, rolled hard. This gives them the gloss and appearance of new silk. Ironing silk hose

always injures the appearance. For black silk, add
a spoonful of ox-gall to the suds. Yellow spots, in
black silk, can be removed by spirits of hartshorn,
mixed with an equal quantity of water. Silk gloves
are to be treated in the same manner.

To take out Soot Stains, or Stove-Pipe Stains.

Wash the place in sulphuric acid and water.

To take Grease out of Wall Paper.

Make a paste, of either potter's or Wilmington
clay, and ox-gall, with water. Apply it to the wall,
and keep it covered with paper, till dry. Renew it
till the spot disappears.

To cleanse Gloves, Down, and Feathers.

Linen, silk, and cotton, gloves, can be washed as
previously directed. Wash-leather gloves should
have grease removed by French chalk or magnesia.
They then may be squeezed through two different
portions of suds, and rinsed, first in warm, and then
in cold, water. If but a little dirty, they can be
cleansed with a sponge and warm suds, and afterward
fair water. White kid gloves can be improved, by
removing grease with French chalk or magnesia,
and then brushing them with a soft brush and a
mixture of powdered fuller's earth and magnesia. In
an hour after, wet them with flannel, dipped in bran
and powdered whiting. Common colored gloves or
Hoskin's gloves, can be cleansed very neatly, by nice
spirits of turpentine, rubbed on with woollen cloths,
rubbing from the wrist towards the ends of the fingers. Hang them several days in the air, and all
the disagreeable smell escapes. They can often be
made to look as well as new. Gentlemen's white
gloves can be cleansed by washing with a sponge,
in white-soapsuds, and then wiping them thoroughly. When nearly dry, they must be stretched on

the hands. Swan's-down capes and tippets, can be washed in white-soapsuds, by squeezing and not rubbing. Rinse in two waters, shake and stretch while drying it. Ostrich feathers can also be thus washed. Stiffen them a very little, with starch wet in cold water, but not boiled. They should be shaken in the air till dry. To curl them, hold them before the fire, while damp, and taking a pair of dull scissors, give each fibre a twitch, turning it inwards and holding it so a moment.

To cleanse and whiten Straw and Leghorn Hats.

Rip them and take out the grease with magnesia or French chalk. Most stains can be removed with cream of tartar. Oxalic acid and water is better. The last must be immediately washed off. Wash the straw first in weak pearlash water, afterwards in soapsuds. Then take a barrel and fasten nails near the bottom so that cords can be stretched across. On these cords, tie the bonnet, while wet with suds, so that, when the barrel is turned bottom side upwards, the bonnet will hang near what is then the top. Turn the barrel, holding the bonnet over a dish of coals, on which roll brimstone is placed, so as to burn slowly. The barrel must be raised on a chip, to admit air. Keep the bonnet in these fumes till it is white. Then let it hang in the air, (it must not be damp, as this yellows the straw,) till the smell of sulphur ceases. Then stiffen the bonnet with a solution of isinglass, or rice-water, or gum Arabic, applied on the inside, with a sponge. When this is dry, press the crown on a block, and the rest on a board, putting muslin between the iron and the bonnet, and pressing very hard. Care must be taken not to make the bonnet too stiff, by trying the mixture on a part of the straw. Simply washing a Leghorn hat, in clear warm water, and then pressing it, improves its looks very much.

To remove Stains from Silk and Worsted Dresses.

Stains made by sweetmeats can generally be removed by pure water and a soft towel. Those made by acids can be removed by spirits of hartshorn diluted with an equal quantity of water. Sometimes it must be applied several times. Stains made by tea, wine, and fruits, can usually be removed thus.

To remove Grease or Oil from Silk or Worsted Dresses.

Slight grease spots can be removed by cold water and a soft towel, or by rubbing with coarse pin-paper. Fine French chalk, scraped on and renewed every few hours, will remove most grease spots. It is still more sure, if left on a day or two, then shaken off, and renewed. Wilmington clay-balls are considered a more certain remedy. These are to be put, in dry powder, on the wrong side, and renewed every hour. Laying an article in water, and changing it till no oil rises, will often remove lamp-oil.

To remove Tar, Pitch, and Turpentine.

Scrape off all that can be removed without injury. Put the spot in sweet-oil, for twenty-four hours, or spread cold tallow over it, for that length of time. After this, wash linen or cotton as usual. Woollens and silks must be rubbed with ether or spirits of wine.

To take out Lamp Oil from Carpets and Floors.

Take fuller's earth, or potter's clay, and spread them in a paste over both sides of the carpet, and on the floor. The floor should be first washed with hot ley or suds. Pin paper over the spots on the carpet. Renew the application several times, till all is removed. Wilmington clay-balls or finely powdered pipe-clay, put on dry, are considered still bet-

ter for a carpet.   The Writer never knew the first
method to fail.   The latter is the most easily tried.
Potter's clay, mixed with an equal quantity of ox-
gall, with water sufficient to make a paste, can be
applied to nice sofas and other articles, to remove
grease, pinning paper over.   It is better to put ox-
gall into paste for carpets, as it preserves the colors.
When dry, it must be taken off, carefully, from nice
worsteds or silk, and brushed with a soft brush.

To remove Oil-Paint.

Dip a piece of flannel in ether, and with it rub
the spot.   Very pure spirits of turpentine is as good.
If the paint be dry, repeat the application, several
times.   Sometimes, dry paint can never be removed.

To remove Wax and Spermaceti.

Wax can be removed by scraping it off and then
holding a red-hot poker near the spot.   To remove
spermaceti, scrape off what can be thus removed,
and, putting a paper over the spot, press the article
with a warm iron.   If this does not perfectly restore
it, rub on spirits of wine.   Wilmington clay, put on
the wrong side, renewing it every three hours, removes spermaceti.

To remove Ink from Carpets and Colored Table-Covers.

Wash the stained place in one teaspoonful of oxalic
acid dissolved in a teacup of hot water.   Repeat this,
if needful, and then thoroughly wash out the acid,
with warm water.   The water must not be hot, as
it may injure the texture.   This acid is a strong
poison, and must be carefully put away.

To remove Stains from Mahogany, and other Wood.

Stains made by setting cups of hot water on varnished furniture, can be removed by rubbing, first

with lamp-oil and then with alcohol. Ink spots can be removed by oxalic acid and water, or, by one teaspoonful of oil of vitriol to one tablespoonful of water. These must be brushed over quickly, and then washed off with milk.

ON COLORING.

There are many articles in a family, which may be much improved by dyeing, and some old articles may thus be apparently transformed to new. The following precautions and preparations are very important. The articles to be dyed must be entirely free from oil and grease of all kinds, and in most cases free from soapsuds. Light colors are best made in brass, and dark ones in iron vessels. Articles must always be put into the dye quite wet, or they will be dyed in streaks; and they must be stirred, and lifted to the air, so that all parts may be exposed to it. The dye must always be carefully strained, before dipping, or the particles of dyestuff will make spots. If the color is too light, dry it, and dip the article again. All the former color must be removed, if possible. Boiling in suds, or, still better, in the soda mixture, will usually secure this.

Pink Dye.

Buy, at an apothecary's, a saucer of carmine, which costs about twenty-five cents. With it you will find directions for using it. This is one of the most beautiful and convenient modes of renewing old silk handkerchiefs, ribands, &c. A little stiffening of gum Arabic in the dye, improves the looks. Balm blossoms, and also the blossoms of the bergamot plant, make a pretty pink dye. Cream of tartar, or oil of vitriol, sufficient to give a slight acid taste, must be put into the water in which the articles are wet before dyeing.

Red Dye.

Take half a pound of wheat bran, three ounces of powdered alum, and two gallons of soft water. Boil them in brass, and then add an ounce of cream of tartar and half an ounce of cochineal, each tied separately, in a bag. Boil fifteen minutes, and then wet the articles in water, and dip them. Brazil wood, set with alum, makes another red dye.

Yellow Dye.

Fustic, and also *Turmeric powder*, which may be found at the apothecaries', make a handsome yellow color. Also, saffron, barberry bush, peach leaves, and marigold flowers. They may be set with alum, putting a piece the size of a small walnut to each quart of water.

Blue Dye.

The hatters and apothecaries keep a " *blue composition*," which is cheap, and makes a good blue for silks and woollens, but injures cottons. Articles, after being dyed in this, must be very thoroughly rinsed. Fifteen drops, to a quart of water, will make a light blue. A dark blue is made by boiling four ounces of copperas in two gallons of water, wetting the articles in this, afterwards dipping them in a strong decoction of logwood, boiled and strained, and then washing them thoroughly in soapsuds.

Green Dye.

First dye a yellow, and then, if the article is made of wool or silk, dip it in the " *blue composition.*" Do not iron the articles, as that changes the color; but rub them with a hard roll of flannel, while drying.

Salmon and Buff Colors.

Tie one teacupful of potash in a bag, and put it in two gallons of hot (not boiling) water. Add an ounce of *anotta* or *arnotto* powder in a bag, and keep it in the hot water for half an hour. Dip the article to be dyed in strong potash-water, warmed, and then dip it in the dye. Dry it, and then wash in soap-suds. Birch bark and alum make another buff. Old cottons, dyed thus, make good linings for curtains, and also good valances. Arnotto, boiled in soap-suds, makes a salmon color. It must be set with alum. Birch bark, boiled in water with a lump of alum, makes a nankeen color. Black-alder bark, set with ley, makes an orange.

Dove and Slate Colors.

Boil a teacupful of black tea, in three quarts of water, in iron, and grate in a teaspoonful of copperas. This makes a dove color. Boil the purple sugar-paper in water, with a piece of alum. Both these make a good dye for ladies' hose.

Black Dye.

Put one pound of chopped logwood to one gallon of vinegar, and let them stand all night. Boil them, and put in a piece of copperas, of the size of a hen's egg. Wet the articles, in warm water, and then boil them, for fifteen minutes, in the dye, stirring them well. Dry them, then dip them again, first wetting them in warm water. Repeat this, till the article is black enough. Then wash it in suds, and rinse till the water comes off clear. Iron nails boiled in vinegar make a black dye, which is good to restore rusty black silks.

Brown Dye.

Put half a pound of camwood in a bag, with two gallons of water, and boil them for fifteen minutes. Then boil the articles, for a few minutes, in the dye. White-walnut bark, the bark of sour sumach, or of white maple, make a brown. Set them with alum.

Olive Color.

Boil fustic and yellow-oak bark together. The more fustic the brighter the olive, and the more oak bark the darker the shade. Set the light shade with a few drops of oil of vitriol, and the dark shade with copperas. Half a teaspoonful of copperas to a quart of water will answer.

CHAPTER XXX.

ON THE CARE OF PARLORS.

Poor Economy of Comfort in this Country, in regard to House Arrangements. Proper Arrangement of Rooms. Finishing of Parlor Walls. House Paper. Carpets, Curtains, and other Furniture, should be selected with Reference to each other. Laying down Carpets. Blocks to prevent Sofas and Tables from rubbing against Walls, and to hold Doors open. Footstools. Sweeping Carpets. Tea Leaves. Taking up and cleansing Carpets. Washing Carpets. Straw Matting. Pictures and Glasses. Curtains. Mahogany Furniture. Unvarnished Furniture; Mixtures for. Hearths and Jambs. Sweeping and Dusting Parlors. Inferior Locks and Keys should not be used. Creaking Hinges. Carriage Wheels; how lubricated. Smoky Chimneys. Cold and Damp Rooms. House Cleaning. Whitewash. Washing Paint, Windows, and Floors. Miscellaneous Directions; Parties, Invitations, Refreshments, Firescreens, Fireboards, Baskets for Flowers, Moss Baskets for Fruit, Varnishes.

It may be questioned, whether there is any point, in which a poorer economy of comfort and money is exhibited, than in the appropriations for parlors, in this Country. In the style of building, most common among persons of moderate wealth, we find two parlors, with folding doors, an eating-room, and a kitchen, on the same floor, while the bedroom and nursery are above stairs. The keeping of the largest and handsomest rooms, to use only when the family are dressed to see company, generally occasions a dull, cheerless, unsociable, eating-room, and the constant passing of the mother and housekeeper, up and down stairs, in her daily cares of nursery and kitchen. Instead of this plan, some, who deem it wisest to enjoy the comforts of their own house, themselves, select the pleasantest and largest room, and use it for both sitting and eating-room, and sometimes keeping another parlor in daily use for company, or for retiring to when the servants eat after the family, in the same room. Instead of an extra parlor, such have a bedroom on the ground floor. It is hoped, that, as the science of domestic economy improves, in this Country, much less money will be laid out in parlors, verandas, porticos, and entries ; and the money, thus saved, be employed in increasing the conveniences of the kitchen, and the healthfulness and comfort of those parts of the house most used by the family.

In finishing the walls of parlors, the cheapest material is common plaster, washed with colored washes of light lemon, straw, or lead colors. These are objectionable, because this wash rubs off on clothing. The next best covering, is wall paper. In selecting paper, choose delicate colors, and small figures. Large figures make a room look smaller, and are out of fashion. The best of all, is a hard-finished wall, painted with oil-paint. This should always be of a light and sober cast, such as gray, stone color, light lemon, or pale olive. Some leave hard-finished walls white ; but this makes the rooms look bare and cold ; and, unless the windows are much shaded, the light of the room is excessive. If hard walls are once well painted, they will last for many years, in perfect order, and all smoke, dirt, and stains, can be easily washed off. In selecting carpets, curtains, and paper, some reference should be had to a correspondence of appearance. Curtains and blinds should always be darker than the walls ; and, if the walls and carpets are light, the chairs should be dark. If some contrast is not thus presented, the room has an indistinct and untasteful appearance. Pictures, furniture, and glasses, always look better against light walls. In selecting carpets, it is poor economy to buy the cheapest. These are made of the poorest wool, and colored with the worst dyes. *Ingrain* carpets, of close texture, are best for common use. The *three-ply* carpets will last enough longer to pay for the extra price, and they are of the best colors and materials. Brussels carpets do not wear so long as the three-ply ones, because they cannot be changed and turned. Wilton carpets are the poorest of any of the expensive kinds, for wear. They soon become threadbare. Venetian or striped carpets are suitable only for stairs and passages.

In selecting colors, black should never be allowed; not even a single thread; as it is almost always rotten. White is not a good color, because it is so easily soiled, and gives a dirty look to the carpet. Very light carpets are never good for common wear. Carpets that are all of medium colors, which make no contrast of light and shade, never look well. The most tasteful carpets, are those, in which there are only two colors, and all shades of these. A carpet, of all shades of brown and yellow, or of blue and buff, or of green only, or of salmon and green, is always handsome. In such cases, sofas and curtains to match add greatly to the beauty of the appearance. The very dark shades, which look like black, should be chocolate or bottle-green, but not a real black.

In laying down carpets, it is a practice, in some parts of the Country, to put straw under them. But this, by making an uneven surface, makes the carpet wear out faster. Where straw matting is used for Summer, it saves carpeting, very much, to lay it on over the matting. This permits the dust to sift through, and makes a soft even surface underneath, while it does not injure the matting. In buying a carpet, always get some yards over, for a portion is always lost in matching the figures. In cutting a carpet, take off one breadth, about three or four inches shorter than the room, to allow for stretching. Then lay it down, and match the figure, exactly, before cutting another; and thus go on, till all are cut. It is generally best to begin to cut in the middle of a figure.

Sew with double waxed linen thread, of a little darker color than the carpet. Sew it on the wrong side, with the *ball stitch*, and it looks better, and wears better, than the common over stitch. The ball stitch is done by taking a stitch on the breadth next you, pointing the needle towards you, and then a stitch on the other breadth, pointing the needle from you. Draw the thread firmly, but not too tight. In fitting a breadth around the hearth, do not cut out the piece, but make two slits, and turn it under. Bind the whole of the carpet with carpet-binding, lapping it over as far as it will reach. In nailing it down, have pieces of kid, or thin leather, to put under the heads of the nails, as it saves the carpet, and makes it easier to draw the nails out. A carpet-fork, such as is kept at hardware stores, is a great assistance, in putting down carpets easily and neatly.

In all rooms, where there are nice walls, or paper, blocks should be covered with carpeting, like that of the room, and be put on the floor, behind sofas, tables, &c., to prevent their being pushed against the wall, and to prevent the wall from being dirtied by the dusting of furniture. A large brick, covered with carpeting, is good to hold doors open. Cheap foot-stools, made of carpeting, for parlors and bed-rooms, can be easily made thus: Have a square or octagon sawed out of a thick plank. Make a cushion of the same shape and size, of stout linen.

Stuff it with hair, or moss and cotton. Then nail its lower edge to the plank bottom, and cover all with carpeting. Make it a foot high, and put worsted handles to the sides.

The carpets of parlors not in constant use, should be swept only once a week, as sweeping wears out a carpet. It should be done with a new light broom. A carpet can often be sufficiently cleaned, without a regular sweeping, by a small whisk-broom and dust-pan. Tea leaves brighten the looks of a carpet, and prevent dust. They should be scattered, and then rubbed about with a broom, and then swept off.

When carpets are taken up, they should be hung on a clothes-line, or laid on thick grass, and whipped with pliant whips, first on one side and then on the other. They should then be rolled up with tobacco, and sewed up in linen, to keep them from moths and cockroaches. This is a sure preservative. Before relaying a carpet, remove all the dust from the floor, and mend all the thin places in the carpet, with yarn of the same colors. Change the position of the carpet, so that the worn spots shall not come in the same place all the year round. Carpets can be washed, and made to look much better, by first shaking them, and then, after thoroughly washing the room, laying them down, and nailing them as usual, and then scrubbing them in cold soapsuds, with ox-gall (a teacupful to a bucket of water.) Then wash off the suds, with a cloth, in fair soft water, making the carpet as dry as possible. Then set open the doors and windows, and let it dry, not using the room for two days or more. Imperial, Brussels, and ingrain, carpets, can be washed thus. Wilton's, or any plush carpets, cannot. Before washing, take out grease, with Wilmington clay or potter's clay, mixed with water and ox-gall.

Straw Matting.

Straw matting is very cool, for parlors and chambers, in Summer, and it is thought to be cheaper than to use woolien carpets through the year. The checked matting, made of two colors, does not wear so well as the other kind. It is poor economy to buy the cheap matting, as the higher-priced wears more than double the time. Frequent washings injure straw matting. Whenever it is washed, it should be with salt-water, wiping it dry. In joining matting, where it is cut, ravel out three inches of each piece, and tie the thread together, and then turn them underneath, and lay one piece close to, or over, the other, nail it with small nails, having kid or leather under their heads. Bind matting with wide cotton or linen binding.

Pictures and Glasses.

In hanging up pictures around a room, they should be placed so that the lower parts are not above the eye of an observer. It prevents defacing a wall, if there are many pictures, to have long brass rods at the top of the wall, from which the pictures can be suspended, by cords or ribands, which should all be of a color.

The glass of pictures should be cleaned with damp whiting, rubbed on with buckskin, and wiped off with silk. Water endangers the prints or paintings. The gilt frames of glasses and pictures can be kept in much better order than in any other way, by varnishing them with such varnish as carriage-makers can supply. A suitable brush for the purpose may be procured of the same persons. After this has been twice put on, and well dried, the frames can be at any time cleansed with warm water, without injury.

Curtains.

Heavy and dark curtains appear well only in Winter. If made of glazed chintz, merino, or worsted, they can be cleansed best by dry wheat bran, rubbed on with flannel. Ottomans and sofas can be cleansed by the same method. Venetian blinds are now made of a light color, to match the walls. The *green* blinds are going out of fashion, as they fade and spot easily. Blinds should be dusted every day, with feathers, and often wiped with a dry cloth.

Plain linen or cotton curtains, to shut out the glare of the sun, are now much used. They are simply a strip of linen or cotton, of the size of the window, suspended from a roller, which has pulleys and cords, so that they can be rolled up or down at pleasure.

Common chambers can be furnished with paper curtains. They are made by pasting wall paper on cotton. Fasten them to a roller at the top, having a cord so attached to it, that, when the curtains are unrolled, the cord will be rolled up around the roller. Then, by pulling the cord, the curtain can be rolled up.

Mahogany Furniture.

Mahogany furniture, made in Winter is very likely to crack. A table, kept near the fire, should be so placed, that the grain of the wood shall run perpendicularly to the fire, and not across it ; as, in that case, it will be likely to be warped. If mahogany furniture is made in Spring, and it stands some months to season, it is less likely to be warped. *Carved* mahogany is mostly out of fashion. When mahogany is much used, by sending it to be scraped and varnished, it will, at a small expense, look almost as well as new. Rose-wood furniture, and also black walnut, are very fashionable. These, as well as mahogany, should usually be rubbed with nothing but a dry cloth. It improves varnished furniture to rub on, occasionally, sweet-oil, and wipe it off thoroughly with a silk or linen rag.

For unvarnished furniture, use beeswax a little softened by the addition of a very small portion of sweet-oil. These articles should be melted together, rubbed in with a hard brush, and polished, first with a woollen, and then with a silk, rag. Another method, is, to rub in linseed-oil. A better way than either, however, is, to mix beeswax in spirits of turpentine, adding a little rosin. Apply this article with a sponge, wiping off with a soft rag. Some persons keep the following mixture in bottles, to apply to unvarnished furniture, whenever it is injured. Two ounces of spirits of turpentine, four tablespoonfuls of sweet-oil, mixed with one quart of milk. Apply with a sponge, and wipe off with a linen rag.

Hearths and Jambs.

Those parts of brick hearths, which are not near the fire, should be painted over with black-lead, mixed with hot soft soap. Those bricks nearest the fire should every day be washed over with a mixture of milk and redding, applied with a painter's brush.

A sheet of zinc cut so as to cover all the hearth, except the parts which touch the fire, looks very neat and handsome, and saves much work. A tinman can fit it properly. Brick jambs can be washed over with a mixture of fine wood-ashes and milk, or with redding and milk. Stone hearths should be occasionally rubbed over with a paste, made of powdered stone of the same color, which may be procured at the stonecutters'. Wet it with water, and when dry, brush it off, with a stiff brush. Wash the hearth first in strong suds. Kitchen hearths are improved by occasionally rubbing in lamp-oil.

Marble jambs and hearths can have almost all stains removed by oxalic acid and water, left on fifteen minutes, and then rubbed dry. Oil of vitriol succeeds nearly as well ; but it must be much diluted. Gray marble is improved by rubbing with linseed-oil. Grease spots can be removed from marble, by potter's clay and ox-gall wet with soapsuds. This mixture improves the marble, if applied to the entire surface, and left on for two days, and then rubbed off. It is made with a gill of ox-gall and a gill of strong suds, thickened with potter's clay. A gill of spirits of turpentine improves it.

On Sweeping and Dusting a Parlor.

When a new domestic takes charge of a parlor, it is well for the mistress of the house to make her do the work in the following order, when the weekly sweeping-day arrives. The most exemplary house-keepers consider a thorough cleansing as demanded for most parlors not oftener than once a week, unless used by children and other careless persons.

First cover the sofas, books, and other nice articles, with old sheets kept for the purpose. Then remove the rugs, and clean the fireplace. Then wash any paint or other articles that require it, and cleanse the mirrors and marble. Then sweep the room, re-moving every article. Then, after the dust is well settled, remove the covers, and, if needful, apply any polishing mixtures to the mahogany furniture. Then, with a duster of old silk, and a dust-brush, dust all the furniture and books, taking care, in dust-ing furniture, not to touch the wall paper. Then take a painter's brush, never used except for this purpose, and brush off the dust, from all narrow cracks and small recesses in the furniture or mould-ings. The cloths for dusting should be washed every week, and shook well after using, or the dirt will accumulate, so as to soil the books and other nice articles. It is best to have the ornaments and nice books dusted with a soft fine brush, kept for that purpose alone. With most domestics, it is necessary to stay with them several times, and superintend till they form a habit of doing this work regularly, thoroughly, and carefully. If they are made to do it in a *regular order*, they will be much less likely to forget and neglect any particulars. And if a proper supply of all conveniences is provided, and kept in a regular place, it will aid in securing thoroughness.

It is poor economy to furnish doors with inferior locks and latches, which soon get out of order. Brass locks and keys are kept in order longest, as they do not rust so easily as iron, and are more thoroughly made. In the end, they are cheapest. In a nice house, provided with good locks and keys, pieces of brass should be tied, with strong cord, to each key, and on the brass a number or name to show the door to which it belongs.

When the hinges of a door creak, put on oil with a feather. The wheels of carriages should be lubricated with black-lead, mixed with grease, which will last twice as long as oil.

Smoky Chimneys.

The following are some of the causes of smoky chimneys :—1. Short and broad flues, running up straight. A bend in a flue and its being made long and narrow, increases the draught. 2. The flues of two chimneys running together; whereas one ought never to open into another. 3. Large openings, at top, which are apt to make the wind draw down, and therefore should have tapering summits put to them, if the chimneys smoke. 4. A house being higher than the chimney. In such cases, the chimney should be raised. 5. Too large an opening at the bottom. This may be remedied, by a false back, or by a sheet-iron front, which diminishes the size.

Cold Rooms and Damp Houses.

The wood used for floors, windows, doors, and subbases to rooms, should be seasoned in the sun, or else with furnaces, through a whole Summer, before being made up. Otherwise, large cracks will appear, which will make the room uncomfortable and unhealthy. When such gaps do occur, they should in winter be calked with cotton, or list. Strips of wood, covered with baize, and nailed tight against a door, on the casing, keep out much cold.

House Cleaning.

This work should never be done, except in warm and dry weather. In damp and cold weather, the health of the family is endangered by it. Whitewash is improved by putting salt into the water it is made with, and a very little blueing in the last coat makes it look whiter. Those who understand this business, will whitewash without dropping any of the wash, so that all carpets and furniture can remain untouched; but as there is always some risk, it is better to cover furniture, and take up carpets.

Before commencing the cleaning of a house, take down all nice glasses, pictures, and ornaments, and cover them. In cleaning paint, use hot suds, and then wipe dry. Take off ink and stains, with oxalic acid. Wash windows with sponges, (as they give off no list,) in warm water, without soap, and wipe them dry. Rub them with whiting on buckskin, and they will look still better. A long brush, to wash the outsides of windows, is useful. Throw water on the outside. A little saltpetre in the water improves the operation. Painted chairs should be wiped with a sponge dipped in warm water. Never wash the floor of a sleeping-room in the latter part of the day, as it endangers health by the dampness.

Miscellaneous Directions.

In writing formal invitations, mention the day of the month and of the week, and also the hour for coming. Provide a place, if possible, for ladies to arrange their dresses, and furnish combs, pins, and a glass. Also a pitcher and tumbler of cold water. In serving tea, the most agreeable mode, for a small party, is, to set the tea on a table, on one side of the room, the lady of the house to pour out tea and the gentlemen to wait on the ladies and themselves. When tea is sent round, always send in with the milk and sugar, hot water, to weaken the tea. Send cold water, also, in tumblers. Rinse the cups, when returned, and keep up a supply of cream and sugar and have the plates well filled. Wipe the waiters, when soiled or wet. Direct the domestic to go first to some elderly lady, or to a stranger guest, and then to all the other ladies, as they come in order, and lastly to the gentlemen. It is hoped, as this Nation advances in refinement, that eating will be made a less prominent object in social gatherings; and ladies of wealth and intelligence should set an example, in this respect. It is important that a room for company be well lighted; but more important that the air be kept pure, by having lamps and candles in good order, and not too numerous. Crowded rooms should never be allowed, unless *very* freely ventilated. Keep a good fire, where ladies put on their outer garments, in cold weather, that they may not go out of doors chilled. Fire and candle screens are very important, for persons with weak eyes. They can be made with a small standard, having light cross-pieces for legs, with a slit made in the upper part, through which the screen (made of stiff ornamented paper) can be slipped. Chairs at table, near the fire, should have back screens, made of stiff paper, hung on their backs, as it is unhealthful to heat the back.

Handsome fire-boards can be made by nailing black foundation-muslin to a frame, the size of the fireplace, and then cutting out flowers from wall-paper, and pasting them on the muslin, according to the fancy.

Pretty baskets, for flowers, on centre-tables, can be made, by knitting various shades of green and brown into a square piece, with large knitting-needles. Then press this with a hot iron, and ravel it out. Then make a basket, of pasteboard, cut these ravellings into bunches, and sew them on, to resemble moss. Then line the basket, and set a teacup of water in it, and in this put flowers. An old waiter, filled with wet sand, raised in a mound in the middle, and then stuck full of flowers, looks prettily on a centre-table. Tissue-paper, of various colors, cut in fancy figures, is pretty to hang in the front of grates.

Large moss baskets, made as above directed, are pretty for holding fruit in parlors.

Many articles of furniture can be improved by varnish, which any lady can apply, by procuring a varnish-brush and some copal varnish, of a chaise or cabinet-maker. Paper and paintings can be varnished, by putting on, with a brush, a previous preparation of isinglass, or fish-glue, (boiling two ounces in a pint of water.) Go over the article, three times, with this, and then varnish. If the varnish sinks in, more isinglass is needed.

Copal varnish is best for furniture, and requires, on wood, no preparation. Put it on thin, or it will be rough. Dilute it with spirits of turpentine.

A white and nice varnish, for paper, is made by mixing one third balsam of fir, one third spirits of wine, and one third spirits of turpentine. First prepare the cloth, or paper, with three coats of isinglass. Strain the isinglass, before using it.

CHAPTER XXXI.

ON THE CARE OF BREAKFAST AND DINING-ROOMS.

Large Closet necessary. Dumb Waiter, or Sliding Closet. Furniture for a Table. On setting a Table. Rules for doing it properly;—for Breakfast and Tea; for Dinner. On Clearing the Table. Waiting on Table. On Carving and Helping at Table.

THE room appropriated to meals, should always have a large closet connected with it, with drawers and shelves, in which should be kept the crumb-cloth, table-linen, dishes, mats, &c. If this closet can be so contrived, as to communicate with the kitchen, by a sliding window, or by a door, it will save much repassing and opening of doors. If it be large enough to have a window, and a small sink, made of marble, or lined with zinc, it will be still better; as, in this case, all nice glass and china can be washed, without being carried into the kitchen. If the house is supplied with water, by pipes, a cock over this sink, for cold water, will be a great convenience. When there is a dumb waiter, or sliding closet, it is well to have it come up here. It can be contrived, so that when it is pushed down, its top will constitute a part of the closet floor, in cases where there is a want of room for it.

Articles of Furniture for a Table.

A table-rug or crumb-cloth saves carpets and floors, very much. It can be of a pepper-and-salt color, which shows dirt the least. Green baize, or heavy brown linen, are often used. In spreading this rug, the same side should always be put uppermost, or else butter or sweetmeats adhering to it, will be trod into the carpet on which it is spread. This rug should be often thoroughly cleansed. Table-mats, of straw, or of oil-cloth lined with baize, are important, to save either waxed or varnished tables from the effects of hot dishes. The India mats, are considered the best. Teacup-mats, or plates, are useful, also, to preserve a tablecloth from the stains of tea and coffee. It is very common for some persons to pour out their drink into the saucer, and then set their dripping cup on the tablecloth ; and when little mats or plates are provided to receive the cup, it *sometimes* happens that such persons will use them. Some persons have *knife-rests*, made of china or metal, laid by the dishes, on which to rest the carving-knife and fork. Butter-knives, of steel or silver, set beside, or on, the butter-plate, are designed to save the butter from the disgusting marks made upon it when each person uses his own knife to cut it. Salt-spoons are also put with salt-stands, for the same purpose. Many persons are much annoyed by a neglect in not having these articles; it is therefore well for a person to notice the habits of a family, and if they seem to be particular in using the butter-knife, salt-spoon, and sugar-spoon, to endeavor to be equally particular. When the family are not careful in this matter, the visiter may follow his own taste. Salt-spoons should always be wiped, as soon as the meal is over, as the salt injures their appearance. A sugar-spoon, or sugar-tongs, should also be kept by, or in the sugar-dish. There is nothing which so much gives a table a neat and tasteful appearance as *clean* table-linen. To secure this, mats and cup-plates are a great aid ; and a set of table-napkins are still more useful. These are usually small towels, folded and laid by each plate, so that each person can spread one in his lap. These, when soiled, can be doubled the other side out, once or twice. A stranger should always have a clean one, and the members of the family always have the same one at each meal. To secure this, napkins are often rolled and slipped through rings, which are numbered, and each person has a particular number. Others mark each napkin with a different number, and in setting the table, take care that each person has the same number, at every meal. Table-cloths, if folded in the ironed creases, when taken off, keep smoother, and look better, than if folded carelessly. They should always be well starched, as should also the napkins. Finger-glasses are used by some persons, in the more stylish circles. They are glass bowls, filled with water, in which the fingers are dipped, and wiped on the napkin, after dining. *Doilies* are colored napkins, for wiping fingers after eating fruit, and are put on only when fruit or sweetmeats are used. Casters and salt-stands should be attended to every morning. The Cayenne needs to be stirred, every day; the holes in the pepper-box unstopped; the vinegar-bottle filled; the salad-oil replenished; the mustard renewed; the salt-stands filled; and the salt and mustard-spoons put in order. No *little* comfort of a table is more desirable, than *fine* and *dry* salt. To secure this, many persons get the finest rock-salt, dry, pound, and sift it, and keep it in a tight tin box, from the air. Salt absorbs water, very fast, in a damp day; and the salt-stands must be often changed, at such times. Very fine and fair table-salt can be procured at the groceries, in most large places. Many persons are very much annoyed, by being obliged to use coarse and impure table-salt. A caster and its glasses in common use should be washed once a week. Salad-oil is apt to grow rancid, unless carefully corked. The mustard-spoon must not be left in the mustard after dinner.

In selecting table-furniture, French china is deemed the nicest; but there is one objection to it, and that is, the shape of the plates, which is such, that butter, salt, and mustard, will not lodge on the rim, but slip into the centre. Knives and forks, which have weights in the handles, so that, when laid down, they will not touch the tablecloth, are very much the best. Handles fastened with rivets, are more durable than any others. Handles made of horn, (except buckhorn,) do not last well. Knives for the table should be sharpened once a month, unless kept sharp by the mode of scouring.

On setting a Table.

Persons who are neat and thorough housekeepers, observe the manner in which a table is set, more than any thing else; and to a person of taste and refinement, who has been accustomed to a table set in a proper manner, few things are more annoying, than to see a table askew; a tablecloth soiled and rumpled, or put on awry; the plates, knives, forks, and dishes, put on without order; the tumblers dirty; the caster out of order; the pitchers soiled on the outside, and sometimes within; the butter pitched into the plate, without care; the salt, coarse, damp, and dark; the bread cut with a mixture of junks and thin slices; and all the other items in similar style. One who wishes to have a table set neatly, and genteelly, must persevere in standing by a domestic, until the habit is formed, of doing it regularly and in proper order. The following directions, put up in the closet or pantry where table-furniture is kept, will secure this object better than any other method.

Rules for setting a Table.
For Breakfast or Tea.

1. Lay the rug *square* with the room, and smooth and even.

2. Set the table square with the room, and see that the legs are properly placed to support the leaves and to stand firmly.

3. Put on the tablecloth, square with the table, and make it lie smooth and even.

4. Put on the waiter, for breakfast or tea, and set the saucers and cups on in two or three piles, and the spoons in the slop-bowl; or, if there are few persons to eat, set the cups in the saucers, with a spoon to each. Set the sugar and slop-bowls and cream-cup the back side of the waiter, and put the spoon or sugar-tongs on the sugar-bowl.

5. Lay the mats on the table, in a regular order, and set the plates around the table, at regular distances, putting at each plate a napkin, and a cup-stand.

6. Put a knife and fork to each plate, laying them even, and all in a similar manner. If meat is used, put the carving-knife and fork and steel by the master of the house.

7. Set the tea or coffee-pot on a mat, at the right side of the waiter, and the dishes on the mats, putting them in a regular order.

8. If meat is used, set the caster in the centre, and at two oblique corners set the salt, between two large spoons crossed. Lay the salt-spoons across the stands, and put the mustard-spoon by its cup.

9. Set the chairs.

For Dinner.

1. Place the rug, table, and cloth, as before directed.

2. Set the caster, salts, and spoons, as above directed. If more table-spoons are needed, put them each side of the caster, or by the dishes.

3. Lay the mats, putting the largest two opposite the master and mistress of the family, and the others in regular order.

4. Put the plates where they will be warmed, if it is cold weather, either in the plate-warmer, or on the hearth, turning the top plate over the others, to keep off dust.

5. Lay the knives and forks at regular distances, and by each place a tumbler and napkin, arranged in similar order. Set the pitcher on a mat on the dining-table, or else on the side-table. Water in glass decanters looks best.

6. Set the principal dish to be carved, on the mat before the master of the house; the other principal dishes before the lady. Place the other dishes in regular order, straight and even. Put a knife and fork by the pickles, and by any dish requiring them.

7. Set the bread on a side-table, if there is a domestic to attend; if not, on the table with the food. It is customary to have bread cut for dinner in small thick pieces. Some take a fork, and lay a piece of bread by each plate on the napkin; others prefer to keep it in a bread-tray, covered with a napkin, and hand it around, as it is thus protected from flies.

8. Set the chairs.

On Clearing the Table.

1. Carry off the largest dishes, and then scrape the plates into a dish, and lay the knives and forks and spoons in a small waiter, kept for the purpose, and carry them out.

2. Put the napkins in their places, and in good order, and put up the caster. Wipe the mustard and salt-spoons, and put them in their places.

3. Set the tumblers on a waiter, and carry them out, or wash them in the room.

4. Remove the mats, shake, and put up the table-cloth and rug.

Waiting at Table.

When persons can afford to keep the requisite number of domestics, it is a great comfort and convenience to have a waiter in attendance at the table, and remain standing by the mistress of the family, until the meal is, at least, half through. It would be well, in this case, to have this domestic, male or female, wear a large clean apron, while in attendance, to be used for no other purpose, and also to require his hands and head to be put in the neatest order. It is peculiarly unpleasant to have food served by an untidy domestic. A small tray should be held by the waiter to carry the articles around. The waiter should announce the meal (when ready) to the mistress of the family, then stand by the door, till all have entered, then close the door, and step to the left of the lady or gentleman of the house. At dinner, when all are seated, the waiter should remove the covers, taking care to lift them so as not to spill the steam on the tablecloth or the dress of the persons near. In serving articles, always go to the left side of the person waited on, and be careful not to pour water, so as to spill or make a tumbler too full. A waiter should notice when drink, bread, or vegetables are wanting, and pass them without being spoken to. When plates are to be removed, do it quickly, but without haste, depositing the knives and forks in a tray provided for the purpose, and setting the plates in piles. Then collect the bread with a fork and plate, then brush off the crumbs, with a crumb-brush. When families do not find it convenient to have a waiter, a light table can be set, so that the mistress of the family can reach it without rising, and on this should be set all the requisite articles.

On Carving and Helping at Table.

It is considered more proper to carve sitting than standing; as an expert carver does not need to stand. The carving-knife should be very sharp, and not thick or heavy. All ladies should learn to carve, as it is very difficult, without, and very easy, with, practice. It is considered a genteel accomplishment, for a lady to carve at her own table.

In carving fowls, which should always be laid on the platter with the breast upward, the common mode is to stick the fork into the breast, having the neck towards the right side of the carver. First take off the further wing and leg. Then, without turning the fowl, cut off the wing and leg nearest to you; then cut off the merrythought, and slices from the breast. Then cut off the collar-bone, then the side bones, and then divide the carcass. Divide the joints of a leg in a turkey. When a fowl is large and tough, it will be necessary to turn it, in carving the wing and leg nearest to you, when beginning. Some persons cut off the wings and legs by running the fork into them without putting it into the breast; but this is more difficult.

In helping, when no choice is expressed, give a piece of the white and dark meat. Help to some of the dressing, and put the gravy, not on the meat and vegetables, but by itself. Do not mix the contents of a plate. In helping vegetables, do not take the water that may have drained into the plate.

In carving a surloin, begin by cutting thin slices from the side next to you, and then cut from the tenderloin, and help to both kinds. Do not give the outside piece, unless requested.

In carving a leg of mutton, begin, by cutting across the middle, to the bone. So also with ham, cutting the latter quite thin. Cut a tongue across, and not lengthwise, and help from the middle part, which is deemed the best.

In carving a forequarter of lamb, first separate the shoulder from the ribs and breast; then divide the ribs. On a loin of veal, begin at the smaller end, separate the ribs, and help each person to a piece of the kidney and its fat.

Carve pork and mutton in the same way. In carving a fillet of veal, begin at the top, and help to the stuffing with each slice. In a breast of veal, separate the breast and brisket, and then cut them up, asking which part is preferred. In carving a pig, it is customary to divide it, and take off the head, before it comes to the table; as, to many persons, the head is very revolting. Cut off the limbs, and divide the ribs. In carving venison, make a deep incision down to the bone, to let out the juices; then turn the broad end of the haunch towards you, cutting deep, in thin slices. For a saddle of venison, cut from the tail towards the other end, on each side, in thin slices. Warm plates are very necessary, with venison and mutton.

CHAPTER XXXII.

ON THE CARE OF CHAMBERS AND BEDROOMS.

Importance of Well-ventilated Sleeping-rooms. Debility and Ill-health caused by a Want of Pure Air. Chamber Furniture. Cheap Couch. Trunks. Washstand. Bedsteads. Beds. Feathers. Straw, or Hair Mattrasses. Pillows and Bolsters. Bedcoverings. *On Cleaning Chambers.* Sweeping and Dusting. To Make a Bed. Domestics should be provided with Single Beds, and Washing Conveniences. *On Packing and Storing Articles.* To fold a Gentleman's Coat and Shirt, and a Frock. Packing Trunks. Carpet Bags. Bonnet Covers. Packing Household Furniture for Moving.

THE importance of well-ventilated sleeping-rooms, cannot be too strongly impressed upon every housekeeper. The debility of young children, the lassitude and indolence of domestics, and much of the ill-health of families, are caused by that most needless of all famines,—a want of pure air. No mistress of a family should allow any person to sleep in a room without an open fireplace, until she makes it certain that free ventilation will be secured in some other way. To accomplish this, a large crack can be made, in the upper sash of the window, by sinking it a little; or a ventilator can be made over a door, or a pane of glass taken from a window, or the door be fastened open into an adjoining room or entry. So many persons are ignorant of the importance of fresh air to health, that the mistress of a family will need to exercise constant care to prevent evil in this direction. Instead of tight fireboards, in chambers, the chimney should either be left open, or the fireboard be made like window-blinds. It is always best, in small rooms, even if they have fireplaces, to have the door left ajar.

As chambers are used most in Summer, straw matting is the best for permanent carpets. In Winter, strips can be laid over the matting around the bed. If a fire is kept in a chamber, it is best to have a woollen carpet. There are many cheap contrivances, to make a chamber look neat and comfortable; some of which will be mentioned. In chambers without closets, a wardrobe is very necessary. This is a large moveable closet, with doors. It is divided perpendicularly into two apartments. In one, two rows of hooks are placed, at different heights, for hanging dresses; in the other, are rows of shelves, for other uses. Some are made with two drawers, at the bottom, for shoes and other articles.

A low square box, set on casters, with a stuffed cushion on the top, and a drawer on one side, is a great convenience for dressing the feet. The drawer is divided into two apartments; in one, is put shoes, and in the other, stockings. An old champaigne basket, fitted up with a cushion on the lid, and a valance fastened to it to cover the sides, can be used for the same purpose.

A very comfortable lounge, for chambers and sitting-rooms, can be made by a common carpenter, at very little expense. Have a frame made, (like the annexed Fig. 31,) of common stuff, five feet long, twenty-six inches wide, and fifteen inches high.

Fig. 31.

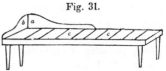

Have the sloping side piece, *a*, and head piece, *b*, sawed out of a board; nail brown linen on them, and stuff them with soft hay or hair. Have these screwed to the frame, and covered with furniture patch. Then have slats nailed across the bottom, as at *c c*, half a foot apart. This will cost two or three dollars. Then make a thick cushion, of hay or straw, with side strips, like a mattrass, and lay this for the under cushion. To put over this, make a thinner cushion, of hair, cover it with furniture-patch, and fasten to it a valance reaching to the floor. Then make two square pillows, and cover them with patch, like the rest.

The Writer has seen a lounge of this kind, in a common parlor, which cost less than eight dollars, was much admired, and was a constant comfort to the feeble mother, as well as many other members of the family.

Another convenience, for a room where sewing is done in Summer, is a fancy jar, set in one corner, to receive clippings, and any other rubbish. It can be covered with prints, or paintings, and varnished; and it then looks very prettily.

The trunks in a chamber can be improved in looks and comfort, by making cushions of the same size and shape, stuffed with hay and covered with chintz, with a frill reaching nearly to the floor.

Every bedchamber should have a washstand, bowl, pitcher, and tumbler, with a washbucket under the stand, to receive slops. A light screen, made like a clothes-frame, and covered with paper or chintz, should be furnished for bedrooms occupied by two persons, so that ablutions can be performed in privacy. It can be ornamented, so as to look well anywhere. A little frame, or towel-horse, by the washstand, on which to dry towels, is a convenience. A washstand should be furnished with a sponge or washcloth, and a small towel, for wiping the basin after using it. This should be hung on the washstand or towel-horse, for constant use. A soap-dish, and a dish for toothbrushes, are neat and convenient, and each person should be furnished with two towels; one for the feet, and one for other purposes.

Bedsteads and Beds.

The recent absurd fashion of very high bedsteads, seems to be passing away; and it would be wise for those, who have bedsteads so high that children endanger their lives in sleeping on them, and stairs are needed to mount them, to saw off the legs, to a reasonable height. High-post bedsteads are best, as it is often important to hang musquito-bars around them, or curtains to protect from cold currents of air. It is in good taste to have the curtains, bedquilt, valance, and window-curtains, of similar materials.

In making featherbeds, side-pieces should be put in, like those of mattrasses, and the bed should be well filled, so that a person will not be buried in a hollow, which is not healthful, save in extremely cold weather. Featherbeds should never be used, but in cold weather. At other times, a thin mattrass of hair, cotton and moss, or straw, should be put over them. A simple strip of straw matting, spread over a featherbed, answers the same purpose. There is nothing more debilitating, than to sleep in warm weather, with a featherbed pressing round much the greater part of the body. Beds, used by children or domestics, should have either a bed-case or a sheet kept between the bed and under sheet, and the bolster should have a case. It is not desirable for young persons to have both bolsters and pillows, as one is better to keep the body in a correct position. Sometimes they are so small, as to need both. Pillows stuffed with papers an inch square, are good for Summer, especially for young children, whose heads should be kept cool. The cheapest and best covering of a bed for Winter, is a *cotton comforter*, made to contain three or four pounds of cotton, laid in batts or sheets, between covers tacked together at regular intervals. They should be three yards square, and less cotton should be put at the sides that are tucked in. It is better to have two thin comforters to each bed, than one thick one ; as then the covering can be regulated according to the weather.

On Cleaning Chambers.

A chamber, and all its appendages, should be thoroughly cleaned, once each week ; every article being moved, in sweeping. On other days, a dustpan and small whisk-broom can be used to collect dust and rubbish. Paper and threads must first be picked, and not swept, up. The domestic, who takes care of the chambers, should go around, both morning and evening, to remove slops, replenish the pitcher with a fresh supply of water, and put the washbowls and other articles in order. Tea leaves are good to throw under a bed to collect the light flue which is apt to fly about, when sweeping. In dusting chambers, as well as other rooms, the ledges, mouldings, doors, and window-sashes, must not be omitted. Clean the plates of looking-glasses with a sponge and pure water.

To Make a Bed.

Few domestics will make a bed properly, without much attention from the mistress of the family. The following directions should be given to those who do this work.

Open the windows, and lay off the bed-covering, on two chairs, at the foot of the bed. After the bed is well aired, shake the feathers from each corner to the middle ; then take up the middle, and shake it well, and turn the bed over. Then push the feathers in place, making the head higher than the foot, and the sides even, and as high as the middle part. Then put on the bolster and the under sheet, so that the wrong side of the sheet shall go next the bed, and the *marking* come at the head, tucking in all around. Then put on the pillows, even, so that the open ends shall come to the sides of the bed, and then spread on the upper sheet, so that the wrong side shall be next the blankets, and the marked end at the head. This arrangement of sheets is to prevent the part where the feet lie from being reversed so as to come to the face, and also to prevent the parts soiled by the body from coming to the bedtick and blankets. Then put on the other covering, except the outer one, tucking in all around, and then turn over the upper sheet, at the head, so as to show a part of the pillows. When the pillow-cases are clean and smooth, they look best outside of the cover, but not otherwise. Then draw the hand along the side of the pillows, to make an even indentation, and then smooth and shape the whole outside. A nice housekeeper always notices the manner in which a bed is made ; and in some parts of the Country, it is rare to see this work properly performed.

The Writer would here urge every mistress of a family, who keeps more than one domestic, to provide them with single beds, that they may not be obliged to sleep with all the changing domestics, who come and go so often. Where the room is too small for two beds, a narrow truckle-bed under another, will answer. Domestics should be furnished with washing conveniences in their chambers, and be encouraged to keep their persons and rooms neat and in order.

Fold a gentleman's coat, thus :—Lay it on a table or bed, the inside downward, and unroll the collar. Double each sleeve once, making the crease at the elbow, and laying them so as to make the fewest wrinkles, and parallel with the skirts. Turn the fronts over the back and sleeves, and then turn up the skirts, making all as smooth as possible.

Fold a shirt, thus :—One that has a bosom-piece inserted, lay on a bed, bosom downward. Fold each sleeve twice, and lay it parallel with the sides of the shirt. Turn the two sides, with the sleeves, over the middle part, and then turn up the bottom, with two folds. This makes the collar and bosom lie, unpressed, on the outside.

Fold a frock, thus :—Spread it on a bed, so that the creases in folding will come behind and before. Smooth it, and lay the hem even, and then fold the shirt lengthwise, in four parts, turning one fold on each side, and then both together. Then begin at the bottom, and double up the skirt, crosswise, and then arrange the waist and sleeves, outside, so as to make the fewest creases. Pin the whole in a napkin.

In packing trunks, for travelling, put all heavy articles at the bottom, covered with paper, which should not be printed, as the ink rubs off. Put coats and pantaloons into linen cases, made for the purpose, and furnished with strings. Fill all crevices with small articles; as, if a trunk is not full, and tightly packed, its contents will be shaken about, and get injured. A thin box, the exact size of the trunk, with a lid, and covered with brown linen, is a great convenience, to set inside, on the top of the trunk, to contain light articles which would be injured by tight packing. Have straps, with buckles, fastened to the inside, near the bottom, long enough to come up and buckle over this box. By this means, when a trunk is not quite full, this box can be strapped over so tight, as to keep the articles from rubbing. Under-clothing packs closer, by being rolled tightly, instead of being folded.

Bonnet-boxes, made of light wood, with a lock and key, are better than the paper bandboxes so annoying to travellers. Carpet bags are very useful, to carry the articles to be used on a journey. The best ones have sides inserted, iron rims, and a lock and key. A large silk travelling-bag, with a double linen lining, in which are stitched receptacles for toothbrush, combs, and other small articles, is a very convenient article for use when travelling.

A bonnet-cover, made of some thin material, like a large hood with a cape, is useful to draw over the bonnet and neck, to keep off dust, sun, and sparks from a steam engine. Green veils are very apt to stain bonnets, when damp.

In packing household furniture, for moving, have each box numbered, and then have a book, in which as each box is packed, note down the number of the box, and the order in which its contents are packed, as this will save much labor and perplexity when unpacking. In packing china and glass, wrap each article, separately, in paper, and put soft hay or straw at bottom, and all around each. Put the heaviest articles at the bottom ; and on the top of the box, write, " This side up."

CHAPTER XXXIII.

ON THE CARE OF THE KITCHEN, CELLAR, AND STORE-ROOM.

Importance of a Convenient Kitchen. Floor should be painted. Sink and Drain. Towels. Washbasins. Dishcloths. Washing Dishes. Conveniences needed. Rules. Kitchen Furniture. Crockery. Iron Ware. Tin Ware. Wooden Ware. Basket Ware. Other Articles. Miscellaneous Directions. *On the Care of the Cellar and Storeroom. Modes of Destroying Insects and Vermin.*

It is very important, for every man who wishes to have his daughters brought up with good domestic habits, to secure a light, neat, and agreeable kitchen. Such an arrangement will make this part of the house more attractive to his daughters, more comfortable for his wife, and better secure the contentment of domestics. For this reason, cellar-kitchens are undesirable, besides being often unhealthful.

A kitchen should have either a smooth, painted floor, or else an oil-cloth, as this saves much labor, and looks much neater than a bare floor. An oil-cloth is best, because it can be removed, to be repainted, whereas when a floor is newly painted, it has to be used, before the paint is sufficiently hardened, and consequently it wears off much sooner, so that the oil-cloth is cheaper in the end. To get this as cheap as possible, make up a kitchen-carpet, of coarse tow cloth, have it nailed to the south side of a barn, and put on it a coat of thin rye paste. Then hire a painter to put on a coat of common yellow paint, and let it dry for a fortnight. Then have a second coat of paint put on, and at the end of another fortnight a third coat. Let it then dry for two months, and it will last many years. Be careful to have the paint well mixed, with a proper supply of drying ingredients.

A kitchen should always have a sink, with a drain to carry away all slops; and this drain should never empty on the surface of the ground near the house, as it is both unhealthful and uncleanly. It is best to whitewash the walls of a kitchen, as it makes it lighter, and tends to remove all bad smells. A roller-towel, to be changed twice a week, and two block-tin basins, one for common and one for nicer uses, are very necessary, in every kitchen. A nicer towel should also be hung near one of these basins.

The sink should be thoroughly washed every day, and often scalded with ley or hot suds. Keep a supply of *nice* dish-cloths hanging near the sink, hemmed, and furnished with loops. There should be one for dishes that are not greasy, one for greasy dishes, and one for pots and kettles. These should all be put in the wash every washing day. If the mistress of the family will insist on this, she will be less annoyed by having her dishes washed with black, dirty, and musty rags. Under the sink should be kept a slop-pail, and on a shelf, close by, should be placed two water-pails, one for hard and one for soft water. A large kettle of warm soft water should always be kept over the fire, and a hearth-broom and bellows be hung beside the fireplace. A clock, in or near the kitchen, is very important, to secure regularity in family arrangements.

Washing Dishes.

Careless domestics are very apt to fail in washing dishes properly. A full supply of proper conveniences, and considerable watchfulness from the lady of the house, will remedy this. A swab, made of candle-wick, or strips of linen, and tied to the end of a stick, is useful to wash small deep dishes. Three dish-cloths, as before described, and two towels, should always be used in washing up the family dishes. Two large tin tubs, painted on the outside, should be provided, one for washing and one for rinsing ; and a large old waiter, on which to drain the dishes. A soap-dish, with hard soap, and a slop-pail, should also be furnished. Then, if directions, like the following, are written, in a large hand, and put up near the sink, they will be some aid in securing the desired care and neatness.

1. Put all the food remaining on the dishes, and which is good, on plates, and set it away for use. Scrape the grease into the soap-grease pot, and the scraps into the slop-pail ; and put the tea leaves into a bowl for use. Save all bits of butter.

2. Make a strong hot suds, in the wash-dish, and wash the nicest articles with a swab, or the nicest dish-cloth, and lay them in the rinsing-dish, which should also be filled with hot water. This is better than to pour hot water on them after the suds is partly dried on. Then take them out of the rinsing-water, and lay them to drain on the waiter. Then rinse the dish-cloth, and hang it up.

3. Pour in some more hot water, take another dish-cloth, and wash all the greasy dishes, rinsing them, and setting them to drain. Then take two towels, and wipe all the dishes, and set them away. Put the knives and forks into a vessel made for the purpose, and wash and wipe them ; or, if no such article is provided, wash them in the water with the other greasy dishes, *taking care not to put the handles in the water.* Wipe them, and put them in the knife-tray, to be scoured.

4. Get a fresh supply of hot suds, and wash the milk-pans and buckets, and then the tins. Then rinse and hang up the dish-cloth, and take another and wash the roasters, gridiron, pots, and kettles. Then empty the slop-bucket, and scald it. Dry the teapots (if of metal) and the tins by the fire. Then

scald out the chamber-bucket, and set it out of doors, to air. Then sweep and dust the kitchen and put the fireplace in good order.

Kitchen Furniture.

Crockery. Brown earthen pans are said to be best, for milk and for cooking. Tin pans are lighter, and more convenient, but are too cold for many purposes. Tall earthen jars, with covers, are good to hold butter, salt, lard, &c. The red earthen ware should never have acids put into it, as there is a poisonous ingredient in the glazing, which the acid takes off. Stone ware is better and stronger and safer, every way, than any other kind.

Iron Ware. Many kitchens are very imperfectly supplied with the requisite conveniences for cooking; and when a person has sufficient means, the following articles are all desirable. A nest of iron pots, of different sizes, (they should be slowly heated, when new;) a long iron fork, to take out articles from boiling water; an iron hook, with a handle, to lift pots from the crane; a large and small gridiron, with grooved bars, and a trench to catch the grease; a Dutch oven, called, also, a bakepan; two skillets, of different sizes, and a spider, or flat skillet, for frying; a griddle, a waffle-iron, tin and iron bake and bread-pans; two ladles, of different sizes; a skimmer; iron skewers; a toasting-iron; two teakettles, one small and one large one; two brass kettles, of different sizes, for soap-boiling, &c. Iron kettles, lined with porcelain, are better for preserves. The German are the best. Too hot a fire will crack them, but with care in this respect, they will last for many years.

Portable furnaces, of iron or clay, are very useful, in Summer, in washing, ironing, and stewing, or making preserves. If used in the house, a strong draught must be made, to prevent the deleterious effects of the charcoal. A spice-box, spice, pepper, and coffee-mill, are needful to those who use such articles. Strong knives and forks, a sharp carving-knife, an iron cleaver and board, a fine saw, steel-yards, chopping-tray and knife, an apple-parer, steel for sharpening knives, sugar-nippers, a dozen iron spoons, also a large iron one with a long handle, six or eight flatirons, one of them very small, two iron-stands, a ruffle-iron, a crimping-iron.

Tin Ware. Bread and cake-pans, a colander, an egg-boiler, a dredging-box, a pepper-box, a large and small grater, large and small pattypans, cake-pans, with a centre tube to insure their baking well, pie-dishes, of block-tin, a covered butter-kettle, covered kettles to hold berries, two sauce-pans, a tin oven or tin-kitchen, a tin apple-corer, an apple-roaster, a large oil-can, with a cock, a lamp-filler, a tin lan-tern, broad-bottomed candlesticks for the kitchen, a candle-box, a funnel or tunnel, a tin reflector, for baking warm cakes, two sugar-scoops, and flour and meal-scoop, a set of tin mugs, three tin dippers, a pint, quart, and gallon measure, a set of scales and weights, three or four tin pails, painted on the out-side, a tin slop-bucket, with a tight cover, painted on the outside, a milk-strainer, a gravy-strainer, a tin box, in which to keep cheese, also a large one for cake, and a still larger one for bread, with tight covers. Bread, cake, and cheese, shut up in this way, will not grow dry as in the open air.

Wooden Ware. A nest of tubs, a set of pails, wooden-bowls, a large and small sieve, a beetle for mashing potatoes, a spad or stick for stirring butter and sugar, a bread-board, for moulding bread and making piecrust, a coffee-stick, a clothes-stick, a mush-stick, a meat-beetle, to pound tough meat, an egg-beater, a wooden ladle for working butter, a bread-trough, (for a large family,) flour-buckets, with lids to hold sifted flour and Indian meal, salt-boxes, sugar-boxes, starch and indigo-boxes, spice-boxes, a bosom-board, a skirt-board, a large iron-ing-board, two or three clothes-frames and six dozen clothes-pins.

Basket Ware. Baskets, of all sizes, for eggs, fruit, marketing, clothes, &c., also chip-baskets. When often used, they should be washed in hot suds.

Other Articles. Every kitchen needs a box containing a ball of brown thread, a ball of twine, a large and small darning-needle, a roll of waste-paper, a roll of old linen and cotton, and a supply of common holders. There should also be another box, containing a hammer, carpet-tacks, and nails of all sizes, a carpet-claw, screws and a screw-driver, gimlets of several sizes, a bed-screw, a small saw, two chisels, (one to use for button-holes in broadcloth,) two awls, pincers, two files.

In a drawer, or cupboard, should be placed cotton tablecloths, for kitchen use, nice crash towels, for tumblers, marked, T T ; coarser towels, for dishes, marked, T ; six large roller-towels ; a dozen hand towels, marked, H T ; and a dozen dish-cloths, hemmed and having loops. Also, two pudding or dumpling-cloths, of thick linen, a gelly-bag, made of white flannel, to strain gelly, a starch-strainer, and a bag for boiling clothes. These last should be put in the washing-closet, if there is one. In this, or another place, should be kept a cotton and woollen ironing-sheet, two iron-wipers, three iron-holders, some beeswax and spermaceti, the common irons and the ruffle and crimping-irons, the bosom-board and skirt-board, and the cases or covers that slip on them ; and, if there is room, the clothes-frames and large ironing-board.

In a closet, should be kept, arranged in order, the following articles. The dust-pan, dust-brush, and dusting-cloths, old flannel and cotton for scouring and rubbing, sponges for washing windows and

looking-glasses, a long brush for taking down cob-
webs, whisk-brooms, and common brooms, a coat-
broom or brush, a whitewash-brush, a stove-brush,
shoe-brushes and blacking, articles for cleaning
tin and silver, leather for cleaning metals, bottles
containing stain mixtures and other articles used in
cleansing.

Miscellaneous Directions.

Clean gold ornaments with hot suds and a soft
brush, and then rub with magnesia. Never wash
pearls, nor wear them on damp hands. Repol-
ish tortoise-shell combs with sweet-oil and fine rot-
tenstone. Cleanse combs and brushes with pearl-
ash-water, wiping them dry. Nothing looks more
slatternly, than a dirty fine-tooth comb. It can be
best cleaned with thread slipped between the
teeth.

India-rubber, melted in lamp-oil, and put over
common shoes, keeps water out, perfectly. Gardening shoes should be thus protected. It can be black-
ened with ivory-black or lampblack.

Keep small whisk-brooms wherever gentlemen
hang up their clothes, either up stairs or down.
Also at the back door. Provide a good supply of
mats.

If a house takes fire, at night, wrap a woollen
blanket around you, to keep off the fire. If you
cannot get out of your room, draw the bedstead to a
window, tie the corners of your sheets together,
fasten them to the bedpost, and let yourself down
out of the window. Never read in bed, lest you fall
asleep, and the bed be set on fire.

When a stable is on fire, blind the horse, and then
he can be led out. Keep young children in woollen
dresses, in Winter, to save from risk of being burnt.
If your dress catches fire, do not run, but lie down,
and roll over till you can reach some article, or the

edge of the carpet, in which to wrap yourself tight, and this will put out the fire.

Boil new earthen in bran-water, putting the articles in when cold. Do the same with porcelain kettles. Never leave wooden vessels out of doors, as they fall to pieces. Lift the handle of a pump, and cover it with blankets, to keep it from freezing.

Broken earthen and china can often be mended, by tying it up, and boiling it in milk. *Diamond cement*, when genuine, is very effectual for the same purpose. Old putty can be softened by muriatic acid. A strong cement may be made, by heating together equal parts of white lead, glue, and the whites of eggs. A cement for iron is made of six parts potter's clay and one part steel filings, formed into a paste, as thick as putty, with linseed oil.

Stop cracks, at the bottom and sides of doors, by nailing down strips of wood covered with baize, tight against the door on the casing. Stuff raw cotton into other cracks. Nail slats across nursery windows. Scatter ashes on slippery ice at the door; or rather, remove it. Clarify impure water with powdered alum, a teaspoonful to a barrel. In thunder storms, the centre of the room, or a bed, is safest, shutting doors and windows. A lightning-rod, if well pointed, and run deep into the earth, protects a circle, whose diameter equals the height of the lightning-rod above the highest chimney, and *no more*.

ON THE CARE OF THE CELLAR.

A cellar should often be whitewashed, to keep it sweet. It should have a drain, to keep it perfectly dry, as standing water in a cellar is a sure cause of disease in a family. The following articles are desirable in a cellar. A safe, which is a moveable closet with sides of wire or perforated tin, in which cold meats, cream, and other articles are kept. If ants are troublesome, set the legs in tin cups of water. A refrigerator, which is a large wooden box, on feet, with a lining of tin or zinc, and a space between the tin and wood filled with powdered charcoal. At the bottom, is a place to put ice, and a drain to carry off the water. It has moveable shelves and partitions. It is used for keeping articles cool. It should be cleaned, once a week.

Filtering jars, to purify water, should be kept in the cellar.

Fish and cabbages, in a cellar, are apt to scent a house, and give a bad taste to other articles.

STOREROOM.

Every house needs a storeroom, in which to keep tea, coffee, sugar, rice, candles, &c. It should be furnished with jars, having labels, a large spoon, a fork, sugar and flour-scoops, a towel, and a dish-cloth.

MODES OF DESTROYING INSECTS AND VERMIN.

Bed Bugs.

These animals can be destroyed, by scalding the places where they are found, with hot water, by washing with tobacco tea, and by anointing, either with quicksilver mixed with whites of eggs, or corrosive sublimate dissolved in alcohol, or camphor dissolved in oil of cedar. The last is probably the most effectual. All cracks and holes in bedsteads should be filled with putty, and in Summer an examination should be made, (if not every day, at least every Monday or Saturday,) of both bedstead and bedding. It is much easier to keep them away, than to get rid of them when they have once been allowed to multiply.

Cockroaches.

These animals can be killed by scalding them, when they accumulate in a place like a sink. They can be poisoned, by setting chloride of lime and water about. Also, by mixing either arsenic or calomel with Indian meal and molasses. These last must be used with care, lest children or others get poisoned.

Fleas.

These animals are generally brought by dogs or swine, or by dry shavings about the premises. A dog can be freed from them, by putting him into a tub of warm suds. The insects will rise to the top, and must be taken and burned, or they will revive. Scotch snuff, sprinkled over a dog, will destroy them. Strong perfumes, like camphor or penny-royal, about the bed and person, will keep them off, or at least diminish their attacks. When caught in the fingers, they are best destroyed by putting them in a basin of water. They often escape, if any other mode is tried.

Crickets.

Scalding, and snuff sprinkled about, are remedies for this annoyance.

Flies.

Flies can be driven out of rooms, by flirting towels or branches with leaves. Then darken a room, and they will not return. Cups containing quassia (four drachms to one quart of water) will drive them off. Also, cold green tea and molasses. Traps can be made, like two large book covers and sprinkled with sugar or molasses. When covered with flies, crush them suddenly together.

Musquitoes.

Nets, made of gauze, or thin muslin or millinet, hung around the bed, are the only perfect protection, at night. Washing the skin in perfumes, will diminish their attacks. Salt and water, camphor, and spirits of hartshorn, are the best remedies to alleviate their stings. The last is best.

Red or Black Ants.

Scalding them, and smearing the places where they resort, with corrosive sublimate, will destroy them. The latter is dangerous, as it is a deadly poison. (Whites of eggs are the antidote.) Setting the legs of a sideboard or safe in tin cups of water will keep them off.

Moths.

Airing clothes does not tend to prevent moths, but rather produces the opposite effect. Furs, feathers, and woollens, in Summer, if sprinkled with camphor, or fine tobacco, and wrapped and sewed tight in linen, are perfectly safe from moths. When moths frequent a particular place, scald it with a decoction of tobacco, and then sprinkle on camphor. Fur and woollens should be put away in April.

Rats and Mice.

A good cat is the best preservative against rats and mice. Various kinds of traps are also useful. Poisoning is also a remedy. Equal quantities of hemlock or *cicuta* and old cheese, mixed and set in their haunts, will drive them off, or poison them. Poison makes a house liable to the smell of dead rats. To remedy this, pour oil of vitriol on some saltpetre, and set it where the smell is most annoying, and shut the room up tight. Chloride of lime answers nearly as well, in most cases. It should be mixed with a little water in a saucer.

CHAPTER XXXIV.

ON SEWING, CUTTING, AND MENDING.

Importance of Young Girls being taught various Kinds of Stitching. Directions for doing various Stitches. Workbaskets, and their Contents. ON CUTTING AND FITTING GARMENTS. To cut and make Frocks, Shirts, and Chemises. Cotton and Linen. Old Silk Dresses quilted for Skirts. Flannel; White should be colored. Children's Flannels. Nightgowns. Nightcaps. Wrappers. Bedding. MENDING.

EVERY young girl should be taught to do the following kinds of stitch, with propriety. Over-stitch, hemming, running, felling, stitching, back-stitch and run, buttonhole-stitch, chain-stitch, whipping, darning, gathering, and cross-stitch.

In doing over-stitch, the edges should always be first fitted, either with pins or basting, to prevent puckering. In turning wide hems, a paper measure should be used, to make them even. Tucks, also, should be regulated by a paper measure. A fell should be turned, before the edges are put together, and the seam should be over-sewed before felling. All biassed or goring seams should be felled. For stitching, draw a thread, and take up two or three threads at a stitch.

In making buttonholes, it is best to have a pair of scissors, made for the purpose, which cut very neatly. For broadcloth, a chisel and board is better. The best stitch is made by putting in the needle, and then turning the thread near the eye, around the needle. This is better than to draw the needle through, and then take up a loop. A thread should first be put across each side of the buttonhole, and also a stay thread, or bar, at each end, before working it. A small bar should be worked at each end. Whipping is done better by sewing *over*, and not

under.   The roll should be as fine as possible, the
stitches short, the thread strong, and in sewing,
every gather should be taken up.

The rule for *gathering*, in shirts, is, to draw a
thread, and then take up two threads and skip four.
In *darning*, after the perpendicular threads are run,
the crossing threads should interlace, exactly, taking
one thread and leaving one, like woven threads.

The neatest sewers always fit and baste their
work, before sewing; and they say they always
save time in the end, by so doing, as they never
have to pick out work, on account of mistakes.

All new garments, that will never be altered in
shape, it is wise to sew close and tight; but some
are more nice than wise, in sewing frocks, and old
garments, in the same style.   However, this is the
least common extreme.   It is much more frequently
the case, that articles, which ought to be made strong
and neatly, are sewed so that a nice sewer would
rather pick out and sew over again, than to be annoyed with the sight of grinning stitches, and vexed
with constant rips.

Workbaskets.

It is very important to neatness, comfort, and
success in sewing, that a lady's workbasket should
be properly fitted up.   The following articles are
needful to the mistress of a family.

A large basket, to hold work; and in it a smaller
basket, or box, fastened, and containing, a needle-
book, in which are needles of every size, both blunts
and sharps, having a larger number of those sizes
most used; also darning-needles, small and large,
for woollen, cotton, and silk; and two tape-needles,
large and small; nice scissors, for fine work; buttonhole scissors; an emery-bag; two balls of white and
yellow wax; and two thimbles, in case one should
be mislaid.   When a person is troubled with damp

fingers, a lump of soft chalk, in a paper, is useful, to rub on the ends of the fingers.

Besides this box, keep in the basket, common scissors; small shears; a bag containing tapes of all colors and sizes, done up in rolls; bags, one, containing spools of white, and another of colored, cotton thread, and another for silks, wound on spools or papers; a box or bag for nice buttons, and another for more common ones; a bag containing silk braid, welting cords, and galloon binding. Small rolls of pieces of white and brown linen and cotton, are also often needed. A brick pincushion is a great convenience, in sewing, and better than screw-cushions. It is made by covering a brick with cloth, putting a cushion on the top, and covering it tastefully. It is very useful to hold pins and needles, while sewing, and to fasten long seams when basting and sewing.

ON CUTTING AND FITTING GARMENTS.

To make a Frock. The best way for a novice, is, to get a dress fitted (not sewed) at the best mantua-maker's. Then take out a sleeve and rip it to pieces, and cut out a pattern. Then take out half of the waist, (it must have a seam in front,) and cut out a pattern of the back and fore body, both lining and outer part. In cutting the patterns, iron the pieces, smooth, let the paper be stiff, and then, with a pin, prick holes in the paper, to show the gore in front, and the depth of the seams. Then, with a pen and ink, draw lines from each pinhole, to preserve this mark. Then baste the parts together again, and in doing it, the unbasted half will serve as a pattern. When this is done, a lady of common ingenuity can cut and fit a dress, by the patterns thus obtained. If the upper part of a dress is too tight, the seam under the arm must be let out; and in cutting a dress, there should be an allowance made, to let it out, if needful, at this seam. The lining of the fore-body must be biassed.

The linings for dresses should be stiffened with cotton or linen.   In cutting bias pieces, for trimming, they will not set well, unless they are exact.   In cutting them, use a long rule, and a lead pencil or piece of chalk.   Welting-cords should be covered with bias pieces; and it saves time, in many cases, to baste on the welting-cord, at the same time that you cover it.   The best way to put on hooks and eyes, is to sew them on double broad tape, and then sew this on the frock-lining.   They can then be moved easily, and do not show where sewed on.

In cutting a sleeve, double it biassed.   The skirts of dresses look badly, if not full ; and in putting on lining, at the bottom, be careful to have it a very little fuller than the dress, or it will shrink, and look badly.   All thin silks look much better with lining, and last much longer, as do aprons, also.   In putting in a lining to a dress, baste it on each separate breadth, and it looks much better than to have it fastened only at the bottom.   Make notches in selvage to prevent it from drawing up the breadth.   Dresses which are to be washed, should not be lined.

Silk dresses are very expensive ; and none but the wealthy should use them, except for a full dress. Any lady will look properly dressed, for almost any occasion, in the beautiful prints which are now to be obtained, and which wash and wear so well, as to make them the most economical dresses, both for Winter and Summer.

Figured silks, do not generally wear well, if the figure is large and satin-like.   Black and plain colored silks can be tested by getting samples, and making creases in them ; fold the creases in a bunch, and rub them against a rough surface, of moreen or carpeting.   Those that are poor, will soon wear off, at the creases.   English satin reps, of the best quality, double Florence, or Marceline, gros d'Afrique, and Turkish satin, are the best silks for wear.

Plaids are becoming, for tall women, as they shorten the appearance of the figure. Stripes are becoming to a large person, as they reduce the apparent size. Pale persons should not wear blue or green, and brunettes should not wear any light delicate colors, except shades of buff, fawn, or straw color. Pearl white is not good for any complexion. Dead white and black are becoming to almost all persons. It is best to try colors, by candle-light, for evening dresses; as some colors, which look very handsome in the daylight, are very homely when seen by candle-light. Be careful, in cutting dresses, to have the figures run in the right direction, and to have all the parts agree. When there is a right and wrong side, and a figure also to be matched, much care is necessary to prevent mistakes. Never cut a dress low in the neck, as it shows that a woman is not properly instructed in the rules of modesty and decorum, or that she has not sense enough to regard them. Never be in haste to be first in a fashion, and never go to the extremes.

To cut and make Shirts and Chemises.

In buying linen, look for that which has a round close thread, and is perfectly white; for if it be not white at first, it will never afterwards become so. Much that is called linen at the shops is half cotton, and does not wear so well as cotton alone. Cheap linens are usually of this kind. It is difficult to discover which are all linen; but the best way is to find a lot, presumed to be good, take a sample, wash it and ravel it. If this be good, the rest of the same lot will probably be so. If you cannot do this, draw a thread, each way, and if both appear equally strong, it is probably all linen. Linen and cotton must be put in clean water, and boiled, to get out the starch, and then ironed. A long piece of linen, a yard wide, will, with care and calculation, make eight shirts.   In cutting it, take a shirt of the right size, for a model, and by it measure the length of seven bodies, not cutting any but the last.   Cut off from this long piece all that is needed to go into the bodies, and from the narrow strip cut out the binders or linings, gussets, and other parts, measuring by the pattern. Then cut out the sleeves, from the original piece ; and when seven shirts are cut out, calculate whether there is enough for the eighth, before beginning to cut it.   Take the model-shirt as a guide, in fitting and basting.   Bosom-pieces, false collars, &c. must be cut and fitted by a pattern which suits the person for whom the articles are designed.   Gentlemen's night-shirts are made like other shirts, except that they are longer.

In cutting chemises, if the cotton or linen is a yard wide, cut off small half gores, at top of the breadths, and set them on the bottom.   Use a long rule and pencil, in cutting gores.

In cutting cotton which is quite wide, a seam can be saved, by cutting out two at once, in this manner.   Cut off three breadths, and, with a long rule and a pencil, mark and cut off the gores thus : from one breadth, cut off two gores, the whole length, each gore one fourth of the breadth at the bottom, and tapering off to a point at the top.   The other two breadths are to have a gore cut off from each, which is one fourth wide at top and two fourths at bottom.   Arrange these pieces right, and they will make two chemises, one having four seams, and the other three.   This is a much easier way of cutting, than sewing the three breadths together, in bag-fashion, as is often done.   The biassed, or goring seams, must always be felled.   The sleeves and neck can be cut according to the taste of the wearer, by another chemise for a pattern.   There should be a lining around the armholes, and stays at all corners. Five yards, of yard width, will make two chemises.

Old silk dresses, quilted for skirts, are very serviceable. White flannel is soiled so easily, and shrinks so much in washing, that it is a good plan to color it a light dove-color, according to a previous receipt. Cotton flannel, dyed thus, is also good for common skirts. In making up flannel, back-stitch and run the seams, and then cross-stitch them open. Nice flannel, for infants, can be ornamented, with very little expense of time, by turning up the hem, on the right side, and making a little vine at the edge, with saddler's silk. The stitch of the vine is a modification of buttonhole-stitch.

Long nightgowns are best cut a little goring. It requires five yards, for a long nightgown, and two and a half for a short one. Linen nightcaps wear longer than, and do not turn yellow as, cotton ones do. They should be ruffled with linen, as cotton borders will not last so long as the cap.

A double-quilted wrapper is a great comfort, in case of sickness. It may be made of two old dresses. It should not be cut full, but rather like a gentleman's study-gown, having no gathers or plaits, but large enough to slip off and on with ease. A double gown, of calico, is also very useful. Most articles of dress, for grown persons or children, require patterns.

Bedding. The best beds, are thick hair mattrasses, which, for persons in health, are good for Winter as well as Summer use. Mattrasses are also made of husks, dried and drawn into shreds. They are also made of alternate layers of cotton and moss. The most profitable sheeting, is the Russian, which will last three times as long as any other. It is never perfectly white. Unbleached cotton is good for Winter. It is poor economy to make narrow and short sheets, as children and domestics will always slip them off, and soil the bedtick and bolster. They should be three yards long, and two and a

half wide, so as to tuck in all around.   All bed-linen
should be marked and numbered, so that a bed can
always be made properly, and all missing articles be
known.

MENDING.

Silk dresses will last much longer by ripping out
the sleeves when thin, and changing arms, and also
by changing the breadths of the skirt.   Tumbled
black silk, which is old and rusty, should be dipped
in water, and after being drained for a few minutes,
should be ironed, without squeezing or pressing.
Cold tea is better than water.   Sheets, when worn
thin in the middle, should be ripped, and the other
edges sewed together.   Window-curtains last much
longer, if lined, as the sun fades and rots them.
Broadcloth should be cut with reference to the way
the nap runs.   When pantaloons are thin, it is best
to newly seat them, cutting the piece inserted in a
curve, as corners are difficult to fit.   When the
knees are thin, it is a case of domestic surgery,
which demands *amputation*.   This is performed, by
cutting off both legs, some distance above the knees,
and then changing the legs.   Take care to cut them
off exactly of the same length, or in the exchange
they will not fit.   This method brings the worn spot
under the knees, and the seam looks much better
than a patch and darn.   Hose can be cut down,
when the feet are worn.   Take an old sale stocking,
and cut it up for a pattern.   Make the heel short.
In sewing, turn each edge, and run it down, and
then sew over the edges.   This is better than to
stitch and then cross-stitch.   Run thin places in
stockings, and it will save darning a hole.   If shoes
are worn through on the sides, in the upper-leather,
slip pieces of broadcloth under, and sew them around
the holes.

CHAPTER XXXV.

ON THE CARE OF YARDS AND GARDENS.

Important Rules for Ladies cultivating Fruits and Flowers. On the Preparation of Soil. For Pot-Plants. To prepare Garden Soil. On the Preparation of a Hot-bed. Planting Flower-Seeds. To plant Garden-Seeds. To transplant Flowers and Vegetables. To transplant Shrubs and Trees. To repot House-Plants.

In undertaking the cultivation of fruits and flowers, the following rules are very important for ladies.

1. As this employment is designed for health and amusement, no more time is to be taken for it, than is requisite for these ends ; and all that exceeds this measure, is to be considered as time misemployed. Before commencing, every lady should decide how much time, each day, it is right for her to give to this fascinating object, and then arrange her plans, so as not to exceed this amount.

2. Any risk of health, in this pursuit, is sinful ; and to avoid this, whenever the ground is damp, flannel drawers and India-rubber shoes, and a warm shawl, should be put on. In a damp and cold air, the neck and jaws should also be covered. Excessive fatigue should likewise be avoided.

On the Preparation of Soil.

Although ladies cannot perform many of the processes which are here mentioned, they need to know how they are to be done, in order to be able properly to direct others.

The common soil, which covers the earth, is called *loam.* If sand predominate in it, it is called a sandy loam, and is a light soil. If clay predominate, it is called a clay loam, and is a cold and heavy soil.

The finest kinds of native soil, are those, in which much decayed vegetable matter is mixed with the loam.   This is the kind of soil in our new Western States ; where, for hundreds of years, forests have been shedding their verdure.   The best kind of soil is made by mixing animal manure, vegetable mould, and common loam, in due proportions.

To prepare Soil for Pot-Plants.

Take one fourth common yellow loam, one fourth manure, and one half vegetable mould, such as is found in woods, under the trees.   The manure must be at least two years old, so as to be thoroughly decayed.   It must first be laid to dry, then broken up fine, and sifted through a *lime screen*, which is a coarse sieve, made of wires one fourth of an inch apart.   These materials must be thoroughly mixed.

To prepare Garden Soil.

If the original soil is a whitish loam, and packs tight and hard during Winter, put on a covering of sand, three inches thick.   Then put on a thick covering of manure, and spade it in, and this will make one of the finest soils for a garden.   A soil which packs hard, and is slow in its growth, is called a cold soil, and needs manure to warm it.   If the original soil is black, and crumbles readily, manure without sand improves it.   In digging a garden, it is important to dig as deep as possible, so as to have the soil soft and loose around the lower roots of the vegetables.   New manure is called *long*, and that which is old is called *short*, manure.   Most garden plants require short manure, and many of them will be almost destroyed by the long.   Corn and potatoes will thrive, with long manure, as well as, or better than, with short.   The soil must be kept loose around plants.

On the Preparation of a Hot-bed.

Hot-beds are very useful, in bringing forward seeds for early vegetables and flowers. A gain of two months is usually secured, by their use. To prepare a hot-bed, make a frame, or box, without a bottom, two feet deep, in front, and three feet deep, behind, with the sides sloping from back to front. To this, must be fitted frames like window-sashes, except that the horizontal bars are omitted, and the panes of glass are lapped over each other, like shingles. Then select a place with a southern exposure, and place four stakes in the earth, for the corners of the bed, which must be made a foot larger than the box, on every side. Between these stakes, raise the bed, by carting on fresh horse-manure, (the old is useless for this purpose.) When it is a foot thick, tread it down hard, and then lay on another layer, a foot thick, and tread it down. Continue this, till the bed is three feet thick. Then set the box upon it, so that the front shall face the south, and throw into the box rich garden-soil, till a layer of six inches is made. In this, plant the seeds. The box must be covered with the glass, when the weather is so cold as to chill the plants; at other times, it must be raised, to admit the air, which is necessary to the growth of the plants. When the sun is warm, the top must be put over and covered with straw matting, or old blankets, from ten to four o'clock, otherwise the plants and seeds will be killed by the heat. In very cold nights the box must be covered with blankets and straw. The bed must be often watered, especially in warm days. The appearance of the soil and plants must be the guide in this matter. Hot-beds should be prepared in the middle of March, in the Northern States, and in the middle of February, in the Middle States. After the frosts are over, the plants can be transplanted into the garden. They must be covered from the sun, two days after transplanting.

Planting Flower-Seeds.

Before planting seeds, prepare sticks for marking them. This is easily done, by sawing a board, planed smooth on one side, into pieces a foot long, and then splitting these into strips an inch wide. On each of these pieces, the name of the seed can be written, with a black-lead pencil, as this is not washed out by the rain. Those seeds, which are large, and have hard coverings, must be soaked in cups and saucers, and be kept in a warm room, till they begin to sprout. When doing this, write the name on one of the above sticks, and place it upon the saucer or cup, to prevent mistake. It is not necessary to sprout seeds in water thus, it only hastens their progress.

When ready to plant the seeds, take a *dibble* or *garden-trowel,* and break up the soil. Make it fine and soft, in a circle of a foot or nine inches in diameter. Then, if the seeds are large, like the sweet pea, scrape off the soil of this circle, an inch deep, and put it in a little pile. Then scatter the seeds over the surface of the circle. Then sprinkle the earth over the seeds, till it is all returned to its place. Then, with the trowel, beat down the earth, over the seeds, to make it press well, and to exclude the light; for seeds sprout much better in the dark than in the light. After this is done, set up the stick, in the middle of the circle, so that the name will be towards the earth. This prevents the removal of the writing by rain. Seeds ought not to be planted, when the earth is very wet. In planting flower-seeds, it is best to put them where they ought to grow, as transplanting puts them back, a fortnight, or more. It may be well to transplant a part, as it will secure a longer supply of the flower, by having some bloom earlier than others. The same object can be secured by planting the same kind of seed at different times, though many plants require a whole season to bring them to perfection. As a long period of wet or cold weather will rot the seeds, it is best to plant only half at once; and if they do not come up, plant more.

When the seeds have come up, and are half an inch high, they should be thinned out. The most thriving should be left to stand, and the rest be pulled up or transplanted. If a large number grow in the same spot, they will all be small and imperfect. Where the plant is large, leave only one in a place; if smaller, four or five; if quite small, leave seven or eight, or more. Small seeds, like those of the poppy, should be scattered on the surface, and be sprinkled with fine earth, enough just to cover them. This should be beat down with the trowel. The largest seeds are put one inch deep, the smallest on the surface; and the seeds of intervening sizes are to be planted accordingly, the larger, deeper, the smaller, nearer the surface. Where seeds are very small, like those of the ice plant, set up some shingles on the south side, to shade the seeds and young plants; and success will be more certain.

To plant Garden-Seeds.

Prepare the beds, laying them out about a yard wide. Take a board a yard long, and a foot broad. Lay it across the bed, and with a stick make a furrow each side of the board, one inch deep. Scatter the seeds in this furrow, and cover them. Lay the board over the top of the covered furrows, and step on it, to press it down hard. This packs the earth around the seeds, and makes them sprout quicker. Lay the board a foot from the furrow, and proceed as before. When the seeds come up, thin them out, leaving the plants at different distances, according to their size. The seeds of fruit-trees must be planted in the fall.

To transplant Flowers and Vegetables.

Transplanting should never be done when the sun is warm. The best time is just before evening, or before a rain. It should not be done in a rain, or in a dry time. Dig up the plants with a garden-trowel, and put them in the place prepared. Set them straight in the ground, a trifle lower than they were before, and press the soil around the roots, firmly, but not so as to make it very hard. Transplanted roots should never be watered, till the sun is nearly down ; and they are more likely to do well if covered from the sun, for two or three days after transplanting. All plants must be watered in a dry time, at evening.

To transplant Shrubs and Trees.

Fall is considered the best time for transplanting. In cold climates, the peach, nectarine, and almond, run less risk of being Winter-killed, if transplanted in the Spring. In transplanting, all the roots should be taken, if possible, especially the small fibres, which are of much more consequence than the large roots. The fibres nourish, while the large roots serve chiefly to hold the tree firmly in the soil. These fibres should never be allowed to get dry. If they are to be carried some distance, the roots should be covered with moss, tied up in cloths, and kept wet. Dig the hole larger than is sufficient to place the roots in their natural position, and take care to cut off any wounded root. Reduce the top one third, and leave the two thirds perfect. Be careful not to set the tree deeper than it was before, and throw in soil, adding one or two shovelfuls of good manure according to the size of the tree. While this is doing, the tree should be shaken, in order to admit the soil among the small fibres.   When the hole is filled, let the ground be trodden hard, and raise a slight mound of earth around the tree, say two or three inches high.   Then make a hollow or basin around the trunk to receive the water, and pour in a little to pack the earth around the fibres.   The common plan of cutting off all the limbs of the tree, and leaving mere poles, under the impression that this will secure more nourishment to what remains, is founded on ignorance of the physiology of plants. There must be a relative proportion preserved between the roots and leaves; and as some roots are lost in transplanting, a part of the leaves must be removed ; but usually not more than one third.   If a dry time follows transplanting, the trees should be watered every three or four days.

To Repot House-Plants.

The earth for pot-plants should be renewed once a year.   The best time for doing this, is soon after their flowering, which is usually in the Spring. First prepare the soil, as previously directed.   Then take the plant out of the pot, and remove the small matted fibres at the bottom, and all the earth, except that which adheres to the roots.   From woody plants, like roses, all the earth should be shaken out. Then hold the plant in the proper position in the empty pot ; and shake in the earth, around it.   While doing this, give several knocks on the side of the pot, to shake the earth in among the roots.   When the pot is full, pour in some water to settle the earth, and heap on fresh soil, till it is at the right height. There must always be a hole at the bottom of the pot, or else water will accumulate and rot the roots. A piece of broken earthen must be laid in the pot, over the hole, or the soil will be carried off when the plant is watered.

CHAPTER XXXVI.

ON THE PROPAGATION OF PLANTS.

Different Modes of Propagation. By Offsets. Cuttings. Layers.
Budding, or Inoculating. Ingrafting;—Whip-Grafting; Split-
Grafting. Inarching. Pruning. Thinning.

MOST plants can be propagated by seeds ; but this
is a slow method, for trees and shrubs. There are
six other methods, namely, by offsets, by cuttings,
by layers, by budding, by ingrafting, and by inarching. Bulbous roots are propagated by offsets.
Some bulbs have little offsets growing on the top of
the bulb, which, after furnishing supplies for them,
decay. Of this kind, are the crocus and the gladiolus. Other bulbs have offsets growing around their
sides, which are to be split off and set out to make
new plants. Of this kind, are tulips, daffodils, and
tuberoses.

Many plants can be propagated by cuttings, or
slips. This is done, by simply cutting off twigs of
the plant, and setting one end in the earth, so that
two or three eyes or buds may be under the soil.
Every variety of apple may be propagated in this
way; but some are more easily propagated than
others. In selecting cuttings, take side shoots from
the lower part of the tree, and choose those which
grow horizontally, rather than those which are perpendicular. Cut them ten inches long, having an
inch or two of last year's growth, and the rest of
this year's. The time for planting is when the sap
is in full flow ; and in setting out the cuttings, put
broken crockery at the bottom of the hole, and let
the lower end rest upon it, pressing the earth firmly
around. At least one eye must be under the soil.

They must be watered, and shaded in hot weather. Limbs of fruit trees can be made to sprout roots, by encircling them with damp soil, kept constantly wet for some weeks. Eventually, roots will shoot out from the limb, into the wet earth. The limb may then be sawed off, and set out, and it will make a shrub fruit tree, as it will grow but little larger than it would have done had it remained on the tree.

Plants are also propagated by *layers*. To do this, take a shoot, which comes up near the root, bend it down, and bring several eyes under the soil, leaving the top above ground. It is better and more surely done, by cutting the shoot half through, at one of the buried eyes, and bending it in the manner exhibited in Fig. 32, in which, *a*, is the place of the

Fig. 32.

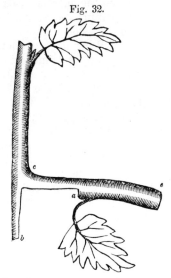

eye where the shoot is cut half through, and *c*, the place where it bends upward. This part must be fastened firmly under the soil, two or three inches deep. At *b*, is the place where the roots will spring out for a new plant. After the roots appear, the shoot can be cut from the parent stock, at *e*, and transplanted. Roses, honeysuckles, and many other shrubs, are readily propagated thus. They will generally take root, by being simply buried; but cutting them, as here directed, is the best method. Layers are more certain than cuttings.

Another mode of propagation is by budding, or inoculating. The time for doing this, is from July to September. To do it, take a shoot, of this year's growth, from the tree whose fruit you wish to secure. From this shoot, cut off, with a penknife, a bud, half an inch above, and half an inch below the bud, cutting a piece of the inner wood adhering under the bud. It used to be the practice to remove this wood; but success is much more certain if it be left. Then prepare the stock, into which you are to place the bud, by making a perpendicular cut in the plant an inch long, and a transverse cut downward, as is shown in Fig. 33. Then insert the bud, in this opening, so that *a*, of the bud, shall pass under the bark to a, of the stock. Then *b*, of the bud, must be cut off square, to match the cut, b, in the stock, and fitted exactly to it. It is the fitting of the bark of the bud and that of the stock exactly together, at this point, which secures success. After fitting in the bud, woollen yarn must be wound around the place, to hold it securely. When the bud has grown awhile, till the bark adheres firmly, take off the yarn.

Peaches, plums, and other fruits, are easily thus propagated. So also are roses, after a little practice. Any lady can secure all the stone-fruit in the neighborhood, by planting cherry and peach-stones in the Fall, and when they are two or three years old, budding them, in July or August, from any fruit tree she may like.

Fig. 33.

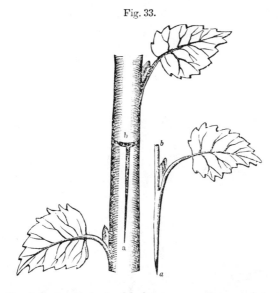

Seed-fruit can be budded into any other seed-fruit; as pears into apples, or apples into the crab-tree. So stone-fruits can be budded into any other stone-fruit, as peaches into cherry or plum trees. But stone and seed-fruit cannot be thus mingled.

Rose bushes can have a variety of kinds budded into the same stock. The branch above the bud, must be cut off, the next March or April after the bud is put in. Seed-fruit, like apples and pears, are more easily propagated by ingrafting than by budding.

Ingrafting is a similar process, and offers this advantage, that it can be performed on large trees, whereas budding can be done only on small ones. There are two kinds of ingrafting,—whip-grafting, and split-grafting. The first kind is for young trees, and the other for large ones.

The time for ingrafting, is from May to October.

The cuttings must be taken between Christmas and March, and kept in a damp cellar. In performing the operation, cut off, in a sloping direction, as seen in Fig. 34, the tree or limb to be grafted. Then

Fig. 34.

cut off, in a corresponding slant, the slip to be grafted on. Then put them together, so that the bark of each shall match, exactly, on one side, and tie them firmly together, with woollen yarn. It is not essential that both be of equal size; if the bark of each meet together exactly on one side, it answers the purpose. But the two must not differ much, in size. The slope should be an inch and a half in length. After they are tied together, the place should be covered with a salve or composition of beeswax and rosin. A mixture of clay and cow-dung will answer the same purpose. This must be tied on with a cloth. Grafts must be selected from horizontal shoots, in the Winter, and be kept from freezing, till they are used. Grafting is more convenient than budding, as grafts can be sent from a great distance ; whereas buds must be taken in July or August, from a shoot of the present year's growth, and cannot be sent to any great distance.

Fig. 35.

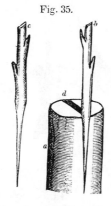

Fig. 35, exhibits the mode called stock grafting ; *a* being the limb of a large tree which is split, and is to be held open by a small wedge, till the grafts are put in. A graft, inserted in the limb, is shown at *b*, and at *c*, is one not inserted, but designed to be put in at *d*, as two grafts can be put into a large stock. In inserting the graft, be careful to make the edge of the bark of the graft meet exactly the edge of the bark of the stock ; for on this, success depends. After the grafts are put in, the wedge must be withdrawn, and the whole of the stock be covered with the thick salve or composition before mentioned, reaching from the top, where the grafts are inserted, to the bottom of the slit. Be careful not to knock or move the grafts, after they are put in.

Fig. 36.

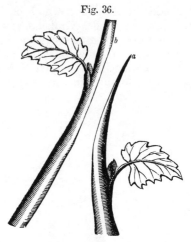

Fig. 36, exhibits the mode of inarching; *a* being the plant cut entirely off, and *b* one which has a place shaved out half through the stock, to match the slant in the other. These are to be bound together, and covered with the salve or composition before named. This is done in plants both having a root. When it is found that they have united, and are growing well, the plant *b* is cut off, below the inarching. All these modes require practice, to insure success; but any lady, after a few trials, will succeed.

Pruning.

The following rules for pruning, are from a distinguished horticulturist. Prune off all dead wood, and all the little twigs on the main limbs. Retrench branches so as to give light and ventilation to the interior of the tree. Straight and perpendicular shoots give little or no fruit, while those which are most nearly horizontal, and somewhat curving, give fruit abundantly, and of good quality. On this account, side shoots are often budded, that new and artificial angles may be formed to obstruct the flow of sap, and secure fine fruit. Superfluous and ill-placed buds may be rubbed off, at any time; and no buds, pushing out after Midsummer, should be spared. In choosing between shoots to be retained, preserve the lowest placed, and on lateral shoots, those which are nearest the origin. The retained shoots should be treated according to the class of fruit to which they belong. If the tree bears on distinct branches and old spurs, they should not be shortened; if it bears only on the last year's wood, (like the apple, apricot, pear, cherry, and plum,) shorten them alternately, year and year, so as always to keep a proper supply of bearers. Shorten strong shoots one fourth, and feeble ones one half. The object of this, is, to secure an increase of fruit. When branches cross each other, so as to rub, remove one or the other. Remove all suckers from the roots of trees or shrubs. Prune after the sap is in full circulation, (except in the case of grapes,) as the wounds then heal best. Some think it best to prune before the sap begins to run. Pruning-shears, and a pruning-pole, with a chisel at the end, can be procured of those who deal in fruit.

Thinning.

As it is the office of the leaves to absorb nourishment, from the atmosphere, they should never be removed, except to mature the wood or fruit. In doing this, remove such leaves as shade the fruit, as soon as it is ready to ripen. To do it earlier, impairs the growth. Do it gradually at two different times. Thinning the fruit is important, as tending to increase the size and flavor of the fruit, and the longevity of the tree. If the fruit be thickly set, take off one half, at the time of setting. Revise in June, and then in July, taking off all that may be spared. On an apple tree, one very large apple to every square foot, is the rule that may be a sort of guide, in other cases. According to this, two hundred apples would be allowed to a tree whose extent is fifteen feet by twelve. If a person thinks this thinning excessive, let him try two similar trees, and thin one as directed, and leave the other unthinned. It will be found that the thinned tree will produce an equal weight, and much finer flavored fruits.

CHAPTER XXXVII.

ON THE CULTIVATION OF FLOWERS.

List of Various Kinds of Flowers, in Reference to Color, Height, and Time of Flowering. Biennial and Perennial Flowers. Shrubs; List of those most suitable for adorning a Yard. Roses; Varieties of. Herbaceous Roots. Care of House-Plants. Shade-Trees for Yards. Creepers; Annual. Care of Bulbous and Tuberous Roots. Laying out Flower-Beds.

THE following list of flowers, taken from the Magazine of Horticulture, Number lxv., will enable a lady to lay out flower-beds, with reference to color, height, and time of blooming. An immense variety of tasteful plans might be devised, in arranging the beds and flowers in yards and gardens.

WHITE.

Plants from six to twelve inches high.

Ice Plant, (Mesembryánthemum cristallínum.) Flowering in July and August. This plant is a great favorite in every garden, its singularly beautiful foliage claiming for it a place in almost every flower-border. The seeds should be planted in pots, early in May, and transplanted into the border about the first of June, and each plant allowed sufficient room to spread its branches. The soil should be light, and the situation rather dry.

Sweet Alyssum, (Alyssum maritimum.) Flowering from June to

October. The sweet alyssum is a tender perennial, but flowers from the seed the first season, and is therefore classed among annuals. The flowers are highly fragrant. If the roots are taken up in a pot, it will flower well in the house.

White-flowered Leptosiphon, (Leptosìphon androsàceus, var. alba.) A new variety with white flowers. Flowering from June to August.

Mr. Walker's Schizopetalon, (Schizopétalon Walkèri.) Flowering in July and August; an extremely delicate plant, with small but singularly beautiful white flowers.

Beautiful Blumenbachia, (Blumenbáchia insígnis.) Flowering from July to September.

One foot to eighteen inches high.

Common white Candytuft, (Ibèris amàra.) Flowers in June and July. To have a succession of flowers, two sowings of the seed should be made, one in April or May, and the other in June.

Pinnate-leaved Candytuft, (Ibèris pinnàta.) Flowers from July till October.

New rocket Candytuft, (Ibèris amàra var.) Flowers in June and July; a new and improved variety, with very large and dense corymbose clusters of blossoms.

White Venus's Looking-glass, (Prismatocárpus spéculum álba.) Flowers from June to August.

Mr. Priest's Schizanthus, (Schizánthus Prièstii.) Flowers in July and August.

Sweet-scented Stevia, (Stèvia serràta.) Flowering in July and September.

White evening Primrose, (Œnothèra tetráptera.) Flowers from June to October. Very pretty.

Eighteen inches to two feet high.

White Petunia, (*Petùnia* nyctaginiflòra.) Flowers from June to October. A showy and handsome annual; the plants should be allowed plenty of room to extend their branches.

White Clarkia, (Clárkia pulchélla álba.) Flowers in July and September. One of the most delicate annuals.

White Chrysanthemum, (Chrysánthemum coronàrium álba.) Flowers in July and September.

Double white Jacobæa, (Senècio élegans álba.) Flowers in July and September; very pretty.

Love in a Mist, (Nigélla damascèna.) Flowering in July and September.

Two feet high and upwards.

White Argemone, (Argemòne mexicàna.) Flowers from July to October. Very showy.

New white Malope, (Málope trifida álba.) Flowers in July and October. New and handsome.

Winged Ammobium, (Ammòbium alàtum.) Flowers from July to October; erect in its habit.

White Lavatera, (Lavátera triméstris álba.) Flowers from July to October. The plants should not stand too crowded.

White sweet Sultan, (Centaurèa moschàta álba.) Flowers from July to September.

New white eternal Flower, (Xeránthemum bracteàtum álba.) Flowering from August to October.

White Helicrysum, (Helicrysum macránthum.) Flowers from July to October; a new and very elegant variety, with white flowers, tipped with blush.

YELLOW AND ORANGE.

Six inches to one foot high.

Yellow Chryseis, (Chrysèis califórnica.) Flowers from June to October; sow where the plants are to remain, as they do not bear removing with success.

Orange-colored Chryseis, (Chrysèis cròcea.) Flowers from June to October; sow where the plants are to remain to flower; thin out to the distance of six inches.

Procumbent Sanvitalia, (Sanvitàlia procúmbens.) Flowers in June and September; of a spreading, dwarf habit; pretty in patches.

Musk-flowered Mimulus, (Mímulus moschàta.) Flowering from June to September. This is a pretty little plant, for small beds, and desirable from its strong odor of musk.

One foot to eighteen inches high.

Drummond's Coreopsis, (Calliópsis Drummóndii.) Flowers from June to October.

New dark Coreopsis, (Calliópsis, var. atrosanguínea.) Flowers from June to October.

Golden Hawkweed, (Crèpis barbàta.) Flowers in June and August.

Showy Sphænogyne, (Sphænógyne speciòsa.) Flowers in July and August.

Stem-clasping Dracopis, (Dracòpis amplexicaúlis.) Flowers in July and September.

Tri-colored Chrysanthemum, (Chrysánthemum tricolor.) Flowering in July and September.

Drummond's Primrose, (Œnothèra Drummóndii.) Flowering from June to September. New and very handsome.

Chrysanthemum-like Oxyura, (Oxyùra chrysanthemoìdes.) Flowers in July and August.

Yellow Cladanthus, (Cladánthus arábicus.) Flowers from June to October; very pretty; grows well in light, dry soil.

Peroffsky's Erysimum, (Erysimum Peroffskyànum.) Flowering in July and September. Bright orange and very beautiful.

Two feet high and upwards.

Golden Bartonia, (Bartònia aúrea.) Flowers from July to October.

Golden Coreopsis, (Calliópsis tinctòria.) Flowering all Summer.

Bright yellow Zinnia, (Zinnia parviflòra.) Flowers in July and September.

Yellow Chrysanthemum, (Chrysánthemum coronària.) Flowers from July to October; requires good soil, and the plants to stand one foot apart.

African Marigold, (Tagètes erécta.) Flowers from June to October; should be planted in good soil.

Yellow sweet Sultan, (Centaurèa suavèolens.) Flowers in July and August. One of the prettiest annuals cultivated.

Bright yellow Argemone, (Argemòne speciòsa.) Flowers from July to October. The plants should be tied to stakes, to prevent their being broken by the wind.

Californian Lasthenia, (Lasthènia califórnica.) Flowers from June to September.

Elegant Madaria, (Madària, [formerly *Màdia*] élegans.) Flowers in July and September. Should be in a rather shady situation, as the sun curls up the flowers.

Great flowering evening Primrose, (Œnothèra grandiflòra.) Flowering in August and September.

Yellow Nasturtium, (Tropæ'olum màjus.) Flowering from June to September.

French Marigold, (Tagètes pátula.) Flowering from June to October.

ROSE.

Six inches to one foot high.

Many-flowered Catchfly, (Silène multiflòra.) Flowers in August and September.

Rose of Heaven, (Lychnis cœli ròsea.) Flowers in July and September, in light sandy soil.

One foot to eighteen inches high.

Drummond's annual Phlox, (Phlóx Drummóndii.) Flowers from June to October.

Mangles's Rodanthe, (Rodánthe Manglèsii.) Flowers from June to September.

Rose-colored Nonea, (Nònea ròsea.) Flowers from July to September.

Cluster-flowered Catchfly, (Silène compácta.) Flowers from June to October. This species does best when the seeds are sown in the fall. The plants come up strong early in April, and in June are in bloom, and continue to display their flowers the whole season. A better soil may be appropriated to this species than the others.

Elegant rose Clarkia, (Clárkia élegans ròsea.) Flowers in June and September. A new and pretty plant, forming a beautiful object in large masses.

Tenore's Catchfly, (Silène Tenòrei.) Flowers in July and September. Like the other silenes, it delights in a light sandy soil.

Lobel's Catchfly, (Silène armèria.) Flowers in July and September.

Two-colored Calandrinia, (Calandrinia discolor.) Flowers in July and September.

RED.

Six inches to one foot high.

Chinese annual Pink, (Diánthus chinénsis.) Flowers from July to October. No annual adds more to the beauty of the border than the annual pink, especially if the seeds are selected from choice flowers. They grow freely, flower profusely, and the great variety and blending of colors, in a large bed, is extremely beautiful.

Virginian Stock, (Malcòmia maritimus.) Flowers from July to October.

Showy-flowered Calandrinia, (Calandrinia speciòsa.) Flowering in July and September. Delights in a light dry soil in a sunny and fully exposed situation.

Rose-colored Verbena, (Verbèna Aublètia.) Flowering in July and September.

One foot to eighteen inches high.

Drooping Catchfly, (Silène péndula.) Flowers in July and August, in a light sandy soil.

Crimson Coxcomb, (Celòsia cristàta.) Flowers from June to October. Plants should be forwarded in a frame or hot-bed, and transplanted into a *very rich* soil, to make them produce handsome heads.

Eighteen inches to two feet and upwards.

Red Lavatera, (Lavátera triméstris.) Flowers in July and September.

Rose-colored branching Larkspur, (Delphínium consólida ròsea.) Flowers in July and September. Plant in very rich soil, and tie up the stems to neat sticks, as the wind is apt to break them down from the profusion of flowers.

Red Zinnia, (Zinnia multiflòra.) Flowers in July and September, in a good soil and open situation.

American Centaurea, (Plectocéphalus Americànus.) Flowers in August and September.

Vermilion-colored Malva, (Málva miniàta.) Flowers in July and September.

Dark red Nasturtium, (Tropæ\olum màjus, var. atrosanguínea.) Flowers in July and September. A pretty plant for training up to a trellis or sticks, &c.; attaining the height, when thus assisted in its growth, of six feet.

Love lies bleeding, (Amarántus caudàtus.) Flowers from July to September.

SCARLET.

One foot to eighteen inches high and upwards.

Scarlet Cacalia, (Cacàlia coccínea.) Flowers from June to September. A bed or patch of this pretty flower, with the plants standing close together, has a very showy appearance; one foot high.

Flos Adonis, (Adònis vernàlis.) Flowers in July and September. The plants may stand close together, as the flowers are not very large, but in masses they make a brilliant show. One foot high.

Scarlet Zinnia, (Zinnia coccínea.) Flowering from July till frost. This variety, when *true*, is one of the brightest scarlet annual flowers; but unless great care is taken in saving the seeds, it soon degenerates to a dull purple, or into various shades between scarlet and purple. The soil should be very rich and light, and the situation warm and exposed to the sun.

Crimson Cypress vine, (Ipomæ\a Quamóclit.) Flowers in August and September. A most exquisitely beautiful annual climber.

LILAC AND PURPLE.

One foot to eighteen inches high.

Elegant Clarkia, (Clárkia élegans.) Flowers in July and September.

Beautiful Clarkia, (Clárkia pulchélla.) Flowers from June to September ; should be planted in light loamy soil.

Dense-flowered Leptosiphon, (Leptosìphon densiflòrus.) Flowers in June and August. Delights in a good loamy soil.

Great-flowered Calandrinia, (Calandrinia grandiflòra.) Flowers in July and September.

Purple Petunia, (Petùnia phœnícea.) Flowers from June till frost. A light rich soil will suit the plant best.

Purple Candytuft, (Ibèris umbellàta.) Flowers in June and August.

Crimson Candytuft, (Ibèris umbellàta var.) Flowers in June and August.

Double purple Jacobæa, (Senècio élegans plèno.) Flowers in July to September. Plant in good rich soil.

Long-tubed Leptosiphon, (Leptosìphon androsàceus.) Flowering in June and August. Both this and the L. densiflòrus delight in a good light loam, and a partially shaded situation.

Hooker's Schizanthus, (Schizánthus Hookèri.) Flowering in July and September. All the schizanthuses are beautiful and exceedingly delicate plants. The seeds may be sown in May, in light, loamy soil, and the plants transplanted early in June. A situation not too much exposed to the wind or the full sun should be selected, and the plants should be tied up to neat green stakes as they proceed in growth. Thus treated, they will be great ornaments of the garden all Summer.

Wing-leaved Schizanthus, (Schizánthus pinnàtus.) Flowering in July and September.

Graham's Schizanthus, (Schizánthus Grahámi.) Flowering in July and September.

Dwarf-branched Schizanthus, (Schizánthus pinnàtus hùmilis.) Flowering in June and August.

Lindley's Primrose, (Œnothèra Lindleyàna.) Flowering in July and September.

Veined Verbena, (Verbèna venòsa.) Flowers in July and September. The roots of this species, if protected in a frame or cellar during Winter, flower very profusely the second season.

Purple eternal Flower, (Xeránthemum ánnuum.) Flowers in July and August.

Eighteen inches to two feet high and upwards.

Globe Amaranthus, (Gomphrèna globòsa.) Flowers from July till frost. Plant in very rich soil.

Purple sweet Sultan, (Centaurèa moschàta.) Flowers in July and September.

Sweet Scabious, (Scabiòsa atropurpùrea.) Flowers in August and September.

Purple Zinnia, (Zínnia élegans.) Flowers in August and September.

Prince's Feather, (Amarántus hypochondrìacus.) Flowers from July till frost.

Great flowering Malope, (Málope trífida grandiflòra.)

Large blue Lupin, (Lupìnus pilòsus.) Flowers in July and August.

Barclay's Maurandya, (Maurándya Barclayàna.) Flowers in July and September. A fine climber.

BLUE.

Six inches to one foot high.

Graceful Lobelia, (Lobèlia grácilis.) Flowers from July to September. To plant this delicate annual, so as to have a fine effect, it should be placed on slightly elevated mounds of rich soil. Lobèlia bicolor is similar to L. grácilis.

Elegant Nemophila, (Nemóphila insignis.) Flowers in July and September. Plant in a half shady moist situation.

Pretty Clintonia, (Clintònia pulchélla.) Flowers from July till frost.

Elegant Clintonia, (Clintònia élegans.) Flowers from July till frost. It should be treated in the same manner as Lobèlia grácilis, to which it is a fine companion.

Atriplex-leaved Nolana, (Nolàna atriplicifòlia.) Flowers from June till frost. This and Nemóphila insignis are fine annuals for planting in beds on turf.

Fine blue Anagallis, (Anagállis índica.) Flowering all Summer.

One foot to two feet high.

Mexican Ageratum, (Agératum mexicàna.) Flowers in July and September.

Azure blue Commelina, (Commelìna cœléstis.) Flowers in July and September.

Azure blue Gilia, (Gília capitàta.) Flowers in August and September.

Spanish Nigella, (Nigélla hispánica.) Flowers in July and September.

Fine blue Eutoca, (Eutòca víscida.) Flowers from July till frost.

Dwarf Convolvulus, (Convólvulus mìnor.) Flowers from June till frost.

Blue Didiscus, (Didíscus cœrùleus.) Flowers in August and September.

LILAC, PURPLE, OR BLUE, AND WHITE.

One foot to two feet high.

Various-leaved Collinsia, (Collinsia heterophylla.) Flowering in June and August. Both of these species are very fine annuals. The plants flower more vigorously, if the seeds are sown early, before warm weather overtakes the young plants. Select a half shady situation, and plant in good mellow loam.

Two-colored Collinsia, (Collinsia bicolor.) Flowering in June and August.

Three-colored Gilia, (Gília tricolor.) Flowers all Summer; one of the most exquisite little annuals cultivated.

Unique Larkspur, (Delphinium consólida var.) Flowering from July to September.

VERY DARK.

One foot to eighteen inches high.

Dark-flowered Lotus, (Lòtus jacobæ'us.) Flowering in August and September. A beautiful plant, which may be treated as an annual.

The seeds should be sown in April, or early in May, and the young plants removed to the border in June. Its dark, almost black flowers, and small linear foliage, render it a very desirable plant.

Dark purple Salpiglossis, (Salpiglóssis atropurpùrea.) Flowering in July and August. A light, loamy soil and half shaded aspect best suits the salpiglossis.

COLORS VARYING.

Six inches to one foot.

Pansy or Hearts-ease, (Viola trícolor.) Flowers all Summer The large flowering varieties are the most beautiful ornaments of the garden all Summer.

One to two feet high.

Г Double German Aster, (Aster sinénsis.) Flowering in August and September. These should be planted in very rich moist soil, and be well watered if the weather should be dry.

Double Balsam, (Impàtiens balsámina.) Flowering from July till frost. Transplant into very rich soil.

Rocket Larkspur, (Delphinum ajàcis.) Flowering all Summer if successive sowings are made. Plants from seeds sown in April will flower in June and July; those from seeds sown in May, or early in June, in July and August; and those sown in October, in May. Sow the seeds where the plants are to bloom, as they will not do well transplanted.

Fine Poppy, (Papáver somniferum.) Flowering in July and August.

Lupin, (Lupìnus sp. and var.) Flowering in July and August. They delight in a light rich soil.

Ten-week stock Gilliflower, (Mathiòla annua.) Flowering all Summer.

Two to four feet high and upwards.

Marvel of Peru, (Mirábilis dichótoma.) Flowers in August and September.

Morning Glory, (Convólvulus màjor.) Flowering in July and September.

Sweet Pea, (Láthyrus odoràtus.) Flower in August and September.

Tall branching Larkspur, (Delphínium consólida.) Flowering in August and September.

Mixed Cyanus, (Centaurèa cyànus.) Flower all Summer.

Biennial and Perennial Flowers.

These bear the second year after planting. Hollyhocks, of various colors, Hibiscus of many colors, Purple and White Foxglove, Purple and White Canterbury Bells, Perennial Pea and Perennial Bee Larkspur.

Shrubs.

The following is a list of the shrubs most suitable for adorning a yard.

Lilacs, purple and white. By budding, the two kinds can be made to grow on the same stalk, thus much increasing the beauty. Syringas, single and double. Snow-balls. Althæas, single and double. Corchorus Japonicus. This has a rich green leaf, bright yellow double flowers, resembling small double roses, bears full early in the Spring, and continues flowering sparingly till Fall. Snow-berry, a beautiful shrub, bearing white wax-like berries, which hang till frost. Double flowering Almond. This is very beautiful, and its abundant bright pink blossoms appear early in the Spring. Shrub Honeysuckles. Very delicate and early. Pyrus Japonica, brilliant crimson flowers, in the Spring. Common Barberry. A fine shrub for yards, having yellow blossoms and bright red fruit. Rose Acacia. A beautiful shrub, bearing large rose-colored clusters and requiring a sandy soil. Yellow Laburnum. An elegant shrub bearing yellow clusters.

Roses. No shrubs are more easily cultivated than roses; and none are more elegant. The following are the most beautiful kinds that will bear our Winter. Moss Rose, White and Red. This is propagated by shoots or suckers, by the roots, by layers, and by budding. But the third year after budding, the shoot will fail, and must be budded again. Buds from the shoot to be renewed, are as good as any; as every bud is, in fact, a new plant. Double Yellow Roses. These must have a light gravelly soil, well manured, and an airy situation in a north or east exposure. A southern exposure is not good. The old wood must often be cut away. The single yellow rose can be more easily cultivated. The Yellow Multiflora is very pretty. Black Roses, of which, La belle Africana is the darkest. Tri-colored, or Belle Alliance. Sweet Briar or Eglantine, single and double. Small Eglantine Rose, used to border beds. Champney's Blush Rose. This is very beautiful, and easily cultivated. It bears large clusters of small double blush roses, in Autumn. At the North, it needs to be covered with straw in Winter. Noisette. This is like the preceding, only more dark, and in larger clusters. It bears the Winter without cover. Greville Rose. This is a splendid Rose, bearing large clusters, containing, in the same cluster, every variety of shade, from the lightest pink to deep red and purple. It grows most luxuriantly, in one case growing eighteen feet in a few weeks. It can easily be obtained in the large cities from flower dealers. Rosa Banksii or Lady Banks. Multiflora. This has an evergreen leaf, small double white flowers, in clusters, and can bear the northern Winter, if covered in the Fall with straw. Besides these, there are the more common, White, Blush, Cabbage, Hundred-leaved, and many others.

With a little practice, a lady can multiply her varieties abundantly, by budding from all varieties within her reach. Some buds do better in one kind of stock, than another. Experiments can be tried to learn how they will best succeed. Inarching can be tried on rose trees. The surest way to propagate roses, is, by suckers, which come from the root, taking a part of the root. Layers prepared as before directed, are the best mode ; budding and inarching the next. In transplanting shrubs, do not bury too deep.

Herbaceous Roots.

Herbaceous roots die to the root, in the Fall, and in Spring again shoot up. Of these, the Artemisia, Fleur-de-lis, Pæonies, Hibiscus, and Lilies, of various kinds, are the finest kinds. Pæonies have varieties of white, crimson, rose-colored, and sweet-scented ; the last having the perfume of a rose.   Of the Lilies, are the White, the Tiger, and the Fire-Lily.   The Artemisias are of great variety, in color and shade.   *The Lily of the Valley* grows best in the shade.   All require a rich soil.

On the Care of House-Plants.

House-plants must have the soil renewed every year, as previously directed.   In Winter, they should be kept as dry as they can be, without wilting. Many house-plants are injured by giving them too much water, when they have little light and fresh air.   This makes them grow spindling.   The more fresh air, warmth, and light, they have, the more water is needed.   They ought not to be kept very warm in Winter, nor exposed to great changes of atmosphere.   Forty degrees is a proper temperature for plants in Winter, when they have little sun and air.   When plants have become spindling, cut off their heads, entirely, and cover the pot in the earth, where it has the morning sun, only.   A new and flourishing head will spring out.   Most house-plants cannot bear the noon sun.   When insects infest plants, set them in a closet, or under a barrel, and burn tobacco.   The smoke kills any insect enveloped in it.   When plants get frozen, cold water, and a gradual restoration of warmth, are the best remedies.

Shade-Trees for Yards.

The Ailanthus or Tree of Heaven, is one of the finest, as it grows the fastest, is most easily propagated, and is not surpassed by any in beauty.   It is easily propagated by all methods.   If trimmed up every Spring, nearly to the top, it will in three or four years grow thirty or forty feet high, bearing on the top a large coronet of long leaves, and very much resembling the palm tree.   If left to grow without trimming, it forms a wide spread and thick shade. In good soil, it will, in two years from the seed, grow ten or twelve feet high. It requires a rich soil. The Locust grows fast, has fine blossoms, and gives a good shade. The Elm and Sugar Maple are the handsomest forest trees, but they grow slowly, and should be mingled with fast-growing trees. The Lime or Linden, is a beautiful forest tree. The Tulip Tree is very beautiful, but difficult to transplant successfully. The Mountain Ash is a beautiful shade-tree.

Those who live in the Western States, can procure, in their own forests, the most beautiful shade-trees and shrubs, such as, in Europe, and at the East, would be cultivated with great care, as rare specimens of beauty. The Red Arbutus, called the Burning Bush, is a shrub bearing evergreen leaves, and bright scarlet berries, which hang on the tree during the Winter. The Bitter Sweet is a creeper, which has a rich green foliage in Summer, and bright red berries which hang on the tree all the Winter. The Dog Wood is a beautiful tree, which bears large white flowers before the leaves are out in the Spring, and has red berries afterwards. The Wild Lenna, or Cassia Marilandica, is an herbaceous plant, bearing orange-colored pea-shaped flowers, with leaves resembling those of the Locust, and is found in sandy soil. The Virginian Creeper, or American Ivy, grows rapidly, and fastens itself firmly into brick walls. This makes it good for covering unsightly back buildings, in cities. The American Judas Tree grows fifteen feet high, and has flowers early in the Spring.

Creepers.

The Sweet-scented Monthly Honeysuckle is the most delightful of all creepers. It is easily raised, and bears blossoms from early Spring to late in the

Fall. The Yellow, White, and Coral Honeysuckles make a fine variety. The White is very fragrant. The Scarlet Trumpet Monthly is a beautiful climber, and bears flowers through the season. Of the Clematis, there are several varieties, all very handsome. The Glycine is a large and splendid creeper, with large blue clusters. The common large Trumpet Creeper must not be trained on houses, either wood or brick, as it injures them. It is the largest and most showy of all creepers. The English Nightshade is a quick and vigorous climber, with blue flowers, and fruit of a bright red color.

Annual Creepers.

Crimson Cypress Vine, ⎫ Very beautiful.
White Cypress Vine, ⎭
White Maurandia, ⎫ Beautiful.
Pink Maurandia, ⎭
White Thunbergia.
Buff Thunbergia.
Morning Glory.
Purple, White, and Scarlet, Flowering Beans.
Sweet Pea of various kinds.

On the Care of Bulbous and Tuberous Roots.

The soil for these roots should be such as is described for pot-plants, well pulverized, and a foot and a half deep. The beds should be raised six inches above the earth around. For common gardens and yards, it is best to plant them in little circles, nine inches or a foot in diameter, putting six or eight in the ring, according to the size. Other flowers can be planted on the same bed, as most bulbs have completed their growth, before other plants draw on the soil. The time of planting is in the months of September and October, for the Hyacinth, Crown Imperial, Lily, Polyanthus, Narcissus, Jonquil, Iris, Crocus, Colchicum, Star of Bethlehem,

Winter Aconite, Snow Drop, Snow Flake, Gladiolus, and most other hardy bulbs. The more delicate bulbs must be kept in dry sand, till April, and then be planted out of the reach of frosts. The depth of planting should be as follows: the measure is made from the top of the bulb.

The Hyacinth, Martagon Lily, and Pæony, should be planted four inches deep; Crown Imperial, and Polyanthus, Narcissus, six inches; Tulip, Jonquil, Colchicum, and Snow Flake, three inches; Bulbous Iris, Crocus, small Fritillary, Pancratium, Gladiolus, and Snowdrop, two inches; Ranunculus, Anemone, and Dog-tooth Violet, one inch deep. In Winter, it is safer to cover bulbs with tan bark, dry leaves, or straw, which should be removed very early in the Spring.

Every three years, bulbs should be taken up, about a month after they have done blooming; and, after cutting off all within an inch above the bulb, dry the tender ones which are to be kept till Spring, in a garret for three weeks, and then keep them each wrapped in a paper, or else put in dry sand, till the month comes for planting them. All except the tender ones should be taken up, and immediately replanted. When replanting, all the little offsets must be pulled off, and set by themselves, as they make new roots, and will bloom the second year after planting.

Bulbs to bloom in pots in the Winter, should be planted in October or November, and be exposed to the open air till it begins to freeze. They should be kept as much as possible in the sun; and water should be sparingly given, or be proportioned to the sun, and fresh air afforded.

Bulbs intended for glasses, should be placed in them about the middle of November; and the glasses should be often filled with pure water, so that the bottom of the bulb may just touch the water.

They should be kept, during the first ten days, in a dark room. The water must be kept pure and never be allowed to freeze. This method injures bulbs, irremediably. Putting them in a garden, for two or three years, partially restores them. Cultivating them in the house, in pots, also injures them, but not so much as keeping them in water.

Dahlias are tuberous roots; and as the plant cannot bear the slightest frost, they must be taken up in the Fall, and be kept in a dry room, free from frost, or in dry sand, in a cellar. They can be raised from seed, so as to bear flowers the same season they are planted. But by this method, no selection can be made, as it is all uncertain whether they prove single or double. They are easily propagated, by dividing roots. This must be done so as to leave at least one eye or sprout with each portion. To do this, wait till they have sprouted, which will be before it is time to set them out; and then, with a sharp knife, divide the roots, giving one or more sprouts to each part. In planting them, dig holes a foot deep, and drive into it a stake, four feet high, to tie them. After fixing the stake, put in the root, so that the sprout will be one inch below the soil, and press the soil firmly around them. An open exposure, and good soil, inclining to sand, is the best. When they are tall, tie them to the stake, and trim off some of the lower shoots. Those flowers which are fullest and roundest, and show least of the centre, are esteemed the nearest perfect. They are the most brilliant and showy of all garden flowers, and are of many varieties of color.

On Laying out Flower-beds.

If flowers are cultivated in a common vegetable garden, let the beds be along the main alleys. Raise the flower-beds nine inches or a foot above the walk, with even and sloping sides. Some put

brick or boards around, to keep the beds in place;
but these materials soon decay, or get out of order;
and it is better to have the beds kept in shape by
the hoe. Beds look very finely with borders made
of the snowdrop, the blue iris, the white and quilled
daisy, Iceland moss, sives, box, and various other
plants. The white and the quilled daisy are very
hardy, and blossom, all the season. They propagate
very fast, by offsets, and are the prettiest of any
thing for a border. They do best when put on a
place which is shaded for half the day.

If flowers are to be put in a yard, where there is
much turf, an oblong, with a *crescent* at each ex-
tremity, cut out of the turf, and raised a foot above
it, looks very finely, among the green grass. If this
is done, a small trench should be made between the
beds and the turf, to keep off the grass. In planting
such beds, much taste can be displayed. As a general rule, the tallest and largest flowers should be
put in the middle, and the lowest on the outside.
The Writer has seen a yard laid out thus : In front
of the house, were two crescents, one on each side
of the walk. These were bordered with the white
and quilled daisy, and blue iris. Bulbs were put in
circles, around the beds, and between the circles
were planted the prettiest of the smaller annuals.
In the centre of each crescent, were planted the
crimson cypress, the Maurandias, and Thunbergias,
which were trained on a fancy trellis, made of young
willow twigs, peeled. In the yard on the other side
of the house, was an ellipse, and two crescents, cut
out in the turf, and raised. Fig. 37, will give an
idea of its appearance. The crescent (*a*) having
dots in it, was planted with five different kinds
of Candytuft,—the purple, white, crimson, sweet-
scented, scarlet, and Normandy, scattered promiscu-
ously, so as to form a thick bed of mingled flowers,
in the shape of a smaller crescent. On the remain-

Fig. 37.

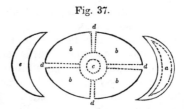

ing border of the bed were planted the various trailing plants, which filled up the remainder of the bed. The Ellipse, *b b b b*, had a centre bed, *c*, in which was placed a clump of various colored Dahlias, and around them, some smaller flowers. Four narrow alleys, *d d d d*, divided the Ellipse, and in the centre of each of the divided parts, *b b b b*, were placed a root of either white lily, pæony, or fleur-de-lis. Around the edges, were planted various annuals. The other crescent, *e*, was arranged *ad libitum*.

By planting the same flower, at different periods, it can be continued a much longer time. Flowers can often be arranged with reference to color, so as to produce a good effect.

The most disagreeable part of gardening, is removing weeds from beds and walks. The Writer recommends that weeding *walks* should be reserved for an early hour, when the beds are too wet with dew to work upon them, and when, before breakfast, active exercise is not good. Have the dibble ground very sharp, and take a cricket to sit upon, and shave off the weeds in the walks with the dibble, and sweep them into a heap, with a broom. Draw the weeds from around the flowers with the hand, and then cut up the weeds in other places with a small hoe, and rake them up and remove them. Be sure and keep the walks and beds free from weeds, and preserve the beds in regular shape.

CHAPTER XXXVIII.

ON NURSERIES AND ORCHARDS, AND FRUIT.

Preparation of Soil. Planting of Seeds. Budding, Grafting, and Transplanting. Training the Limbs. Attention to the Soil. Manuring. Caution needful, lest too much manure be used. Washes. Apples. Pears. Peaches. Quinces. Apricots and Nectarines. Plums. Cherries. Filberts. Figs. Currants. Gooseberries. Raspberries. Strawberries. Grapes. To preserve Fruit.

THE most experienced nursery-men teach, that the soil for a nursery should be rich and well dug. It should also be protected from the coldest winds. The manure should be well decayed. Plant seeds in Autumn in ridges, four or five feet apart, beating down the earth firmly over the seeds. They should be planted from an inch and a half to two inches below the surface. While they are growing, thin them out, leaving the best-looking about a foot and a half apart. The soil must be kept soft and free from weeds. In two or three years, or when the stems are of the size of a pipe-stem, they may be budded or grafted. A year after this epoch, they may be transplanted. Peach trees bear in four years from planting, and two years from budding. In a year after transplanting, some pains must be taken to form the heads aright. It has been found, by long experience, that straight upright branches produce what are called gourmands, or twigs bearing leaves and no fruit, and that it is chiefly the horizontal and curved branches which yield the fruit. For this reason, those having the care of young nurseries, take pains to train limbs in a curving direction; and when they train young trees, they cut off those limbs which are least likely to take a curving direction. The last of June, is the best time for directing and pruning

limbs.   The more the earth is kept open and loose
about the roots, to admit air, the better they flourish.
Grass should never be allowed to grow around fruit
trees.   A space of four feet each way from each tree,
should be kept loose and free from grass and weeds.
Opening the soil, with a spade, in the Fall, to admit
air, moisture, and frost to the roots, is a great advantage in destroying insects, and promoting healthful
growth.   When this is done, straw should be put
over the roots in the Spring, to prevent too much
evaporation from the soil.   Fruit trees do best in a
warm, loose, and deep soil.   They are not so flourishing in a cold and stiff soil ; and they fail entirely
on one that is very wet or very dry.   The nature of
the earth under the soil has much influence.   If it
be rock, or what is called *hard pan*, the trees will
deteriorate.   The best site for an orchard is a southern exposure, protected from the coldest winds.
Manuring improves fruit.   But there may be two
much employed.   Manure should not constitute one
fourth of the soil, and often less than this will be
injurious.   Orchards should have the trees twenty-
five feet apart.   Young trees must be tied to stakes,
or they will be injured by the wind.   Ley and soapsuds applied to fruit trees are good.

Apples.

The best wash for an apple tree, is strong ley,
applied with a brush to the body and limbs, in June.
It destroys the insects and parasitic plants.   Cater-
pillars should be destroyed by cutting off the nests
on a wet day, or by burning sulphur on a wadding
at the end of a pole.

The following are the best kinds of apples for an
orchard.   The Summer Sweeting, the Harvest
apple, the Early Chandler, and the Juneating, ripen
in July and August.   Besides these, are the follow-

ing, selected by Judge Buel,* as the best apples to be found in the Country. The Bough, Summer Queen, Early Pearmain, Summer Rose, Codling, Maiden's Blush, Hagloe Crab, Romanite or Rambo, Cataline, Fall Pippin, Doctor apple, Wine, Late Pearmain, Burlington, Greening, Bell Flower, Newark Pippin, Pennock, Michael Henry, Spitzenburg, Newtown Pippin, Priestly, Lady Apple, Carthouse, Tewksbury, and the Winter Blush. The Newtown Pippins, as raised in New York or Ohio, are the best for keeping, as they can be preserved, in perfect flavor, for a whole year, till they come again. In a dry cellar, they can be thus preserved, without extra care. In a damp cellar, they must be packed in dry sand, as elsewhere directed.

The Pear.

This excellent fruit tree is subject to the *Fire Blight*, or Bru lere, which causes it to turn black, and wither ; but for which, a remedy has lately been discovered. It consists in cutting off the blighted parts, and then some of the main roots. It is said to be caused by excess of sap, which cutting off the roots remedies. The Citron des Carmes, Jargonelle, Seckle, and Summer Rose, ripen in July or August. The Belle et Bonne Virgalieu, White Doyenne, Flemish Beauty, and Neille, ripen in September. The Autumn Bergamot, Ashton Town, Capiaumont, Beurre d'œil, Duchesse d'Angouleme, and Marie Louise, ripen in October. The Forelle, Gloux Morceau, Napoleon, and Colmar, ripen in November. The Nilia Dasse Colmar, Beurre Vait, and the Beurre d'Aremberg, ripen in December. The Easter Beurre, Beurre Rance, and Chaumohlette, are

---

* The last and best work of this lamented Author,—his 'Farmer's Companion,' is issued by the Publishers of this volume. It forms the sixteenth volume of the larger series of ' THE SCHOOL LIBRARY,' publishing under the sanction of the Board of Education of the State of Massachusetts.

late Winter and Spring pears; and the Catillac, Chaptel and Bezi d'Hui are good for baking and stewing.

Peaches.

The soil best adapted to peaches is a rich sandy loam. Grass around their roots is very destructive. A worm at the root, or the *yellows*, often destroys the tree. Examining the root, every Spring, and Autumn, to remove the worm, and throwing lime and ashes freely about the root, is a remedy for the first. Ashes or tanner's bark should be put around peach trees, to *prevent* the attack of the worm. A plaster of cow-dung and clay should be put on any wounds made by a worm. The Yellows is a disease which is spread by the pollen of the blossom. If a tree is attacked thus, its leaves will turn yellow. It should then be removed, before it blossoms again, or it will spread the contagion to all the other peach trees around. All its roots, also, should be removed. When the trees are very full of young fruit, it should be thinned out, or the tree will be weakened, and all the fruit be inferior in quality. It has lately been discovered, that planting tansy or wormwood around the roots of peach trees, will effectually protect them from worms at the root, by preventing the moth from depositing her eggs upon them.

The farmers in New York save their peach trees from being Winter-killed, by a heap of stones around the tree, four feet in diameter, and as thick as the usual depth of snow. A mound of earth it is said has a similar effect. But these must be removed in Spring, to give air and warmth to the soil. Too much manure injures peach trees; and many orchards never succeed, because the soil is too rich. A sandy soil is best.

The best peaches are the Early Ann, Heath, Noblesse, Coolridge's Red Rareripe, Early Royal

George, Kenrick's Clingstone, Lemon Clingstone, and the Teton de Venus.

The Quince.

There are four varieties of quince;—the pear, the apple, the mild, and the Portuguese. The last is the best.

Apricots and Nectarines.

These trees require the same sort of management as the peach. They are apt to produce too much fruit, and should be thinned out.

Plums.

This fruit does well in any soil, except a very sandy, or a clayey soil. A light rich soil is best. Plums are very extensively destroyed by the *Curculio*, which also often attacks peaches, nectarines, and apricots. Paving around a tree, as far out as its limbs reach, is recommended as a remedy, by most cultivators; though some say it is ineffectual. Keeping hogs under plum trees, is said to be the best remedy, as they eat up the plums as fast as they fall and thus destroy the insect. Tin troughs, filled with water or oil, placed tight around the trunk of the tree, and the chinks, between it and the trunk, filled with tow, prevent the insects from ascending, as they rarely fly, but crawl up the body of the tree. Huling's Superb, is the largest plum. The White and Green Gage, Purple and White Magnum Bonum, and Large Queen Claudia, are among the best plums.

Cherries.

A rich sandy loam is best for cherries. When the trees are old, they should be cut off, to a stump eighteen inches high, and one of the shoots be trained for a new tree.

The best cherries, are, the Black Tartarian, May Duke, Spanish, Davenport's Early Red, Elkhorn, Downer, Napoleon Bigarreau, Belle et Magnifique, Plumstone Morello, and Late White Heart.

Filberts.

This favorite nut can easily be raised in any part of this Country. Seed-nuts can be procured in our large cities.

Figs.

This fruit can be raised in our Middle States, by covering the tree in Winter. To do this, loosen half the roots on one side, bend the tree down, lay it on the earth, and cover it with a mound of straw, earth, and boards.

Currants.

This fruit grows in any soil, except a very wet one. It is chiefly propagated by cuttings, which should have the eye cut off the joints that go below the soil. In Autumn, the old wood should, be thinned out, and some manure put around. They can be trimmed into small trees, thus improving their appearance, and the fruit.

Gooseberries.

These are propagated by layers and cuttings, cutting out the eyes of the joints below the soil. They do best when shaded from the noon-sun. It is best to train a single stem like a tree, and it should be kept free from suckers. One third of the old wood should be removed every Autumn. Where the Summers are hot, a northern aspect is best.

Raspberries.

These are propagated by cuttings, layers, and suckers. A situation which is shaded, during part of the day, is best. There is a kind, called the

Monthly Raspberry, to be obtained in Cincinnati, and probably in other cities, which bears constantly till late in the Fall.

Strawberries.

The soil for this fruit should be light, and manured chiefly with vegetable mould. Common manure, well decayed, is better than none. April or September is the best time for transplanting Strawberries. In doing this, cut off the old leaves, preserving the centre leaves. Set the plants eight inches from each other, and in rows nine inches apart, in beds two feet wide, each bed separated from the next by a narrow alley. There are two kinds, which always grow together;—the *bearers* and the *non-bearers.* Those which bear, can be distinguished in blossom-time, when care should be taken to pull out the non-bearers. Some gardeners leave a part of the non-bearers, in the proportion of one to ten. Other gardeners think it needless to leave any, claiming that the plant is *Monœcious.* The non-bearers have large flowers, with showy stamens and high black anthers. The bearers have short stamens, and a great number of pistils ; and the flowers are every way less showy. They must be selected in blossom-time. Many persons have beds which never bear, because they consist chiefly of non-bearing vines. All weeds should be kept out of the vines. In two or three years after setting out beds, when they have become matted with young plants, it is the practice of some to dig over the beds in cross lines, so as to leave some of the plants standing in little squares, while the rest are turned into the soil. This is less work than transplanting, as it thins out the bed, in some places, and leaves the old roots standing in other places. This should be done over, the second time, the same year, as it serves to keep the soil mellow, and free from weeds.

Grapes.

The soil must be made mellow, two feet deep, and well manured. A gravelly or sandy soil is better than a harder one. A south, or southwest, exposure, is the best. The Spring or the Fall is the time for transplanting. The roots must be kept moist, and the holes dug two feet deep, and two feet square. The young vine should be pruned, the first year, so as to have only one or two main branches, and all the side shoots should be taken off, as soon as they appear. In October or November, shorten these main branches, till there are only three or four eyes remaining. This last pruning must be done in Winter or late in the Fall. In the Spring of the second year, the earth must be loosened around the roots, with care, so as not to injure the roots. During the second Summer, allow only two of the most promising shoots to grow, and every month prune off all the side shoots. When the side shoots are strong, leave the first joint remaining, lest too much sap be turned into the main stem. In the Fall, take off these remaining parts. In October or November, of the second year, cut off the main stems to eight buds for the strongest and six for the weakest vines. After the second year, no other pruning is needed, except to reduce the side shoots, in order to increase the fruit. All pruning of the grape, (except nipping side shoots,) must be done in the Fall or Winter, when the sap is not running, or the vines will be killed or seriously injured. Vines should be trained on latticed fences, or on poles, freely to give them air and sun. Tender vines must be covered in the Fall after they are pruned. Uncover them in April and restore them to their places. Grapes may be propagated, by cuttings, layers, or seeds. For cuttings, select well-ripened wood, of the previous season, and cut it in pieces, each having four or five joints. Bury these out of the reach of frost, till early in April, and then soak them some hours in water. They may be set out, so that all the eyes are covered except the top one. Of course they must be set in the ground, sloping, and not perpendicularly. The following are the best for common use: Isabella, Catawba, Munier, Black and White Sweetwater, Bland's, Alexandria, Elsinburg, Worthington, and Scuppernong.

To preserve Fruit.

Currants, Gooseberries, and all fruits of such kind of skin, can be preserved in the following manner. Gather them in a dry warm day, before they are completely ripe. Take off the stalks, and put them in perfectly dry junk bottles. Set them in a large kettle of cool water, without corks. Gradually raise the water to the boiling point; then cork the bottles, and after that, take them from the water. Then drive in the corks, more firmly, and cover them with rosin, and keep them in a dry place, where frost will not reach them. The success of this process depends upon keeping out air and water.

Apples, Grapes, and the like, can be preserved by packing in dry sawdust, or dry fine sand. First, put a layer of sand or sawdust, then a layer of fruit, (it must be entirely dry, not soft nor very ripe;) cover the fruit, entirely, with another layer of sand or sawdust, and thus go on, till the box is filled, putting sand on the top, three inches thick. The sand or sawdust must be first dried in an oven. The Writer has seen, in the most popular receipt books, some receipts for preserving fruit in bottles; in one case directing the bottles to be corked and sealed, before putting them in the water, (which, of course, would burst the bottles;) and in another directing to have hot water poured into them after the fruit is put in, which must rather hasten, than retard its decay.

CHAPTER XXXIX.

ON GARDEN VEGETABLES.

Potatoes. Sweet Potatoes. Turnips. Indian Corn. Cucumbers. Onions. Melons. Peas. Beans. Beets. Celery. Cabbages. Carrots and Parsnips. Lettuce. Egg-Plants and Tomatoes. Pumpkins. Radishes. Rhubarb, or Pie-Plants. Salsify, or Vegetable Oysters. Squashes. Herbs. Asparagus. Planting Garden-Seeds. Culture. Gathering. On laying out a Garden.

Potatoes.

THE best soil for potatoes, is a sandy loam, in a cold climate, and a clay loam, in a warm climate; both being well manured. They should be planted in rows, running North and South, that the sun may reach both sides. The rows should be a foot and a half apart, and each potato nine inches from the next. The largest and best potatoes must be selected, for planting; and the largest leading eyes must be put upward, as this will secure the strongest shoots. They must be kept free from weeds, with the hoe, making a slight hill or ridge about them. The best potatoes are the Kidney, or Foxites, the Pink-eyes, the Mercer's and the Loux St. Marie. Long manure is better than short, for potatoes. Potatoes should not be planted twice in the same spot.

Sweet Potato.

It is best to sprout these first in a hot-bed, and then transplant them. When the potato has sent up its shoots, take it up, and divide it into parts, having at least one sprout on each, and plant these parts in high hills or ridges. In weeding, take up the running tops, and wind them around the top of the hill; and do not let the vines throw layers into the ground. They must be kept, when gathered, in a dry place, and no frost allowed to reach them. Packing in dry sand is best.

Turnips.

Turnips should be planted in beds, in rows, and thinned out according to their size. A dry sandy soil, well manured, is best. The Yellow Malta is fine for the table; also the Early White Stone, and the Yellow Altringham.

Indian Corn.

A sandy soil, and long manure, are best for corn. Gypsum, or Plaster of Paris, is very good for it. In raising corn, the following directions, from a celebrated cultivator, may be a guide. Take the seed from plants which have ripened two or more ears. Take the middle grains, and not those on the ends. Steep the seeds in nitre, for twenty-four hours. Plant three grains in each place, three feet, each way, from the others. Hoe every fortnight, and do not hill up the corn, which is now regarded as a bad practice. Put on gypsum, in small quantities, at the first hoeing.

Cucumbers.

Raise them, at first, in a hot-bed; and then transplant them. If no hot-bed is used, plant twenty seeds in each hill, and thin out, leaving the two largest plants to a hill. The hills must be six feet apart, and three or four inches high. The seed should be sowed three or four different times, to have successive crops. The soil should be very rich, with manure. The Early Frame, and Long Green, are the best. The Small Gherkins, are best for pickles.

Onions.

A rich moist soil is best for onions. They should be planted in beds, in rows eight inches apart, and thinned out, leaving six inches between each. Tie them in strings, or bunches, and hang them in a dry place, free from frost. The Yellow Dutch and White Portugal are best.

Melons.

To succeed well with melons, dig holes in a sunny spot, two feet square, and two feet deep. Fill the hole with sand, stable manure, and vegetable mould, in equal quantities. In this, plant the seeds, say twenty to each hill, the hills being seven feet apart. Thin out the plants, when an inch high, leaving three of the largest to each hill. When the melons are formed, pick off all but three or four to each vine, and put a piece of glass, or thin stone, or slate, under each melon, to have both sides ripen alike, and avoid an earthy taste. Muskmelons and Cantalupes are ripe when the stem appears a little withered. The Watermelon, when ripe, has a peculiar hollow sound, if snapped with the finger. Save the seeds of the best melons, and dry them in their juice, in the shade. The best Watermelons are the Long Island, or Jersey, the Carolina, and the Early Apple-seeded. The best Muskmelons and Cantalupes are the Early Yellow Cantelupe, the Long Yellow Musk, Skillman's Fine Netted, (very fine,) Stone's fine Mixed, Minorca Netted, Murray's Pine-Apple, the Green Nutmeg, and the Citron.

Peas.

A sandy soil with but little stable manure, is best for Peas. Vegetable mould is better than animal manure, mixed with the sand and loam. They should be planted an inch and a half deep, in rows four feet apart, and each plant six inches from the next. When six inches high, they should be bushed. The best Peas are the Early Frame, the Large White Marrowfat, Knight's Tall Honey, the Tall and the

Dwarf Sugar. The pods of the last two are good, if boiled with the Peas, unshelled. Peas should be planted at intervals of three weeks, to keep up a supply.

Beans.

Beans flourish best in a moist and well-manured soil. They should be planted (for poles) in hills six feet from each other, four plants to a hill. More must be planted than are needed, and the best selected to remain. Get poles, nine or ten feet long, for them to climb on. The Lima bean must not be planted till frosts are over. Bush beans must be planted in rows, each plant six inches from the next. The best beans, for poles, are White Dutch, Case Knife, and Large White Lima; for bushes, Early China, Red-eye, and Large White Kidney.

Beets.

These should be planted in beds, in rows a foot apart, and thinned out to be a foot apart. They are tender, and at the North, should not be planted till May. The best are the Early Blood, Turnip Rooted, and the Long Blood. They require a rich dry soil.

Celery.

Plant this in hot-beds, not very thick. Give it air, every day, if not too cold. If it grows rank and spindling, it must be put in the open air. If no hot-bed is used, sow in a rich moist soil, the last of April, (as far North as New York,) in a sheltered situation. Plant one quarter of an inch deep, rather thick, and beat down the soil lightly. When the plants are two inches high, transplant, (three inches apart,) into well-manured soil. In doing this, rub off side shoots around the bottom, and cut off the ends of the roots. This last is very important. The first week in July, transplant to the trench.

If the plants are too weak to bear up the tops, cut them off, and shade from the sun. But if transplanted from the seed-bed, as above directed, into good soil, they will need no trimming. Make the trench eighteen inches deep, and fifteen inches wide. Fill up six inches with *old manure*, and dig over, to mix it with the soil. Then put on an inch of good soil, and set the plants in it, six inches apart. Keep adding soil, as they grow, leaving only the green leaves above the soil, till the trench is *nearly* filled. Then do not add any more soil, till the first or second week in September; and then cover all but the leaves. When taken up, cut off the fibrous roots, and *all* the green of the tops. Dry it two days, in an airy shed, turning it every day. Then pack it in dry sand.

Cabbages.

These require a rich moist soil. Transplant them when they are three inches high, putting each one three feet from the next. Press the soil firmly about the roots, and water after sunset. The Cauliflower and Turnip Cabbage require frequent watering, to make them do well. Broccoli is as good as Cauliflower, and easier to raise. The best Cabbages are the Early York, the Large Late Drumhead, and the Green Globe Savoy. The Red Dutch is good for pickling. The best Cauliflowers are the Fine Early, and the Large Late Dutch. The best Broccoli is the Early Purple Cape.

Carrots and Parsnips.

These should be treated like the beet. The best are the Early Horn, and the Long Orange, Carrot, and the Long Dutch Parsnip.

Lettuce.

Plant this in hot-beds, and transplant. If the hot-bed is not used, plant on the summit of ridges three feet high. The best varieties, are the Early Curled, the Royal Cape Head, and the Large Drum-head, or Cabbage ; the last is the best.

The Egg-Plant, and Tomato.

These should be started in a hot-bed, and not transplanted till frosts are past. If the hot-bed is not used, plant so as to avoid frosts, and then thin out, till the plants are three feet apart. Train the tomato on a trellis. Thin out some of the branches, and the fruit will be much better. Both require a rich soil. The best tomatos are the Large Red, and Large Yellow. The Cuba or Spanish is best for Pickles. The Egg-Plant has two varieties, the Purple and the White. The Purple only is used to eat; the White for ornament. Start in hot-beds, and transplant three feet apart, in rich soil.

Pumpkins.

These do best in a sandy loam, well manured. Put two vines to a hill, and let the hills be eight or nine feet apart. Leave only two or three pumpkins on one vine. The best kind, is the Large Cheese. The best for pies, is the Seven Year, or Long Keeping.

Radishes.

These require a very dry sandy soil, well manured. Plant several times. The best are the Early Scarlet Short-Top, the Long Salmon, and the Scarlet Turnip-Rooted.

Rhubarb or Pie-Plant.

This is propagated by seeds and offsets. It requires a sandy soil, well manured. The stalks, alone, are used for Pies, being peeled, cut up in inch pieces, and stewed like gooseberries.

Salsify or Vegetable Oyster.

A moist clay soil, well manured, is best for this plant. Sow the seed in rows, a foot apart. Thin

out, leaving each plant six inches from the next.
To procure the seed, leave the plant in the ground,
in the Fall, and cover it with straw. The next
year it will yield seed. This plant must often be
watered, in dry weather.

Squashes.

Plant, and treat in the same manner as directed
for Pumpkins. The best Summer Squash, is the
Early Bush Scollop. The best Winter Squashes,
are the Valparaiso, and Acorn. For some climates,
the Winter Crook-Necks are best.

Herbs.

Balm, Fennel, Caraway, Lavender, Sweet Marjo-
rum, Sage, Wormwood, Summer Savory, Saffron,
Catnip, and Thyme, should be planted in a garden,
for sickness, and for cooking.

Asparagus.

Manure, abundantly, with short manure, the space
devoted to Asparagus. Begin on one side, and dig
the earth more than two feet deep, and continue till
the whole space is made soft and mellow, two feet
in depth, and leave it thus through the Winter.
Very early in the Spring spread on short manure,
three inches deep, and dig it over, as deep as the
spade will reach, mixing well. Level, and divide
into beds a yard wide, separated by narrow alleys.
Sow the seed, or plant the roots, in rows, a foot
apart, and each plant fourteen inches from the next.
If seed is planted, sow it thick, and thin out afterward. Plant the seed one inch deep, the root three
inches deep. In the Fall, mow off the young Asparagus, and cover with stable litter, to keep it
warm. In the Spring, take off this, and keep the
bed loose, and free from weeds. The third year
from planting the seed, begin to use sparingly.

After this, manure every third year. Brine, poured around the plants, is very useful.

In planting garden-seeds, they must be put in deep, according to the size, and the earth must be pressed down firmly over them. In a very dry time, they must be watered. Keeping the earth loose and light, to admit air, is very essential, and *weeds* always subtract from the size and excellence of the vegetable, by using up the nourishment of the soil. In procuring seed, always select the finest plants. Many vegetables do not yield seed till the second year.

In gathering in the vegetables for Winter, the beets and carrots must be got in before frost. The parsnips and salsify may be left in the ground through the Winter, as they are then better than when put in the cellar. The potatoes should be dug before the tops are injured by frost. Turnips must be gathered before hard frosts, or else covered with straw. Cabbages can be preserved in the garden, by turning them upside down, and burying the heads. This preserves a house and cellar from their unpleasant odor. Broccoli and Cauliflower must be put in the cellar. Celery may be covered with straw and left out. A part may be gathered and put in sand. Pumpkins and Squashes must be brought in before frost, and kept in a dry place, free from frost. Herbs must be gathered in blossom, except those whose seed is used.

On laying out a Garden.

Select a spot having a southern exposure, and one not much shaded. Some shaded spots are useful, for plants that require partial shading. Secure a supply of sand, of clayey earth, and of vegetable mould from the woods, and of both long and short manure.

Have them deposited in a convenient place, and then use them for the various beds, according to the demand. If there are any low and moist spots, reserve them for the plants that demand such a soil. It is best occasionally to change the location of each kind of vegetable, as a *rotation of crops* is deemed very important in the economy of agriculture, some plants extracting one principle from the soil, and some another. This method saves considerable labor in manuring the soil.

CHAPTER XL.

ON THE CARE OF DOMESTIC ANIMALS, BARNS, ETC.

A Knowledge of this Subject often of great Value to a Woman. Care of a Horse. Rules for Riding, for a Lady. On the Care of a Cow. Dog and Cat. Poultry. *On Barns and Barnyards.*

It may, at first glance, appear that this kind of knowledge is not needed by a woman. But how often is it the case, that the death or absence of a husband, or a father, throws all the care of a whole establishment on a woman. In such cases, if dumb animals are left to the sole care of domestics, they will often suffer, unless the mistress of the family has the knowledge which fits her to direct respecting them.

On the Care of a Horse.

Hot and foul stables are very injurious to horses. Very dark stables are bad, occasioning inflamed eyes. Very glaring light is also injurious. The stall for a horse should be twelve feet high, and at least six feet wide. The floors should never be made of brick or stone, which injure the feet. The best floors are made of sand mixed with clay. Next to these, plank floors are best. The floor of a stable should incline a very little, to let the urine run off; but not much, as it will strain the muscles of the limbs, in standing. The stable should be airy, and cool, but protected from a current of air. It should be thoroughly cleaned every morning. The hay should be put in a box behind the feeding trough, so as to be on a level with the horse, instead of being raised above his head; as, in the latter case, the seeds will fall into his eyes.

The farmer's horse needs little more cleaning than washing the dirt from his legs. A horse turned into the field needs no cleaning. A horse kept in a stable and irregularly exercised, should be curried and brushed every day. Nothing refreshes a horse more than rubbing his skin, especially his legs. Every horse needs daily exercise, say, as much as to trot two miles or more. When a horse is over ridden, bloody spots appear in the whites of his eyes.

Food should never be given immediately after labor; time must be allowed for the body to cool. When a horse is very warm, very cold water is dangerous; and large draughts of water should never be allowed. A little at a time, at considerable intervals, is safe. Well-mixed cut hay, chaff, sheaf-oats, shorts, corn-meal, and bran, are the best common food for a horse. Oats may be given when he works or travels, but very little or none, when he does nothing. No horse should have oats till four years old. When travelling, a horse should have six quarts of oats in the morning, four at noon, and six at night. A little salt should be put in his water when he is warm, and he should not be watered, as a general rule, except at his regular meals. The common practice, of stopping to water horses, on the road, in travelling, is a bad one, as is taught by the best writers; and is passing into disuse.

If horses' feet are not cleaned, a disease is induced, in which the legs swell, and sometimes crack. Keeping the legs clean, prevents this. The remedy is, to wash in soap and water, scrape off the dandruff, and rub on a mixture, consisting of one drachm of sugar of lead united with an ounce of lard. If cracks appear, wash in alum-water, four drachms to a pint of water. If very bad, use a poultice of oil-cake or boiled carrots. Washing the legs in cold weather, without rubbing them dry, is bad. The better way, is, to brush off the mud and dust, with a stiff brush. The hair should be cut off from the heels of road horses, but not of farm horses.

When a horse drinks too much cold water, or eats too much grain, while very hot, it produces what is called *foundering*, which is shown by stiffness in the limbs, and a fever. The remedy is bleeding, and then one pound of Glauber's salts, in two portions, in a pailful of water. Keep the horse walking. When a horse is kept long in a stable, and is very fat, hard driving sometimes causes a muscular spasm, over the body. Unless it is very bad, he will get over it with rest and a drink of salt water, otherwise, he must be taken to a farrier. A horse should be completely new shod, every six or eight weeks. Fish-oil on the skin, or strongly perfumed oil, like tansy or pennyroyal, prevents horses from being bit by the flies. Sometimes horses are made fractious by having a check rein drawing too tight, so as to weary the muscles of the neck. Sometimes the bit hurts the jaws.

Rules for Riding, for a Lady.

In riding, hold the reins in the left hand, laying the hand in the lap, and holding the whip in the right. The right hand also is to lay on the lap, except when cantering ; and then it should hang by the side, or, in case of danger, rest on the horn of the

saddle. Let the stirrup be long enough for the limb
to hang nearly straight, and do not hang on the horn
of the saddle, but learn to balance the body and accommodate yourself to the movement of the horse.
Ladies are apt to sit too far over to the right. The
mode of mounting, by stepping on a gentleman's
hand, is very simple and easy, after a little practice.
The gentleman should ride on the right side of the
lady.

On the Care of a Cow.

A cow-house should be airy, but not open to currents of wind. The floor should incline a very little
to a gutter at the end, for the urine to run off. Oats
and bran mixed with hay, potatoes, carrots, and
boiled corn, are all good food for a cow. Turnips
and cabbage give a bad taste to the milk. A handful of salt should be mixed twice a week with the
food. Pure water is very important. A cow, if
well fed, will give nearly half as much again, by
being milked three times a day, instead of twice.
If cows are stripped a second time, fifteen minutes
after milking, they will give another quantity of
almost pure cream. It does not injure the health of
a cow to give a great quantity of milk, if she is well
fed; but such cows are usually thin in flesh. A
cow well fed, will give three or four times as much
milk, as if kept on a spare diet. A cow should go
unmilked two months before calving, and her milk
should not be used till four or five days after calving.
The calf must run with the cow two or three days,
and then be shut up from her, except twice or thrice
a day, when it must be allowed to take as much
food as it wants, and then the cow must be milked
clean.

The Dog, and Cat.

A bull-dog should not be kept for a watch-dog, as
he attacks in silence, and may kill a child or inno-

cent person. Setters and pointers and cur-dogs are good for watchers. Dogs can be made neat and cleanly, by proper care in punishing them. They can be freed from fleas, by putting them in a tub of hot soapsuds. The insects will float on the surface, and must be burnt, or they will recover. Sprinkling with Scotch snuff is another remedy. Madness or hydrophobia is indicated by frequent attempts to pick up straws, bits of paper, and very small objects. The eyes become red, the ears and head hang down, the dog is dull and melancholy, and sometimes howls. When suspected, a dog should be shut up. If he proves mad, he will snarl, bite, and be distressed at the sight of water, because, although longing for it, he cannot swallow it. Sometimes dogs have fits, and also what is called the distemper. When not very bad, three spoonfuls of sulphur, mixed with molasses, is a remedy.

Cats sometimes have fits, and fly about as if they were crazy. Catnip is the best remedy for diseases of this animal. Cats should not be allowed to sleep with children, as they sometimes do them injury, and it is never a healthful practice.

On the Care of Poultry.

When poultry have proper care given to their food and accommodations, they lay much more, and their flesh is much better. The following is the best method of taking care of them, having the sanction of those who make it a business, and are most successful. Provide a yard, which is dry, and protected from cold winds. Surround it with a very high picket-fence, so that they will not fly out. On the North side, put up a poultry-house, in which there should be perches for them to roost upon, so placed, that one shall not be over another, as a matter of cleanliness.

Covered boxes should be put around this house,

for nests, having a side or back entrance, so that the hen can go in unobserved. In the bottom of these boxes, put a thick layer of ashes, to retain the heat when the hen is sitting. Over this, put a layer of fine bruised straw or hay. On one side of the yard, place a heap of ashes for the poultry to roll in, to keep off vermin. Near by, place some unslacked lime, and also small gravel, which they will eat. It is said that hens do not lay as much in Winter, as in other seasons, because the snow prevents their having access to lime for the shell of the egg, and if this is supplied, they will lay all the year.

Hens sit twenty days. The eggs for sitting should not exceed a month in age, and should be of middle size, and smooth. The number should vary from ten to fifteen, according to the size of the hen. Mark the eggs with ink, and when the hen is off, take away any new ones which may have been laid. If an egg be broken, cleanse those remaining with warm water, and remove all that part of the nest which is soiled. Give corn and water to a sitting hen once a day, as she will often suffer for want of food, if it is not brought to her. The chickens first hatched should be taken away, and put in wool, in a basket, in a warm place. This is to prevent the hen from leaving before the whole brood is hatched.

There is no need of feeding chickens, for twelve hours after they are hatched. When the brood is all out, put the hen in a coop, in a dry sunny place, and do not put two broods near together, as the chickens will mingle, and the mothers will injure those that do not belong to them. Insects and angle worms, thrown occasionally to fowls, are very good, to preserve health. Chopped meat answers the same purpose. An egg-shaped lump of chalk is good for a nest-egg, as it spoils an egg to be used for this purpose. Oats are better for hens than corn, though both are good. The first food for young chickens should be coarse corn meal, *dry*. All watery food is improper for very young chickens. Clean water should be kept in pans. As they grow older, feed with Indian meal, or boiled potatoes, mixed with sour milk. The best food for ducks is buckwheat, grass, and corn.

The diseases of poultry are generally caused by bad food and want of care. Chickens, in cold wet weather, have the *chip*, when they lose feathers, shiver, and chip. Worms and peppercorns are the best remedies. When hens have the *pip*, a white scale grows on the end of the tongue. To cure this, pull off this scale, and rub the tongue with salt. The *flux* is cured with solid and some animal food. Constipation is cured by scalded bran mixed with a little sulphur. Vermin are consequent on a want of cleanliness. The *croup* is caused by bad weather. This is indicated by swollen eyes and running nostrils. The cure is warmth and peppercorns, for three successive days. Turkeys are difficult to rear, as wet and cold weather frequently kills them. They must be kept warm, and well housed, till six weeks old; and then allowed to roam. Their proper food is barley meal or oatmeal mixed with milk, and in some cases only with water, as milk is not then so good. In case of chills, give caraway or coriander seed.

ON BARNS AND BARNYARDS.

A barn should be at a distance from the house, as a matter of taste and cleanliness, and to escape the risk of fire. Hay and grain should always be kept under cover. Large plank bins should be made, to keep rats from the grain. In some places, rats will in one year consume the cost of the bins, if this precaution is not taken. The barn-floor should be close and tight, for the purpose of threshing.

A cellar under the barn is useful, for storing vegetables for cattle.   Cisterns, made of brick, and coated with water-lime, are useful in a yard, to catch, from the eaves of the barn, water for the use of the cattle. This saves the labor of drawing water.   The barnyard should be on the South side of the barn, and two other sides of it should be sheltered, by sheds for the cattle.   The following directions for making a proper barnyard, are furnished by a successful agriculturist.

Make a hollow place in the centre, four or five feet deep in the middle, and sloping upward on every side.   Line the bottom of this with clay, well beat down.   In this basin, throw all the refuse of the barn, house, and garden.   This makes fine manure, in Spring.   It should be put on, and ploughed in immediately, as manure loses its virtues, if left to the influence of sun and rain.   All manure should be kept covered, either by a shed, or in a cellar under the barn, or it loses its most valuable properties.   The drain of the stables should be conducted to the manure-heap.   When manure cannot be put under cover, it should have earth thrown over it.

THE END.